Andrew Wilson is a j … *rdian*,
the *Daily Mail*, the *N* … d the
Observer. He is the a … *utiful*
Shadow: A Life of Patr … *arold*
Robbins: The Man Wh …

Also by Andrew Wilson

Beautiful Shadow:
A Life of Patricia Highsmith

The Lying Tongue

Harold Robbins:
The Man Who Invented Sex

SHADOW OF THE TITANIC

The Extraordinary Stories of Those Who Survived

Andrew Wilson

SIMON & SCHUSTER

London · New York · Sydney · Toronto · New Delhi

A CBS COMPANY

First published in Great Britain by Simon & Schuster UK Ltd, 2011
This paperback edition published by Simon & Schuster UK Ltd, 2012
A CBS COMPANY

1 3 5 7 9 10 8 6 4 2

Simon & Schuster UK Ltd
1st Floor
222 Gray's Inn Road
London WC1X 8HB

www.simonandschuster.co.uk

Simon & Schuster Australia, Sydney
Simon & Schuster India, New Delhi

A CIP catalogue record for this book is available from the British Library.

ISBN: 978-1-47111-185-3

Typeset in Baskerville by Hewer Text UK Ltd, Edinburgh
Printed and bound by CPI Group (UK) Ltd, Croydon, CR0 4YY

CONTENTS

To M.F.

INTRODUCTION

The sound of the screaming was the worst thing, they said. For those who survived the *Titanic* disaster – which took place in the dying hours of 14 April and the early morning of 15 April 1912 – the awful noise of fellow passengers calling out into the dark night was the one thing they could never forget.

Jack Thayer, a seventeen-year-old boy who lost his father in the sinking, compared the wail to the continuous high-pitched hum of locusts one might hear on a midsummer night in the woods near his home in Pennsylvania. Second-class passenger Charlotte Collyer, who was travelling with her husband and daughter, described the noise as being like a gigantic swarm of bees; 'the bees were men, and they had broken their silence now,' she said. 'Cries more terrible than I had ever heard rang in my ears.'[1] For crew member George Kemish the sound was forever seared on his consciousness. 'A hundred thousand fans at a Cup Final could not make more noise,' he said.[2] Similarly, third-class passenger Frank Goldsmith, who was only nine years old at the time, likened it to the roar of a crowd at a baseball game. He grew up near Tiger Stadium in Detroit, but when he became a father he could not bring himself to take his three sons to a game. It reminded him of the screams of that night, says his son, Thomas.

Four days after the sinking of the *Titanic*, George Rheims, who was travelling in first-class, wrote a letter to his wife, Marie, detailing precisely what happened. After rushing to his cabin to save a photograph of his wife, he ran back up on deck where he undressed to his shirt and undershorts. The bow of the liner was already in the water and he knew the ship did not have much time left. Nearly all the lifeboats had left the *Titanic* – any remaining places were reserved for women and children only. Water was pulling the bow of the majestic vessel down with an almighty force, he said, and the stern was gradually rising into the sky. An explosion from the bowels of the ship threw him into a pile of ropes and chairs. His only chance was to try and swim and so after taking a running start he jumped overboard. He thought his fall would never end, but then after what seemed like minutes, he hit the icy water. He was pulled under, but after a long dive finally came to the surface. He swam away from the ship, fearful that the sinking would suck him under. Then he turned to witness the liner's final few moments.

'Suddenly, I saw the *Titanic* go down, straight up, with horrible explosions and excruciating screams . . . There was then a huge swirl, then silence. Suddenly [there] rose a dismal moaning sound, which I won't ever forget; it came from those poor people who were floating around, calling for help. It was horrifying, mysterious, supernatural.'[3]

Marjorie Newell Robb, who was twenty-three at the time of the disaster and who lost her father that night, watched the sinking from lifeboat number six. Interviewed about the disaster in 1981, when she was ninety-two, she recalled the visceral impact of the sounds. 'I can remember, to this day, the noise the ship made as it went under,' she said. 'You could actually feel the noise, the vibrations of the screams of the people, and the sounds of the ship.'[4]

For Hugh Woolner – a first-class passenger who jumped into collapsible D fifteen minutes before the ship went under – the noise of the sinking was like thousands of tons of rocks tumbling down a metal chute. 'Every light went out and the roaring went on for about a minute,' he wrote a few days after the event. 'Then arose the most fearful and bloodcurdling wail. It was awful. One thousand seven hundred men in the dark, going down amid that ghastly turmoil! I can never forget it.'[5]

Thomas Patrick Dillon, a crew member who gave evidence at the British inquiry into the disaster, desperately clung to a handrail as the ship went down. A wave of water washed over him, sweeping him into the sea, and as he looked around he saw over 1,500 people struggling to stay alive in the ocean. 'The air was filled with sharp, pitiful groans,' he said, recalling how one young man near him repeatedly called out for his mother. Another man clutched him round the neck and Dillon had to battle him off, finally seizing him by the throat in a bid to save his own life. He was in the freezing water for approximately twenty minutes before he was pulled into a lifeboat. 'I was told afterwards that I was unconscious for a long time,' he said. 'I would rather die a hundred times than go through such an experience and live.'[6]

As survivors recounted their experiences, the horror of the loss of the *Titanic* came to be encapsulated by an auditory, rather than, visual memory. Passengers seemed able to erase, to some extent, the surreal sight of the ship – then the biggest moving object in the world – splitting in two and then disappearing under the surface of the Atlantic, but not the awful, nightmarish cries that accompanied the sinking. 'The concerted cry of despair that came from the direction of the liner as she plunged into the ocean is ringing in my ear this minute,' said silent screen actress Dorothy Gibson, who escaped in lifeboat seven, and who recounted her memories in a newspaper interview on her arrival in New York. 'I cannot describe it. It sounded like a mighty wail.'[7]

Recalling her memories of the disaster at the United States

Senate Inquiry, passenger Daisy Minahan described the cries as 'horrible',[8] while George A. Harder recalled the noise as a 'continuous yelling or moaning'.[9] Ruth Becker Blanchard, then a twelve-year-old girl travelling from India to Michigan with her mother and siblings, could still hear the noise in her ears more than seventy years later. The screams, she said, were the 'most terrible noise that human beings ever listened to – the cries of hundreds of people struggling in the ice-cold water, crying for help with a cry we knew could not be answered.'[10] Second-class passenger, twenty-seven-year-old Edwina Troutt, later Corrigan, wrote in a 1958 letter of how crew member Joseph Henry Bailey rallied the survivors in lifeboat sixteen to raise their voices in an effort 'to help drown out the cry of death', as well as singing the popular song 'Pull for the Shore'.[11]

Yet, for some, the sound of the screams had seeped so deeply into their psyches that there was no escaping them. Chief baker Charles Joughin – who drank a bottle of spirits before simply stepping off the sinking ship, reportedly without even getting his hair wet – said later that he was haunted by the cries throughout his life. 'All those years, and I could never put that noise out of my head. Not even drink could put it out.'[12] For third-class passenger Gus Cohen, who wrote of his memories fifty years later, the sound of the cries 'is never out of my ears'.[13]

After witnessing the sinking of the ship from lifeboat fourteen, seven-year-old Eva Hart, who had been travelling on the *Titanic* as a second-class passenger with her parents, and whose father died in the disaster, turned to her mother and commented on the harrowing nature of the cries. 'I'll always remember her reply,' said Eva years later. '"Yes, but think about the silence that followed it" . . . because all of a sudden the ship wasn't there, the lights weren't there, and the cries weren't there . . . Silence. The silence was worse.'[14]

This stark contrast – between the unbearable noise of the

cries and the complete stillness that came after – could almost serve as a symbol of the way in which survivors responded to the event. At the same time as remembering the experience, many repressed certain elements of that night. For example, second-class passenger Albert Caldwell, who was twenty-six in April 1912, was happy to relive the tragedy for the benefit of friends and family. His great niece, Julie Hedgepeth, recalls how Al loved to talk about his time on the *Titanic* – he was, she recalls, far from melancholy or morbid about it. However, one day she asked him about something he never mentioned, something he deliberately left out of his narrative – the noise the passengers made after being thrown into the water. 'Finally I saw him turn sombre. "You have to forget the screams," he said quietly. "You have to forget the screams or you'd go crazy."'[15]

This forced forgetting – the conscious or unconscious suppression of memory – was one of many strategies employed by those who survived. For them, the experience was like a closed book, a text that had been placed in a strongbox and locked away from both prying strangers and curious family members. It was a subject not open for analysis or discussion. When, in the 1950s, historian Walter Lord contacted a number of survivors for the first of his two books on the *Titanic*, he encountered a certain amount of resistance. Typical is the response from the daughter of first-class passenger Leila Meyer, who escaped in lifeboat number six and who lost her husband, Edgar. 'Under no circumstances can she be approached on the subject of the *Titanic*,' she wrote of her mother. 'She has no written account of any kind, and never discusses it.'[16]

J. Bruce Ismay – the chairman of the White Star Line who survived the disaster in ignoble circumstances when he accepted a place in a lifeboat rather than going down with the ship – would not countenance discussion of the incident. The very name of the liner – a ship that was to be the pride of his company, the last word in technology, opulence, and efficiency – was forbidden to be mentioned in his presence. The shock of the loss of the vessel – the contrast between its exaggerated presence and its sudden absence, the excessive enterprise of the venture and the extraordinary fall and concomitant shame – was too much to endure as it symbolised the sinking of his own reputation.

Of course, this enforced forgetting – this desperation of survivors to wipe the incident from their consciousness – could not be successfully achieved without consequences. In its least severe form the repression led to a type of self-erasure, in which individuals were reduced to mere shadows of their former selves. Ismay is one such example – a man who has been described, inaccurately, as a 'recluse' in the years after the *Titanic*. It's true he did spend increasing amounts of time at Costelloe Lodge, his summer home in County Galway, Ireland, where he indulged his passion for fishing, and was largely rejected by the society that had previously embraced him. Yet the label 'recluse' does not capture the strangeness of his new personality. The truth of the matter is that Ismay became a ghost, more of a spectre than a man. In his spare time, he would haunt the parks of London, where he would sit on benches in the hope of meeting down-and-outs; post-*Titanic* he identified with the disenfranchised and the marginal. When he travelled by train he would reserve a first-class cabin to himself, refusing to venture into the dining car and insisting that his servant close the blinds to the windows so that the general public could not see him. His granddaughter, the historian and writer Pauline Matarasso – who remembers him from her childhood – has gone so far as to describe him as a 'corpse'.

She says: 'Having had the misfortune (one might say the misjudgement) to survive – a fact he recognised despairingly within hours – he withdrew into a silence in which his wife made herself complicit, imposing it on the family circle and thus ensuring that the subject of the *Titanic* was as effectively frozen as the bodies recovered from the sea.'[17]

Constance Willard was another survivor whose whole being seemed to have been snuffed out by the enormity of the experience. Larry Boyd, an instructor in physical education and recreation at Las Campanas Hospital – an expensive and discreet institution in California that specialised in the treatment of mental illness – remembers her as a silent, shadowy figure; a prematurely old woman with long white hair, who always wore a nightgown, even during the day. 'I was not too successful in getting her interested in any activities, but sometimes, late in the afternoon, she would go for short walks with me out to the tennis courts or the rose garden,' he says. 'She didn't want to be seen by visitors to the sanatorium.'[18] She was first admitted to Las Campanas – whose most famous patient was Judy Garland, the actress who once occupied the room next to Constance's – in the 1930s, when she was in her forties, suffering, it seems, from a total disintegration of the personality. Her only interest, noted Boyd, was the feeding of 'her' cats – creatures that lived in the lush grounds of the sanatorium. Every Friday night the patients were invited to attend a film evening and, on one occasion, the chosen movie was *A Night to Remember*, the 1958 film made from Walter Lord's book of the same name. Boyd remembers feeling worried that she might react badly to the film, but she sat through it in silence; afterwards she never mentioned the *Titanic*. 'I knew better than to ask about the *Titanic*, and the subject never came up,' he recalls.[19]

In April 1962 – on the fiftieth anniversary of the sinking of the ship – the staff of Las Campanas were instructed to look out for reporters keen to seek an interview with Constance Willard. But no one tried to hunt her down and the day passed quietly. However, around the time of the anniversary, the *Los Angeles*

Times published a number of photographs taken on board the *Carpathia*, the rescue ship that transported the 705 survivors to New York. Boyd remembers looking closely at the pictures to see if any of the young ladies was Constance, and later that day he showed the images to one of the doctors. 'He told me that he had already confirmed that one of the ladies was Miss Willard,' he says. 'I imagine when she was sitting on the hatch of the *Carpathia*, she could never have believed she would end her life in a sanatorium in distant California.'[20]

Today there are few traces left of the shadowy figure of Constance Willard. We only seem to know what she *didn't* do – she never married, never had children, never had a job. Her only friends were a few cats and the staff of a psychiatric institution in California, far from her birthplace of Minneapolis, Minnesota. Apparently, that cold night in April 1912, when she was ordered by an officer to jump into a lifeboat, at first she refused to get in. 'Don't waste time – let her go if she won't get in,' the officer is recorded as saying. Constance then ran back to the first-class deck to search for her friends, none of whom she found. Although she did eventually board a lifeboat, which she shared with seven men, twenty women, and several children, it was as if she left a piece of herself behind on the stricken ship, a fragment of her identity that sank with the liner to the bottom of the Atlantic.

How people remembered the event can be traced back to the manner in which they survived. Each of the 705 survivors responded in their own individual way according to a matrix of factors based on gender, class, economic status, personality type, past experience and future expectations. As passengers configured and reconfigured their memories of that night so too did they lay the foundations of the method of their psychological survival. After the tragedy, some were so desperate to find something good amidst the emotional wreckage of the disaster that they suffered from a sort of mass hysteria, a collective need to create a positive narrative of the event, a trend that also reflects the expectations of society at that time. In a way, these stories not only helped the survivors to cope with their surreal experience; the world at large benefited too. The sinking of the *Titanic* was so shocking, so negative, so alien to the securities of Edwardian society that almost as soon as the disaster was reported, myths began to spring up like fragments of driftwood from the sea. As first-class passenger May Futrelle – a writer who lost her husband, the crime novelist Jacques Futrelle, in the sinking – noted, many of the news clippings from the time were nothing more than 'the wild imaginings of frustrated reporters who could not get facts from survivors and had to write something'.[21]

These narratives, often questionable in their veracity, tended to be stories of self-sacrifice, anecdotes that illuminated the innate goodness of mankind. The band, some said, stood on the deck of the sinking ship and played until the very end with the strains of 'Nearer My God to Thee' echoing over the dark ocean. The Captain, Edward Smith, swam over to one of the lifeboats with a baby in his hands, ensuring its safety, before slipping under the waves. A young woman gave up her place in one of the lifeboats to a mother with a young child.

'I often think it all over again and again, the things I saw as plain as if they were printed on my brain,' recalled Bertha Watt (later Marshall), a twelve-year-old second-class passenger. 'I know now that I learned a great deal of the fundamentals I have built a happy life on, such as faith, hope and charity, just in one short week of my life, listening to people talk and hearing answers my mother gave to me and others and later thinking how some behaved.' Writing about the experience in 1963, she remembered the diverse reactions of some of the adults in her lifeboat, particularly the unexpected hypocrisy of a man of the cloth and the shallowness of one of the first-class women on board.

'There was the minister who hid under the seat in our boat, walking stick and small suitcase included,' she wrote. 'When we were well on our way he appeared and sat bemoaning the fact that he had lost so many years of sermons on the *Titanic*. Another woman was worrying about her jewels when all of a sudden another woman yelled, "Give me back my husband and son and I'll buy you jewels." Those few days before we landed in NY were a life all their own. Tragedy affects people in so many different ways.'[22]

One of the aims of this book is to show the impact of the *Titanic* disaster on the lives of its survivors. For the majority the experience was nothing short of traumatic; women, especially those in second and third class, lost husbands, brothers, fathers, sons. Their lives would never be the same again. Writing in 1955, Marjorie Dutton – who travelled aboard the *Titanic* in second class as an eight-year-old girl – described how her life seemed to be blighted or cursed. 'My father was drowned taking our worldly wealth with him, as in those days people were not as bank minded as they are now,' she said. 'Since that time I have been blessed with bad luck and often wonder if it will ever give me a break, but it just seems to be my lot . . . I think my name was published at the time as having been drowned.'[23]

In a number of letters written to Walter Lord in the 1950s, Marjorie described her straitened circumstances – the fact that she could not claim any money from the Titanic Relief Fund because of her marital status (even though her husband had died fifteen years previously), her ill health (she had had a stroke in 1953), and the loss of her part-time job. She was unable to meet her day-to-day expenses, she could no longer pay the mortgage on her house in Chilworth, Surrey, and feared she was so low on money that she could not afford to buy food. 'I cannot help thinking that if it had not been for the *Titanic* affair I might have now been in America in very different circumstances,' she wrote. 'I'm afraid one cannot help feeling at times that life can be very unkind through no fault of one's own.'[24] In the final letter of the series, she seems particularly distressed. 'I am now in desperate straights [sic], as I have now lost my job and the people I had living in my house to pay expenses are leaving,' she says. 'I feel that, after all, I am still a survivor and also lost my father on the *Titanic*. I do hope you will forgive me for writing to you like this, but I feel so desperate I do not know what to do.'[25] Marjorie Dutton died nine years later, aged sixty-one, after a period spent living in a nursing home in Gosport.

Yet for others, the memory of that night spurred them on to greater things. After coming so close to death – and encountering so many of its markers (the unknowable iceberg itself, the sinking ship, the ink-black sea, not to mention the unforgettable screams and the ocean littered with corpses) – it was as if some survivors chose to squeeze every last drop of experience out of life. For instance, journalist and author Helen Churchill Candee went on to travel in China, Japan and Cambodia; she became fascinated by the mysterious ruined temples of Cambodia and in 1924 published the travel book *Angkor the Magnificent*. Indeed, after the death of their husbands in the sinking, many women were forced to adopt new forms of independence. Renee Harris – who lost her husband, the Broadway producer Henry Harris, that April night – transformed herself into America's first female theatre manager and producer. The details of her career, she said, were never of much interest to people, 'but let them learn that I am a survivor of the *Titanic*, then I am the center of attention,' she said. 'This, unfortunately, is consistent with the public's appetite for violence and horror.'[26] Until her death in 1969, aged ninety-three, Renee looked upon that night as a defining moment; either she could let herself be consumed by grief or she could make a future that was, at least, endurable. Writing in an unpublished document in 1977, she said, 'That fateful night that engulfed me fifty years ago has never entirely disappeared, though it has become buried under the many events that have accrued through the years. There is no doubt in my mind that what I went through that harrowing night in 1912 was a test to find out if I should go through life without my beloved or just give up.'[27]

For the privileged, cynical few the *Titanic* was nothing more than an experience to be mined, an opportunity to turn tragedy into profit, dolour into dollars. Although there is a general perception that the Edwardian era – and its equivalent in America, the gilded age – was less obsessed with scandal and sensation than we are today, in fact nothing could be further from the truth. Within four weeks of the sinking, the first-class passenger and silent screen star Dorothy Gibson had made the first film about the disaster, starring herself, and sporting the same dress that she had worn that very night. Perhaps this was her way of surviving. By turning the event into a performance, an 'act', Gibson was able to transform experience away from reality – a territory full of painful memories, murky emotions and unpleasant sensations – into a place of fantasy. What happened to Dorothy Gibson – and her mother Pauline, who was a fellow passenger – after the *Titanic* contains all the elements of melodrama: illicit love, passion, ambition, intrigue, accusations of spying and even internment in a concentration camp during the Second World War. Similarly, many of the survivors went on to lead fascinating lives – lives that will be explored in this book in relation to the wider cultural context.

Most accounts of the *Titanic* story stop at the point when the rescue ship, the *Carpathia*, docks in New York. This book shows what happened later, after the newspaper reporters had moved on, after the glare of attention had dimmed. In many respects, it is an untold story, or series of stories, which is uncovered using many documents (letters, diaries, memoirs) that have never been published before.

Survivors said that after the ship went down the sea was as calm as a millpond. However, for many passengers the echoes of that night continued to reverberate throughout their lives, the memories refusing to completely die away. The Countess of Rothes, for example, recalled dining out with friends a year after the disaster when she 'suddenly felt the awful feeling of intense cold and horror' that she associated with the sinking of the *Titanic*. She realised that the orchestra was playing *The Tales of Hoffman*, the last music she had heard at dinner on the night of 14 April 1912.[28] Disassociation was a common complaint, a feeling of disembodiment and disconnection. Second-class passenger Lyyli Silven, from Finland (who lost her aunt and uncle), remembered that often, when she related what had happened to her, she would be left with an overwhelming feeling of unreality, as though 'the whole thing is like a dream'.[29] For many survivors, the spectre of the *Titanic* would forever cast a shadow over their lives.

One

A FANCY-DRESS BALL IN DANTE'S HELL

Sunday 14 April 1912 dawned bright and clear. There was a feeling of optimism in the air, a sense that anything was possible. The ship seemed to glide over a sea of glass. For first-class passenger Colonel Archibald Gracie, the RMS *Titanic* was a 'floating palace',[1] a high-class hotel that cut through the waters of the Atlantic with a majesty and power he had never experienced before. As he stood on the first-class deck, he noticed that the sea was so level he could barely make out a ripple.

Since Wednesday, when the ship had departed Southampton on its maiden voyage to New York, Gracie had taken advantage of every luxury. After all, this was a liner that had cost $7.5 million to build, a ship that carried 800 bundles of asparagus; one and a quarter tons of fresh green peas; 36,000 oranges and 16,000 lemons; 75,000 pounds of fresh meat; 11,000 pounds of fresh fish; 4,000 pounds of bacon and ham; 7,500 pounds of game and poultry; 1,000 sweetbreads; 40,000 sausages; 40,000 fresh eggs; 6,000 pounds of fresh butter; not to mention the 1,500 bottles of wine, the 20,000 bottles of beer and stout or the 850 bottles of spirits. For the gentlemen on board there were 8,000 cigars, which they could enjoy while putting the world to rights.

It's not surprising then that on that Sunday morning, after a few days of self-indulgence, Colonel Gracie felt he should take a spot of exercise. He rose early, before breakfast, and played a half-hour game of squash with Fred Wright, the professional racquet instructor, followed by a swim in the heated salt water swimming pool. The exercise refreshed his body and his spirit, erasing, for a few moments at least, a slight uneasiness that hung over him. 'The pleasure and comfort which all of us enjoyed . . . seemed an ominous feature to many of us, including myself,' he said, 'who felt it almost too good to last without some terrible retribution inflicted by the hand of an angry omnipotence.'[2]

Lady Duff Gordon – the London-based couturier known as 'Lucile' – remembers how extraordinary it was to see and taste strawberries in April in mid-ocean, while another first-class passenger, Marjorie Newell Robb, was still able to recall in 1981, at the age of ninety-two, the feel of 'carpets that you could sink in up to your knees', the 'fine furniture that you could barely move', and the 'very fine panelling and carving'.[3] Many second-class passengers spent their time riding between floors in the elevator, which was described as 'a great new attraction on the boat'.[4] The tang of novelty hung in the air – in fact, one could even smell it. In a letter, second-class passenger Marion Wright wrote to her father from the ship on 11 April and said, 'It is lovely on the water, except for the smell of new paint, everything is very comfortable on board.'[5]

For thirteen-year-old Madeleine Mellenger (later Mann) the ship was nothing short of a floating miracle. She was travelling with her mother, Elizabeth Anne, in second class to make a new life for themselves in America. Her father, Claude Alexander Mellenger, a London journalist, had brought the family to the point of ruin through years of what she later described as 'his extravagance and high living'. After Mellenger finally deserted them, Elizabeth was forced to take a position as a lady's maid and travelling companion with the wealthy Colgate family of America. For Madeleine, the *Titanic* became a symbol of promise, a sign of new beginnings. 'I could write forever about *Titanic* and how it changed my life,' she wrote in a letter nearly sixty years later. 'A little while ago I started a "Story of my Life" kind of thing and I had to stop as it was running into dozens of papers and I wondered if I could finish it.'[6] That Sunday morning she remembers Charles Jones, the Colgates' superintendent who did not survive the disaster, knocking on the door of their cabin on E deck and showing them a series of beautiful photographs of the family's grand estate in Bennington, Vermont. At eleven o'clock the mother and daughter attended the Divine Service, which was held in the first-class dining room.

Captain Edward J. Smith – a distinguished, bearded man whose plan it was to retire after the *Titanic*'s maiden voyage, following fifty years at sea – led the passengers through the service, which included the 'Prayer for Those at Sea' and the hymn 'O God, Our Help in Ages Past'. After the service, Madeleine Mellenger remembers going back to her cabin with her mother in order to get ready for lunch and, as she walked along the wide corridor that ran the length of the ship, seeing a door open. 'I saw Captain Smith and his officers coming toward us in full regalia, lots of gold braid, and I knew him, as he looked so much like Edward VII, beard and all,' she said. 'I asked, what they were doing and was told they were inspecting the airtight compartments and doors. That was his last inspection."[7]

As was customary, Captain Smith and his men would meet at noon each day to take a series of sun measurements. With the use of sextants the officers were able to work out the precise position of the ship and, as a result, chart the distance they had travelled in the course of twenty-four hours. Those passengers who had bet on the ship's sweepstake would then meet in the first-class lounge to hear the results – the ones who had picked a figure closest to that day's passage (which came in at 546 miles) could collect a tidy sum.

The sweepstake was just one of many diversions offered to discerning passengers on what was considered the world's most sophisticated ship. On board there were Turkish baths, a fully equipped gymnasium, a lending library, a smoking room, a reading and writing room and a wide range of restaurants. The first-class dining saloon – a magnificent room 114 feet long and 92 feet wide – was decorated in a style inspired by English Jacobean houses such as Haddon Hall and Hatfield, 'but instead of the sombre oak, which the sixteenth- and seventeenth-century builders would have adopted, the walls and ceiling have been painted white'.[8] The room had a series of 'recession bays', which in effect formed 'a number of separate private dining rooms, where families or friends can dine together practically alone, retired from the busy hum of surrounding conversation'.[9]

Many first-class passengers also commented on the grandeur of the main staircase, which measured 60 feet high and 16 feet wide. The walls were covered with oak panelling, which, although simple in character, was 'enriched in a few places by exquisite work reminiscent of the days when Grinling Gibbons collaborated with his great contemporary, Wren'. On the top landing stood a clock, flanked by two female figures, 'the whole symbolizing Honour and Glory crowning Time'.[10]

Not only was it the last word in luxury, but the *Titanic* was also a massive 46,000-ton signifier of technological mastery. With its revolutionary design – the liner possessed a series of watertight doors which its designers assumed would protect it from virtually every calamity – a writer in *Shipbuilder* magazine of 1911 proclaimed it 'practically unsinkable'.[11] By the time passengers boarded the liner, less than a year later, the word 'practically' had been erased from the collective consciousness. Sylvia Caldwell, who was travelling in second class with her husband Albert and ten-month-old son Alden, remembers asking a deck hand who was carrying luggage on board whether the vessel really was unsinkable. The man turned to her and said, 'God himself could not sink this ship.'[12] Captain Smith, in an interview five years before his final voyage aboard the *Titanic*, stated, 'I cannot imagine any condition which would cause a ship to founder. I cannot conceive of any vital disaster happening . . . Modern shipbuilding has gone beyond that.'[13]

The ship was enveloped by a sense of safety and security. In fact, the vessel was seen by many passengers to be a symbol of social order. The liner's passengers were stratified by class – the third class at the bottom of the ship, the second in the middle, the first at the top – and, for the most part, did not mix with one another. Each person was content with his or her place; those in third class knew better than to aspire upward, those in first would not dream of looking down below. These were days when, for the majority, God was still in his heaven and everything was right with the world.

As seventeen-year-old Jack Thayer, an American who had been visiting Europe with his parents, wrote in a privately printed memoir in 1940, 'Upon rising in the morning, we looked forward to a normal day of customary business progress. The conservative morning paper seldom had headlines larger than half an inch. Upon reaching the breakfast table, our perusal of the morning paper was slow and deliberate. We did not nervously clutch for it, and rapidly scan the glaring headlines, as we are inclined to do today. Nothing was revealed in the morning, the trend of which was not known the night before . . . There was peace, and the world had an even tenor to its ways.'[14]

That Sunday, Jack could see his future mapped out as plain as the clear, straight line of the distant horizon. After graduating from Haverford School outside Philadelphia, he would attend Princeton, then travel in Europe, returning home to

America to practise private or commercial banking. As he said, 'It could be planned. It was planned. It was a certainty.'[15]

He spent most of the day walking around the deck with his mother, Marian, and his father, John Borland Thayer, who was second vice-president of the Pennsylvania railroad. The family stopped for short conversations with various acquaintances such as Thomas Andrews, the ship's chief designer, J. Bruce Ismay, the chairman of the White Star Line, and Charles M. Hays, the president of the Grand Trunk Railway of Canada. Like many passengers, Jack noticed that, as the afternoon wore on, the temperature seemed to plummet. 'I remember Mr Ismay showing us a wire regarding the presence of ice and that we would not reach that position until around 9 p.m.,' he said.[16]

Ismay had been given the wire by Captain Smith just before lunch, during which first-class passengers could choose from fillets of brill, egg *à l'Argenteuil*, grilled mutton chops, or, from the buffet, salmon mayonnaise, potted shrimps, Norwegian anchovies, roast beef, veal and ham pie, corned ox tongue, galantine of chicken, and a selection of cheeses including Gorgonzola, Camembert and Cheddar. The message had been sent by the *Baltic*, another White Star Line ship. Transmitted at 11.52 a.m., the message read: 'Have had moderate, variable winds and clear, fine weather since leaving. Greek steamer 'Athenai' reports passing icebergs and large quantity of field ice today in latitude 41.51 N., longitude 49.52 W.'[17]

Ismay did not seem unduly worried about the threat of icebergs. When he met Marian Thayer and her friend, Emily Ryerson, later that afternoon, he seemed animated and excited. According to Emily Ryerson's statement, dated 18 April 1913, after a short, polite conversation about the suitability of their accommodation, Ismay took the Marconigram from his pocket and brandished it with a flourish at the two women. The gesture was motivated, according to Marian Thayer, by a need to show the two socially prominent passengers 'who he was'. This sense was reinforced by Mrs Ryerson, who stated, 'Mr Ismay's manner was that of one in authority and the owner of the ship and that what he said was law.'[18]

The icy temperatures forced many passengers to stay inside their cabins; those in first class were fortunate enough to have staterooms complete with heating. Edith Rosenbaum (later Russell), a thirty-three-year-old fashion journalist and buyer, was so cold she remained in bed until four o'clock that afternoon, at which point she decided to dress and take a short walk around the deck. As she stood by the stern she noticed the enormous propellers – they weighed around thirty-eight tons each – that churned up the darkening waters below. 'The foam whirled in a great cascade, made blood-red by the rays of a glorious setting sun,' she recalled. 'It looked like a crimson carpet stretching from the ship to the horizon.'[19]

She then returned to her stateroom, A-11, to dress for dinner. In Edith's mind, clothes were much more than mere garments to warm and protect the body; fashion was both a source of joy and a complex language of individual expression. In addition, fashion was how she made her living – on this trip she had with her a number of trunks packed with exquisite gowns that she had ordered in Paris for clients and businesses in America. Her original plan was to travel on the *George Washington*, sailing from Cherbourg on 7 April, but her editor at *Women's Wear Daily* in New York wanted her to file a report on the fashions at the Easter Sunday races in Paris. She had discovered she could book a passage on the *Titanic*, leaving Cherbourg on 10 April, and she would still arrive in New York on the same day as the *George Washington*.

As she had stepped on board the train at Saint-Lazare station in Paris, bound for Cherbourg, she noticed a man and a woman rushing towards her, waving. It was Laurent, the head tailor at Paquin, the couturier on the Rue de la Paix, together with the head tailoress. Just as the train began to ease itself out of the station they passed over two huge white boxes tied with tapes, carrying heavy lead seals, containing a number of garments that she had ordered but which she assumed would not be finished in time. The boxes accompanied her on to the *Titanic*, boxes that, as she later remembered, 'were never unpacked and went down with the ship just as they were delivered'. Before the voyage she had tried to insure her collection of clothes, but she was told, in no uncertain terms, that 'it was ridiculous to spend money for insurance when travelling on an unsinkable vessel'.[20] The opinion – the invincibility of the vessel – was echoed on the tender that had ferried her out from Cherbourg to the *Titanic*. As they approached what appeared to her like an enormous building, almost a skyscraper, John Jacob Astor IV, the richest passenger on the liner, told her that the ship had cost 'ten million dollars to build, and [had] emphasised that she was unsinkable, a miracle of modern shipbuilding'.[21]

Yet, as she had embarked, something unsettled her – an awful sense that all was not right. The night before she sailed she had visited Madame de Thebes, one of the most famous fortune-tellers in Paris, who had told her she was about to endure a 'dreadful experience' during which she would lose her possessions and many, many friends. At the time she had felt highly sceptical, but as she set foot on the boat she was not so sure. Certainly the ship had every luxury one could think of and was, as she wrote to her secretary in Paris in a letter on 11 April, as big 'as from the corner of the Rue de la Paix to near the Rue de Rivoli . . . [it has] bedrooms larger than any Paris hotel room, and altogether is a monster. I cannot say I like it, as I feel as though I were in a big hotel, instead of on a cosy ship'.[22] She also remembered the words of an Arab fortune-teller who had told her, while reading grains of sand, that she would be in a 'very grave sea accident'. She had been so troubled that day that she asked Nicholas Martin, the general manager of the White Star Line's Paris bureau, whether she could get off the ship. He had informed her that she could disembark, but her luggage would have to stay on board. 'My luggage is worth more than I am,' she said. 'I had better remain with it.' And so he had arranged for her to have a stateroom where her trunks could be stored.[23]

In the late afternoon of 14 April, first-class passengers were in the process of getting ready for the gala dinner that Sunday evening. The men wore dinner suits, white shirts complete with collar studs and cufflinks, while the women sported a dazzling array of dresses. 'On these occasions, full dress was always *en règle*,' noted Colonel Gracie, 'and it was a subject both of observation and admiration, that there were so many beautiful women . . . aboard the ship.'[24] Helen Churchill Candee noted that the prettiest girl in the room wore a 'glittering frock of dancing length, with a silver fringe around her dainty white satin feet'.[25] Edith Rosenbaum chose to wear a white satin evening gown, together with velvet slippers topped with imitation diamond buckles.

At around 7.30 p.m., Bruce Ismay dined with the ship's doctor, Dr William O'Loughlin, in the first-class à la carte restaurant. During the meal, the doctor mentioned that the ship had 'turned the corner', meaning that the liner had reached a certain point in the Atlantic where it started to head directly for New York. Later, this conversation would be analysed for evidence that Ismay knew about the intricacies of navigation; if that point could be proved then it would demolish his later defence that he had been travelling on board the *Titanic* as a mere passenger rather than in any official capacity. At dinner, Captain Smith asked Ismay for the

Baltic's Marconigram regarding ice so he could share it with his fellow officers on the bridge.

That evening Ismay was in a boisterous, confident mood, telling Sir Cosmo and Lady Duff Gordon that 'undoubtedly the ship would establish a record'.[26] The liner continued to cut through the dark Atlantic waters at a speed of around 22 knots – the *Titanic's* top speed was in the region of 24 knots – while, in contrast, a number of other ships had dropped anchor for the night on account of the dangers of ice. In addition to the message from the *Baltic*, the *Titanic* had received a flurry of ice warnings during the course of that Sunday, and while the Captain had taken heed of them – he had already plotted a course that took the ship ten miles south of the normal shipping lane so as to avoid drifting ice – it seems as though he too had been intoxicated by the air of hubris that powered the vessel.

In the second-class dining room, a group of around one hundred passengers filed into the saloon for the Sunday evening service. Marion Wright, a young woman from Somerset, England, who was travelling to America to marry her sweetheart and start a new life in Oregon, walked to the front of the room and sang 'There is a Green Hill Far Away' and 'Nearer My God to Thee'. Before each hymn, Reverend Earnest Carter, who led the service, explained a little about the circumstances surrounding their composition. Lawrence Beesley, a schoolmaster from Dulwich College, recalled that it was curious that so many of the hymns dealt with dangers at sea. Included in the service that night was 'Lead, Kindly Light', which the Reverend said had been composed after a shipwreck in the Atlantic, and 'Eternal Father, Strong to Save', which features the lines, 'O hear us when we cry to Thee/For those in peril on the sea'.

Young Jack Thayer seemed entranced by the beauty of the ocean. After dinner, he decided to take a few turns around the deck, with a new acquaintance, Milton C. Long, the son of

Judge Charles M. Long of Springfield, Massachusetts. In June 1911, Long had been travelling on the SS *Spokane* – which was cruising from Seattle to Alaska – when the ship hit an uncharted rock off Seymour Narrows. The majority of passengers had had a lucky escape – all but two of the 160 tourists were accounted for – but perhaps that experience had shaken Long's belief in the invulnerability of modern shipbuilding; he, for one, had experienced the possibility of death at sea. Yet, as Jack and his new friend looked out at the perfectly still ocean, they assumed that the evening would end as peacefully, and as comfortably, as the previous four nights on board the ship.

'It was a brilliant, starry night,' Jack recalled years later. 'There was no moon and I have never seen the stars shine brighter; they appeared to stand right out of the sky, sparkling like cut diamonds. A very light haze, hardly noticeable, hung low over the water . . . I have never seen the sea smoother than it was that night; it was like a millpond, and just as innocent looking . . . It was the kind of night that made one feel glad to be alive.'[27]

Elizabeth Shutes, a forty-year-old governess, could not sleep because of the biting cold. There was something strange about the air that night, she recalled, an edge to it that unsettled her. The smell of it reminded her of the air inside an ice cave on the Eiger glacier that she had once visited. She lay in her bed, unable to banish a sense of anxiety that clawed at her consciousness, until finally she got out of her berth and switched on her electric stove. The red glow of the heater cheered her for an instant, before a sense of nervousness returned.

Up on the promenade deck, the mood was rather different. Silent film actress Dorothy Gibson was playing bridge with a party that included her mother, Pauline; Frederick Seward, a prominent marine lawyer from New York; and William

Thomson Sloper, a stockbroker from Connecticut. As Dorothy later remembered there was a 'great deal of merriment on board' that night.[28] The ripple of laughter danced through the air, sounding a top note to the light melodies provided by the ship's band. The accompanying conversation was as sparkling as the ice-cold champagne that seemed to flow all night. 'Inside this floating palace [there was] warmth, lights and music, the flutter of cards, the hum of voices, the gay lilt of a German valse,' noted Lady Duff Gordon – 'the unheeding sounds of a small world bent on pleasure.'[29]

After the gala dinner, Lady Duff Gordon and her husband, Cosmo, retreated to their staterooms on A deck. Across the ship, passengers prepared for bed, changing out of their clothes, whether it be evening dress or more workaday garments, into nightgowns and pyjamas. By eleven o'clock, many were either in bed reading or fast asleep, lulled by the steady rhythmic pulsation of the ship's engines. Jack Thayer, after putting on his pyjamas, said goodnight to his parents in the next room. Before climbing into bed, he opened slightly the porthole of his cabin and noticed that the breeze made a 'quiet humming whistle' as it entered his room.[30] It was, he said, 'a fine night for sleeping', and, what with all the fresh air he had had that day he was tired.

For some members of the crew, however, the day was just beginning. On the boat deck, in the cramped surroundings of the Marconi room, Harold Bride, the twenty-two-year-old junior wireless engineer, heard the sound of his colleague, Jack Phillips, tapping out a series of traffic messages on the wireless system. Without bothering to dress fully, Bride got out of bed and started work. There was an enormous backlog of messages that had to be cleared. Earlier that day the Marconi system had broken down and it had taken the two men seven hours to fix it.

At around eleven o'clock that night, the Marconi operator

from the *Californian*, which was in the near vicinity, sent a message to Phillips that the ship had stopped and was surrounded by ice. Phillips, tired and overworked, was nearly deafened by the blast of noise that came from his equipment. He was also furious that the *Californian*'s operator hadn't bothered with the usual etiquette of asking whether it was acceptable to interrupt transmission and Phillips had replied with a curt 'Shut up! Shut up! I am busy.' As a result, the message from the *Californian* never reached the bridge of the *Titanic*.

In the crow's nest of the ship, twenty-four-year-old Frederick Fleet stared into the darkness. At ten o'clock that night he, and his fellow 'eyes of the ship', Reginald Lee, had relieved Archie Jewell and George Symons. He had been told to keep a sharp lookout for small icebergs and growlers. The cold bit into him, chilling him to the marrow. As the night wore on, a slight haze settled over the water line, but it was, as he remembered later, 'nothing to talk about'.[31] Although the ship was equipped with binoculars, the set was not at hand and was later said to have been mislaid; if Fleet had been able to use them it's highly likely that he would have spotted the iceberg much, much sooner.

At around 11.40 p.m., Fleet saw an object loom out of the night, something 'even darker than the darkness', high above the water line.[32] With each moment, the indefinable, unknowable mass seemed to grow bigger. The moment of revelation – when the thing revealed its true identity – would haunt him for the rest of his life. Without a moment's hesitation, he rang the bell in the crow's nest three times – a sign that something lay in the path of the ship – and then rang down to the bridge.

'What do you see?' asked an officer.

'Iceberg right ahead,' he replied.[33]

Fleet had heard about time slowing down, but he had always dismissed it as a romantic notion. Now, for the next half a minute or so, he endured the agony of being a witness to time seemingly stretching out before him. With each second the liner sped towards the iceberg, a dark mass that now towered above the ship; surely, collision was certain. Then, just as it seemed too late, the vessel turned. Fleet watched as slithers of ice cascaded down on to the forecastle and well decks, before the iceberg glided by and disappeared once more into the night. 'That was a narrow shave,' said Fleet to Lee, assuming that the ship had suffered minimal damage.[34]

Around the ship, passengers experienced the collision in a variety of ways, each recalling the moment differently. One described it as though the *Titanic* had passed over a thousand marbles, while another compared it to the sound of someone tearing an enormous piece of calico. Second-class passenger Sylvia Caldwell was woken up with a start; she later said that the sensation was like 'a large dog had a baby kitten in its mouth and was shaking it'.[35] Martha Eustis Stephenson, who was lying in her bed in first class, immediately felt something was terribly wrong as the sensation brought back to mind the early morning, almost six years ago to the day, when she had witnessed the city of San Francisco reduced to rubble during an earthquake.

Governess Elizabeth Shutes, who had been made so anxious by the curious smell of the cold, described it as a 'queer quivering' that seemed to run under her feet, the whole length of the ship. A moment later, her employer Edith Graham, knocked on her cabin, and announced that she had just seen an iceberg pass by. Although everything was then 'sepulchrally still', Elizabeth remembers watching her charge, nineteen-year-old Margaret Graham, trying to eat a sandwich; her hand shook so badly that the 'bread kept parting company from the chicken'.[36]

Up on A deck, Dorothy Gibson felt a 'slight jar', but the movement seemed so insignificant that she, and her group, continued to laugh and converse for a full fifteen minutes before she noticed that the stewards and officers had started to behave with 'considerable nervousness'. She then said goodnight to her party and stepped out on deck, with the intention of having a brief stroll. As she came out of the saloon she noticed that 'the great ship was leaning heavily on one side'. As she walked, she saw 'passengers engaged in card playing and other forms of divertissement'. The night was beautiful, the moon 'shining brilliantly and the stars twinkled without being obscured by a single cloud'. Yet, in the ocean, there were 'icebergs around us and the water seemed filled with the shattered remains of others'.[37]

Jack Thayer remembered the moment that occurred just as he was going to bed. He seemed to sway ever so slightly and then he heard the engines stop – it was this 'sudden quiet' that he found more startling and disturbing. All was silent except for the breeze whistling through the half-open port window. A moment later, he heard the distant noise of running feet and muffled voices, followed by the sound of the engines starting up again. But there was something odd about the timbre that emanated from deep within the ship, as if the engines functioned not 'with the bright vibration of which we were accustomed', but as though they were tired.[38] Curious, he quickly threw on his heavy overcoat and put on his slippers, and after calling out to his parents to tell them that he was going up on deck to 'see the fun', he left his cabin to find out what had happened to the ship. His father said he would follow shortly.[39]

Renee Harris, who was married to a successful Broadway producer, was playing double Canfield with her husband in her cabin. Earlier that day, she had taken a tumble down a flight of stairs and had suffered a compound fracture of the elbow. Despite the pain, and the trauma of having her arm set, she had made an appearance at dinner that night, but had left early to return to her cabin. She had heard the talk of ice and had thought to herself how strange it was that the ship should sail at such a speed. 'The door of the clothes closet had been left open and I noticed my clothes swinging to a marked degree,' she remembered, 'so I said, "We're going awfully fast to have my dresses sway like that – much too fast among icebergs," when at that very moment the ship stopped.' Her husband said that he and Jacques Futrelle, who had the room opposite, would go out and see what all the fuss was about, and so he asked May Futrelle to sit with Renee in his absence. 'It is not an ordinary event to have a ship suddenly stop in the middle of the ocean so I was alarmed,' she said.[40]

Laura Mabel Francatelli – 'Franks', Lady Duff Gordon's secretary – was getting into bed in her cabin on E deck when she felt an almighty crash. 'The collision shook me, as well as everything else in my room.' She put on her dressing gown and opened her door to see several people standing in the corridor, all wearing 'night attire'. Two gentlemen approached and told her that although they had hit an iceberg there was no reason to be concerned and that she ought to return to bed.[41]

Some passengers claimed to have seen the iceberg itself. Edith Rosenbaum had finished writing a batch of letters in the drawing room, when she returned to her cabin to get ready for bed. Just as she was about to turn on the electric light in her cabin she felt a 'very slight jar, then a second, a little stronger, and a third, accompanied by a heavy shock, strong enough to make me cling to my bed-post'. She noticed the floor seemed to list and that the ship had come to a dead stop. As she opened her porthole and looked out she saw a 'huge white mass, like a mountain' drift by.[42] Virginia Clark, from California, had just climbed into bed when she felt a sudden jolt. As she looked through the window, instead of seeing the blackness of the ocean and the sky, she saw a 'perfectly white background', which she assumed was 'a tremendous ship with its white bow at the window'. Anxious to discover more, she stood on her bath to look out of the porthole, but saw nothing but the night, 'which shows the rapidity with which the ship must have passed the huge white thing after it was hit'.[43]

According to quartermaster George Rowe – who was stationed on the poop deck, the raised deck at the stern of the ship – the iceberg was in the region of one hundred feet tall. Just before the collision he noticed that the light seemed to take on an extraordinary quality, as if the air was full of minute ice particles, 'like myriads of coloured lights', a phenomenon that sailors called 'Whiskers round the Light'. At 11.40 p.m. he felt the ship shudder, a movement that he compared to the sensation of buffing up against a dock wall. At first sight he thought that the large object that passed by was a Windjammer, a type of sailing ship, but as it came closer he realised it was an enormous iceberg. Despite this, at the time he 'did not think the collision was serious'.[44]

In fact, many passengers took advantage of the drama to have a bit of fun. Some scooped up chunks of ice into their hands and proceeded to have snowball fights, while one passenger in the second-class smoking room asked a friend whether he could fetch him some ice to top up his highball. In general, the whole thing, as Edith Rosenbaum observed, was regarded as a great joke; she recalled throwing snowballs with an acquaintance on board, twenty-seven-year-old Robert Williams Daniel.

Even the chairman of the White Star Line did not think the ship was in danger at first. Ismay was asleep in his cabin when he felt a jarring movement. Assuming that the liner had dropped a propeller, he pulled on a pair of trousers over his pyjamas and threw on an overcoat and went straight to the bridge to speak to the Captain. Smith told him the ship had struck ice. Was she seriously damaged, Ismay asked. 'I'm afraid she is,' Smith replied. Before Ismay had arrived on the bridge the Captain had checked the commutator, a piece of equipment 'like a clock to tell you how the ship is listing'.[45] The device showed Smith that the liner was already listing two degrees down by the bow and five degrees to starboard. On seeing this, Captain Smith was heard to say to himself, 'Oh, my God.'

Smith, together with Thomas Andrews – the managing director of Harland and Wolff, the Belfast-based company that had built the *Titanic* – began their descent into the bowels of the ship to inspect the damage. With each discovery the prognosis worsened. The cargo hold at the front of the ship was flooded; the mail room was deep in water; the freezing-cold sea was seeping into boiler room number five, and boiler room number six was already fourteen feet under water; even the racquet court where Colonel Gracie had played a game of squash earlier that morning was filling with water. Back on the bridge, Andrews calculated that the iceberg had ripped a three-hundred-foot hole, or series of holes, along the starboard side of the ship. Although the crew closed the liner's watertight doors, five of the ship's compartments had been damaged, meaning that seawater started to weigh down the vessel, allowing yet more water to flow over the top of the bulkheads. If only four of the compartments had been flooded, *Titanic* would have survived. But, as Andrews realised, 'she could not float with all of her first five compartments full'.[46]

The *Titanic* would not last the night.

Laura Mabel Francatelli realised something was seriously wrong when she overheard a man in her corridor tell a passenger that the hold, luggage and mail had 'gone'. She dressed quickly and opened her door to find water running down her corridor. When she reached the cabin of her employer, Lady Duff Gordon, she found 'Madame' wearing two dressing gowns for warmth and Sir Cosmo in the process of getting dressed.

A minute or so later a member of the crew knocked on the door to tell them that the Captain had issued an order for all passengers to wear their life preservers. 'The next instant they were putting one on Madame, and I,' the secretary wrote to a friend. 'Oh, Marion, that was a sickening moment, I felt myself go like marble, but Madame and I prayed together, for God to look after us, and keep us safe, if it was his will.' Sir Cosmo accompanied his wife and 'Franks' to the top deck, which was already full of people. 'I looked over the side of the boat and tried to penetrate the blackness,' she remembered, 'and noticed the water was not such a long distance away from us, as we had always remarked at what a height it [the ship] was. I said to Sir Cosmo, "I believe we are sinking." He said, "Nonsense, come away," and then we walked more to the bow of the boat.'[47]

Among the crowd was Dorothy Gibson, who observed Thomas Andrews 'run to and fro with a face of greenish paleness'.[48] Mary Sloan, a stewardess from Belfast, recalls the look of horror in Andrews's eyes that night; although the chief designer was trying to control his emotions and his fear, it was possible to discern from his demeanour the fate of the ship. 'I read in his face all I wanted to know,' she said.[49] Andrews told Jack Thayer and his father that the ship would not last more than an hour. The two men returned to their staterooms to find Marian Thayer and her maid dressed. Jack hurried into his clothes – 'a warm greenish tweed suit and vest with another mohair vest underneath my coat' – and tied a life preserver, which he described as a kind of large, thick cork vest, around him, before putting on his overcoat. The family rushed to the lounge on A deck, which had become crowded with people. There, Jack saw his new friend, Milton Long, who asked if he could join the Thayers. 'There was a great deal of noise,' said Jack. 'The band was playing lively tunes without apparently receiving much attention from the worried . . . audience.'[50]

When Edith Rosenbaum was told to put on her life jacket and leave her cabin she didn't have time to get fully dressed. She was still wearing her evening dress – a style which the women of the day called 'potato sacks' or 'hobble skirts'– her velvet slippers and thin silk stockings. She donned a fur coat, fur scarf and a knitted wool cap and, before locking her trunks, rushed up to the lounge. 'Shall I ever forget my last look into my stateroom?' she wrote years later. 'The soft pink light of a table lamp, the pink down quilt, the warm radiator casting a soft glow, everything so cosy, so comfortable. How I hated to leave it.'

On her way to the lounge, she walked past the open door of a friend who had recently bought a dog in France. She heard the animal whining and so walked into the cabin and stroked it, tucking it under the bed cover, before closing the door. She then met her bedroom steward Wareham, and asked him whether he would return to her cabin to fetch her lucky mascot – a toy musical pig that played the popular song 'La Maxixe'. Although fellow passengers who overheard the exchange looked at her with distaste – how could she think of such a trifle when the boat was sinking? – the toy had special meaning for her. In August 1911, Edith had been seriously injured in a car accident on the so-called 'hill of death' between Deauville and Paris. Her friend at the wheel, a German gun manufacturer named Ludwig Loewe, had been killed instantly as the car ploughed headlong into a tree; she only survived because she had been tossed from the vehicle and landed on a tyre. 'My mother, having heard that the pig was considered a symbol of good luck in France, and feeling that good luck was just what I needed, presented me with this toy pig, the size of a big kitten and covered with white fur and black spots,' she said later.[51]

Although Edith heard the order for all women and children to go to the boat deck, she ignored the command, choosing instead to settle down in a cosy armchair in the lounge. She still

gone so far as to take her daughter to Europe to try and separate them – Behr was having none of it. After following Helen halfway across the world – and inventing a business trip in Europe – he wasn't about to part from her now.

As she approached lifeboat number five, which was surrounded by around twenty crew members, Mrs Beckwith heard Ismay calling out for more passengers. She walked up to Ismay and asked him quietly whether each member of her party, men included, could get into the lifeboat. 'Of course, Madam,' Ismay replied, 'all passengers, men and women, go in these boats.' The statement was not quite true, however, as three men – Captain Edward Gifford Crosby, Frank Warren and Engelhart Ostby – were already standing on the deck and waving goodbye to their wives and daughters. The three men would lose their lives that night.

Just as the crew started to lower lifeboat five, Dr Henry William Frauenthal – distressed at being parted from his wife, Clara, or perhaps finding himself unable to live and die by an Edwardian code of honour – jumped down into the boat, together with his brother, Isaac, and two other men. As he landed, Frauenthal – a heavily overweight man who was wearing two life jackets – hit first-class passenger Annie May Stengel. The impact of the fall broke two of her ribs and rendered her unconscious. Someone shouted out, 'Throw that man out of the boat,' but it was too late, and the boat continued to be lowered.

Apart from this incident, perfect discipline seemed to prevail, remembered Behr, as each of the passengers assumed that it was simply a case that they would spend an hour or so in the lifeboat before returning to the *Titanic*. Lifeboat number five, which left the ship at 12.55 a.m., carried around forty people – again, apart from a handful of crew members, all of them came from first class.

'Nearly all the men saved with their parties were in these

first few boats, all this before the lack of organisation and realisation of danger was felt,' said Behr. 'This was after explained by the fact, then unknown to us, that the Captain had ordered all passengers to A deck, the one below, while we were on the top boat deck on the side which had been struck, the star-board.'[56]

Over on the port side of the ship, Charles Herbert Lightoller – the ship's Second Officer – was busy preparing lifeboat six. He called out for women and children, and slowly they came forward. He saw a young English couple – Tyrell and Julia Cavendish – looking dazed and confused. She was wearing nothing but her husband's overcoat, a wrap and a pair of thin shoes. The couple looked at each other for a brief moment, before Lightoller gently took hold of Julia's hand and directed her towards the boat. When she looked back her husband had disappeared into the crowd; she never saw him again.

Helen Churchill Candee was the next passenger to secure a place in the boat. Candee – a fifty-three-year-old American writer – had been travelling in Europe when she had heard that her son, Harold, had been injured in an aeroplane accident. On board the *Titanic*, she had attracted the attentions of a number of men, some of whom had appointed themselves as her protector. Candee, however, was an independent woman – a divorcee, she had written the bestselling guide *How Women May Earn a Living*. She was not, however, immune to the joys of romance, and it seems that on the ship she had dallied with the affections of two men – Hugh Woolner, a forty-five-year-old London investor, and Edward Austin Kent, a fifty-eight-year-old architect from New York. In her account of the disaster published in the magazine *Collier's Weekly*, Candee refers to herself and her unnamed companion as 'the Two'. As she was walking up the grand staircase, she bumped into Kent, and gave him an ivory cameo of her mother and a small gold flask, engraved with the Churchill crest. The items were later found on his body when it was recovered from the sea and brought to Halifax, Canada.

Boarding the lifeboat proved difficult for Candee. As she climbed into it, she lost her footing, and landed on the oars lying lengthwise in the boat, hurting her ankle. Yet she did not make a fuss and kept the painful injury to herself.

Lightoller then spotted Margaret 'Molly' Brown – a first-class passenger who later became the subject of a musical and Hollywood film – who looked as though she was about to walk away from lifeboat six, towards the starboard side of the ship. He grabbed hold of her with the words, 'You are going, too,' and physically manoeuvred her into the lifeboat. By the time Lightoller had managed to direct around two dozen women – plus two crew members, quartermaster Robert Hitchens, and Frederick Fleet, the lookout who had first spotted the iceberg – into the boat he ordered it to be lowered. As it began its uncertain descent, Hitchens called up to say that he could not handle the lifeboat with only one other man. Lightoller called out for a crew member to step forward, but as he got no reply, a middle-aged man, Major Arthur Peuchen, a Canadian manufacturer of chemicals, announced that although he was no seaman, he was a yachtsman. 'If you're sailor enough to get out on those falls and get down into the boat, go ahead,' said Lightoller. Peuchen hesitated for a moment, before jumping out a distance of some ten feet, grasping the ropes and sliding down into the boat. In his cabin, he had left behind a tin box containing $100,000 worth of stocks and $200,000 in bonds, choosing instead to take only a good luck pin and three oranges.

Those in third class, however, did not have the luxury of being able to choose what to take with them; in fact, they would be lucky if they escaped from the ship with their lives. Eighteen-year-old Gus Cohen, an unemployed printer who was emigrating from England to America in search of work, went to bed at 10.30 p.m. that Sunday night. He shared his cabin with six other Englishmen; he would be the only one to survive the disaster.

At 11.40 p.m. Gus had been awoken by a crash, but assumed, like many others, that it was a minor problem in the boiler room, and so he went back to sleep. Even later, when he was woken by the master-at-arms and told to put on a lifebelt, he didn't worry. He walked up to the third-class deck, where he saw great lumps of ice, and realised that the ship had struck an iceberg. He heard the call for women and children to take their places in the lifeboats and saw a number of people praying and holding rosaries. He thought to himself, 'I will pray when I am rescued.' People seemed to be in a daze, as if trapped in some odd sort of dream. He worked out that if he stayed on the third-class deck he would almost certainly die. 'I could see that the first-class passengers were looked after first,' he remembered. 'I tried to get to the first-class deck, but was barred by sailors from going there.' Finally, through a circuitous route, he did manage to find a way up to the first-class deck, but by then, he said, 'things were hopeless'; he knew that he would not be allowed into a lifeboat. He would have to do something. For the moment, however, he didn't know what.[57]

Those third-class passengers who occupied cabins at the front of the ship felt the full impact of the collision. Bertha Mulvihill, who was sharing her room with Margaret Daly, was nearly thrown from her berth. Eugene Daly – Margaret's cousin, and a friend of the Mulvihill family from Athlone, Ireland – was also woken by the crash. He went to the girls' quarters to check on them and found them 'awake and confused'. He then returned to his cabin and put on his life jacket. When he stepped into the corridor, however, he discovered that he was the only passenger wearing a life preserver and immediately became the butt of jokes. Daly grabbed his thick black overcoat, with its astrakhan fur collar – a garment he later credited with saving his life – and urged his cousin and friend to get dressed. Margaret pulled on a coat over her night-gown and went out into the corridor. When she heard the call for all passengers to put on life jackets she went back inside and retrieved a life preserver.

The three friends then started to climb upward, finally reaching the deck above. But almost as soon as they arrived, Margaret realised she had left a number of precious keepsakes in her cabin. She wanted to go back and retrieve them, and although Eugene tried to stop her, she was adamant. Margaret, however, was in for a shock – her cabin was now under five feet of water and the expedition left her legs soaking wet.

On rejoining her friends Margaret had to wait for what seemed an eternity as the group was 'held below deck for the longest time'. According to Bertha, 'Every time we went up a stair they were locked.'[58] Finally, Eugene managed to find an open route towards the lifeboats on the upper deck. The other problem, according to Eugene, was that many women in third class believed the reassurances of the stewards that the ship could not sink. 'Most of the women believed these statements,' said Daly, 'until it was too late. That is why so many of the women in the steerage [third class] were drowned. When they finally realised that the ship was sinking they tried to reach the boats, but could not get through the crowd of other frightened passengers.'[59]

As the water continued to gush in, the crew knew that time was running out and so they worked quickly to launch the boats. With each moment, the situation proved more desperate. *Titanic* was carrying 2,228 people, yet her sixteen lifeboats (plus four Englehardt collapsibles) provided enough space for only 1,178. Loss of life would be inevitable.

Between 12.45 a.m. and 1.10 a.m., six lifeboats were lowered that contained only first-class passengers, with accompanying crew members. One lifeboat, the one carrying Sir Cosmo and Lady Duff Gordon, launched at 1.10 a.m., contained only five passengers (all from first class), together with seven crew members. It was designed to hold forty people. Laura Mabel Francatelli – Lady Duff Gordon's secretary – was one of the passengers in this lifeboat. 'Presently an officer started to swing off a little boat called the "Emergency" boat, quite an ordinary little rowing boat,' she wrote in a letter to a friend a few weeks later. 'He saw us and ordered us in, they were then firing the last rockets beside us, we had to be nearly thrown up into this boat, two other American gentlemen jumped in, and seven stokers, they started to lower us, we had not gone a few yards when our little boat got caught up by a wire rope on my side and in a few minutes we should all have been hurled into the sea, had it not been for that brave officer still up on deck. He shouted cut it with a knife, but nobody had one, and we were all in black darkness, hanging in midair, he shouted mind your heads, and threw a piece of heavy iron which shook our boat, and so set it free, we then went rapidly down to the water.'[60]

Despite the marked tilt and list of the ship, many passengers were still reluctant to get into the boats. Edith Rosenbaum was one of them. When, at around 1.20 a.m., Bruce Ismay spotted her, he shouted, 'What are you doing on this ship? I thought all women and children had left! If there are any more women and children on this ship, let them step forward and come over to this stairway immediately.' Ismay then, according to Edith, practically threw her down a narrow iron stairway to the deck below. There, two crew members grabbed hold of her and tried to throw her into one of the waiting lifeboats. She became frightened and in the struggle lost her velvet slippers. Her legs went rigid and she refused to move. 'Don't push me!' she screamed. One turned on her, spitting out the words, 'If you don't want to go, stay!' She looked about in the gutter of the deck for her slippers, and finally found them, minus an imitation diamond buckle.[61]

As she studied the remaining lifeboats, all hanging at a height of a seven-storey building above the sea, she couldn't imagine ever being able to climb into one. One insurmountable problem was her skirt; at the bottom, near her feet, it was less than a yard wide. She was, she said, 'a prisoner in my own skirt'.[62] She could only just walk in it, never mind jump, and so springing from the deck, across a wide gap, and into the nearest lifeboat, seemed to her 'a feat that only an acrobat could perform'.[63] Just then, one of the sailors spotted that she was cradling something in her arms. Thinking it was a baby, he wrenched it from her and threw it into the lifeboat. Edith froze in fear.

Watching the scene unfold was the painter Philip E. Mock, who, in a soft, gentle voice, asked her whether he could assist her. If she raised her leg and put her foot on his knee, and her arm around his neck, he could lift her up to the rail, from where she would be able to jump into the lifeboat. She nodded her assent, and a moment later she found herself flying through the dark night. There, at the bottom of the lifeboat in which she landed, she found her lucky mascot, her pig, with its little legs broken and nose chipped, but its musical ability intact.

'Looking up from the lifeboat, the *Titanic* seemed the biggest thing in the world . . .' she said. 'As we drew away, everything was calm and still, with the reflection of the lights on the water, passengers leaning over the rails . . . Nothing to predict the horror of the next few minutes.'[64]

Second-class passenger Charlotte Collyer also refused, at first, a place in one of the lifeboats. She was travelling from Southampton with her husband, Harvey, and her daughter, Marjorie, eight, to Idaho, where they planned to establish a fruit farm. As she stood on deck, contemplating the dark sea, one image from that night would not leave her: the sight of a stoker with all five fingers of one hand missing. 'Blood was running from the stumps and blood was splattered over his face and over his clothes,' she said. 'The red marks showed very clearly against the coal dust with which he was covered.' The stoker told her in no uncertain terms that the ship would sink. 'At this moment I got my first grip of fear – awful sickening fear,' she said. 'That poor man with his bleeding hand and his speckled face brought up a picture of smashed engines and mangled human bodies.'[65]

Despite this, she refused to leave her husband, ignoring the repeated calls of 'Women and children first'. However, at just before 1.30 a.m., she was standing on the port side of the ship with her family, when a sailor, responsible for filling boat fourteen, spotted her daughter. He caught up Marjorie in his arms and threw her into the boat. 'You too!' the sailor then yelled at her. 'You're a woman, take a seat in that boat or it will be too late.' Charlotte clung desperately to her husband, but the couple were wrenched apart by two crew members. 'Go, Lotty, for God's sake be brave and go!' said her husband. 'I'll get a seat in another boat.' As she landed in the boat, she bruised her shoulder, but stumbled to her feet to see her husband turn and walk away into the mass of people on the deck.

Just as lifeboat fourteen was about to be lowered away, a young boy, 'a pink-cheeked lad', jumped in and crawled under one of the wooden seats. Charlotte and another female passenger covered the boy with their skirts, but the crew member in charge, Fifth Officer Lowe, had spotted him. The boat was almost full to capacity and he was afraid that taking on any more people would destabilise it; that, and from Lowe's point of view, the last-minute stowaway was more of a man than a boy. Furious, Lowe dragged the adolescent to his feet and thrust his revolver in his face. 'I give you just ten seconds to get on to that ship before I blow your brains out,' he said. Marjorie pulled Lowe's jacket and begged him not to shoot. The boy started to plead with him, maintaining he wouldn't take up very much room. Lowe then lowered his revolver and told him to be a man. Defeated by the heavy code of Edwardian behaviour, the youngster finally climbed back on deck, where he lay down and wept.

Panic was now in the air. Panic and the acrid smell of fear. A male passenger – described as 'Italian' by Charlotte Collyer – hurled himself into their lifeboat, falling upon a young child with such force that he injured her. Lowe also ejected this man from the lifeboat, pushing him back on to the ship where he fell into the hands of a mob of second-class men who started to beat him senseless. Before lowering the lifeboat away, Lowe fired his revolver into the air – three warning shots that echoed through the night. It was the sound of desperation.

Bruce Ismay had spent the last one and a half hours working to fill and lower the lifeboats on the starboard side of the ship. In doing so he had helped to save the lives of dozens of passengers, including Dorothy and Pauline Gibson and honeymoon couple Dickinson and Helen Bishop (in boat seven); Karl Behr, his sweetheart Helen Monypeny Newsom, and her mother (in boat five); governess Elizabeth Shutes, and her charge, Margaret Graham, together with her mother (boat three); May Futrelle, the wife of novelist Jacques Futrelle, and Marion Wright (in boat nine); and, in boat eleven, Edith Rosenbaum, together with ten-month-old baby Philip Aks, who had become separated from his mother, third-class passenger, Leah.

By 1.40 a.m. all the lifeboats on the starboard side of the ship – except for collapsible C – had left the *Titanic*. As the bow of the liner sank further into the ocean, tons of water continued to gush into the front section of the ship. Around collapsible C, an ugly fight broke out as mostly male third-class passengers and a number of stewards tried to jump into the boat. A purser shot his revolver into the air as a warning and some kind of order was restored. Ismay, together with Officer Murdoch, then helped women and children – including Emily Goldsmith and her nine-year-old son, Frank – into the boat. When the men were satisfied that there were no more women and children nearby, Ismay, together with fellow first-class passenger William Carter, climbed into the collapsible. That small, seemingly innocent step towards survival would have enormous repercussions for Ismay in the months, and years, to come.

Jack Thayer, who was standing nearby, later claimed that Ismay pushed his way into the lifeboat. The seventeen-year-old interpreted Ismay's gesture as one of determined aggression, the triumph of savage instinct over breeding and behaviour, morals and manners. 'It was really every man for himself,' said Thayer.[66]

Thayer and his friend, Milton Long, debated whether or not to try and fight for a place in one of the last remaining lifeboats, as they could see the ship slowly sinking by its head. Amidst all the confusion – the shouting, the panic, the gunshots, the sudden storming of the lifeboats by hysterical mobs – he doubted whether the last few vessels would be safely and successfully launched. Another option was to jump into the sea – he saw a number of dark figures pitch themselves into the water from the back of the ship – but he was worried that the impact of hitting the surface would stun him. 'Three times I made up my mind to jump out and slide down the davit,' he recalled, 'and try to make the boats that were lying off from the ship, but each time Long got hold of me and told me to wait a while.'[67]

Unknown to Jack, his mother, Marian, had managed to

secure a place in lifeboat number four, which left the ship at 1.55 a.m. With her were first-class passengers Emily Ryerson, Virginia Clark, Florence Cumings, Madeleine Astor and Eleanor Widener – all six women would lose their husbands that night (Eleanor Widener her twenty-seven-year-old son too). After seeing his wife into the lifeboat, John Jacob Astor asked if he could accompany her as she was pregnant. Lightoller replied he could not, as it was a boat for women and children only. 'The sea is calm,' Astor said quietly to his wife. 'You'll be all right . . . I'll meet you in the morning.'[68]

Renee Harris witnessed this scene, before Astor, who she called 'an unsung hero', joined her and her husband, Harry, on deck. As the group walked towards the port side of the ship, Captain Smith spotted her. 'Why aren't you in a boat?' he said, angrily. 'How can your husband save himself and you too, with a broken arm?' She told the Captain she didn't want to leave her husband. 'You get into that boat, it is the last one,' said Smith. 'And lose no time – give your husband a chance.'[69]

At the port side of the ship Renee saw collapsible D. Around it stood a ring of sailors, guarding it against the sudden rush of the mob. Renee tried to persuade Ida Straus – the wife of Isidor Straus, the co-owner of Macy's department store – to get into the boat with her, but she refused to be parted from her husband. Isidor said, 'We've been together many years so when we must go, we'll go together. You are young – you have your whole life ahead of you. You go and may God go with you.' At that moment, Harry lifted Renee in his arms and threw her towards a sailor, who pushed her into the collapsible. At 2.05 a.m. it was launched from the ship, the last boat to be lowered from the *Titanic*.[70]

The ship would stay afloat for only fifteen minutes more. There were still around 1,500 people on board.

* * *

Jack Thayer had already gone through the motions of saying goodbye to Milton Long, the new acquaintance who by now felt like one of his closest, oldest friends. He had thought of all the good times he had had in his short life, and had reflected on future pleasures he would not experience. He looked at himself, he said, as though from some far-off place, unable to understand the strangeness of what was happening around him. Yet, amidst all of this – the sweet memories of life, the love for his family, the overwhelming sense of self-pity – part of him was able to detach itself from the horror of the situation and analyse how to maximise his chances of survival. 'We still had a chance,' he said, 'if only we could keep away from the crowd and the suction of the sinking ship.'[71]

Second Officer Charles Lightoller also knew he had to resist the urge to climb towards the rising stern of the ship. Crowds of people, terrified by the approaching mass of water that weighed down the front of the liner, had started to push backwards. If he joined them, 'it would only be postponing the plunge, and prolonging the agony – even lessening one's already slim chances, by becoming one of a crowd'.[72] He had done everything he could to help the passengers and soon he would have to battle for his own survival – alone. 'It came home to me very clearly how fatal it would be to get amongst those hundreds and hundreds of people who would shortly be struggling for their lives in that deadly cold water.'[73]

On deck, Lightoller heard the Captain giving his last command. 'Men, you have done your full duty,' he said. 'You can do no more . . . Now it's every man for himself. You look out for yourselves. I release you. That's the way of it at this kind of time. Every man for himself.'

Harold Bride, the junior wireless officer, looked out of the Marconi room to see the boat deck completely awash with water. His colleague, Phillips, continued to send a frenzied dispatch of SOS messages, even after the Captain had released him from his duties, even after the sea had started to seep into the cabin. As Phillips worked, Bride hurriedly packed a bag for him, but as he did so he noticed a stoker steal into the cabin and quietly try to slip the life jacket from his colleague's back. The sight infuriated Bride to such an extent that he, together with Phillips, started to attack him. 'I suddenly felt a passion not to let that man die a decent sailor's death,' he said. 'I wished he might have stretched rope or walked a plank. I did my duty. I hope I finished him. I don't know. We left him on the cabin floor of the wireless room, and he was not moving.'[74]

There was not much time left now, only a matter of minutes. The water was all-consuming, taking possession of the front of the ship, swallowing the bridge, destroying everything in its path. It pushed the crowd further towards the stern. The instinct to survive was strong, even to the very end. 'We were a mass of hopeless, dazed humanity,' observed Jack Thayer, 'attempting, as the Almighty and Nature made us, to keep our final breath until the last possible moment.'[75]

Lightoller was not about to wait and let his destiny be decided for him. He looked at the sea and dived in. Hitting the freezing water was like being stabbed by a thousand knives, he said. For a moment, he felt he was slipping away, before he forced himself back to consciousness. He saw the frame of the lookout cage poking out of the water – this was normally situated a hundred feet above the ocean – and was tempted to swim towards it before he realised that it would be foolish to try and hold on to anything that was part of the ship. He started to swim away from the *Titanic* as fast as he could.

On the ship, Jack Thayer contemplated the night. The lights on the *Titanic* were still blazing, but the noise of the exhaust steam pumping out from the liner's funnels had stopped. One could hear the discordant sounds of panic and praying, mixed with the strains of the ship's band in the background. Then, almost without warning, the *Titanic* jolted forward at an angle that Thayer estimated was around fifteen degrees. From somewhere deep within the ship came the sound of stifled roars and muffled explosions. 'It was like standing under a steel railway bridge while an express train passes overhead,' said Thayer, 'mingled with the noise of a pressed steel factory and wholesale breakage of china.'[76]

Thayer and Long shook hands and wished each other luck. Jack hurriedly took off his heavy overcoat, while Long climbed over the starboard rail and dived into the sea, which was now only twelve or fifteen feet below them. Jack followed, ten seconds later. 'I am afraid that the few seconds elapsing between our going,' said Jack, 'meant the difference between being sucked into the deck below, as I believe he was, or pushed out by the back wash. I was pushed out and then sucked down.'[77]

The shock of the icy water took the breath out of his lungs. Down he went into the darkened ocean, spinning in all directions. When he surfaced again his lungs felt as if they were about to burst. But he was alive.

Now the ship was sinking fast. The weight of the water pulled everything on and in the ship – boilers, china, children, clothes, wine bottles, pianos, pot plants – towards the bow. The remaining passengers clung desperately to whatever they could get hold of – rails, pillars, staircases, each other – yet many were swept away by wave after wave of encroaching freezing water. Rhoda Abbott, a thirty-five-year-old third-class passenger, desperately tried to hold on to her two sons, Rossmore, seventeen, and Eugene, thirteen, as she was swept from the deck. But in the swirling maelstrom she lost her grip. She never saw them again.

As water dragged down the front part of the ship, the liner began to split apart. The noise of the internal wrenchings echoed over the ocean, as boilers exploded, thundering down to the bottom of the ocean, and funnels began to topple. One witness out at sea in a lifeboat likened the noise to 'an immense heap of gravel being tipped from a hopper'.[78] As the sea sucked down the bow, the stern began to rise into the sky, higher and higher until it reached a fully perpendicular angle. 'All the passengers were sticking like flies to the stern,' said George Rheims, who jumped overboard at the end and witnessed the sinking from the water.[79] Jack Thayer described the panicked, terrified crowd as a cluster of 'swarming bees'.[80]

The stern of the ship, still fully lit, looked like a lone New York skyscraper; an image Charlotte Collyer later described as having a 'terrible beauty'.[81] It paused there, as if contemplating its fate, before it began its final journey down to the ocean floor. From lifeboat eleven, Edith Rosenbaum listened with horror to the dying cry of the *Titanic*.

'Just before the ship went down, there came a huge roar from her, as though from one's throat,' she said. The men in her boat – in an effort to try to protect the women from the awful screams of the dying – asked all the women to cheer. 'Saying that what we heard were shouts of joy indicating that all aboard had cleared the ship and were saved,' she recalled. 'And everyone in our boat did actually cheer three times. This, of course, was surely a device to distract us from the awful sound as the ship went down, and it did at least serve that purpose. Somehow or other we were still quite incapable of realising the full extent of the tragedy in which we were participants.'[82]

Two

THE SHIP OF WIDOWS

From her lifeboat, Irene – or Renee as she preferred to be called – Harris watched as the *Titanic* slipped into the sea. The screaming stopped and an uncanny silence descended on the scene. She recalled the words Isidor Straus had said to her just before she had left the *Titanic*. 'God go with you,' he had said, before accompanying his wife back to their cabin where they would die together. At that moment, Renee, who had just become a widow at thirty-six, thought to herself, 'No, God is not with me. He is with you and my beloved . . . He too went down with the *Titanic*.'[1]

Renee had met her husband, Henry Birkhardt Harris, one of New York's most famous theatrical producers, while she had been working as a legal secretary and had married him in 1902. The couple were devoted and Henry had once said of his wife, 'I never take an important step without consulting Renee. If anything happened to me, she could pick up the reins.'[2] However, she had no time to think about her future as she sat in collapsible D, the last lifeboat to leave the ship, and watched as it began to fill up with water. The women in the lifeboat started to scream, as did the two Navratil boys, children who had been snatched away from their mother by their father and who were travelling in second class on board the *Titanic* under an assumed name. The forty-four passengers squeezed into the makeshift lifeboat thought that, just as they had escaped one sinking, they were about to experience another.

'The water was above our ankles and as fast as it was bailed out it would fill up again,' recalled Renee. 'How long this kept up I can't remember – interminable hours it seemed to me – when a voice from a distance resounded, "Keep yelling – we will locate you." It was impenetrably dark, so not until there was a little ray of daylight were we found by a lifeboat. They lightened our boat by taking a few of our women. They were not filled to capacity as were most of the lifeboats, and the officer in charge tied us to his stern – and together we rowed on a sea as calm as a pool – until daylight.'[3]

Across the dark ocean, in boat five, Karl Behr was busy rubbing the feet of Helen, his sweetheart. Covered by only a thin sheen of stocking, her flesh felt frozen. Suddenly, Behr felt someone nudge him. He turned round to see a man holding a nickel-plated revolver, which he had concealed close to his body. The stranger leaned over towards him and whispered in his ear, 'Should the worst come to the worst, you can use this revolver for your wife, after my wife and I have finished with it.' The words were spoken in a composed and calm fashion and later Karl would look back and recall how natural it had seemed for the man to extend this courtesy towards them. After all, no one knew how long it would take for a rescue ship to reach them or whether one would locate them at all. During that long night, Behr remembers seeing lights all around them, but they were only the flashlights from some of the other lifeboats. The cold ate into their bones as the boats drifted across the darkened sea.[4]

The situation was especially bad in collapsible A, the Englehardt, which had been washed off the *Titanic* as the ship sank. A few survivors had managed to crawl over its canvas sides to sit amidst the frozen waters that slopped about inside its wooden keel. One of these was first-class passenger George Rheims, who had jumped off the ship in the moments before it sank. 'We had to balance ourselves, from left to right, to prevent the raft from turning over,' he wrote to his wife. 'I remained there for six hours, in my shirt, freezing to death. I almost let myself go and fall in the water two or three times, but the thought of you prevented me from doing it. I got my courage back, and for I don't know what reason, I took command of the raft. What a horrible night that was! We had to push back about a dozen fellows who wanted to get on the raft; we were loaded to the limit. Eight persons died during the night, from cold or from despair! I will spare you the details, which were horrible.'[5]

One of the passengers who did not have the strength to survive was Edith Evans, a thirty-six-year-old single woman who, just as the ship was sinking, had given up her place in one of the last lifeboats for the sake of a friend who had children. After the ship had gone down, Evans had made a desperate bid to swim towards collapsible A, eventually hauling herself out of the icy sea and into the boat. Rheims tried to help keep up her spirits, but Edith was finding it increasingly difficult to remain standing. 'He told her, "We have to stand to balance the boat or we will drown,"' related Edith Rosenbaum, who heard the story directly from Rheims. 'She stood a little longer. Her body bent closer and closer to the water until finally she was submerged. She lay dead at his feet for some time, then a wave carried her body out of the boat to the open sea. There was nothing they could do to recover her without upsetting the boat.'[6]

Although the sea was calm, and the stars were bright, the cold descended like a second wave of death. Charlotte Collyer, in boat fourteen, lost consciousness due to the freezing temperatures. As she lay slumped in the bottom of the boat, her hair became tangled in an oarlock. The force ripped a large chunk of hair from her scalp and although she did not feel a thing at the time, the accident affected her badly afterwards. 'She did not recover from that for a long time,' remembered her daughter, Marjorie.[7] Joseph Duquemin, a twenty-four-year-old stonemason from Guernsey, had given his overcoat to seven-year-old Eva Hart while on board the ship. Now, he sat shivering in collapsible D – indeed, his legs were so badly frostbitten that he would have to have both of them amputated. Harold Bride, the radio operator, also suffered from frostbite in his feet. 'I lay there, not caring what happened,' he said. 'Somebody sat on my legs. They were wedged in between slats and were being wrenched. I had not the heart left to ask the man to move . . . I lay where I was, letting the man wrench my feet out of shape.'[8] At some point over the course of the following few hours, his colleague Jack Phillips passed away from exposure.

Interrupting the silence of the dark night, Harold Bride and the fellow survivors in his lifeboat, started to say the Lord's Prayer. 'Our Father, who art in heaven, hallowed be thy name . . .' they chanted. 'Thy kingdom come; thy will be done, on earth as it is in heaven . . .'

A few miles away, the *Carpathia*, which had picked up one of Bride and Phillips's SOS signals, altered its course and steamed towards the scene of the disaster. The journey was a dangerous one, as the ocean was awash with icebergs. Captain Rostron suspected the worst – that the *Titanic* would have gone by the time his ship arrived – but he hoped to rescue as many survivors as possible. He gave orders to prepare the ship for their arrival – and, in the middle of the night, the vessel buzzed with activity. Stewards carried armfuls of blankets and pillows to public rooms; tables were set for hundreds of people, while others were laden with row upon row of coffee and tea cups and glasses of brandy. After this was done, Rostron called his men to the first-class saloon where he explained what had happened, that the *Titanic* had hit ice and that they would do everything in their power to help. By 4 a.m. they were near the spot of the collision; from the deck of the *Carpathia* the crew launched a spectacular array of rockets and Roman candles in order to attract the attention of the survivors.

'All eyes were strained at the darkness,' recalled Robert H. Vaughan, who worked as a mess steward on board the *Carpathia*, 'and soon we could make out the dim shape of a lifeboat not far off. The *Carpathia* shut down her engines, and it was not long before the first boat load of survivors came alongside. It was only then that we knew the worst – the *Titanic* had sunk.'[9]

Passengers on board the *Carpathia* – which was on its way from New York to Gibraltar – gradually emerged from their cabins to witness extraordinary scenes. At 4.10 a.m., lifeboat number two drew up towards the ship and the first survivors began to climb on board, by means of a rope ladder and slings; babies and children were lifted by using canvas bags or coal sacks. 'Some were so cold it was impossible for them to climb up the ladders and had to be put in bags to be hauled up,' remembered one passenger on the *Carpathia* at the time.[10]

As dawn broke over the horizon, Captain Rostron and the crew of the *Carpathia* noticed that the sea was covered with icebergs, some up to two hundred feet tall. 'These little mountains were just catching the early sunshine which made them take on all manner of wonderful aspects,' wrote Rostron later. 'Minarets like cathedral towers turned to gold in the distance and, here and there, some seemed to shape themselves like argosies under full sail.'[11] From the perspective of one of the lifeboats, thirteen-year-old Madeleine Mellenger compared the icebergs to the mountains that rose out of the Italian lakes.

Over the course of the next four hours, lifeboat after

lifeboat arrived. The survivors were still enveloped by shock; Captain Rostron noted an atmosphere of stillness that accompanied the passengers, many of whom seemed to have been reduced to mere spectres or shades by the experience. 'Through it all that quietness reigned,' he said, 'as though the disaster were so great that it silenced human emotion.'[12] Rostron cruised around the site of the disaster, in the hope of finding more survivors, but there was nothing to be seen on the surface of the water except for what witnesses describe as a slight brownish discoloration, some fragments of wood, a scattering of straw, the cork from macerated lifebelts and the occasional deck chair.

Reunions were a mixture of joy and heartache. 'Gladness and sadness were mixed in strange ways, as the survivors tumbled aboard,' recalled Robert H. Vaughan. 'They were glad to be alive – yet crushed by the loss of fathers, sons, brothers, husbands and so many dear friends.'[13] As Jack Thayer climbed up the ladder and set foot on the *Carpathia* he saw his mother. She assumed that her husband would be with her son; the shock he was not hit her badly. Yet during the journey back to New York, Marian Thayer convinced herself that her husband was still alive, certain that some other boat had picked him up.

An Italian woman became hysterical in the third-class dining room, repeatedly calling for her 'bambino'. Mother and child were reunited, only for her to continue crying. She held up two fingers; an indication that another was missing. Finally, that child was located too – 'in the pantry on the hot press, where it had been left to thaw out'.[14]

Survivors of the *Titanic* strained their eyes for the sight of other lifeboats in the hope that their loved ones might yet be saved. But none arrived. 'All were looking for a husband, son, brother or sweetheart,' recalled second-class passenger Albert

Caldwell, 'who never came.'[15] Augusta Ogden, a passenger on board the *Carpathia*, remembered taking coffee and brandy to two women, dressed in grey coats, and sitting by themselves in a corner. As she offered them the drinks, one of them said, 'Go away, we have just seen our husbands drown.'[16]

Grief settled over the ship as the realisation of the scale of the loss sank in. Captain Rostron decided to hold a burial service for the three bodies he had taken on board and for the one man who had subsequently died that morning. The service of the dead was read by Father Roger Anderson of the Episcopal Order of the Holy Cross, and the bodies were committed to the sea. 'Some of the *Titanic*'s passengers turned away from the rail as the first of the weighted forms fell into the water,' wrote *Carpathia* passenger Carlos F. Hurd, a journalist from the *St Louis Post-Dispatch*.[17] 'It would have been hard for anyone present not to have been moved,' said mess steward Robert H. Vaughan. 'Even Captain Rostron could hardly continue, he was so overcome by emotion.'[18]

The survivors had escaped the *Titanic* with only the clothes they were wearing that night, and they wandered around the rescue ship in various states of dress. As one first-class passenger observed a few days later, 'for four days the company lived together . . . in this strange assortment of undress costume, some in ball gowns, many in night dresses and only a few fully clothed'.[19]

The passengers and crew did everything in their power to make the survivors comfortable. Captain Rostron made his cabin available to three widows, one of whom was Marian Thayer (her son, Jack, slept on the floor). Steward Joseph Zupicich gave away his towels, shirts, trousers, even underwear to the men who had arrived on the ship lacking basic clothing. Yet nobody could take away the pain of the women who had lost their husbands and their children. With each mile the

Carpathia sailed away from the scene of the disaster – and the watery graves of the dead – so their grief intensified. 'It is useless and I don't think wise to tell you of the awful suffering that a great number of the rescued have been and are going through now, but it is heartrending,' wrote survivor Marion Wright to her father. 'I believe as far as can be made out there are about 150 widows on board, some with children, some none.'[20] *Carpathia* passenger Mrs Paul Schabert observed at the time, 'It is pitiful to see so many young widows sitting about weeping.'[21] Karl Behr even went so far as to state that, 'Although the sinking of the *Titanic* was dreadful, to my mind the four days among the sufferers on the *Carpathia* was much worse and more difficult to try and forget.'[22]

Twelve-year-old second-class passenger Bertha Watt remembers her mother trying to comfort Mathilda Weisz, who had just lost her husband Leopold, a sculptor. 'The first day on the *Carpathia* – she was in a very bad way and was ready to jump,' she wrote years later. 'My good mother must have walked miles with her up and down the decks while the ship stayed around all day Monday hoping to pick more up.'[23] Second-class passenger Jane Laver Herman also threatened to commit suicide when she learned of the loss of her husband, Samuel, a butcher and hotelier from Yeovil. She could not be comforted by her twin daughters, Alice and Kate, who were also grief-stricken at the death of their father. 'Their mother was quite old and had never been separated from her husband one night in all her married life,' recalled *Titanic* survivor Madeleine Mellenger. 'She was almost insane on the *Carpathia*. I know as I was shut up in someone's cabin with her all day not knowing where my mother was . . . Mrs Herman threatened to commit suicide and to me, a child, that was unforgettable. I cried all that day for my mother who was unconscious in hospital . . .'[24]

Later that night, members of the crew toured the ship and

took a ledger of names, a list of survivors, which duly made its way round the world. By this point, Madeleine had been joined by her mother, and they prepared for a night's sleep on the floor of the library. Next to them was her namesake, Madeleine Force Astor, a widow at eighteen. 'She was quite sick from an injured arm when getting into the lifeboat,' recalled Madeleine Mellenger, who also learned that the young woman was pregnant. 'I loaned her a little bottle of smelling salts which Mum had in her purse. Next night she did not sleep on the floor, [she] got a cabin, but we did, only on the dining room floor, more room. Food was very scarce.'[25]

Edith Rosenbaum, used only to the very best whenever she travelled, had to make do with a makeshift bed on a dining room table. She recalled a sad conversation with May Futrelle, the widow of the novelist Jacques Futrelle. May told her how they had been childhood sweethearts, and how they had married when he was only twenty, she eighteen. 'We have had eighteen years of complete happiness,' she added. 'My forte is writing love stories. How can I continue writing romances when the only real romance I have ever had in my life lies at the bottom of the sea?'[26]

From the *Carpathia*, the *Titanic* widows sent a stream of wireless messages – telegrams that encapsulated the progression from hope to despair. On 17 April, Marian Thayer wrote, 'Jack [her son], Margaret [her maid] and I safe no news yet of Mr Thayer.' A day later she wrote, 'Jack, Margaret and I safe. No news Johnny,' and then finally a message, which was not sent, 'Let any one meet us but not children. My hope gone.'[27] Renee Harris sent a wireless message to her father-in-law telling him that she was still hoping that her husband had been picked up by another steamer. She knew, of course, that Harry was dead; she would rather that than live with the knowledge that he had taken the place of one of the women in the lifeboats.

When Dr Henry William Frauenthal, the doctor on the *Titanic* who had set Renee's broken arm, came into her cabin on the rescue ship to see if he could help her in any way, she made her feelings clear. As he started to explain how he had been saved – he had jumped into lifeboat number five and landed, all 250 pounds of him, on top of another first-class passenger, breaking several of her ribs – Renee cut him short. 'I wouldn't have my husband back at the cost of a woman's life,' she said, 'and he made such a hasty exit I didn't see him again either on the *Carpathia* or ever after.'[28]

On Thursday, 18 April, the *Carpathia* arrived in New York. The city was enveloped in fog, but as the liner drew closer, passengers could dimly make out the brilliantly lit skyscrapers of Manhattan. In the distance they could hear the mournful tolling of bells. Edith Rosenbaum recalls that 'we were told, upon leaving the ship, to go immediately to the partitions where the initials of our surnames were displayed. I went straight to "R" and looked round. I shall never forget that pier. There were thousands of people there, but not a sound – an intense silence, a silence of death . . . The quiet of the scene was broken by cries and sobs. Many doctors and nurses were in attendance. Apparently, it had been expected that a number of survivors would have to be carried off the *Carpathia* on stretchers, but nearly all those who had been saved were able to walk down the gangway. It is difficult to describe the cruel intensity of that spectacle; the huge, but quiet pier, the crying and sobbing among those who had come to meet the ones they loved, buoyed up by a hope to be confirmed or broken. All the time the bells kept tolling, and outside there was a cold drizzle of rain. Under these circumstances, the cannonade of flashes from photographers' lamps as we went into the street seemed a cruelly inappropriate thing.'[29]

Renee Harris only recalled fragments of what happened

next. She remembered being taken from the ship by her husband's father, her brother and their doctor, and uttering the words, 'I have come back alone.' After that, for a period of two months, her mind was a complete blank. Later, friends told her that she had attended memorial services for her husband at his theatre, the Hudson, on 44th Street, but she had no recollection. 'My first awareness was when I was taken by my doctor and a nurse to the theatre and was seated at his desk and for the first time (so I was told) went into a paroxysm of hysteria,' she said. 'The first tears I had shed.'[30]

Many widows still refused to believe their husbands were never going to come back. A few days after returning to America, Marian Thayer wrote of her desperation – would she ever see her husband again? 'My reason tells me *No*, but how can we give up all hope until some days yet go past of this cruel torture,' she wrote in a letter to President William Howard Taft, whose military aide Major Archibald Butt perished in the disaster. 'Today is my husband's fiftieth birthday. Oh, he is young to go and leave us he so loved.'[31]

New York – together with London, Southampton and countless other towns, cities and villages around the world – underwent its own period of mourning. On 20 April a memorial service for those lost at sea was held at St Paul's Chapel, situated at Fulton Street and Broadway. Reverend W. Montague Geer, the curate at the church, used the service as a way of pledging his support for the widows and orphans who were now, for the time being at least, guests of the city. 'They will be most tenderly cared for, but their hearts are with their beloved dead off the Newfoundland Banks; at the bottom of the Atlantic Ocean,' he said. The Reverend led a prayer for the widows and fatherless children, many of whom he suspected were wishing that they were 'now with their husbands and fathers out of the bitterly hard struggle for life, and at rest and peace forever more.'[32] Cardinal Farley, the Archbishop of New York, announced that prayers for the *Titanic* dead would be said in all churches that Sunday and directed that, the next day, each priest in the city would hold a silent requiem mass for the repose of the dead.

The widows needed practical and financial support too, as many had been left penniless by the loss of their husbands. By June, the American fund – under the banner of the Red Cross Emergency Relief Committee – had distributed more than $130,000 to *Titanic* survivors and relatives of victims, a total of 350 people or families. 'Most of the payments are necessarily to be administered in the form of pensions, and must be intrusted to the continuing oversight of responsible agencies,' said Robert W. de Forest, the committee's chairman. 'Assistance of this character has been especially necessary for the families of widows. Seventy-two are already known to the committee, of whom sixty-three lost their husbands in the disaster. Eight or ten have returned or will return to England or other parts of Europe and will obtain the larger part of relief from the funds raised abroad.'[33]

The Relief Committee heard from eighty-three families whose main loss was property, which in some instances was 'so serious as to leave the families quite helpless'. Some stories, such as that of the young Daniel Burke from Chester, England, were particularly heartbreaking. As an orphan – he had lost his father a number of years ago, and his mother had died two months before – he and his sister, Catherine, had decided to chance their luck in America and had booked steerage passage on the *Titanic*. By some stroke of luck, Daniel had managed to sneak aboard lifeboat number four, where Madeleine Astor took it upon herself to protect him, throwing her coat over his head to disguise him as a woman. When the other men on board the boat discovered Burke was a boy in his teenage years, they wanted to throw him into the sea, but Mrs Astor pleaded for him to be saved. It was obvious that the boy was in distress, as he had lost his sister in the tragedy.

He described all this to W. Frank Persons, who was in charge of the Red Cross fund, and provided a detailed description of his sister, together with the fact that she was wearing a gold chain around her neck with a golden sovereign inscribed with her initials, ACB – Alice Catherine Burke. Persons was moved by the story, especially when he discovered that the body of Catherine Burke had been recovered from the sea. Yet Persons felt something was not quite right about the account. After asking a doctor from the Children's Society to examine him, his suspicions were confirmed – the boy, instead of being fourteen years old as he had claimed, was more likely in his late teenage years or even early twenties. In addition, Catherine's sister, who had identified her body, told the committee that this young man was a stranger to the family. Finally, it was concluded that the boy was, in the words of the committee, a 'high-grade imbecile' and that 'every word of his story had been concocted from newspaper accounts'. His fate was to be sent to a 'home for the feeble-minded' on Randall's Island, New York.[34] 'In a few cases bold impositions were tried,' said one report, 'and in a few rare instances absolute deception was attempted, but such cases were quickly discovered.'[35]

On Thanksgiving Day 1912, widows and orphans received wireless messages informing them of the money amassed by the *Titanic* Relief Fund. Created by newspaper magnate William R. Hearst, this fund totalled $62,010, ten thousand of which had been set aside as a gift to Arthur Rostron of the *Carpathia*. 'Through the fund a great number of half orphans and widows will be assured of a good start in life,' said Victor A. Watson, the fund's manager.[36]

On the other side of the Atlantic, the British fund had reached the much higher figure of $2 million by August 1912. From Southampton – where a large majority of the crew had come from – there were claims from 239 widows, 532 children under the age of sixteen and 213 other dependants. Petitions for financial help had also been received from the dependants of 461 people whose lives had been lost in the disaster. A breakdown of this figure shows the international diversity of transatlantic travel at the time. Two hundred and thirty-two were British or Irish; there were 12 Austro-Hungarians; 3 Danes; 18 Belgians; 2 French; 1 Italian; 16 Norwegians; 36 Russians; 72 Swedes; 19 Swiss; 33 Bulgarians and 17 Syrians.[37]

However, no amount of aid could help salve the emotional wounds suffered by the widowed or the orphaned. On the first anniversary of the sinking, a large number of survivors gathered together for a memorial service at St Thomas' Church, at Fifth Avenue and 53rd Street. Observers noted the bravery of Emily Ryerson – who had been travelling back to America on the *Titanic* in order to attend the funeral of her twenty-one-year-old son, Arthur Jr, who had died in an automobile accident and who also had lost her husband in the sinking – and the absence of Vincent Astor, whose family had a pew at the church. The service opened with a rendition by the vested choir of the hymn 'Guide Me, O Great Jehovah', with additional songs that included 'Until the Day Breaks', 'Crossing the Bar', and 'Nearer My God to Thee', which by now, in the popular consciousness at least, had become inexorably linked with the Titanic. As Reverend Ernest M. Stires started to preach, the lights of the church were dimmed.

'One year ago today a great ship was crossing the ocean from the Old World to this land,' he said. 'It represented the climax of skill and luxury. There was every comfort and every protection. The officers were selected from among the ablest. The ship was "unsinkable". Then came the warnings, the warnings were ignored. In the night the great ship was struck and there occurred the greatest tragedy recorded in the marine annals of the world. It meant much to me personally. On that ship were ten men that I knew and loved, and not one reached this shore. There were a dozen women I knew. All came home safe.'

He recalled the scene as the *Carpathia* docked in New York, and its mournful cargo of widows that disembarked in a seemingly never-ending stream. He turned to the survivors – the widows and their children – and praised them for their bravery, strength in adversity and their sure-footed religious belief, commending them for the fact that they had not questioned the existence of God or His role in the tragedy. 'This should be a memorial both to those who died and to the divine courage of those who survived and those whose character has stood the test of the last year,' he said. He hoped that certain lessons – practical, philosophical and moral – had been learned from the disaster and that the sinking of the ship, and the concomitant loss of life, would not go in vain.

'Our life in New York City is in a large degree marked by that same luxury which resulted in the loss of the *Titanic*,' he said. 'There are many warnings, but they are unheeded. This is no far-fetched comparison. You may not see the shipwrecks of humanity, but the physicians see them and the clergymen see them. Men and women are allowing themselves to be carried along by unseen currents in our complex life in this greatest city of the world. I say the dangers are there. We will imperil our lives to prevent physical suicide, but look on too often unmoved by moral suicide. But a great help and inspiration has come to us. And I suggest to you that, conscious of the dangers of our city, conscious of the unheeded warnings, conscious of the fact that the shipwrecks are among our friends, that we go out among the perils and show that our confidence in God is complete. Don't wait. Go forth and bear witness to the truth. The lessons that those brave men and women taught by their sacrifice are the legacy they have left us. Will our characters meet the test? Or will they behold our disloyalty with the waters of luxury whirling around us?'[38]

That April, a number of *Titanic* widows braved the cold Atlantic once more as they set sail from Boston harbour out to the spot where the liner sank. Those on board included May Futrelle and Gertrude Maybelle Thorne, who had been travelling on the liner as the mistress of George Rosenshine, an importer of ostrich feathers in New York. At just after 2.15 on the morning of 15 April, exactly one year after the sinking, the widows tossed baskets of flowers and wreaths into the sea, while they sang 'Nearer My God to Thee'. Although Renee Harris had been invited on the journey, she had rejected the offer in no uncertain terms, saying that she 'was too deeply affected to even think of making such a trip'.[39]

In truth, the death of Henry Harris had presented his widow with a raft of seemingly insurmountable problems. Although Harris owned the Hudson Theater – a grand building with a Renaissance-style façade designed in 1903 by architects J.B. McElfatrick, Israels and Harder, with an interior that featured Greco-Roman motifs, Tiffany glass, and a marble box office – and he had had great success with a number of productions starring some of the biggest names on Broadway, when his lawyers finally settled his estate it was discovered that he was over $400,000 in debt. Many women in the same situation would have been destroyed, and Renee nearly was, as she herself recognised. 'For months, after the sinking of the *Titanic*, I was in a dreadful state of nerves and thought I should never be able to concentrate upon anything again,' she said. 'It was a frightful sensation. Then one memorable day I recalled the words of Mr Harris: "You are a better businessman than I am.'[40] She decided she had no choice but to be strong; after all it was what Harry would have expected of her. 'I knew then what I was going to do,' she said. 'I was going to carry on his work and make the theater a monument to his memory.'[41]

The choice of her first production, *Damaged Goods* – a translation of *Les Avariés* originally written by Eugène Brieux, which dealt with the taboo subjects of prostitution and syphilis – was an interesting one. As Renee read the play for the first time she must have been struck by the parallels between syphilis and the iceberg that hit the *Titanic* – both were silent killers that selected their victims largely according to their sex. Conservative estimates put the extent of syphilis at around 7 per cent of the population, the majority of sufferers being men from the 'upper and middle ranks and among the casual labouring poor'.[42] The death toll numbered at least 1,502: of these, 1,327 were men, 111 were women, and 54 were children. Post-*Titanic*, some religious figures condemned the sinking as a symbol of the decadence of the modern age – it was God's way of showing his dislike for the overreaching pride of man – in the same way that moralists likened the fatal venereal disease to a tool used by the Almighty to wipe the earth clean of sin. As George Bernard Shaw wrote in the preface to the play: 'Now the diseases dealt with in *Damaged Goods* are doubly taboo, because the sacrifices are ignorantly supposed to be the salutary penalties of misconduct. Not only must not the improper thing be mentioned, but the evil must not be remedied, because it is a just retribution and a wholesome deterrent.'[43]

In some respects at least, Renee could empathise with those syphilis victims whose lives had been upturned by fate. Why had her husband been taken from her? Was it his fault in some way? Should she have died with him? How could God exist in a world that seemed so brutal, so cruel? All these questions, and more, raced through her mind as she read the play. On a purely practical level she had to ask herself whether it was even possible to stage it. The greatest obstacle, she realised, was one of public decency, as the very word syphilis was unspeakable in the public arena. 'My father-in-law . . . felt that the play was too daring for a woman to present,' she said and so she decided to produce it under the auspices of the Medical Society. The play – which starred Richard Bennett – also had a social message that appealed to Renee Harris. Just as the *Titanic* exposed the extraordinarily wide class divisions of Edwardian society so the play uncovered the hidden inequalities of contemporary life. '*Damaged Goods* contains more than an exposé of venereal disease,' wrote the Russian-born anarchist and author Emma Goldman in 1914. 'It touches upon the whole of our social life. It points out the cold-blooded indifference of the rich toward those who do not belong to their class, to the poor, the workers, the disinherited whom they sacrifice without the slightest compunction on the altar of their own comforts. Moreover, the play also treats of the contemptible attitude towards love not backed by property or legal sanction. In short, it uncovers and exposes not only sexual disease, but that which is even more terrible – our social disease, our social syphilis.'[44]

In 1914, Bennett reprised his role in the film version, directed by Tom Ricketts, one of the many silent movies that no longer survive. Yet posters publicising the film do exist – images that contain resonances of the *Titanic* disaster: 'WE MUST SAVE THE MOTHER AND THE CHILD' reads one; 'THE INNOCENT SUFFER FOR THE GUILTY!' screams another; and 'A VITAL DRAMA OF MORAL UPLIGHT' proclaims a third.

Throughout her time as a producer, Renee was attracted to works that somehow counterpointed the disaster she tried so hard to forget. The pull was a subliminal one, a force that flowed under the surface of her life, but all the stronger for that. As she watched her productions of *Cobra* by Martin

Brown and *The Noose* by Willard Mack, she would have been struck by the underlying moral dilemmas that she had experienced during and after the *Titanic* disaster. The first play, which ran at her theatre between April and June 1924 and starred William B. Mack, Judith Anderson and Louis Calhern, tells the story of a man who finds himself divided between his lustful impulses and his feelings of loyalty towards a good friend. What should he do? Follow his desires and bed his friend's wife (Elise Van Zile, played by Anderson) or try to control himself and reject a woman who declares her love for him? He decides not to betray his friend and stands up his lover, refusing to go along to the hotel where the two had decided to meet. That night, there is a fire in which Elise dies; his choice was the right one, after all – if he had given in to his animal instincts he too would have lost his life.

The moral dilemma at the heart of *The Noose* centres on a family – son Nickie Elkins, his dishonest father, Buck Gordon and his mother, who has left the chaotic home to remarry the respectable Governor Bancroft. When Elkins discovers that his father is going to blackmail his former wife and her new husband, he kills him in order to save his mother from disgrace. The choice is a difficult one for Mrs Bancroft: if she tells the truth she will bring about the ruin of her new husband, while if she says nothing her son will be hanged. The production – which also starred former chorus girl Barbara Stanwyck as Dot, Nickie's sweetheart, in one of her first Broadway roles – was a smash hit and ran from October 1926 for nine months.

Although Renee tried to blank the *Titanic* from her consciousness, the ship – and the memory of her husband – kept resurfacing. What preyed on her mind more than anything was whether she had done the right thing in leaving her husband on the ship to die. She felt so divided about the issue that, although friends constantly assured her that she had behaved entirely appropriately, finally she decided to explore her feelings in an article for the *American Weekly*. After recounting the day of the sinking – how she had broken her arm late that afternoon, how she had been playing cards when the iceberg hit, how Harry had slit the right sleeve from her blouse in order for her to pull on the lifebelt – she detailed her last few moments on deck. She recalled hearing one man say to the officers that he was going to help his wife into one of the lifeboats; he had evidently sneaked into a lifeboat as the next time Renee saw him he was on board the *Carpathia*. Her husband could have saved himself in the same cowardly manner, but his sense of right and wrong was too strong for that, she said. At first, she refused to get into the lifeboat without him, but finally her husband persuaded her to escape in collapsible D, the last boat to be lowered from the ship. He could always get on to one of the rafts, he assured her; if she didn't go, it would be hard for him to save her too, what with her broken arm. What could she do? she asked herself. 'It was the most awful moment I had ever known,' she wrote. Harry then lifted her into the collapsible and told the crew member of her injury. 'For years after that my heart was numb with grief. And always one question haunted me: Should I have remained aboard the *Titanic* and died at sea with Harry?'

When she thought of her own dilemma she recalled the situation of another couple she had read about in a newspaper report. A husband and wife were on their way to the movies near Chicago when the woman got her foot caught in a railway track. Although the man tried to free his wife's trapped foot, it wouldn't move. Then, they heard the whistle of a train, quickly followed by a rumble. Within seconds, the train was approaching. Frantically, the man – who had three children at home – pulled at his wife's foot, but still it did not move. As the train thundered towards them, he had to make a decision – whether to stay with his wife or save himself. His choice? 'To remain with his wife beneath the wheels of the train,' said Renee. 'Was he right? I've never known what to think.'

In order to prompt a debate, Renee invited readers of the magazine to write in with their own thoughts and feelings. 'Should I have stayed on the ship?' she asked. 'Or was I right in leaving it? What do you, the reader, think? I would like to know – and I'm sure the Editor would like to know, too.'[45] An overwhelming majority believed that Renee had behaved correctly in saving herself. Most of those who agreed with her decision defined themselves as fatalists. 'I believe that when it is our time to go, we go,' wrote one woman from Baldwin Park, California. 'And if it is not our time to die, we live. I believe that had you remained at your husband's side, you still would have lived and he would have gone . . . anyway.' God played a central role in the debate. 'To have stayed on the *Titanic*,' said a man from North Bergen, New Jersey, 'would have been suicide on your part. According to God's teachings, it is sinful to destroy ourselves.' Many believed that it was the duty of a wife to love, honour and obey her husband and they commended her for doing all three. 'You did as he asked,' said a woman from Hornell, New York, 'and I feel he died a happier and more heroic man knowing his beloved was saved.' One letter even came from a fellow survivor, that of John Hardy, a second-class chief steward who was also one of Renee's fellow passengers in collapsible D. His point of view was a straightforward one – believing that 'the old tradition of the sea, "women and children first", should prevail'.

The feature concluded with a letter from a man in Seneca Falls, New York, who summed up the response of the bulk of readers with his wish that Renee Harris lead a happy and fruitful life. 'If I had been in your husband's position,' he said, 'and were speaking to you from the other side of the divide, I would say to you: "The last thing in the world I want you to do is spend your life in self-condemnation and unhappiness. Find a new happiness, new interests. It is your obligation to yourself."'[46]

Renee tried to do just that. She immersed herself in the theatre business, reading about ten new plays each month, often laughing to herself when she flicked through the pages of some of the more amateur submissions. 'I do enjoy reading the poor plays,' she said. 'They are usually sincere attempts, and contain situations which are funny, but impossible to produce.'[47] She had an active social life and enjoyed the company of actors and journalists, men such as Ward Morehouse, Vinton Freedley and Robert Breen. And, although she always maintained she still loved her dead husband, she made an effort to reshape her personal life. In May 1916, in Greenwich, Connecticut, she married Lester Consolly, a former assistant manager at the Hotel Claridge, New York, and then a businessman, whose main interests included the Commonwealth Hotel Construction Company, based at 18 East 41st Street. That marriage did not last, however; nor did either her subsequent marriages to L. Marvin Simmons and Zach C. Barber. It seems the ghost of Henry Harris – whose body was never found – would not stay beneath the surface of the sea. 'After all, I had ten wonderful, happy, superb, unforgettable years with my first husband,' she said. 'He spoiled me for any other man in the world. I have had four marriages – but really only one husband.'[48]

Renee continued to spend money as if she was still married to a successful theatrical producer. She had a yacht, an apartment on Park Avenue, houses in Long Island and Palm Beach, but for many years she simply lived beyond her means, her self image boosted by the confidence that came with the knowledge that she had a fortune invested in the stock market and the belief in the high real-estate value of her theatre. In the late twenties, she was offered $1.2 million for the Hudson, but she turned down the offer, believing that it was worth closer to $2 million. In the summer of 1929, while enjoying a trip around the world, she received a cable from her business manager pleading with her to return home. In October of that year, the stock market crashed, and as Renee said, 'Depression had set in and my business manager was in a state of collapse as he couldn't get an attraction to fill the theater. From 1929 until 1932 I could get nothing but 'turkeys' to put into the theater.'[49] Her one great chance came in late 1929, when playwright Marc Connelly invited her to attend a rehearsal of his new play, *Green Pastures*, which was based on the short stories, *Ol' Man Adam an' His Chullun'* by Roark Bradford. Renee loved the play – which portrayed episodes from the Old Testament as seen through the eyes of a young African-American child in the South – and immediately signed a contract to stage the production at the Hudson. Problems started, however, when work began on constructing the elaborate set – one scene called for a treadmill to be built and during the construction process it was discovered that this could not be done without damaging the foundations of the theatre. Connelly cancelled the contract and moved the production to the Mansfield Theatre, where between February 1930 and August 1931 it ran for a total of 640 performances. The play went on to win the Pulitzer Prize for drama. 'That play would have carried me over the tough years, but it was not to be my fate,' Renee said.[50]

By 1932, when her bank foreclosed on her mortgage by demanding an immediate payment of $500,000, she had no option but to sell the theatre, which she still thought of as 'a monument to Harry B. Harris'. Although it was subsequently owned by the broadcasters CBS and NBC, over the years it gradually declined, and by the sixties it had reached its lowest point – a venue for pornographic films. 'When I'm on 44th Street, I turn my back on the Hudson,' she said. 'It's a movie house with sex pictures.' In her mind, the image of her first husband had been tarnished; there was no greater sin than questioning the reputation of Henry B. In fact, this had proved central in a nasty row that broke out between Renee and her friend and fellow *Titanic* survivor, Lady Duff Gordon.

The two women had known each other before they had sailed on the *Titanic*, as Lucile (the pseudonym of Lady Duff Gordon) had designed a number of costumes for some of Henry's productions. After the disaster the two continued to enjoy a close professional and personal relationship; photographs show the women in the dressing room of the actress Bertha Kalich after the first-night production of *The Riddle: Woman* at the Hudson in October 1918. However, when Lucile – who came under attack from the popular press after it was alleged that her husband, Sir Cosmo, offered the crew in his lifeboat a bribe not to return to help save the dying – published her memoirs in 1932, she included a couple of sentences that Renee took to be a direct attack on her and her husband.

'Even in that terrible moment I was filled with amazement at nearly all the American wives who were leaving their husbands without a word of protest or regret, scarce of farewell,' wrote Lucile. 'They have brought the cult of chivalry to such a pitch in the States that it comes as second nature to their men to sacrifice themselves and to their women to let them do it.'[51]

Renee was outraged and, in a spirit of literary revenge, penned a vicious portrait of the Duff Gordons in a piece she wrote for *Liberty* magazine in April 1932, twenty years after the disaster. She alleged that they had escaped the *Titanic* in a lifeboat piled high with luggage (an accusation that proved to be untrue) and recalled seeing them on the *Carpathia* dolled up in evening dress. The couple may have saved themselves, yes, but how much joy did they get out of living, she asked. Two months later, still gripped by the need to vent her anger towards her former friend, she wrote her a letter. Significantly, it is addressed not to Lucile, but to Lady Duff Gordon, and it is written in ink the colour of envy – green. Renee said that she found Lucile's statements regarding American women to be 'despicably low and mean'. She outlined how she, together with her compatriots, did not bid careless farewells to their husbands and reprimanded her for stating that American women were unfeeling.

'How dare you say such a thing when so many of us lost our husbands. You know how dear Harry was to me. I will never recover from his loss which left me penniless as well as bereaved. Harry was a great champion of yours and did much to help you gain your initial prominence in theatrical circles in New York. He thought so much of you. It would have agonized him to know of your ill-treatment by the press after the disaster.'

She concluded by reiterating her anger at Lucile's words, which she found 'spiteful in the extreme'. She expressed her sympathy for the fact that her former friend had fallen on hard times – without confessing that, after building up the business, she was experiencing the very same financial troubles as Lady Duff Gordon – yet surmised that Lucile must now be an extremely unhappy and bitter woman. Old age, she added, obviously did not become her. 'I have nothing more to say,' she said. 'Only I will not suffer privately should you publish any more cruel criticisms.'[52]

By 1940, Renee had been reduced to living in a single room in a New York welfare hotel. Yet friends testify that, in the face of adversity, her spirit remained strong. She became particularly close to Walter Lord, the author of *A Night to Remember*, who recalled that she would often walk over from the Spencer Arms Hotel at 140 West 69th Street, across Central Park, to the author's apartment on East 68th Street. One day he was writing at home when there was a call from the doorman who asked him whether he was expecting an elderly lady holding a shopping bag. She was in the lobby and he wondered whether she might be homeless. Walter took the elevator down to find Renee sitting in a chair in the foyer. 'I was in the neighborhood and wondered if you might want something,' she said. The two would often take tea together and it is obvious he relished her company. She was tough and gutsy and fun, even to the last. In 1961, after his book on the Alamo was published, Lord inscribed a copy to her with the words, 'For Renee, who has done everything in her full and exciting life except defend the Alamo'.[53] Renee died on 2 September 1969, aged ninety-three, at the Doctors Hospital, New York.

Five years before her death, one afternoon at the end of May 1964, Lord interviewed her about her experiences on the *Titanic* and then persuaded her to write out a fuller description of her life. In that account, which remains unpublished, Renee told a story of how one day, on the anniversary of the sinking, she was walking into her New York apartment block when the doorman stopped her and told her he had seen her name in that morning's paper. He didn't know she had been a passenger on the *Titanic*. Another woman, standing nearby, was curious to learn more. Was she really on the *Titanic*, she asked. Yes, replied Renee. Had she been saved? No, she said, and walked away.

Three

A LIFE TOO FAR-FETCHED FOR FICTION

The life of Madeleine Force Astor reads like something that could have been written by a romantic novelist, perhaps even by fellow *Titanic* survivor May Futrelle. It contains all the elements of a classic love story – a chance encounter between an innocent, fresh-faced girl just out of school and a fabulously wealthy older man; a whirlwind courtship played out against the backdrop of gilded-age New York, followed by a marriage in the elaborate ballroom of one of America's grandest houses; a lavish honeymoon in Europe and Egypt; and then the shared joy that the couple would soon be parents. As in all the best love stories, tragedy played its part too; on the return voyage from Europe to America aboard the world's biggest and newest liner, the husband loses his life and goes down with the *Titanic*. However, if one read about Madeleine's life post-*Titanic* in a novel one would have to discount it as being too far-fetched even for fiction of the lowest kind. Who could believe that she could be a bride, a widow, an heiress and a mother all in the course of a single year? That she would renounce her right to the Astor millions in favour of marrying a childhood sweetheart? And that, in turn, she would divorce her second husband for a penniless Italian boxer, who would use her as a punch bag?

Madeleine, born on 19 June 1893 in Brooklyn, New York, was the youngest daughter of William Force, head of a large shipping and forwarding business, and an aspirational mother, Katherine Talmage. Until 1910, Madeleine lived in what, in contrast to her later life, can only be described as a state of blissful ignorance: she went to school, played with her sister, Katherine, spent her summers in Bar Harbor, Maine, where she enjoyed playing tennis and riding, and dreamt about the forthcoming pleasures of married life. Her first seventeen or so years went largely unnoticed by the press – she simply existed within the confines of her own experience; later, she would discover, first with fascination and then horror, the consequences of a life reflected through the prism of the mass media.

To begin with, of course, her fame was all rather exciting. In fact, it seems Madeleine initially regarded her relationship with Colonel John Jacob Astor – who was nearly three times her age – as nothing more than a summer dalliance. For his part, after the nightmare of a disastrous first marriage to Ava Willing, with whom he had had two children (Vincent and Alice), Astor was looking for a spot of light relief. The multi-millionaire heir of the Astor millions (the family, originally from Germany, had made a fortune from fur trading and real estate) and the ingénue met in the summer of 1910 in Bar Harbor, soon after the Colonel, accompanied by his son, Vincent, had arrived at the resort by yacht. Father and son were standing by a tennis court at one of the exclusive country clubs when two young girls started to play a game. Astor was immediately attracted to the teenage girl and asked a friend to introduce them. Moments later the foursome were playing a match of mixed doubles. 'Young debutante Madeleine was quite dazzled by the famous Colonel's attentions as he grew more and more interested in her,' observed one commentator, 'but the idea of falling in love with a man nearly three times her age probably did not occur to her. However, Mrs Force, her strong-minded and socially ambitious mother, had other ideas as to what was best for Madeleine in the way of love.'[1]

Over the course of the following few months, Astor courted the 'rather tall, graceful girl with brown hair and strong, clean-cut features',[2] introducing her to the splendours his wealth had to offer. By the summer of 1911, the couple were engaged, and the Colonel presented her with a magnificent diamond ring as a symbol of both his love and his seemingly unlimited riches. On 2 August, Astor – together with Madeleine and her mother – left New York on his luxurious steam yacht *Noma* bound for Newport, Rhode Island. Just before sailing, the Colonel, who had received his military title after supplying arms and horses during the Spanish-American war, responded to a barrage of questions from a mass of newspaper reporters. When were the couple going to marry? 'The matter has been discussed,' he replied, 'but no date has been fixed. At present it looks as though the marriage would take place in the Fall. It may happen sooner.'[3] Keen observers of fashion noted that Madeleine was wearing an outfit of 'pink lingerie', paired with a blue hat, while gossips speculated that father and son, John Jacob and Vincent, would organise a double wedding with Madeleine and her sister Katherine – an idea that did not materialise. The next morning the couple arrived in Newport, where they were joined by Vincent Astor for breakfast on the yacht. After a brief stopover at Beechwood, the Colonel's 'cottage' in Newport, where the couple looked over the mass of congratulatory telegrams and cables together with the acres of flowers sent by the great and the good in the summer colony, Astor took his fiancée back to a boat bound for New York. 'Miss Force looked radiant in a pongee outing dress, with a coat effect,' wrote one correspondent, 'and wearing a small black straw hat, with red roses.'[4]

As can be gleaned from this and other reports, as soon as

Madeleine arrived on the scene she became the subject of intense press scrutiny. Every outfit was detailed in the social pages of the newspapers and every gesture analysed as observers searched for clues to her personality and the nexus of seemingly hidden charms that had attracted one of the richest men in the world. Readers wanted to know just what it was that made her so special. After all, she came from the middle classes – her parents were well-off, but not rich and certainly not socially well-connected – and although she had youth on her side, she did not seem to be especially beautiful. She was tall, athletic (she loved the outdoor life) and had a certain style. In many ways, she functioned as a real-life counterpart to the silent film stars of the era – as Madeleine rarely gave interviews, the public were forced to read her through the images and text of the newspapers. She was studied, discussed, gossiped over, photographed and written about until any meaning or identity she had once possessed seemed leached out of her.

Even from the beginning of her story, an air of sadness seemed to linger over Madeleine, as if she knew, or understood, the nature of the pact she was entering into when she married John Jacob Astor. Her wedding, instead of being a jubilant affair, was a low-key, muted event; although the setting was spectacular – the white and gold ballroom of Beechwood complete with a mass of American beauty roses – the ceremony, which took place on the morning of 9 September 1911, was attended by only a handful of people. Earlier that morning, while still on board his yacht, Astor had been served a writ by two sisters whose brother, Eugene McCrohan, had been killed while repairing telephone wires at Beechwood in the summer of 1910. The union was also overshadowed by the background murmur of society gossip – the grand families of America's East Coast did not approve of the match – and the last-minute dash to find a church official who would marry them. Astor's church, the Protestant Episcopal, refused to bless the couple, and the divorced Colonel was reduced to offering a minister from a Congregational church in Providence, Rhode Island, a $1,000 fee to officiate. For those interested in symbolism, it was curious to note that the union was conducted in a room decorated with images of water babies, dolphins and Poseidon, the God of the Sea – a room which in turn overlooked the Atlantic, the ocean that would claim the life of Astor seven months later. 'As the bridal pair stood in the ballroom with their right hands clasped they could watch the gathering gray rain clouds which blew in from the ocean,' reported the *New York Times*.[5]

Before the couple left Newport by yacht, the Colonel made a statement that attempted to quieten the society gossips. 'Now that we are happily married I don't care how difficult divorce and remarriage laws are made,' he said. 'I sympathize heartily with the most straight-laced people in most of their ideas, but believe that remarriage should be possible once, as marriage is the happiest condition for the individual and the community.'[6] By all accounts, this did little to appease those who disagreed with the union and soon the couple found themselves the subject of a whispering campaign. So unpleasant was it for Madeleine – who, in the gilt-edged drawing rooms of New York, Newport and Philadelphia, was branded a gold-digger at best, a whore at worst – that she persuaded her husband to take her on an extended honeymoon to Europe and Egypt. The couple left New York on the *Olympic*, the *Titanic*'s sister ship, on 24 January 1912. Fellow passengers included Margaret 'Molly' Brown and J. Bruce Ismay (who gave up his suite to the Astors), both of whom would survive the sinking of the *Titanic* – and a week later the party arrived in Cherbourg, from where they made their way to Paris, and finally to Egypt.

One day, while sailing down the Nile, the group stopped to

take some refreshments, when Astor's pet dog, Kitty, an Airedale who wore a collar with her name and address (840 Fifth Avenue, NYC) engraved on it, went missing. Although he spent hours looking for her, finally Astor had to call off the search. 'Nothing was heard of Kitty until his return trip [up the Nile] when on passing another [dahabieh], Col. Astor spied Kitty making herself at home on board,' wrote one journalist at the time. 'The Astor boat was stopped and Kitty found her master with joyous barks.'[7] From this moment on, Astor kept his dog at close quarters, and the pet even slept with him in his cabin aboard the *Titanic*.

During the delayed honeymoon, Madeleine started to experience symptoms of morning sickness and the couple decided it would be best if they returned to New York. They booked passage on the *Titanic*, boarding at Cherbourg, together with Rosaline Bidois, Madeleine's maid, Caroline Endres, a nurse, and Victor Robbins, the Colonel's manservant. The Astors occupied a suite of rooms, C62–C64, that cost $4,350 (about $99,000 today), and for long stretches of the journey Madeleine confined herself to her quarters. Perhaps it was Madeleine's delicate condition that prompted stewardess Violet Jessop to observe of her: 'Instead of the radiant woman of my imagination, one who had succeeded in overcoming much opposition and marrying the man she wanted, I saw a quiet, pale, sad-faced, in fact dull young woman arrive listlessly on the arm of her husband, apparently indifferent to everything about her. It struck me for the first time that all the wealth in the world did not make for inward contentment.'[8]

On the evening of 14 April 1912, Madeleine retired to her suite as she had not been feeling well since earlier that afternoon. At around twenty minutes to midnight she was awakened by a slight jolt, and then noticed that the engines of the ship had stopped. She asked her husband if there was a problem and he told her he was sure it was nothing and that she should go back to sleep. Astor looked out of the window and noticed ice in the sea. It was bitterly cold, he said. Then he dressed immediately and hurried up to the bridge to see the Captain, who informed him of the situation. He then returned to his suite and told Madeleine that although the liner had struck an iceberg, he was sure they were in no danger. Later, on deck, Astor noticed his wife shivering and ordered his valet Robbins to fetch some warmer clothes. After she had changed into a heavier dress and coat, the Colonel tied a lifebelt around Madeleine's waist. As he did so, he felt the slight curve of her belly and realised that, most probably, he would not live to see his unborn child.

'He was perfectly cool and collected, his only thought being for her comfort,' wrote William Dobbyn, Astor's secretary, who heard Madeleine's account first hand. 'When, at last, an officer ordered her into a boat, she did not want to go without him, and the officer took her arm and made her go, the Colonel reassuring her by telling her that he would go with her. (He did it, I'm sure, only to get her to go.) She got in the boat, thinking he would follow for there were a number of vacant places, and the deck about them deserted. He asked the officer if he might go with her, and was refused. She was terribly frightened when she found herself alone, and the boat being lowered.' As Madeleine looked up towards the deck she saw Kitty, her husband's Airedale, pacing the decks of the *Titanic*. 'She remembers his [Astor] calling to her if she was all right or if she was comfortable, and that he asked the officer the number of the boat [number four], and he said something that she could not hear,' recalled Dobbyn. 'Her boat had gone a little way when the *Titanic* sank. She thought she heard him calling and she stood up and cried that they were coming, but the people in the boat made her stop and apparently they made no effort to go back towards those cries for help. There was no light in her boat and anyone in the water, only a few feet away, could not see them. You would be terribly sorry for her if you could see her and hear her tell the awful tragedy. She is so young and she cared so much for him.'

On the *Carpathia*, fellow survivors remember Madeleine lying on a sofa and sobbing continuously. The mood on board the rescue ship was not helped by the fact that after a terrible storm, the ship was shrouded in dense fog. The journey back to America was accompanied by the discordant sound of cries, underscored by the intermittent wail of the foghorn.

Meanwhile in New York, the Astor and Force families felt trapped in a wretched limbo, a state of anxiety and uncertainty. Vincent, the Colonel's son, and William Dobbyn 'haunted' the offices of the White Star Line and the Associated Press, waiting for news. Sudden exhilaration – an early report stated that practically all the passengers had been saved – was quickly followed by shock when it was learned that 1,500 or so travellers had lost their lives. When Vincent learned that his father was not on the *Carpathia*, nor had he been picked up by any other ship, it was reported that he collapsed and had to be taken home.

There was nothing to be done but wait for the arrival of the rescue ship. On 18 April, Vincent, now slightly more composed, stood with Madeleine's sister, Katherine, William Dobbyn, two doctors and a nurse; an ambulance was standing by to whisk Astor's young widow straight to hospital as it was rumoured she was ill and in a terribly depressed state. As they waited, they saw the red lights of the *Carpathia* approach the dock and listened to the 'ominous stillness' that descended over the crowd. 'Then as the people came off, such scenes as one can never forget,' recalled Dobbyn. 'It was several minutes before Vincent, who had received permission to go on board, could force his way through the crowd, but he finally got on the ship where he found Mrs Astor waiting, and brought her down. She could walk, and we had no need of the ambulance. I never saw a sadder face or one more beautiful, or anything braver or finer than the wonderful control she had of herself.'[9]

The group avoided the crush by taking the young widow down from the pier in one of the freight elevators. Waiting outside was the Astor car, which transported her first to her parents' house, at 18 East 37th Street – at this point in his life William Force could not walk and was unable to go and meet his daughter in person – and then to the Astor home at 840 Fifth Avenue. The press seized on the story and revelled in the ironies of the Colonel's fate. He was one of the richest men in the world but even his wealth could not save him from the tragedy. Yet over the course of the following weeks and months, he became a symbol of the nobility and self-sacrifice of the upper classes; in contrast to J. Bruce Ismay, whose life was ruined by his survival, Astor's demise represented the very best way to die and history would view him as one of *Titanic*'s heroes. Of course, there were those who saw his death as the act of a revenging God – such as one American minister who viewed his marriage to Madeleine as sinful ('Judgment of God on Astor Says Pastor Who Denounced Marriage' ran one headline) – but, for the most part, John Jacob Astor was seen as a brave and courageous man, who met death with dignity. 'We congratulate you that as your mouth was stopped with the brine of the sea, so you stopped the mouths of carpers and critics with the dust of the tomb,' wrote one commentator. 'If any think unkindly of you, be he priest or plebian, let it be with finger to his lips, and a look of shame into his own calloused heart.'[10]

Astor's family were particularly keen to recover his body from the sea and it was reported that millions could be spent on the mission. As it turned out, this was not necessary as the

White Star Line organised for its agents in Halifax, Nova Scotia, to charter a boat, the *Mackay-Bennett*, from the Commercial Cable Company to retrieve what bodies they could find from the ocean. The ship was equipped with enormous quantities of ice, a stack of coffins, and staffed by a local reverend, who would perform some of the services for the unidentified bodies buried at sea, and an embalmer. As the ship sailed out of port, towards the site of the wreck, the crew noticed the sea becoming crowded with icebergs and growlers. On 20 April, five days after the disaster, cable engineer Frederick A. Hamilton noted in his diary that they were 'very near were [sic] lie the ruins of so many human hopes and prayers'.[11] The sea was strewn with shards of wood, chairs and bodies, and in the course of the first day's recovery, the crew retrieved the corpses of forty-six men, three women and two children. At eight o'clock the bell on board the *Mackay-Bennett* tolled repeatedly as the bodies were being prepared to be committed to the deep. (There was it seems discrimination even in death as it was decided to preserve the bodies of all first-class passengers and bring them back to land, while those in third class, and crew members, were consigned to the depths of the ocean.) The next day, as the ship continued its grim mission, Hamilton observed that, floating on the surface of the sea, was a greater proliferation of splintered woodwork, cabin fittings, mahogany fronts of drawers, elaborate carvings, all of them wrenched away from their original fastenings. Fog settled over the ocean as they recovered yet more bodies from an area of thirty square miles.

The atmosphere was uncanny, almost supernatural. 'The hoarse tone of the steam whistle reverberating through the mist,' wrote Hamilton, 'the dripping rigging, and the ghostly sea, the heaps of dead, and the hard, weather-beaten faces of the crew, whose harsh voices join sympathetically in the hymn tunefully rendered by Canon Hind, all combine to make a strange task, stranger. Cold, wet, miserable and comfortless, all hands balance themselves against the heavy rolling of the ship as she lurches to the Atlantic swell, and even the most hardened must reflect on the hopes and fears, the dismay and despair, of those whose nearest and dearest, support and pride, have been wrenched from them by this tragedy.'[12]

On 30 April, the *Mackay-Bennett* returned to Halifax harbour, complete with its macabre cargo. As it sailed into shore, the city's church bells tolled and flags flew at half-mast. A total of 305 bodies had been recovered, noted Hamilton, while 116 of those had been buried at sea; other ships subsequently brought in to help the recovery raised the number to 323 with 119 of them being committed to the deep. (A month after the sinking, bodies were still being sighted. On 13 May, Shane and Seymour Leslie, sailing on the *Oceanic* to New York, claimed they saw three figures lying in a lifeboat. 'Two sailors could be seen, their hair bleached by exposure to salt and sun, and a third figure wearing evening dress lying flat on the benches,' said Shane. 'The boat was full of ghastly souvenirs, rings, watches and children's shoes from those who had died unrescued and been consigned to the ocean one by one.' His brother, Seymour, wrote in his diary at the time: 'The arms came off [the corpses] in the hands of the *Oceanic* boarding officer . . . The bodies were buried at sea and the prayer service read.'[13] Later, the bodies were identified as thirty-six-year-old first-class passenger Thomas Beattie, and two crew members, all of whom had died during that first night in collapsible A. When Fifth Officer Harold Lowe transferred passengers from the collapsible to lifeboat fourteen he left these three bodies behind.)

After docking, a continuous procession of hearses took the bodies from the *Mackay-Bennett* to a makeshift morgue in the

Mayflower ice rink, where relatives were free to claim them. The first body to be released was that of John Jacob Astor, who had been discovered wearing a brown flannel shirt with his initials embroidered on the collar, a blue suit, brown boots and a belt with a gold buckle. In his pockets or on his person, he carried nearly $2,500 (the equivalent of around $57,100 today), $225 in notes, together with a diamond ring, a gold watch and a pair of gold cufflinks. His son, Vincent, had chartered a special train to Halifax and it was on this that the body travelled to New York state for a funeral. On 4 May, a service was held at Rhinecliff on the Hudson, where the Colonel had been born, and the next day Astor's body was buried at Trinity Cemetery, Washington Heights, in a family tomb near to his mother's final resting place. It was reported at the time that it had been decided to omit one of the Astors' favourite hymns from the service – that of 'Nearer My God to Thee', which had been played at family funerals for generations – because of its association with the *Titanic*; relatives feared that its melody, which had supposedly been played by the bandsmen as the ship went down, could bring about the mental or physical collapse of his young widow.[14]

If this wasn't enough, Madeleine then had to endure the public controversy surrounding her dead husband's will, details of which were published in the press just three days later. At first sight, it looked as though she would benefit handsomely from the settlement – the income from a $5 million trust (around $114 million today), plus an immediate payment of $100,000, together with the bequest of the Colonel's horses, livestock, carriages, harnesses, stable furniture, and automobiles. Yet, on closer inspection, the will carried with it a deadly sting in its tail: Madeleine would only reap the benefits of the sizeable trust fund – and would only be able to continue living in the Fifth Avenue mansion – if she remained a widow for the rest of her life. A bleak future indeed for a girl of only eighteen years. Even more disturbing was the fact that her unborn child would only be entitled to a $3 million trust fund rather than share equally a slice of the Astor millions. The bulk of the fortune – estimated to be in the region of $150 million in 1912 (the equivalent would be around $3.4 billion today) – was left to Vincent, who would inherit the bequest when he came of age on 15 November 1912 and who would, in effect, become the largest individual landowner in the world. Legal experts debated the intricacies of the will, particularly the fact that Madeleine would lose her home and the income from the trust fund if she remarried.

'The unusual legal situation brought about through the fact that Madeleine Force Astor became an heiress, a bride, and a widow all in the course of a single year caused many lawyers familiar with litigation growing out of will contests to turn to their law books yesterday,' stated the *New York Times*. 'They agreed that there had been no exact or even approximate precedent for the case of Col. John Jacob Astor's widow. One view, somewhat generally held, was that the rule of the "interests of society" ought to be invoked in this case, since it was obviously unfair to a twenty-year-old girl to compel her to go through life as a widow or make a tremendous money sacrifice. It was pointed out that no father has been able to make a will that would hold where it stipulated that a son or daughter should not marry in order to gain certain benefits.'

After a reporter from the paper outlined Madeleine's unfortunate situation, lawyer John P. Cohalan, stated, 'Practically every one will agree that it is not fair to Mrs Astor that at the age of 20 she should be bound through the provisions of a will to remain a widow or suffer a tremendous money loss. Her natural status is of course with the young people, for whom the State has made provisions stronger than the wills of their forbears . . . The view may be easily held that Col. Astor in making the will never dreamed what a situation it was to bring about.'[15] In the years to come these would prove to be prophetic words indeed.

For the next four years, from almost the moment she was ferried from the *Carpathia* to her Fifth Avenue mansion, Madeleine Force Astor played the role of the grieving widow to perfection. She ordered a number of fashionable all-white crepe mourning dresses, which she alternated with those in 'dull-finished white crepe meteor',[16] and prepared herself for the birth of her child. On 31 May 1912, she invited Captain Rostron of the *Carpathia*, together with Frank McGee, who had been the surgeon on board the rescue ship, to her home for lunch as a way of showing her appreciation for their gallant efforts; other guests included Marian Thayer, who was 'dressed in heavy mourning', and Madeleine's mother. The atmosphere was sombre and respectful, the enormous windows in the grand dining room darkened since her husband's death, yet the air was full of the delicate scent of pink roses, which had been paired with marguerites and smilax. At four o'clock, the guests left the house, Captain Rostron travelling with Marian Thayer by train from Pennsylvania station to her home in Haverford, Philadelphia, for a few days.[17]

Each afternoon, Madeleine, accompanied by her nurse, would take her customary drive in her chauffeur-driven car through Central Park. By the first week of August, the sight of the young, heavily pregnant widow was enough to provoke an outbreak of mass hysteria. The public couldn't get enough of the story of 'the coming of the stork' as it was described in the press, and photographers regularly gathered outside the house, hoping to capture her image. One day the crowd was so large that, on returning from Central Park, the chauffeur was forced to drive to the back of the house, by way of Madison Avenue; as a result, Madeleine was reported by the *New York Times* to be greatly 'inconvenienced by the curious'.[18] However, the appetites of the public were satisfied, for the time being at least, when on 14 August, four months after she became a widow, Madeleine gave birth to a baby boy, weighing seven and three-quarter pounds. On 2 December, the boy was christened John Jacob Astor VI – the first Astor to carry the name was born in Waldorf, Germany, in 1763 – in the library of the house on Fifth Avenue. The child's godmother was named as Mrs M. Orme Wilson – Colonel Astor's sister, Caroline – while its godfathers were her son, Marshall Orme Wilson Jr, and Madeleine's cousin, Philip Lyndon Dodge. Each person who took part in the ceremony was given a selection of bonbons inside a dainty little white and pink box, bearing the initials J.J.A, outlined in gold, and decorated with a baby's head surrounded by cherubs. The event, of course, was more than just a christening; the news made the front pages of the newspapers and served as a highlight in the social calendar.

Madeleine may still have been in mourning, but it was important to observe the etiquette that underpinned the social network of east coast America. The young widow was still quite naive and the Colonel's sister, Caroline, took it upon herself to help Madeleine negotiate the strict rules of high society. In January 1915, Caroline orchestrated Madeleine's first formal entertainment at the Astor mansion – 'a ball . . . to let the world know she had laid aside the widow's weeds the sinking of the *Titanic* brought upon her'.[19] It was Caroline's 'dearest wish . . . to make Madeleine Astor the real social arbiter of New York'.[20] Competing for the prime position as the queen of the east coast were three women who all had claim to the Astor name – Madeleine Force Astor; the Colonel's divorced wife, Ava Willing; and Vincent Astor's new wife, Helen Dinsmore Huntington. The battle was a bitter one, with Ava Willing – who insisted on calling herself Mrs John Astor from the winter of 1915 – refusing to recognise her former husband's widow. 'Teas are the machine guns of social war,' proclaimed one newspaper at the time, as it analysed which one of the three women would win the 'three-cornered war for society's crown'.[21]

Maintaining this kind of profile did not come cheap and, in the summer of 1915 and the spring of 1916, a list of Madeleine's expenses came into the public domain. One report showed that between August 1912 and the end of 1914 Madeleine had spent $166,000 on maintaining her household. She seemed particularly distressed at having to pay for the rent of her Bar Harbor house and the upkeep of the family's numerous cars out of her own money, rather than the income from her son's trust fund, 'from all of which,' she said in a legal document, 'he has received substantial benefit and with a reasonable proportion of which expense . . . the said infant might properly be charged. From this it will be seen that the expenditures I have incurred for the benefit of said infant are far in excess of the money received by me.'[22]

Particularly noteworthy was the amount of money that she spent on her son – a staggering $27,593 a year ($608,000 in today's money). Written in the small print of little John Jacob's trust fund was a clause that forbade his mother from spending more than $20,000 of its income each year, a sum which Madeleine found wanting. To make up the difference, she had to spend exactly $7,593.20 from her own pocket. The figures were broken down as follows: $11,843.33 which accounted for one-third of the taxes on her home at 840 Fifth Avenue; one-third of the cost of maintaining the household came to $9,666.67; then there was the $2,544.94 on federal tax on the trust fund; $176.09 on federal tax on money received from trustees; $299 on doctors' fees; $720 on a nurse; $1,256.75 on lawyers' fees; $225 on the cost of a guardian's bond; and $861.42 on merchants' and other accounts.

In a legal document, Madeleine outlined her case: 'The above report shows that I have expended for the benefit of said infant, from Dec. 31, 1914, to Dec. 31, 1915, from my own resources, in addition to the amount received by me for his account, the sum of $7,593.20 . . . The estate so occupied is maintained at great expense, taxes for 1915 amounting to $35,920, and the expense of maintaining said establishment during the year 1915 for employees, upkeep, supplies and household expenses being approximately $29,000.' In effect, the cost of the four-year-old's upkeep was an astonishing $75.80 a day ($1,728.24 today). 'By the provision made in the eighth clause of the will of my late husband for the creation of a trust fund of $3,000,000, for the benefit of each child of mine that might survive him,' she added, 'it clearly appears that it was his intent for the upkeep and maintenance of said infant to secure everything for the comfort, welfare, and education of such child that money could provide.'[23]

The publication of the young widow's request in the newspapers shocked society – it was vulgar enough to mention money, let alone ask for more of it from one's own baby son – but two months later Madeleine had the whole world talking again when she decided to renounce her title as the reigning queen of New York and Newport society by announcing her marriage to childhood friend and sweetheart, William Karl Dick. In addition, she would also have to relinquish her right to live in the Fifth Avenue house as well as the regular stream of money that poured into her bank account from her generous trust fund. 'Now, at the very opening of the Newport season, now, with the stage all set,' wrote one observer in the *Chicago Daily Tribune* in June, 'she calmly makes her plans to marry young Mr Dick, tosses aside her $5,000,000 trust fund, a burdensome bauble withal, gives up the Fifth Avenue mansion, from which vantage point Col. Astor's mother for so many years issued the mandates that ruled New York society, and becomes, in place of a spectacularly interesting young widow, a mere matron of the younger set. Her marriage to Mr Dick does not place Madeleine Astor outside the charmed circle by any means, but it does rob her of the social prestige of the Astor name, and that means a lot.'[24]

If Madeleine's first marriage had been dictated by the lure of infinite wealth and the prospect of social enhancement, then her second was largely the result of something the general public could identify with: love. She may have taken a few steps down the society ladder, but ordinary men and women took her to their hearts. Not only had she lost a husband and survived the *Titanic*, but she had the courage to turn her back on a fortune in favour of the flutterings of her heart. Astor's sister, of course, was furious for what she saw as nothing short of a betrayal; after all the hard work she had put into orchestrating her position in society, Madeleine had thrown it all back in her face with not so much as a handwritten thank you note.

Her new husband, whom she married on 22 June in Bar Harbor, Maine, was described as 'sphinxlike'. To the gossip columnists and society commentators he was very much an unknown quantity. They knew the facts – he was twenty-eight, the eldest son of Mr and Mrs J. Henry Dick of 20 East 53rd Street, New York, and was the vice-president of the Manufacturers Trust Company of Brooklyn, and director in the Broadway Trust Company, the Cord Meyer Development Company, Citizen's Water Supply Company, Lake Charles Rice Milling Company, vice-president of the McKee Refrigerator Company, and secretary and treasurer of Rigney and Co. – but little of his personality. He was rich in his own right – his grandfather, William Dick, had made a fortune from sugar refining – yet his wealth could not match that of the Astors. Although they had known one another since childhood – and he was a regular guest at some of Madeleine's parties in New York and at her house in Aitken, South Carolina – there was little indication to suggest that the relationship had progressed from friendship to a greater intimacy. 'The friendship of their early days was renewed and it began to be noticed that he was rather often in her company,' said the *New York Times*. 'Still, so carefully was their secret guarded, that when this was commented upon the matter could be turned off lightly as the natural result of old friendship, and society has not suspected even since they have actually been engaged.'[25]

Fashion observers noted that her wedding trousseau included a black and white checked sports skirt, a white evening dress edged in black, and a black and white striped yachting jacket; apart from her signature style of black and white, other colours she favoured included ecru, cerise, lemon, jade, pervenche blue and candy pink. After a month-long honeymoon in California – Madeleine travelled across America in an ordinary Pullman rather than the Astor private train she had been used to – the couple returned to Dick's country house, Allen Winden, Islip, Long Island. Perhaps for the first time since she had met John Jacob Astor, Madeleine had a taste of 'ordinary' life. She was no longer followed around by packs of photographers and she did not feel she had to conform to the narrow strictures of society. In short, she experienced a freedom to simply exist. Friends testified that she was extremely happy and the couple proceeded to have two sons, William Karl Jr and John Henry. By 1924, however, Madeleine started to tire of her 'ordinary' existence; she realised she yearned for the glamour and excitement of her old life. Perhaps a trip abroad would satisfy her longings? In June,

Dick booked passage on the Cunard liner, the *Berengaria*, bound for Europe. In addition to Madeleine's three sons and her mother, fellow passengers included film producer Jesse L. Lasky, who was carrying a movie version of *Peter Pan* to show its author J.M. Barrie; the actress Jeanne Engels; the writer Anita Loos, and the novelist Edna Ferber. Despite the sights, sounds and flavours of Europe, Madeleine returned dissatisfied. Although she despised the popular press, she couldn't get used to a life that didn't feature her in its pages. Was it this desire that brought about the next – and most shocking – phase of her life? Or had she become so frustrated by conformity that she felt she had no other option but to reject polite society completely? Perhaps the loss of John Jacob Astor in the *Titanic* disaster had warped her mind to such an extent that she felt she needed to continue punishing herself. Or did she feel that she should have died with her first husband? Whatever the reason – and it was probably a messy cluster of all of the above – Madeleine initiated a series of events that would bring about her destruction.

Curiously enough, her bad romance started at sea. In early 1932, Madeleine decided she needed to escape from her failing marriage and try and improve the delicate state of her health. She had told her doctor, who always travelled with her, that the *Titanic* had 'ruined her nerves' and, as a result, she regarded herself as something of an 'invalid'. A trip to Europe would do her the world of good, she said, and in January of that year she booked a first-class cabin on the *Vulcania*. One night, during the transatlantic voyage, her doctor, the 'bluff and hearty' Moullowd, asked Madeleine whether she would like to make the acquaintance of a rather interesting and good-looking man, the Italian prizefighter Enzo Fiermonte, who was travelling in second class. At first, she refused, believing that it would be inappropriate to invite such a man to sit at her table, but finally she relented. The attraction between the thirty-nine-year-old woman, who already looked late middle-aged and quite dowdy, and the strapping, dark-haired boxer, who seemed even younger than his twenty-four years, was instant. She lusted after his youth, his earthy vigour and his sexual promise, while he was intrigued by the symbols of her wealth: the large diamonds on her slender fingers, the string of rare pearls around her neck, the orchids pinned to her jacket that had been brought to the ship especially for her.

'I suppose I stared at her,' said Fiermonte of that first meeting. 'She was different in a peculiar way. I could not decide how old she was. When she smiled she looked extremely young, and when she was serious she might have been past middle age. Perhaps she noticed my scrutiny and misunderstood, for suddenly I was aware that her pale blue eyes were fixed on mine, and that she was looking at me as no woman had ever done before. Her look went straight through me. I became a hundred and sixty pounds of blushing confusion. I couldn't even speak. And all the time we were together she continued to stare at me.'[26]

That night, when Fiermonte returned to his cabin, he vowed never to see Madeleine again; despite the attraction he felt for her he had a wife, Tosca, and son, Gianni, back home in Italy. The next day, when Moullowd, a boxing fan who knew Fiermonte through the fighter's manager, asked him to Madeleine's cocktail party he at first turned down the invitation before the doctor persuaded him the event might be good for his career. That night, the couple talked, and at the end of the evening Madeleine said that he was 'the most interesting person I've met for a long while'. To her friends, she observed, 'I don't think we realize how bored we are until we meet some real people.'

The next day, the couple played deck tennis and backgammon, during which their hands touched accidentally.

When she smiled, Enzo told her that she was beautiful. 'I suppose you tell all women that,' she replied. 'I know I'm very ordinary. They say I was quite good looking once, but I've had too much trouble in my life to keep my good looks.'

After dinner that night, Fiermonte led her out on deck where he kissed her. 'I suddenly lost control of myself,' he recalled. 'It was as if I had to gasp to breathe . . . We stayed for a long time under the moon. We were absolutely alone in a world of our own. To say we were both happy would be an underestimation. We were in a misty, romantic heaven.'

Yet moments later, after he had retired to his cabin alone, he was struck down by an overwhelming feeling of guilt. Each time he resolved to break it off with Madeleine, she seduced or tempted him to return. While he constantly vacillated between desire and contrition, lust and remorsefulness, Madeleine made it clear that she wanted him. She simply would not take no for an answer, and as the ship docked at Naples, where Fiermonte disembarked, she forced a promise out of him that he would join her at the Lido in Venice. He travelled on to Rome where he met his wife at the family's home on the Via Nomentana. He felt wretched, burdened by guilt, yet unable to confess his feelings to his family. Madeleine was incapable of waiting any longer for her new lover and promptly dispatched a telegram that read, 'Darling come and see me. If not I am going to Rome.' Fiermonte took a train to Venice and checked into the Excelsior on the Lido, where, later that night, the couple reunited. The boxer's description of the scene makes for steamy reading.

'That night in Venice is memorable,' he said. 'The air was full of the mysticism of romance. It was a long time before either of us spoke. We stood there as if we were both looking into the purple darkness and seeing a new vista of life open itself up to our eyes. She was different. Everything about her was subtly changed from the woman I had met on the ship. It was as if the years had slipped away from her. I saw her as a young and beautiful girl.

'We took a gondola and were soon gliding silently toward the old city of Venice, listening to the melodious guitars. I was no longer a boxer, and she was not a twice-married, rich woman. We were just boy meeting girl and, for us, time and age had stopped.

'Venice is made for love. Everywhere about us was music, light and color. The soft ripple of water, the warm-throated singers, the tinkle of music in the distance; these are the pleasures of a Venetian night.'

Then, the gondolier began to sing an Italian love song, which Madeleine asked Fiermonte to translate. He did not wish to interrupt the moment – translating the aria would have been like trying to warm up a soufflé, he said – and so he took her into his arms and kissed her. 'The memory of that kiss is a jewel I shall carry in my treasure chest of memory until my soul says goodbye to this earth,' he said.

From Venice, the couple travelled first to Cortina d'Ampezzo, where Madeleine found it too hot, and then to Villa d'Este, where she was met by her sons from her second marriage. After supper on a terrace overlooking Lake Como, Fiermonte finally unburdened himself of the secret that had been eating into him for the last few months – that he was married and that he had a son. 'My dear, so am I,' she responded. 'And I have three sons. Is that all? It would be more serious to me if I thought you were getting tired of me.' Enzo tried to interrupt, telling her that he was in love with his wife, but she refused to listen to him. 'Oh dear, how delicious you are,' she said. 'So I've made you feel a naughty boy? It's strange, after all these years, to find a man with a conscience. I like you all the more for that. You're quite precious.' She went on to tell him that her second marriage had been a 'big mistake', something she regretted terribly, and surmised that her young lover had spoken to her in this fashion in a bid to make her jealous. 'You want to hurt me,' she said, 'all Latin lovers do it.' Madeleine sat in silence, staring out across the black water of the lake, before she came up with an idea.

'But you can get a divorce, Enzo,' she said.

'Impossible!' he said. 'I'm a Catholic. My wife is devout, and there is no divorce in our church.'

'What a ridiculous country!' she replied. 'You must come to America. Or perhaps you can get a divorce in France. You can if you want to. I want you to get a divorce, Enzo, and I will get one too. Then I'll marry you!'

Fiermonte did everything in his power to resist her – informing her that he would never give up boxing, that a divorce would be out of the question, that they would never be happy together – but perhaps the promise of untold riches was too much for him. Finally, he confessed everything to his wife, Tosca, who told him that ever since he had met the rich American lady he had changed. 'I suppose I'm a very ordinary, simple woman to you now, Enzo,' she said.

On 28 September 1932, after spending time in Paris, the couple sailed on the *Olympic*, a journey that must have been quite surreal for Madeleine as the liner was a virtual copy of its sister ship, the *Titanic*. Back in New York, Fiermonte reiterated the fact that their marriage would be an absolute impossibility; the division between their material worth was just too wide to bridge. 'I don't agree with you,' said Madeleine. 'We should get on exceedingly well. We're such a change for each other. I've never got on with any one so well as I have with you. As for money, it really doesn't matter. You have brains, and I have enough money for both of us.' Madeleine proposed a deal: if he didn't want to accept her wealth as a gift, she could lend him a sum to set him up in business, which he could then pay back to her. Whatever the case, Enzo would have to give up boxing, a profession that Madeleine found disgusting. 'All that dirt – and those men who fought, they're nothing but animals,' she said, after watching her lover fight. 'It made me sick when I saw them put that rubber thing in your mouth and throw water over you from that horrible bucket. I'm sure you'll catch some awful disease . . . It's a shame to think of you mixing with these people. They'll make you coarse and ugly, and you'll never be anything. Get your divorce and we'll be married. Then you can go into business and live like a gentleman.'[27]

From New York, the couple moved to Palm Beach for the winter, where Madeleine rented a fifteen-room mansion overlooking Lake Worth. But the life of the idle rich bored Enzo. He did not think much of Madeleine's social circle – he regarded her acquaintances as superficial and dishonest – and he began to loathe himself. 'I would rather be a yard dog for life than a Pekingese for a day,' he said. After the arrival of Jack Astor – Madeleine's twenty-year-old son by her first marriage – the house was transformed into a battle zone as arguments raged between mother and child. Then, Madeleine's new doctor and Jack turned on Fiermonte and advised her that the boxer was a highly unsuitable choice of partner. Enzo could stand it no longer and so left for New York where he resumed his training. When Madeleine returned to the city, he tried to resist her charms – or rather the charms of her bank balance – but one night, after a hard day's work at the gym, he came out of the building on 66th Street to find a car drawing up outside. 'The window glass was lowered, and a white-gloved hand beckoned to me,' he said. 'I knew who it was, and obeyed the impulse to run out and greet her. The chauffeur opened the door and I got in, as happy as a schoolboy on a holiday.' They drove to Madeleine's house on East 84th Street, which he described as a gloomy six-storey building packed with antiques. 'The place depressed me,' said Enzo. 'It seemed like a dull mirror that reflected the cares of its owner.'

Still the couple continued to argue about the suitability of their union. Madeleine was so focused on the idea that she planned for Fiermonte to go to Reno to get a divorce, and organised to settle a large sum of money on her lover's son. Enzo duly wrote to his wife in Italy, outlining that he would never return to her and pleading with her to grant him a divorce. Tosca wrote back to tell him she would never consent to such a thing. Four months later, however, after reporters had begun to pester her for comments on her husband's scandalous relationship with the American millionairess, she relented. A lawyer drew up a contract, arranging for Madeleine to transfer $10,000 to Fiermonte's young son. Elsa Maxwell, the gossip columnist, sniffed out the news of the transaction and wrote, snidely, 'John Jacob Astor's widow finally used part of her fortune to buy herself an Italian boxer for a husband.' Fiermonte felt disgusted with himself but still continued to play the part of passive possession to perfection, travelling to Reno to start the divorce process. 'Reno was a crazy, unreal place, full of unreal people,' he said. 'It reminded me of a Hollywood movie set, with the extras from every film ever made running wild. With its cowboy roisterers, its Mexicans, dark-haired European swains, fake college boys, professional gamblers and blackmailers, all set on distracting and plundering the women waiting to qualify for divorce, it presented one of the most bizarre and sorry sights in the whole of the United States. Reno has more shyster lawyers than it has lamp posts.'

By June 1933, Madeleine and her second husband were officially separated and they divorced a month later. To celebrate, Madeleine and Enzo went to stay in a bungalow on the shores of Lake Tahoe, into which they threw her wedding ring.

The news of the split only served to increase public interest in her scandalous love life and soon the papers were full of the racy relationship between the *Titanic* widow and her so-called 'Italian Adonis'. One morning, Enzo opened the door of the rented bungalow to find the property besieged by journalists. 'Reporters swooped down on me like a flock of starlings on a worm,' he recalled.[28] The boxer denied the rumours of a relationship, describing the story as a 'lot of boloney' and stating that he hardly even knew Mrs Astor Dick.[29] Again, Fiermonte tried to leave Madeleine, but she had become so obsessive that she put a detective on his trail. When they met again, the boxer told her in no uncertain terms that he would never marry her. The couple quarrelled violently, he made a statement to a newspaper reporter about how she was too old for him, and Madeleine broke down at her suite in the Hotel Pierre. Yet still Madeleine continued to pursue the young boxer, inviting rejection at every turn.

'One morning the Reno lawyer telephoned,' recalled Fiermonte. 'Poor devil, he thought he was giving me good news! He couldn't have the least idea that he was crashing my life . . . He announced, triumphantly, that Tosca had signed the paper, and if I would settle ten thousand dollars on my son, he could get my divorce as soon as I arrived in Reno.'

In the two weeks before his next appointment with his lawyer in Reno, Fiermonte finally questioned himself about the basis of his attraction to Madeleine. Was it because of her fame, her money, or was it something within him that compelled him to love a woman he found difficult, and who actually scared him. After returning to Reno – 'the city of marital bad dreams' – for his divorce he felt so depressed and powerless that on the flight back to New York he secretly fantasised that his plane would crash. From New York he sailed to Bermuda on the slowest boat he could find, to the triumphant Madeleine. As he looked at the ocean he toyed with the idea of throwing himself into the sea, but he doubted whether he would have the courage to drown. He realised then that he did not love Madeleine, rather he had been motivated by the darker emotions of 'passion and fear'. Again, he resolved he would leave her – this time he planned on travelling to London to pursue his boxing career, yet when he arrived at the island and told her of his proposal, Madeleine became hysterical.

'I've been dead for a year,' he confessed, 'and I can't live in a grave. Let's be reasonable – part friends and give each other a chance. You should marry someone in your own circle and of your own station.'

'You mean I'm too old!' she shouted back, her face white, her eyes frantic.

'No, it's not a question of age . . . Your idea of living is wrong. Your life is wrong.'[30]

He told her that he did not want to be reduced to a mere possession, but as he walked towards the door she grabbed hold of his hair and told him that he could not leave her. Fiermonte brought both of his arms down to force her to release her grip on him, not realising his own strength. Madeleine fell on to the floor, fracturing her left arm. The boxer immediately regretted what he had done and scooped her up, shouting for the doctor that always travelled with her, who then called an ambulance. On arriving back in Manhattan, Madeleine was photographed on a stretcher. 'What a hungry mob of vultures you are!' screamed her secretary, Edith Searle, at the pack of newsmen that surrounded her. 'What dirty dogs! What torturers and persecutors!'[31]

However, the only true torturers and persecutors were Madeleine and Enzo themselves. She refused to admit to herself or to the public what he had done, telling the world that she had simply slipped on the highly polished floor of the house in Bermuda. Enzo, for his part, felt guilty at having reacted with such force. Instead of agreeing to separate, the couple decided to go through with their union. On 27 November 1933, from the confines of her bed at the Doctors Hospital, the couple married. Not surprisingly, the match generated a rash of ugly headlines and acres of snide comment.

'Just what led Mrs Dick to leave her quiet and successful husband in 1933 to become the wife of an Italian prizefighter half her age is not easy to figure out,' wrote one journalist. 'Of course, young Fiermonte is handsome, and he has a romantic name which seems to mean "fiery mountain" in Italian. But having neither money, social position, nor promise for success even in prizefighting, he hardly seemed a match for the widow of John Jacob Astor. Perhaps somewhere in Madeleine's heart she still terribly resented the domination of her mother which led to her first marriage. Perhaps she determined to show the world she was independent by ignoring all the dictates of convention and accepting happiness where she found it – which happened to be with Enzo Fiermonte.'[32]

Her family, it seems, tried to do everything to prevent the alliance. Her stepson, Vincent Astor, even went so far as to try and ban Fiermonte from entering America by petitioning the help of his friend President Roosevelt. The marriage must have been galling for Madeleine's sons, particularly for her first born, John Jacob, who the week after his mother's unwise union announced his own engagement to a Manhattan debutante Eileen Gillespie. Perhaps it was the scandal surrounding his mother's marriage to the young, penniless boxer that was responsible for the breakdown of this relationship; six months later, in July 1934, John Jacob married Ellen Tuck French, a cousin of William Vanderbilt. Those listed as 'notably absent' at the Newport wedding included his half-brother,

Vincent Astor, his former fiancée and his new stepfather, the 'pugilist' Fiermonte.

Despite objections from Madeleine's family – and from Madeleine herself – Fiermonte insisted he wanted to pursue his career as a boxer. At the beginning of July 1934, he maintained he would start training at Asbury Park, New Jersey, but by the end of the same month he announced that he was 'through with the ring forever'.[33] Two weeks later he declared he wanted to break into the movies, but, despite travelling to Los Angeles, he was unable to get any studio to take him seriously. After only seven months together, the couple's marriage started to disintegrate. Fiermonte was spotted in LA with American journalist, screenwriter and novelist Adela Rogers St Johns – who herself would interview another *Titanic* survivor, silent screen star Dorothy Gibson – while his wife was sailing for Europe. On 10 August 1934, it was reported that he 'had two divergent ideas in his mind yesterday. One is to break into films and the other is to be divorced by his wealthy and socially-prominent wife, Mrs Madeleine Force Astor Dick Fiermonte.'[34]

If some marriages are sometimes described as rocky, this one was positively Himalayan. Each week – practically every day – one or both of them would try for a reconciliation only for it to be met by rejection or abandonment. It was clear why Enzo had married Madeleine, for the same reasons that she had agreed to marry John Jacob Astor: money and prestige. When Madeleine realised the truth she felt repelled by her own lack of judgement, but no matter how hard she tried to extract herself from this most toxic of relationships she was unable to do without her fix of Fiermonte, the fiery mountain. In January 1935, Enzo booked a passage on the Italia liner *Roma*, bound for his home country; when his wife discovered his intentions she chased after him, buying a last-minute ticket on the same ship. It wasn't until the liner was at sea that Fiermonte discovered the truth. 'Wife is aboard,' he wired a friend. 'God help me.'[35] Yet, a few days later, he changed his mind again, this time sending a wire to the Associated Press to say that the couple had 'effected a reconciliation'.[36] The appeasement was short-lived, as Fiermonte embarked early, at Genoa, where he met his first wife and son, a meeting that was described as 'affectionate'. As he stepped on to Italian soil, the police seized his documents – he had skipped his compulsory military service while living in the United States – and ordered a team of detectives to be placed on his trail. 'As he has no American passport, but merely a provisional repatriation permit from the Italian consulate in New York, he is completely under Italian jurisdiction,' explained one source. 'He cannot return to the United States without special dispensation.'[37]

This was just the beginning of his problems in Italy. On 12 February, the Italian authorities impounded his passport and forbade him to leave the country. The crux of the matter was that Italy did not recognise the divorce from his first wife. The implication for Madeleine was serious – legal experts advised her that there was a possibility that she could be prosecuted on grounds of bigamy and that it would be best if she left Italy immediately. The Italian lawyer Francesco Montefredini told Madeleine that 'she might face a sentence of from one to five years for participating in bigamy, since Italian laws do not recognise divorce'.[38] In addition, the authorities made it known that Mussolini himself disapproved of Fiermonte's behaviour – 'When he [Enzo] went to America he acted in a way Italy cannot approve,' said a spokesman. 'Because he is not considered desirable to represent Italians abroad and to make sure he meets his obligations, his passport will not be returned.'[39]

Fiermonte was desperate. He knew that if he was ever to extract himself from Italy he would need money and connections, things that only Madeleine could supply. On 15 February he announced, 'My wife and I have both made mistakes in the past, but we have reached an understanding . . . As soon as my papers are returned we will start our second honeymoon and go back to America.'[40] By early March, Madeleine's lawyer had managed to retrieve Fiermonte's passport – and organise the settlement of a regular monthly payment to his first wife – leaving the couple free to travel. From Italy, Enzo and Madeleine journeyed to France, where they checked into a smart hotel in Menton. On the surface, everything appeared to be back to normal – whatever that meant in their highly unstable, emotionally turbulent world – and Fiermonte was excited to take delivery of a Duesenberg, a car that would prove particularly useful when his first wife turned up, fresh from the Rome express, unannounced at their hotel. 'She explained in strong language that she had come to reclaim Enzo,' said one witness. 'There was considerable argument. Mrs Fiermonte No. 1 waxed vituperative. But the management was firm. She finally compromised by taking a room near the honeymoon suite. Fiermonte and wife No. 2 meantime slipped out of the side door, ran to the garage, jumped into the racer and vanished.'[41]

From Menton the couple drove to Paris, where Fiermonte issued a series of disclaimers to the press. He denied that he had ever seen his first wife while in Italy, that he had alimony trouble with his former wife or that he or Madeleine had ever faced bigamy charges, and concluded by rejecting the rumours that he and his wife were about to separate. By the summer of 1935 they had returned to America where Madeleine tried to introduce her husband to those few friends in society who still accepted her. 'Not even the shifting of the Gulf Stream has caused such variation in the Newport temperature as the presence of the Enzo Fiermontes,' wrote one commentator.[42] The strain was obviously taking its toll; although she was still only in her early forties, friends began to comment on how she had lost her freshness. 'The path she has chosen for herself is not easy, and her face well shows it . . .' wrote one observer. 'Her deeply furrowed face gives little hint of the great beauty with which she charmed Colonel Astor shortly before the war.'[43] In private, Madeleine was suffering her own secret hell. Fiermonte constantly demanded money and, when it was not forthcoming, he started to hit her. Underneath her fine garments and elegant outfits, Madeleine's pale skin began to be covered by an ugly bloom of dark, purple bruises. For his part, Fiermonte resented his role as a rich woman's plaything; of course, he enjoyed the trappings of her wealth, but he hated himself for the sordid exchange. It was clear by this stage that he no longer found her attractive – if anything he was repelled by her lined skin, her ageing body – and he felt frustrated and angry with himself. The only way he felt able to cope with the situation was to lash out and Madeleine bore the full force of his rage.

In July 1937, Fiermonte was sentenced to five days in New York's Rikers Island prison for failing to answer a three-year-old speeding charge, and on his release he hit a press photographer, John Dennan. The pressman filed a civil suit against the former boxer, a case that was settled out of court on payment of a four-figure sum. By the end of the year, Madeleine could stand no more. Her body ached from the regular beatings and her bank account had been drained by his increasingly frequent demands for money. According to court records, 'once he broke her wrist, on another occasion he broke her ribs. She frequently was left bedfast by his attacks, her bills charged. Their final separation was late last year [1937] when Fiermonte . . . beat her senseless.'[44] In May 1938, while staying in Palm Beach, Florida, she decided to make him a final severance settlement of $150,000 and file divorce papers on grounds of 'extreme cruelty'. Witnesses said that Fiermonte 'used her as his punching bag, often breaking her bones in their five years of marriage . . . Although he is a youth of great personal beauty, his prize ring record shows that his wife was the only opponent he was able to flatten successfully.'[45] Other reports confirmed that 'on various occasions he had 1) knocked her down, 2) broken her wrist, 3) hit her with his fist after a dance; been 'exceedingly unpleasant'.[46] On the same day the divorce was granted, Fiermonte – who was in France with a party of three women – crashed his car into a tree near Auxonne. He suffered minor injuries, while one of his companions, twenty-six-year-old American actress Marion Whitworth, had to be taken to hospital. The crash resulted in yet another prison sentence.

Madeleine, her heart and body bruised, assumed that after the divorce had been finalised she would have nothing more to do with her former husband. But then, in early 1939, came a betrayal worse than any barbed insult or petty infidelity: he sold the story of his marriage to *True Story Magazine*. The serialisation, entitled 'Kept Husband', and running in the February, March and April issues of the popular magazine, detailed every aspect of their relationship. Claiming to stand as 'one of the most startling and illuminating commentaries on life among the idle rich ever written', Fiermonte's testimony devastated Madeleine. Her reputation ruined, she felt depressed, almost suicidal. Then, in August, she heard the news that her mother had died after a long illness. Over the course of the following few months she became increasingly dependent on prescription drugs. In January 1940, she travelled from her house in Charleston to Palm Beach, where on 27 March she died. She was forty-seven years old. The official cause of death was given as heart failure, but those close to her suspected that she had taken an overdose of sleeping pills; as she left no note behind no one could be sure whether it was an accident or suicide. As Fiermonte – who went on to fulfil his dream of becoming an actor (he starred in over one hundred films and television series between the 1940s and 1980s) – said of his former wife, Madeleine 'carried her doubts with her always, like her pearls'.[47]

In her will, she split her $1,149,142 estate between her two sons with William Dick, as she believed that her son by Colonel Astor had already been amply provided for by the terms of his trust fund. She did, however, leave John Jacob – who at this point was living at the Hotel Plaza – a diamond solitaire ring worth $50,000 and a pearl necklace valued at $1,525.

The *Titanic* baby had grown up to be, in the words of Enzo Fiermonte, a 'poor little rich boy, if ever there was one . . . tall, fair, sleek, lackadaisical'. The problem was he had no purpose in life; with little to do but spend money he dedicated himself to satisfying the most trivial of desires. He wore four watches – one on each wrist and one in each inner pocket of his suit and, when he came into his inheritance, he bought a fleet of cars. 'When I met him he gave me the impression of never having enjoyed anything in his life,' said Fiermonte. 'No, perhaps I am mistaken. His hero was Napoleon. He had read everything he could find about the little Corsican . . . The last time I saw Jack was in Newport. He was nearly happy, I should think. He had his ten cars and four chauffeurs, standing by. He would drive one car for awhile, then dash into the garage, jump out, leap into another and drive off, and so on, until all the vehicles had had an airing. He was as serious about their exercise as a groom who has ten horses that must be walked each day.'[48]

Jack grew to loathe his half-brother Vincent, who had inherited the bulk of the Astor fortune after the death of his father on the *Titanic*. 'He [Vincent] had the legal, not the moral right to keep all the money,' he said.[49] After a life as turbulent as his mother's – including three failed marriages, an allegation of bigamy and a bitter legal battle over Vincent's will – John Jacob died in Miami Beach, in June 1992.

In many ways, Madeleine and her son can be seen as victims

of the *Titanic*, both forced to live in the shadow of the doomed liner. For her part, Madeleine struggled with the burden of unconscious guilt and punished herself for surviving. John Jacob chose the opposite route – indulging in a lifetime of pleasure, an existence of hedonism. Neither strategy proved successful. For Jackie Astor – the daughter of John Jacob – the event is clouded in so much sadness that she prefers not to discuss it. 'My father has not mentioned the *Titanic* in years and I assure you he wouldn't discuss it now,' she said a few months before her father's death. 'It was all so sad and tragic for his mother [Madeleine] and the whole family. You know, his parents were very much in love, and I think the memory of it all has affected his whole life. Why can't people just forget the *Titanic*?'[50]

Four

FALLING IN LOVE IN THE SLIPSTREAM OF THE *TITANIC*

The *Titanic* disaster separated hundreds of couples in the most appalling manner. However, what is extraordinary is the way in which it affected the survivors in the aftermath. The sinking generated a maelstrom of emotion and as the survivors struggled to make sense of the tragedy, many found themselves swept along by a host of invisible undercurrents. It was almost as if the vortex that had sucked the *Titanic* under the water had somehow manifested itself as a series of intangible forces that had the power to align or destroy relationships. Some love affairs blossomed, others withered and died. Bereaved individuals sought out other survivors, drawn together by an experience so profound that they had no option but to turn to those who had witnessed the same terrible event. Couples produced children who would otherwise not have been born. The *Titanic* was a constant presence in their lives.

Soon after the *Carpathia* had docked in New York, twenty-six-year-old second-class passenger Marion Wright scanned the mass of people surrounding the pier. She had left her home town of Yeovil, Somerset, and set out for New York on the *Titanic* to meet her sweetheart, Arthur Woolcott, whom she planned to marry. With each frantic turn of the head she saw anxious, tortured faces, and although she tried to convince herself that Arthur would be somewhere among the crowd, finally she had to accept that he was not there. Her new friend, fellow second-class passenger Bessie Watt – who, with her twelve-year-old daughter, Bertha, had escaped the ship in lifeboat number nine – persuaded her to go with her to a relative's house in New York. As Marion had no other friends or family in America, she felt she had no choice.

Arthur had been travelling from Buffalo to New York by train to meet Marion when he heard news of the disaster. Some of the newspaper reports claimed that scores of passengers were maimed – while many had died on board the *Carpathia* – and he feared for Marion's life. But, when he arrived at the pier to meet the rescue ship, she was nowhere to be seen. He had to keep a firm check on himself, he said; falling apart would do no one any good. With as steady a hand as he could manage he began to call each of the New York hospitals to ask if they had admitted a young woman by the name of Marion Wright. With each apology – sorry, there was no one there under that name said each of the receptionists at the various hospitals – came a sense of relief, soon followed by anxiety. By the end of Thursday, 18 April, Arthur was downcast and exhausted, but that night, in his bed at the Grand Union Hotel, he was so worried he could not sleep.

Marion was equally distraught. After arriving at the home of Bessie Watt's brother, Henry Milne, at 204 West 128th Street, she spent the day ringing round the Manhattan hotels. Finally, on Friday afternoon, she discovered Arthur at the Grand Union. He was not in and so she duly left a message where she could be reached. Later that day, he turned up at her friends' apartment and the two fell into each other's arms. The sight of Arthur was enough to dispel, for a few minutes at least, the awful memory of the *Titanic*. Since the night of the sinking she hadn't been able to get the image of the ship out of her mind; she likened it to a tired, dying animal slipping into the sea.

From the moment of their reunion the couple were buoyed

along by preparations for their wedding. Marion's survival invested the occasion with a certain mania, a high-spirited sense of what it meant to cheat death. Arthur wrote to the vicar of the church where they were to be married, mentioning the fact that his fiancée had been a passenger on the *Titanic*; the word acted like a talisman, speeding up the process and drawing gifts from strangers. Marion's outfit comprised a new blouse and skirt, 'the latter given me by the clothes committee on the docks, who also gave me handkerchiefs, stockings, combinations, vest and comb,' she said.[1] In addition, certain members of the Relief Committee gave her a donation of $225 – money that came directly from particular individuals, not from the general fund – while the White Star Line forwarded a first-class train ticket from New York to Oregon, her new home. Twelve-year-old survivor Bertha Watt served as her bridesmaid, while Henry Milne gave her away, and after the ceremony a couple of church ladies pressed into her hand a prayer book and a hymn book, while a member of the congregation gave her a 'beautifully bound teacher's Bible'. Later, while staying at the Grand Union, a stranger rang to say that she had a present for the newly married couple, a silver nut-stand that had been one of her own wedding presents. Marion could not help but think about her trousseau, and her trunks, full of wedding presents, which now lay at the bottom of the sea.

Witnesses described her as being cheerful and brave. 'She was very cool,' said the Reverend J. Wilson Sutton, who conducted the marriage service. 'She could not have been less frightened at the prospect of matrimony than if she had to experience another *Titanic* wreck.'[2] Indeed, as Marion herself admitted, 'Everybody says that I don't look much like anyone who has been through such a terrible experience.' Surface appearance was one thing, inner feelings quite another. 'I can't very well say in a letter or even put into words quite what I feel about it all, but the memory of it all will never go, I'm sure,' she wrote to her parents.[3] For the moment, however, she had her new life with her husband to look forward to; memories of that awful night on the *Titanic* could be pushed to one side.

The train journey from New York to Oregon was spectacular, and Marion particularly enjoyed the stretches along the Colombia River and through the Willamette Valley. 'For a day and a half we were crossing the Rockies, covered in snow and the prairie beneath them, a very wild part I can assure you,' she said.[4] The couple arrived at Cottage Grove, Oregon, in the early morning on 2 May, and were immediately met by one of Arthur's friends, Curtis Veatch, who took them to his house to meet his wife and have breakfast, before driving them to their new home, an eighty-acre fruit farm. 'We both felt very tired with the train journey and Arthur had almost lost his voice . . .' she said. 'It is alright now though and we both feel rested.'[5] Neighbours went out of their way to make the newly married couple welcome, baking endless rounds of cakes and whipping up rich milk puddings. The day after they arrived Arthur drove his new bride into Cottage Grove to pick up their baggage. 'I have a nice stock of underlinen, boots, shoes, coat and skirt, dresses . . . mackintosh, then we got sheets, pillow cases, the latter I have to make up, we are sleeping in cotton blankets at present and they are so "comfy",' she wrote home. 'The household things such as jugs, table silver!, towels, quilt etc and if we get our claim from the White Star Co. we will be able to get by very well indeed.'[6]

Her letter writing duties were interrupted by new friends dropping by and the demands of country living; the cow had somehow escaped through the fence and so she had to be coaxed out of the nearby woods. There was no doubt, however, that Marion responded to the abundance of nature that Oregon offered; while in the woods she recalled picking bunches of flowering currant iris. 'There are any quantity of flowers of varied kinds here, the colum vine, arum lily, large corn flowers etc, look so pretty in the field up Arthur's hill,' she wrote. 'The mountains are grand and today is such a lovely day, bright hot sun. I have been wearing a cotton dress ever since I arrived here and find it plenty warm enough (short sleeves and low neck) . . . The first morning, while we were having breakfast, a humming bird came and hovered just outside one of the windows. They are sweet little birds, then that same morning I saw two flocks of geese flying north . . .'

Curious, but well-meaning neighbours from the local church group organised an official welcoming party for her on 8 May, during which they wanted her to say a few words about her experiences on board the *Titanic*. 'Although I don't care about it *at all* yet as they are being so kind I feel I must make a slight return and so have said I will . . .' she said. 'I have told them that such things are better not talked about as it all seems so terrible.'[7]

She managed to cope as best she could, she said, as she went on to explain how she gave the talk. She related her time on board the ship: the memories of the smell of the new paint, the friendships she made, the singing of the hymns on that fateful Sunday, the impact of the iceberg, the gradual recognition that the ship would sink, the sight of the liner slipping into the sea, the awful night in the lifeboat and the eventual rescue. At the end of her talk the good people of Cottage Grove presented her with an aluminium chain purse containing the sum of $20, 'to make up for part of losses they said'.[8] The following Saturday, around one hundred people came to the house, each family bearing cakes and flowers. Marion, for her part, made a big vat of ice cream, using six gallons of milk, three dozen eggs, sugar and vanilla.

She wrote of her new life in Oregon while sitting down by the creek, describing the refreshing breeze that came off the snow-covered Cascade mountains, the blossom of the fruit trees – 'there are three big apple trees just near the house, in fact the branches overhang the verandah and almost peek into the kitchen windows' – and the interior of her new home. 'The sitting room has three windows, we made curtains of white spotted muslin last week and put the same up in our bedroom, and things begin to look cozy and home like,' she said. 'The wallpapers are very pretty, purple in the sitting room and golden in the bedroom, two rooms are not papered as yet. Arthur thinks we should wait for the wood to dry. Yesterday we got quite alarmed for a second or so as we heard slight crackling sounds and thought of fire at once, but it was the boards cracking under the heat of the sun and the muslin giving on the walls that are papered . . .'[9]

As is obvious from her letters, Marion's love of domesticity – the delight with which she describes the details of her daily routine – was a channel through which she could express her new-found happiness. She had a husband, a home, land, abundant fruit from the orchard, friends, cakes and puddings galore, swathes of time in which she could devote herself to home-making (while Arthur concerned himself with ploughing or fixing up new telephone poles). She had nearly died – what more would she need, she asked herself, than the simple comforts of everyday life? Never would she yearn for more, she told herself; never would she aspire to the trappings of material wealth or the stimulants offered by the modern world. The quotidian, the simple, the everyday was enough for her, and so she continued to live. She gave birth to three sons, John, Russell and Bob, all of whom, according to a local journal, 'were raised English, dressed for school in knickers and the same wool caps that Arthur wore'. Her children say that she never wanted to volunteer information about the *Titanic*. 'This was a very traumatic thing for her,' says her son Russell Woolcott. 'She tried to put it behind her.'[10]

Yet, for all her efforts to erase that night from her mind, the memory of the *Titanic* continued to shape her life. When her sons left home during the Second World War, Marion took out her thick wool coat that she had thrown over her nightdress as she escaped the ship, and cut a piece from its side. She fashioned the cloth into three little bags 'for testaments' and gave one to each of her sons. If she had survived, so too would her sons, and each of the bags served as a kind of talisman to protect her children from danger. (Today, one can see Marion's sturdy brown coat in a display cabinet at the Cottage Grove Museum, together with typed transcriptions of some of her letters home.)

In April 1962, on the fiftieth anniversary of the sinking, Marion gave an interview to a local newspaper, the *Eugene Register-Guard*. 'I can't believe it has been half a century since that terrible night,' said Marion, whose husband had died in 1961. 'The events are so etched in my mind that it seems like it happened yesterday.'[11] She died on 4 July 1965, at the age of eighty, and although the couple never raised enough money to realise Marion's dream of returning to England, by all accounts they lived a happy and contented life. Marion did not let the *Titanic* define her life, and neither did she deny it. Not only did she survive the night, but she also survived the aftermath.

Another young couple who were drawn together by the *Titanic* were fellow passengers Karl Howell Behr and Helen Newsom. On the boat he had shadowed his sweetheart, rarely letting her out of his sight, and as the ship was sinking he accompanied her into lifeboat number five. Not only had he had to contemplate death on board the *Titanic* – as a first-class male passenger he must have realised that the law of the sea dictated that he should stay behind until all the women and children had been rescued – but also while in his lifeboat he had been offered the use of a revolver if the situation proved unbearable. He had been forced to ask himself: if it looked as though they would never be rescued and would die of starvation and cold, would he be able, and willing, to shoot his sweetheart in the head and then himself? The thought of losing Helen before they had had a proper chance of spending any time together was agonising. And as for the prospect of killing her? It was beyond the realms of possibility.

The sense of relief on being rescued by the *Carpathia* was overwhelming, but he did not relax. Instead, Karl busied himself by helping to form a relief committee. 'We were occupied mainly with the steerage passengers; obtaining clothing, blankets and arranging places for them to sleep,' he said. 'It was harrowing to talk with these despairing people from whom I had to get names, home addresses and the names of lost relatives.' He described the journey home to New York as 'four days of suffering and sorrow', and the sight of people mourning the loss of their loves only heightened his own feelings for Helen.[12]

On the second night, no doubt dreaming of a blissful future with his sweetheart, he was awakened from his 'bed' on top of a table in the smoking room by a terrible crash. He was certain that the *Carpathia* had collided with another ship or even, God forbid, another iceberg. 'I rushed out of the door, starting for Helen,' he said. 'As I hit the deck it was pouring rain – suddenly a flash of lightning almost knocked me down. It was followed by another crash of thunder. I turned back to the smoking room; never before had a violent thunder-storm been more welcome.'[13]

Karl arrived in New York to see the heavens weeping. As he walked down the gangway to the crowded dock into a waiting room he described as 'frantic', he was led by his friends to his father, who was so weak that he was unable to raise himself from his chair. 'His face appeared to have shrunk to half its size,' remembered Karl. 'I shall never forget the indelible imprint of suffering. He was too feeble, my vigorous father, to get up to greet me. He just held out his arms, the tears streaming down his face.'[14]

Yet Karl did not allow the trauma of the disaster to disrupt his life. Rather than internalise the event, he made an effort to look outward. Conscious of his sense of social duty, he did everything in his power to help pursue the legal case for compensation against the White Star Line on behalf of the steerage passengers. Using his background – he had been awarded a Ph.B. from Yale in 1906 and an LL.B. from Columbia in 1910 and entered the Bar in 1911 – he fought for the rights of the third-class passengers, arguing that 'the *Titanic* had taken unwarranted risks in ice filled waters by refraining from slowing down . . . The result of this litigation was the recovery of substantial damages for loss of life and baggage by the steerage passengers.'[15]

In May 1912, when the *Carpathia* arrived in New York from Naples – the first time the Cunard liner had returned to the port of Manhattan since the rescue – Karl, together with the rest of the relief committee members, presented Captain Rostron with a silver cup as a mark of the survivors' deep regard. At 10.30 a.m. on 29 May, Karl stood by and watched as the Captain issued orders for all hands to muster in the first-class dining saloon. Of the 320 sailors who had been on board the *Carpathia* during the rescue mission, 70 had disembarked at Fiume, and so the remaining 250 crew members stood in two neat lines to await the presentation. 'It was a striking picture,' wrote one observer, 'that of the brawny, weatherbeaten old bo'sun and the quartermasters and sailors in their blue uniforms mingling with the soot-begrimed firemen and coal passers who had come direct from the stokehole. In addition to the gold-laced uniforms of the officers and engineers, the cooks, in their white caps and aprons, were there with a big array of stewards.'[16]

The chairman of the committee, Frederick Seward – the lawyer who had left the *Titanic* in the company of actress Dorothy Gibson and her mother – thanked the Captain and crew for saving their lives. 'The eyes of the world are upon you and were upon you when you came to us on the open ocean,' he said, 'when we saw the *Carpathia* coming to us out of the dawn, and to all of you we wish to give our heartfelt thanks. For your hospitality, for your devotion, for your unselfishness, and for all that was done for us we never can be adequately grateful.'[17]

As Karl learned of some of the more heart-rending stories – children who had been orphaned, women who had been widowed, sweethearts who had been separated – he felt increasingly thankful that his own experience had had a happy ending. Like Marion Wright, he felt determined to squeeze everything out of life. Marriage to Helen seemed like a glorious inevitability. After all, if they had survived the *Titanic* disaster, then surely they would be equipped to endure whatever life had to throw at them? Luckily, Helen felt the same way and, after his proposal was accepted, the preparations began in earnest for their wedding.

On 1 March 1913, at three o'clock in the afternoon, the couple were united at the Church of the Transfiguration in New York. Helen wore 'a gown of white satin charmeuse with a long veil of duchess point that was draped in with the gown in pannier effect, the lace being carried down into a train', according to a report in the *New York Times*, while the bridesmaids, Gertrude Behr, Karl's sister, and Beatrice Cook, a friend, wore 'frocks of palest eau de nil chiffon over very pale pink and hats of white lace, having pink bows and all sorts of odd little Spring flowers caught in bunches here and there'. As Helen's father, Logan Newsom, had died some years before, the bride was given away by her stepfather, Richard Beckwith, who had also survived the *Titanic* by escaping the ship in the same lifeboat as his wife and stepdaughter.[18]

A year later, in 1914, Karl H. Jr, the first of their four children was born, followed by Peter in 1915, James in 1920, and Sally in 1928. As the years passed, the *Titanic* faded into the background of their lives – Helen was busy with the children, while Karl continued to work as a director of his father's company, before becoming, from 1925, vice-president of the investment bankers Dillon, Read. Yet Karl would occasionally allow himself to think about how his future would have shaped itself if he had not pursued Helen to Europe and had not returned with her on the *Titanic*. He was sure that he was in love with her before that journey but would either of them have had the willpower, strength of commitment or the frenzied emotional energy generated by survival? Would the passion simply have fizzled out? Would he, or she, have met someone else? How would their lives have changed if they hadn't been united by the *Titanic*? He couldn't answer that. But the image of that nickel-plated revolver – the gun shown to him by a fellow passenger in his lifeboat, a weapon that was offered to him so that he could put an end to Helen's life and then his own – often came to him in the early hours when he could not sleep.

The shared experience of cheating death at close quarters had forged a deep psychological bond between them, a connection that was finally broken when, on 15 October 1949, at his home on East 72nd Street, New York, Karl Behr died, aged sixty-four. Helen did not want to let her husband go – surely this was part of the reason she later married one of Karl's good friends, Dean Mathey. To the end of her life she lived with Mathey in Princeton, New Jersey, where she died on 7 September 1965, aged seventy-two. Both of them passed away due to natural causes, and, if one believes in the relativity of death – that one way to die is better than another – as both Karl and Helen did, then it was at least a comfort for them to pass away knowing that they had never had to endure the terrible deaths they had witnessed in the early hours of 15 April 1912.

'Quite suddenly it seems to me now,' wrote Karl of the sinking, 'her bow started to slide under and her stern rise as her lights went out. We heard with anguish the screams and moaning of those plunged into the icy water. Within a very few minutes all shouting and noise over the water had ceased . . .'[19]

Eighteen-year-old first-class passenger Eloise Hughes Smith was on her honeymoon on board the *Titanic* when the ship struck ice. The daughter of James A. Hughes, a Republican Congressman to the House of Representatives, she was born in August 1893 and grew up in Washington, living at the Willard Hotel, opposite the White House. As a precocious child, she initiated private audiences with President Theodore Roosevelt and, after attending a number of exclusive schools in America, she spent a year in Europe. On her return, in January 1912, she was officially presented to the highest echelons of Washington society. The following month she married Lucian Philip Smith, the twenty-four-year-old heir to a coal-mining fortune from Huntington, West Virginia. Their honeymoon was spent in Europe but after only a few months Eloise wrote to her parents that her new husband wanted to return to America. 'We leave here Sunday . . .' she wrote in April of 1912. 'By boat to Brindisi, by rail to Nice and Monte Carlo, then to Paris and via Cherbourg either on the *Lusitania* or the new *Titanic* . . .'[20]

On the night of 14 April, Eloise stayed up until 10.30 p.m., at which point she left her husband talking to some friends outside the Parisian Café. She was asleep when the collision occurred, she said. 'It did not awaken me enough to frighten me; in fact, I went back to sleep again,' she said. 'Then I awakened again, because it seemed that the boat had stopped.' At this moment, her husband entered the room and she asked him why the boat was no longer sailing. 'We are in the north and have struck an iceberg,' he replied. 'It does not amount to anything, but probably [it will] delay us a day getting into New York. However, as a matter of form, the captain has ordered all ladies on deck.' That frightened her a little, she confessed, but she was reassured that there was no danger. She took her time dressing, putting on her 'heavy clothing, high shoes, and two coats as well as a warm knit hood'.[21]

As she walked down the corridor to make her way up on deck, she told her husband she wanted to return to her cabin to fetch some of her jewels. He told her not to worry over such trifles, but Eloise rushed back and grabbed two rings, one which included a 'flawless diamond [Lucian] had purchased for her in Amsterdam'.[22] After witnessing the first few lifeboats leave the ship, Eloise approached Captain Smith and asked whether her husband could go with her. The Captain ignored her, but continued to shout into his megaphone the message of women and children first. Lucian then turned to her and said, in a serious tone, 'I never expected to ask you to obey, but this is one time you must; it is only a matter of form to have women and children first. The boat is thoroughly equipped, and everyone on her will be saved.' Eloise asked him if he was being absolutely honest with her and he said, 'Yes.' She felt a little better then as she had total confidence in him. He kissed her and, with the assistance of one of the officers, placed her in lifeboat six, which left the ship at around 12.55 a.m. 'As the boat was being lowered he yelled from the deck, "Keep your hands in your pockets, it is very cold weather,"' she recalled later. 'That was the last I saw of him, and I remember the many husbands that turned their backs as the small boat was lowered, the women blissfully innocent of their husbands' peril, and said good-bye with the expectation of seeing them within the next hour or so.'[23]

As the ship sank, Eloise remembered hearing awful cries, but she assumed they were the screams of members of the crew or steerage passengers who had stayed asleep until it was too late to leave the ship. It never occurred to her that her husband might be one of the poor souls left to die as the *Titanic* went down. 'It was bitterly cold, but I did not seem to mind it particularly,' she said. 'I was trying to locate my husband in all the boats that were near us. The night was beautiful; everything seemed to be with us in that respect, and a very calm sea. The icebergs on the horizon were all watched with interest; some seemed to be as tall as mountains, and reminded me of the pictures I had studied in geography. Then there were the flat ones, round ones also.'[24]

In the early hours of the morning of 15 April, she and her fellow survivors were rescued by the *Carpathia*. She was lucky to be assigned her own cabin aboard the ship – a lady gave up her berth for her – and she said that she was 'as comfortable as can be expected under the circumstances until we arrived in New York'.[25] At what point she met fellow *Titanic* survivor Robert Williams Daniel – whom she would marry in August 1914 – is unclear. In fact, a great deal about the survival of this twenty-seven-year-old banker from Philadelphia is shrouded in mystery. Witnesses recall the pride with which he talked of a champion French bulldog he had bought on the Continent and which he was bringing back on the *Titanic* – the animal was insured for $750 – while Edith Rosenbaum recalls having a snowball fight with him on deck after the iceberg struck. But his actions in the minutes after the sinking of the ship and his appearance in lifeboat number seven are still largely unaccounted for.

'As a little girl, my father had told me never to mention the *Titanic* to Old Bob [Robert Daniel] which only increased my curiosity,' says his great-niece, Helen Rodman.

'I have found several interviews he gave. In one, he jumped, swam away from the ship and was picked up by a lifeboat; in another he clung to ice for an hour, and in another he escaped in a collapsible boat.'[26] One report said that he left the ship wearing only his thick woollen undergarments, with his father's watch hung around his neck for good luck, while another said that he was completely nude when he was picked up by a lifeboat. In 1992, in order to try and seek the truth, Helen Rodman wrote to the renowned *Titanic* historian Walter Lord. 'It was impossible for him to have jumped off the ship and clung to a piece of ice until he was picked up,' replied Lord. 'The temperature of the water was 28 [degrees] and none of those who sank with the ship survived more than half an hour.'[27]

Despite a lineage that dedicated itself to the correct procedure and practice of law – his great-grandfather, Peter V. Daniel, was an associate justice of the United States Supreme Court and his great-great-grandfather, Edmund Randolph, was the first Attorney General of the United States and Secretary of State – Robert Daniel's own moral behaviour was questionable. Did he sneak – or jump – into lifeboat number seven? Is that why he could never provide a satisfactory – and coherent – account of his escape from the *Titanic*? Certainly, people in his home town of Richmond, Virginia, thought there was something odd about his story. 'The stigma of his survival as a male first-class passenger is still felt in Richmond, Virginia, where he was born and grew up,' says his great-niece.[28]

Whatever the truth, while on board the *Carpathia* Robert

Daniel struck up a close friendship with Eloise. He comforted her in her grief, listened to her talk about her memories of her husband, and reassured her that she could depend on his support. By the time the ship docked in New York, he walked down the gangway with Eloise on his arm. She returned to her home in Huntington, West Virginia, in full mourning and hundreds of people turned up to stare at her as she stepped down from the train at Chesapeake and Ohio station. According to one source, 'Police were needed to escort her safely to her automobile then home to the seclusion of her grandmother's house.'[29]

On 12 May, Eloise attended the memorial service for Lucian Smith, the man she had married only three months earlier. Just over a week later, her affidavit regarding her experiences on the *Titanic* was read to the Senate Hearings into the disaster. In her statement, she criticised the behaviour of quartermaster Robert Hitchens, who was supposedly in charge of her lifeboat – in fact all he did was wrap himself in a blanket and let the women take charge of the rowing. He was, in her view, a 'lazy, uncouth man, who had no respect for the ladies, and who was a thorough coward'. She also took the time to castigate the chairman of the White Star Line, Bruce Ismay, especially his actions, or rather lack of action, on board the *Carpathia*. 'I know many women who slept on the floor in the smoking room while Mr Ismay occupied the best room on the *Carpathia*, being in the center of the boat, with every attention, and a sign on the door, "Please do not knock",' she said.[30]

The whole business distressed her, including the press coverage – one headline stated, 'Congressman Hughes' Daughter Has Only Words of Scorn for the Creature Ismay, Who Lived while Hundreds Died'. Indeed, she wanted to put the experience behind her, asserting 'that no good could be derived by reviving memories of the awful night'.[31] Yet she was comforted by the attentions of Robert Daniel, and by the knowledge that she would soon be a mother; she had conceived on her honeymoon and she regarded the baby as her husband's last, most precious, gift. Her son, Lucian Junior, was born on 29 November 1912. Robert Daniel welcomed the boy into the world almost as if he was his own son. Photographs show the family sitting under a tree in the dappled shade, the child situated between Daniel's legs in a relaxed and comfortable manner. By his side sits Eloise, concentrating on her knitting, and near them plays a handsome French bulldog, similar to the animal that had perished on the *Titanic*.

Although Eloise's father was opposed to the match, he finally relented and towards the end of 1913 he gave his permission for Daniel to marry his daughter on one condition – the engagement had to be kept secret. Congressman Hughes was helping his daughter receive financial support from the family of Lucian Smith and he, quite rightly, believed that if she were to marry her new status would affect her chances of financial help.

On 19 May 1914, Eloise launched her legal bid in the courts of Uniontown, Pennsylvania, to claim a portion of her dead husband's father's estate. However, during the lawsuit, it came to light that Lucian Smith had not been quite as wealthy as everyone had assumed and that he had only received an allowance of five hundred dollars a month; in addition, it was discovered that Smith's father had no real money of his own, but managed to convince the world he was rich by the wily use of a family stipend. The family duly dropped the case, and Eloise and Robert Daniel married on 18 August 1914, in a private ceremony at the Church of the Transfiguration in New York, the same church where Karl Behr married his sweetheart, Helen Newsom. Yet the ceremony was kept secret from the world, partly due to the fact that immediately after the union Robert had to make an urgent business trip to London.

He expected to be gone for only a number of weeks, yet the outbreak of the First World War in September kept him away until October.

'On August 18, Mrs Smith and I were married in New York,' said Daniel. 'The following day I was compelled to go to London on urgent business. Owing to the war I considered that it would be difficult to care for Mrs Daniel abroad, so I left her in this country. It was my intention to return within three weeks, but I was held up more than two months. My hurried trip prevented us from making a formal announcement of our wedding, and today we were making arrangements to make it tomorrow. Our intimate friends have known of the wedding so it will not come as a surprise to them.'[32]

Journalists, keen to report on the sensational story, asked for more details: quotes about how each of them felt, what it meant to be survivors of the *Titanic*, how they had met on board the *Carpathia*, how their relationship had flourished after the death of Eloise's first husband during the sinking, and their thoughts of their future life together. But neither one wanted to indulge the appetites of the popular press. However, that did not stop some newspapers from writing about their case. 'Mr Daniel met his future bride in the agony of her first widowhood,' wrote one reporter. 'Her honeymoon had ended in the drowning of her first husband on their return trip from Europe.'[33] The facts were inaccurate, as most of the victims died from hypothermia, not drowning. Another journalist added, 'He was pulled into the lifeboat containing Mrs Smith and Mrs John Jacob Astor as he was sinking.'[34] In fact, each occupied a space in a different lifeboat: Daniel in number seven, Eloise Smith in number six, and Madeleine Astor in boat number four.

Despite these factual errors, the newspapers simply reflected the public's appetite for this extraordinary story, a tale that became more bizarre with each passing year. After falling in love in the slipstream of the *Titanic*, the couple came to symbolise the essence of modern romance – they even lived in a house in Philadelphia with the fairy-tale name Rosemont – yet in the years following their marriage their narrative moved away from the genre of the romantic towards something more gothic. Within the space of four years, their relationship had broken down and the couple had started to lead separate lives. They divorced in March 1923, apparently after Eloise discovered Robert living with an attractive blonde woman in New York. Neither partner remained single for long – in 1923 Eloise married Lewis H. Cort, of Huntington, Virginia, a former Pennsylvania State athlete and a war veteran, while Robert, then vice-president of the Liberty National Bank, married Mrs Marjorie Durant Campbell of Park Avenue, New York.

Although they were divorced, and living with new partners, Eloise and Robert still seemed strangely connected. It was almost as if the experiences of one reflected the other – existence seen through the prism of a series of distorting mirrors in a gothic House of Fun. One night, in 1924, at their winter home in San Diego, California, Eloise and her new husband, Lewis, were asleep when they were mysteriously drugged by an intruder who stole jewels worth $10,000. As she began to wake from her slumbers, Eloise saw the thief getting away with the precious diamond she had saved from the *Titanic*. Five years later, Lewis died from injuries sustained in the First World War and Eloise, at the age of thirty-six, was a widow once more.

In 1926 in Virginia, Robert Daniel had purchased one of the state's oldest and most established estates, Brandon, with its stairway designed by Thomas Jefferson and a long history of visiting presidents. Yet within two years the relationship with his new wife, Marjorie, with whom he had a daughter, had broken down, and the couple divorced in September 1928. Robert apparently believed the marriage failed due to a 'charm which had unintentionally been broken at the old estate'. According to an old legend, 'a bride of long ago who was married beneath the chandelier in the stately main room of the mansion died on her wedding night.' After her death, her wedding ring was hidden in the ceiling; those who disturbed it would meet with bad luck in love. When Robert ordered the room to be renovated, workmen disturbed a piece of plaster in the living room, dislodging the wedding ring from its hiding place. 'The workmen took it to Mr Daniel, who had it cleaned and polished and then placed it back beneath the chandelier . . . he was aware of the legend and feared of the results of disturbing the ring. Two years later he was divorced.'[35]

Both Eloise and Robert married yet again – she to C.S. Wright, the State Auditor of West Virginia, and he to Mrs Charlotte Bemiss Christian, the niece of a former Controller of the Currency – yet Eloise could never forget her first husband. Her fourth marriage collapsed and she once again took the name of her first love, the man who had perished on the *Titanic*. She died of heart failure in Cincinnati, Ohio, on 3 May 1940, while Robert Daniel passed away later that same year, on 21 December, due to a circulatory ailment after an illness of eight weeks. She was forty-six, he fifty-six. 'We used to say that Eloise was probably the only woman in the world who in just a year's time made her debut, got engaged, married, survived the *Titanic*, became a widow and then a mother,' said her relative, Z. Taylor Vinson.[36]

Eloise's son, Lucian, whom she was carrying when the *Titanic* went down, grew up 'in the shadow of his mother's grief' and never felt comfortable discussing the disaster.[37] Yet, in many ways, it was his existence that gave her the strength to survive. In 1933, on the occasion of his twenty-first birthday, Eloise wrote to her son, 'Twenty-one years ago, I was waiting for you. When you did put in an appearance, you were the loveliest thing on earth. You were so adorable and such a gift from God to assuage all my grief and sorrow in those few seconds.'[38]

In April 1966 – fifty-four years nearly to the day after the *Titanic* disaster – Lucian, together with his wife and two daughters, Cathy, thirteen, and Betsy, eight, were enjoying a Caribbean cruise when their ship, the Norwegian *Viking Princess*, caught fire. The family were sleeping when there was a knock at their cabin, telling them to make their way to the boat deck. 'There were no lights and no alarm with the generators not operating,' said Lucian, who lived in Sarasota, Florida. The light from the crewman's flashlight was all that was available for them to locate their life jackets and find their way up to the deck. There was no time to get dressed – the two girls quickly put life jackets over their nightgowns and Lucian escaped wearing only a pair of tennis shorts. 'The only people dressed were members of the crew and passengers in evening wear who had been attending a masquerade ball the final night of the cruise.' There was a call for 'women and children first', an eerie echo of that night in 1912, during which Lucian's father had died, but thankfully the lifeboats were equipped with enough space to hold all the five hundred or so passengers before they were picked up by a German freighter, the *Cap Nort*. During the night, however, two people died of heart attacks brought on by the stress. For several hours afterwards, the rescue ship cruised the waters, just off Cuba, looking for more survivors, before making its way to the US naval base at Guantanamo. From there they were flown to Miami. As he reached his home in Venice, Sarasota, Lucian told reporters, 'We're just glad to get back home safe.' He did not elaborate, and neither did he go into details about the fate of his father, whom he had never known.[39]

* * *

Like Eloise Smith, nineteen-year-old Helen Bishop was sailing back to America after spending her honeymoon in Europe. On the night of 14 April she was asleep in her first-class cabin, with her husband, twenty-five-year-old Dickinson Bishop by her side reading, when the iceberg struck. The couple dressed and went up on deck, but could see nothing untoward. 'We noticed the intense cold . . .' she told the US inquiry. 'It was uncomfortably cold in the lounge. We looked all over the deck; walked up and down a couple of times, and one of the stewards met us and laughed at us. He said, "You go back downstairs. There is nothing to be afraid of. We have only struck a little piece of ice and passed it." So we returned to our stateroom and retired.' About fifteen minutes later, fellow passenger Albert Stewart, who would die in the disaster, knocked on their door and told them to go up to A deck. There, they met Colonel Astor, whom Helen saw approach Captain Smith walking down the Grand Staircase. 'The Captain told him something in an undertone,' she remembered. 'He [Astor] came back and told six of us, who were standing with his wife, that we had better put on our lifebelts.'[40]

Helen returned to her cabin to join Dickinson, who had gone down to the cabin to retrieve a fur muff for his wife and her dog, Frou Frou, which she had bought in Florence. She adored her new pet and was delighted that the steward had given her permission to keep the small dog in her cabin rather than in the ship's kennels. She had even arranged two suitcases together in her stateroom to fashion a small bed for it. But what should she do now? She had few qualms about leaving behind her property, valued at $20,000 – her three gold purses worth $1,500, a platinum chain with a diamond plaque, a pearl necklace with an emerald drop, sixteen rings set with diamonds, sapphires, rubies and emeralds, a string of pearls, a string of corals, a platinum bracelet and two or three sets of emerald and pearl earrings. What she couldn't bear was the thought of abandoning her dog. But she knew she had no choice. 'I realized . . . that there would be little sympathy for a woman carrying a dog in her arms when there were lives of women and children to be saved,' she said.[41] 'I feel the loss of my little dog most of all. I will always remember how she tugged at my dress when I started to leave. She wanted to go with me so much.'[42]

With tears stinging her eyes, Helen went back on deck, with her husband following close behind. At 12.45 a.m. she found herself, according to her testimony, being pushed into one of the lifeboats – number seven, the first to leave the *Titanic* – with her husband. Although she told newspaper reporters that someone, perhaps a member of the crew, had called for brides and grooms to be placed in this lifeboat, and that three newly wed couples were in that vessel, she made no mention of this in her official statement to the US Senate Inquiry into the disaster. Records show that, in lifeboat seven, there was only one other honeymoon couple – John Pillsbury Snyder, who was twenty-four, and his wife, Nelle, twenty-three. For the most part, the boat – which contained only twenty-eight people, leaving space for another thirty-seven – carried those with an overwhelming sense of self-preservation, including Robert Williams Daniel, silent screen actress Dorothy Gibson, and her mother, Pauline, and the self-styled Baron von Drachstedt, whose real name was Alfred Nourney, a twenty-year-old man from New Jersey. 'There was a German baron aboard who smoked an obnoxious pipe incessantly and refused to pull an oar,' said Helen. 'The men were worn out with the work, and I rowed for a considerable time myself.'[43]

According to Helen, some of the female passengers in the lifeboat became worried that the sinking of the ship might suck them to their deaths and so she began to tell a true story of her recent encounter with a fortune-teller in Egypt. She had been reliably informed that she would survive a shipwreck and an earthquake, before being killed in an automobile accident. Surely, she asserted, as she had just witnessed a sea disaster, she would have to live in order for the rest of the prediction to come true.

'The water was like glass,' she said. 'There wasn't even the ripple usually found on a small lake. By the time we had pulled away 100 yards the lower row of portholes had disappeared. When we were a mile away the second row had gone, but there was still no confusion [on the *Titanic*]. Indeed everything seemed to be quiet on the ship until her stern was raised out of the water by the list forward. Then a veritable wave of humanity surged up out of the steerage and shut the lights from our view. We were too far away to see the passengers individually, but we could see the black mass of human forms and hear their death cries and groans.'[44]

Helen Bishop also remembered the dignified behaviour of George Hogg, a lookout on the *Titanic* and fellow passenger in her lifeboat, who lost his brother in the disaster. As the ship slipped beneath the sea, Hogg simply held his hand over his face to hide his grief. 'Immediately after she sank he did the best he could to keep the women feeling cheerful all the rest of the time,' she said. 'We all thought a great deal of that man.'[45]

During that long, bitterly cold night, Helen and Dickinson clung to one another in the lifeboat. To try and keep her spirits up, Helen thought of her wedding day, which had taken place on 7 November 1911. She had worn a gown of white satin in a princess style with a court train, while the aroma of orange blossoms, fastened to her bridal veil, had enveloped her as she walked down the aisle at St John's Episcopal Church in Sturgis, Michigan. The only child of wealthy chair manufacturer Jerrold Walton, Helen had enjoyed her wedding day, which was described as a grand affair, 'the most notable ever held in Sturgis'.[46] She thought back to her journey on board the *Adriatic*, the liner that in January of 1912 had taken her and her new husband from New York City to the Azores, Gibraltar, and Egypt, where she had met that fortune-teller. She prayed to herself that the prophecy would come true; she had no thoughts of the automobile accident that was said would kill her, assuming that this would be many, many years in the future. From Egypt, the couple had toured Italy, Spain and France, where, after a few days in Paris, they had travelled to Cherbourg to board the *Titanic*.

Dick was preoccupied with darker thoughts, his mind clouded by memories of his first wife, Mary Beckwith Lee, his childhood sweetheart whom he had married in June 1908. Her father, Fred Lee, had been one of Dowagiac's richest men, the owner of the Round Oak Stove Company, and their wedding, which had taken place at The Rockery, the Lee family home, had been a major event of the social calendar. The whole of the first floor of the neo-Romantic stone house had been filled with a mass of white and pink roses, palms and asparagus ferns, and Mary's mother had worn a dress made from material imported from Denmark. On the wedding day, his father-in-law had given Dick 50 per cent interest in his company, a gift that would ultimately serve as something of a curse. Dick and Mary had enjoyed a honeymoon in which they toured the world and on their return, in 1909, they had bought a large house in Dowagiac, Michigan. This they tore down to make way for a twenty-eight-room English-style mansion, complete with tennis court, Japanese gardens and an artificial lake. On 15 September 1910, Mary gave birth to a baby, Pauline Lee Bishop, but the girl died that same day. Thirteen days later, on 28 September, Mary also died, despite a surgeon's repeated efforts to repair the injuries she had suffered during childbirth. The death of his wife meant that Dick would now inherit half of his father-in-law's company, something that made Fred Lee increasingly bitter – a bitterness that had mutated into anger when the young man met and married Helen.

Escaping the sinking ship was certainly a good omen, wasn't it? It was only a matter of time before he and his wife would be rescued, Dick told himself and sure enough, in the early hours of 15 April, he saw the lights of the *Carpathia* twinkling in the gloom. Arriving in New York, the couple were met by the bride's parents, who accompanied them to the Waldorf Astoria hotel. They stayed in New York for a couple of weeks, 'replenishing their wardrobes', and testifying before the American inquiry, before driving in their chauffeur-driven Lozier to Buffalo; but, because of adverse weather conditions, they were forced to take a train from there to Dowagiac. Everything seemed to be infused with a spirit of optimism, especially after the confirmation that Helen was expecting a child. The birth would help erase the pain of the loss of Dick's first daughter; it would be a new beginning.

On 9 December 1912, Helen gave birth to a son, Randall, but at ten o'clock the next day the child died. The loss brought back the awful memories for Dick of the death of his first wife's daughter. Would Helen go the same way? He wondered how he would cope if she were to perish too. Thankfully, she recovered from the physical ordeals of childbirth, but the emotional scars left behind after giving birth to an infant who died so soon took longer to heal. She felt low in spirits and lifeless, but doctors said that she might benefit from a vacation to somewhere with a warmer climate. The couple settled on California, but while there in 1913, they experienced a minor earthquake – reviving the memory of the fortune-teller who had now accurately predicted that Helen would survive two disasters. And what of the third part of the prediction? The thought of dying in a car accident preyed on her mind, but she wouldn't allow herself to think of it. Dick told her that she should try and enjoy herself, relax a little, let her hair down. Helen tried to follow his advice and on 4 November 1913, the couple attended a dance at the Kalamazoo Country Club, Michigan. The party was fun; there was dancing, music and an endless flow of drinks but as the night wore on, Dick became tired. He told Helen he would see her at their hotel and left her in the company of his cousin, Bartlett Dickinson. At three o'clock in the morning, the partygoers returned to their cars to find that their windshields were covered in frost and ice. In those days a driver would lower the windshield in order to be able to see out, but perhaps because of the intense cold, Bartlett did not do so. Helen climbed into the back of the car with a friend, Dan Eaton, while Bartlett started the engine and set off into the night.

As Bartlett drove at high speed round a sharp corner situated between Kalamazoo's West and Lovell Streets, he lost control of the car and it smashed into a tree. The force of the impact threw him through the windshield and he sustained a number of serious cuts, while Eaton hit the back of the front seat. Both men were left unconscious and Eaton suffered from concussion. But their injuries were minor compared to Helen's. As the car crashed into the tree, she was thrown out over the front of the vehicle and through a mass of branches before landing on her head on a cement walkway some thirty feet away. Witnesses crowded round the scene of the accident and tried their best to help the injured passengers. A doctor who lived nearby, Dr William Tomlinson, rushed out and arranged for the crash victims to be carried into his house. 'It was at first difficult to see how seriously Helen was injured as she appeared to be bleeding from a large bruise on her head, but once she and the two men were sped by ambulance to Borgess Hospital, it became all too apparent.'[47]

Helen's skull had been crushed and she also suffered a number of internal injuries. Her condition was critical. Friends located Dick at the Burdick Hotel, who when he learned of the accident arranged for the family physician, Dr George W. Green, to examine Helen immediately. 'The doctor was rushed to Kalamazoo at top speed in the Bishop automobile with Chauffeur Earl Patterson at the steering wheel,' reported one newspaper. 'The doctor reached the bedside of Mrs Bishop in less than an hour after he first received the message . . . An operation was performed upon her by Dr Green and a number of Kalamazoo physicians, and portions of skull and brain were removed. It was found that paralysis had already set in, and that no definite hope could be held out that the injured woman would survive for many hours.'[48] The *New York Times*, on 6 November, went even further and stated that Helen Bishop was dying. After all, her prognosis was not good; the surgery, to extract the fragments of skull that littered her brain, also necessitated the removal of healthy brain tissue. Her parents stood by her bedside waiting for the moment of her death, but despite doctors' predictions her condition started to improve. The following morning she regained consciousness and spoke a few broken words to her mother and by 7 November she seemed to be able to breathe normally once more.

Doctors gathered round Helen's bedside as they debated what would be the best course of action. Finally, they agreed to try a revolutionary new technique: the fixing of a silver plate over her skull to protect the damaged section of brain. Again, Helen defied the medics' expectations and by the end of December she was ready to be released. This time, however, she was struck down by appendicitis. Yet, by January 1914, she had recovered enough to leave hospital. The local newspaper commented: 'Mrs Bishop's miraculous escape from the sinking of the *Titanic* nearly two years ago, her recovery from the almost fatal injuries received in the automobile accident, and coming through the recent operation for appendicitis, seem to place her in the class immune from fatal results.'[49] As she recovered, Helen pondered the nature of the fortune-teller's prophecy, and how she had been lucky to cheat death three times over. She was at times giddy with the promise of life, and some friends described her behaviour as 'erratic'. She wore a wig to hide the silver plate that now covered her head, but occasionally if she wanted to disarm people – for example, when she wanted an advantage at bridge – she would remove the hairpiece. Meanwhile, relations between Helen and Dick worsened; he couldn't cope with his wife's increasingly irrational behaviour, while Helen felt dismayed by his brutishness. She was also irritated by the constant talk of the snide gossips who said that Dick had only managed to escape the *Titanic* because he had dressed as a woman, an accusation that had been levelled at a number of men from first class. Things finally came to a head and on 18 January 1916, the couple were granted a divorce, she citing grounds of 'extreme cruelty' and his 'habitual drunkenness'. Dick settled on her a one-off payment of $100,000, a sum she said she was going to use to enjoy herself. She booked a residential suite at the Blackstone Hotel in Chicago and spent Christmas in Danville, Illinois, at the house of her friend, Mrs O.W. Cannon, whom she also persuaded to accompany her on a cruise on the *Pastores*, a journey through the Panama Canal to the West Indies. During the vacation, it came to Helen's notice that the steward in the steamer's bathroom was Philip Edgar Grant, a former student of Cornell and the son of a family friend, who had 'strayed from home and fallen from fortune'. She used all her charms to bring about a reconciliation between his parents from Rochester, New York, and the handsome, athletic young man – yet talk of a romance was denied.

Helen's future looked bright. She seemed the very definition of a survivor – of the *Titanic*, of an earthquake, of a near-fatal car accident. But her luck was finally about to run out. After arriving back at the Illinois home of Mrs Cannon on 10 March 1916, Helen tripped over a rug in her friend's sitting room. As she desperately tried to right her footing – before the silver plate that had been screwed into her head collided with a hard, sharp surface – she had a few seconds to come to terms with her fate. The fortune-teller in Egypt had been right, in a way. The 'old accident trouble [was] the main cause'.[50] It was impossible to cheat death; she should have known that when she had witnessed the dreadful loss of life aboard the *Titanic*. As she lost consciousness she suffered a brain haemorrhage and started to fit. She died on the morning of 15 March 1916.

In a final cruel irony, the local newspaper that reported her death also carried a story on the same page of the marriage of her former husband, Dickinson Bishop. With his new wife, Sydney Boyce, the daughter of a newspaper publisher, he would enjoy over thirty years of happy marriage until her death in November 1950. After his own death, in February 1961, his relatives maintained that Dickinson never talked about the *Titanic*; neither did he ever mention the car accident that contributed to the death of his twenty-three-year-old former wife.

Helen – described by Dickinson's sister as 'attractive, vivacious and fun' – had survived the large-scale tragedies of life, including the greatest sea disaster of the modern age, but it was the most banal act that finally killed her. A step in the wrong direction, the corner of a carpet slightly rucked up, that's all it took for Helen's life to be snuffed out. She had survived the *Titanic*, but an untidy rug proved to be her undoing.

Five

THE WOMAN WHO ROWED AWAY FROM THE DROWNING

Lady Duff Gordon looked down at her lavender silk kimono in distaste. The evidence of her seasickness was all too obvious, the delicate fabric splattered with patches of vomit. The garment, described by fellow survivor and fashion expert Edith Rosenbaum as 'very beautifully embroidered',[1] embodied, in many ways, the spirit of its owner: fashionable, exotic and more than a little bit showy. Like the kimono, Lady Duff Gordon, also known as 'Lucile', was something of an unusual specimen. She adored artifice and flourished in the heightened reality of haute couture. Dressed like a butterfly, the tiny, flame-haired woman defined herself, and others, through clothes – she was the one, after all, who had coined the word 'chic' – and, on this occasion, she was distressed to find that the sheen of her normally perfect world had been soiled. The smears that dirtied her kimono would never quite disappear.

Similarly, the stains on her reputation and her husband's, Sir Cosmo Duff Gordon, which resulted from their actions in the minutes immediately after the sinking of the *Titanic*, would stay with them for the rest of their lives. The couple would be haunted forever by the same litany of questions: why had Sir Cosmo written a cheque for five pounds to each of the seven crew members in their lifeboat? Was it a gesture of compassion, as the Duff Gordons claimed – simply a way of giving them the means to replace their lost kit, or was the money a bribe to persuade the crew to row away from the dying? Why, in addition to the seven members of the crew, were there only five passengers in the lifeboat (all of whom were from first class), when the vessel could have held forty?

In an attempt to try and explain the actions of her husband – who was accused of bribery, cowardice and lying (any one of this trio of sins would be enough to ruin a man in Edwardian society) – Lady Duff Gordon maintained it was her stream of light-hearted chit-chat about fashion which was, unwittingly, to blame. In an effort to take her mind off her seasickness she first of all fixed her attention on the sinking ship. She recalled seeing the 'dark hull towering like a giant hotel' and watched in horror as the lights disappeared from the ship's portholes one deck at a time. She heard a 'dull explosion' shake the air and then from the vessel 'there arose an indescribable clamour'. She saw the stern of the ship rise high into the air, where it stayed for a few moments, accompanied by the 'agonized cries' of its passengers. Then 'with one downward rush' the liner 'plunged to her grave', the sinking counterpointed by 'those awful shrieks' followed by silence. At this moment, she felt her reason 'tottering' and she lapsed into unconsciousness.[2]

On coming round, she felt nauseous once more, and in a second attempt to recover she tried to engage her secretary, Laura Francatelli or 'Franks', in conversation. She commented on the strange assortment of clothes she herself was wearing – a kimono and a moleskin coat – and then, in order to try and lighten the mood, she said to Franks, 'Just fancy, you actually left your beautiful nightdress behind you!'[3] Her secretary laughed as though her mistress had said something witty, even though, as she recalled, 'in our hearts we felt very far from laughter'. Then, leading on from the remark about the night-dress, members of the crew started to voice their concerns about the loss of their own belongings. For them, it was not a trivial matter, something that could be laughed off with a light witticism. 'You were lucky to come away with your lives,' one crew member said, 'don't you bother about anything you had to leave behind.' Another went so far as to state, in a voice heavy with bitterness and class resentment, 'You people need not bother about losing your things, for you can afford to buy new ones when you get ashore. What about us poor fellows? We have lost all the kit and our pay stops from the moment the ship went down.' It was at this moment that Sir Cosmo tried to reassure the men. He was sure, he said, that the sailors would get employed by another ship. He then added, 'I will give you a fiver each towards getting a new kit.'

Those twelve words effectively destroyed the reputations of the Duff Gordons the world over. The sentence was delivered, recalled Lucile, with Cosmo's 'characteristic impulsiveness, and I don't think anybody thought much of it at the time, but I remember every word of that conversation, for it had a tremendous bearing on our future. I little thought then that because of those few words we should be disgraced and branded as cowards in every corner of the civilized world.'[4]

Later, Cosmo's comments would be repeatedly analysed and deconstructed in an effort to get to the truth. At that moment, however, the passengers of lifeboat number one were more concerned with surviving the night. Sir Cosmo calmed his nerves and tried to keep warm by puffing his way through a few cigars. The dark shadows of icebergs surrounded the boat, which towards morning was also being buffeted by choppy waves. The sight of the twinkling lights of the *Carpathia* in the distance came as a blessed relief, and the occupants of the lifeboat began to row towards it with all their strength. One crew member began to sing and the passengers, according to Lucile, became 'nearly hysterical with the reaction from our miseries of the night'.[5] As dawn began to break, 'stretching fingers across the grey of the sky, lighting up the icebergs till they looked like giant opals', they noticed that the sea was dotted with a dozen or so lifeboats. Lucile assumed that most of the *Titanic*'s passengers had been saved, and 'not one of us even guessed the appalling truth'.[6]

After boarding the *Carpathia*, Lucile was taken into a cabin where she was given a sedative. There she fell into a 'stupor' and she did not wake up until the morning of the following day. At first, as the light streamed into the porthole, she was disorientated, not knowing where she was and having no memory of the events of the last two days. The cabin looked unfamiliar and it was only when a stewardess knocked on her door and delivered her tray of morning tea that she realised that this girl was not the lovely Irish girl who had served her so wonderfully on the *Titanic*. 'Suddenly everything swept over me in a tide of remembrance,' she said. 'I saw the *Titanic* as I had last seen her, plunging to her grave under the Atlantic, I heard again those heart-rending cries from her decks, and burying my face in the pillows I sobbed uncontrollably. It was the first time that the full realization of the disaster came to me.'[7]

With an American woman, who was occupying the next-door cabin, Lucile walked out on deck to see other survivors, most of whom were talking about the disaster. The stories of 'horror' seemed to be endless, as each survivor related the death of a friend, husband, brother, son. Set within this epic human tragedy, talk of the loss of one's possessions seemed trivial, offensive almost, yet Lucile could not help herself. With *Titanic* survivor Edith Rosenbaum, she 'exchanged compliments about our appearance and swapped style information . . . All her designs as well as my own had gone to the bottom of the sea, but we both acknowledged that panier skirts and Robespierre collars are, after all, at a discount when stranded in mid-ocean.'[8]

Lucile's ability to make a joke in the midst of adversity can be interpreted in two ways: either as an insensitivity to the suffering of others or as a survival mechanism, a coping strategy. Perhaps it was also a way of dealing with the anxiety of having lost a pearl necklace, which she had placed in the purser's safe – an item she had neither paid for nor insured. Lucile had seen the piece, valued at $50,000, at her jeweller's in Venice and had asked whether she could secure it on loan, with the future possibility of purchase. Lucile's great-niece, Susan Rhys-Williams, believes that the couturier had never intended to buy the necklace at all. Her motives were rather more suspect. 'As I see it . . . [she] had borrowed it just for the trip, meaning to impress the wealthy passengers who were potential customers for "Lucile" Ltd . . .'[9]

Meanwhile, on the *Carpathia*, Cosmo continued to worry about the loss of the crew's kit. He had given his word to do his best for the crew members of lifeboat number one and so, on the second day aboard the *Carpathia*, he reminded his wife of his promise. The next day, he said, he would present each of them with a cheque for five pounds. 'Neither of us could have guessed that that simple little act of kindness was forging a powerful link in the chain of evidence which was to be used with such deadly force against us,' she wrote later.[10]

Wouldn't it also be splendid, suggested Lucile, if the crew members wrote their names on her life preserver, and that the presentation be marked by a photograph? A wonderful idea, Cosmo agreed, and so it was settled. Franks went ahead and wrote out seven cheques, while he signed them and a photograph of the event was taken by the *Carpathia*'s surgeon, Frank McGee. The photograph is blurred and of quite poor quality, yet one can still make out the strange atmosphere that haunts the image. Each individual looks away from the camera, their faces drawn and strained, their body language awkward and wooden, almost as if they are trying to absent themselves from the situation. This is not a photograph that memorialises an event of which these people are proud; rather, it speaks of shame, remorse and regret. Indeed, its message is confused: its very existence, brought about by the insistence of Lucile, should serve as a marker of the crew's heroism and the Duff Gordons' beneficence, yet its form actually suggests the opposite. This ambivalence – this uncertainty surrounding the nature of the Duff Gordons' escape from the *Titanic* – would be explored during the London inquiry into the disaster. For the rest of their lives, Lucile and Cosmo were viewed as dubious, slippery characters. In a sense, the *Titanic* had turned them into walking question marks – elusive, enigmatic, shifty, untrustworthy.

On arriving in New York, with their reputations for the moment still intact, the Duff Gordons witnessed the harrowing scenes at the Cunard Line pier: the 'white anxious faces and desperate eyes', the strange juxtaposition of millionaires and their wives wrapped in expensive furs standing next to 'men and women from the slums'. Those who awaited the arrival of the *Carpathia* were joined together, 'allied in a common sorrow' and the hope that their loved ones would walk down the gangplank towards them. 'Most of the women were crying,' noted Lucile, 'and the men stared straight ahead with set, white faces.'[11]

Meeting the Duff Gordons off the ship was Bainbridge Colby, Lucile's American lawyer, who said that they 'sauntered off in apparently excellent condition of health and courage'.[12] He took them to the Ritz, where that night the couple dined, together with a group of friends, and they drank a quantity of champagne; everyone, said Lucile, was 'very gay'. Every so often the telephone would ring with messages of congratulations on their escape, while she was kept busy by the seemingly endless delivery of bouquets of flowers and other presents that showered down upon them. Carried away by high spirits, Lucile described her and her husband's experiences on the *Titanic* to her party of friends. Perhaps her language was a little too colourful, her descriptions of events rather over-stated, but, fuelled by a few glasses of champagne, she thought she was simply telling the dramatic story to a few good friends over dinner. Unfortunately, one of these friends was Abraham Merritt, an editor at the *American Weekly*, who, after supper, relayed the information to his boss, William Randolph Hearst. Later that same night, Merritt telephoned Lucile and asked her permission to put together a story out of what she had told him for publication in the next day's newspaper. Without giving it much thought she agreed, at which point Merritt in turn rang a reporter who quickly shaped her words into an even more dramatic form. The resulting splash, which ran under Lady Duff Gordon's byline and which included her signature, would only go to fuel the controversy surrounding the couple.

Nasty rumours about the behaviour of the Duff Gordons soon began to circulate around New York and then, on 22 April, while applying for financial assistance from the New York City Hall, *Titanic* deck hand Robert Hopkins stated that had he been in lifeboat number one he would have had no need to seek charity. When questioned by reporters, Hopkins said that one of the crew members who escaped with the Duff Gordons had told him that their lifeboat was known as 'the money boat', as each of the men had been promised a sum of money if they 'put right away from the *Titanic*', even though there was plenty of room for more passengers. Although he refrained from naming the millionaire briber, he did state that one of the passengers was Sir Cosmo. 'The crew did as requested by the millionaire,' said Hopkins, 'and after they had boarded the *Carpathia* the millionaire gave each of the *Titanic*'s crew who had handled his boat a check for five pounds . . . If anybody can get hold of one of these checks the identity of the millionaire will be established.'[13]

Fellow passenger Charles Henry Stengel, of Newark, New Jersey – who had accompanied the Duff Gordons in lifeboat number one – immediately rubbished Hopkins's accusations. 'He must be looking for sympathy or money,' said Stengel. 'I know Sir Cosmo Duff Gordon did give the crew something after we were taken on board the *Carpathia*, but it was merely a reward for the work they had done.'[14] Yet his support did little to calm what was, in effect, a growing sense of hostility towards the upper classes, something that Lucile herself recognised. 'The horror and grief which had shaken the whole American nation resolved itself into a sort of hysteria,' she wrote. 'Everyone looked for a victim to blame for the tragedy, and class hatred ran high . . . the names of men who had been drowned were heaped with the vilest abuse, they were proclaimed far and wide as cowards, and in some cases their relatives were booed and shouted at in the streets . . . It was said that Colonel Astor and George Widener had been shot aboard the *Titanic* while fighting with women to get into the lifeboats [and] that a boatful of women had been turned out to make room for the pet dogs and luggage of Mrs Astor.'[15]

It's not surprising that there was a feeling of resentment from some quarters. After all, these were the days when the 'lower' orders were not only segregated on ships, but treated as almost a sub-species. As one appropriately named well-born lady, the horsewoman and author Lida Fleitmann Bloodgood, who went to school with Madeleine Force Astor, described it, 'The world has grown to be a better place since the days of the *Titanic*. I myself am old enough to recall throwing apples and bananas down to the people in the Steerage on such ancient boats as the *Princess Alice* and *Kronprinz Wilhelm*, on which, as on all other lines, these unfortunate immigrants to America were battened down below decks in the prow of the ship like so many cattle.'[16]

In the days following the arrival of the *Carpathia* in New York, it became obvious that one's chance of surviving the *Titanic* had depended largely on which class one came from. As Charles Dienz, who had been head chef in the Ritz-Carlton restaurant on the SS *America* and who had many friends in the kitchens on the *Titanic,* wrote in a letter in 1955, 'The order was women and children first, but that really meant always the first-class first and second, steerage and crew can wait.'[17]

Out of a total of 143 first-class women, only 4 died in the disaster (and 3 of these chose to remain on board the ship). In second class, 154 men perished out of a total of 168, and in third class, 381 men died out of 456, while 89 of 165 women did not survive. When we look at these figures, a number of intriguing patterns emerge – 2.7 per cent of first-class women died, compared to 15 per cent in second class and 53 per cent in third class. Yet more second class men died (91 per cent) than third-class men (83 per cent). Was this due to the good manners of the middle classes? According to research published in 2009 and carried out by Bruno S. Frey of the University of Zurich, and David A. Savage and Benno Torgler, both from Queensland University of Technology, the nationality of passengers, apparently, also had a bearing. British good manners – the propensity to happily form a queue in almost any situation – almost certainly contributed to the lower survival rates among people from the United Kingdom. As the researchers write, 'The sinking of the *Titanic* in April 1912 took the lives of 68 per cent of the people aboard. Who survived? It was women and children who had a higher probability of being saved, not men. Likewise, people travelling in first class had a better chance of survival than those in second and third class. British passengers were more likely to perish than members of other nations.'[18]

This kind of analysis was not what interested the general public at the time. What they wanted to know was why and how Sir Cosmo Duff Gordon, this scapegoat of the whole of the upper classes, had survived. The most startling thing was not that the Duff Gordons had money, but that, allegedly, they had been prepared to use it to bribe their way out of a difficult situation. Instead of going to the rescue of the dying in the water, they had used their economic advantages to save their own lives at the expense of others'. There was something fishy about it all, according to the papers. On their return to England in May 1912, on board the *Lusitania*, the Duff Gordons were greeted by a rash of ugly headlines: 'DUFF GORDON SCANDAL', 'COWARDLY BARONET AND HIS WIFE WHO ROWED AWAY FROM THE DROWNING', 'SIR COSMO DUFF GORDON – SAFE AND SOUND WHILE WOMEN GO DOWN IN THE *TITANIC*'. As they boarded the boat train for London they heard the constant cry of newsboys shouting, 'Read about the *Titanic* cowards! Read about the *Titanic* cowards!' Sir Cosmo's face, recalled Lucile, was 'stricken', and the couple travelled up to London feeling 'wretchedly dispirited'. At their house in Lennox Gardens, SW1, they were greeted by letters and telegrams of support from friends and vicious missives of abuse from strangers. Newspapers around the world carried an awkwardly phrased anonymous verse that said it all:

Did You
Sir Cosmo Duff Gordon
On that night of tragedy
Behave as a gentleman or a coward?
And restive hands
Made so in regret of lost souls

You might have saved
But, for all craven and selfishness,
You did not?

After talking to their son-in-law, Lord Tiverton, it was decided that it would be best if the couple put themselves forward as witnesses at the British inquiry into the disaster, which would take place in London between 2 May and 3 July 1912. The objective of the British Board of Trade's investigation was to try and set out the possible causes of the disaster and to examine ways of preventing such a tragedy occurring ever again. 'It is only fair that you should,' he said. 'You must have a chance of showing how false these abominable stories are. Of course Esmé [his wife, Lucile's daughter from her first husband] and I knew that there was not a shade of foundation in them, but they have given rise to a lot of nasty gossip.'[19]

However, the case against them was not based solely on rumour and hearsay. On the tenth day of the official British inquiry into the disaster, Charles Hendrickson, a fireman, who had escaped with the Duff Gordons in lifeboat number one, appeared before the court. Central to his evidence was the claim that he had called out, just as the *Titanic* was sinking and pitching its passengers into the sea, that they should go back and attempt a rescue. 'It is up to us to go back and pick up anyone in the boat,' he said. This appeal, he claimed, was overturned by the Duff Gordons. Hendrickson was asked whether this was a momentary impulse? 'No, it came across me after I heard those cries,' he replied. Where was Lady Duff Gordon sitting in relation to him in the lifeboat? She was in the second seat away from him, he explained. And she had heard what he said? 'She must have heard me to answer me,' he replied. Did any of the other crew reply? 'None of them, none of them,' he said. The allegation was a serious one, an accusation the Duff Gordons were ill prepared to defend themselves against.[20]

As the couple drove to the inquiry, held at the Royal Scottish Drill Hall, Buckingham Gate, Westminster, Lucile thought about the delights of the weather. It was a glorious May day, the trees were budding and the flowers were bursting forth. In fact, it was difficult, she said to herself, to believe that she was not going to some 'pleasant social function'. Indeed, when she stepped inside the court, she was delighted to see the presence of so many friends and acquaintances including Prince Leopold of Battenberg, Margot Asquith (the wife of the Prime Minister), and Lady St Helier. However, she soon realised that her so-called friends were there not so much to support her as to watch the spectacle; the Duff Gordons had become a source of entertainment. Indeed, the *Daily Sketch* reported the event as if it were a night at the theatre, describing how the society women settled down in their seats and watched the event with unabashed glee, while the *New York Times* reported that the occasion had the atmosphere of a fashionable matinee in aid of a popular charity.

'Looking at them all as I went in I recognized many who had regarded themselves as my intimate friends,' said Lady Duff Gordon, 'yet it came to me that they were rather enjoying the novelty of seeing two people standing in a moral pillory, watching for us to make some slip in our evidence.' The couple were, she was forced to admit, 'absolutely alone' in their moment of sorrow.[21]

Sir Cosmo was the first to take the stand. The Attorney General, Sir Rufus Isaacs, asked a number of general questions about the night of the collision, before turning his attention to the issue of the number of passengers in the Duff Gordons' lifeboat. Was there room for more? 'There would have been more room if the oars and masts had been thrown away,' replied Cosmo. Was he suggesting that there was not room for more people? 'Of course there was room for more people,' he said, 'but we should have had to put away the oars and mast and sail, I think, and some boat hooks, and a lot of things that were lying alongside us.' Why was the boat, containing so few passengers, lowered away when there were so many people still left on the ship? 'There were no people visible, I am quite sure of that, when I got into the boat,' said Sir Cosmo. At this point, the Commissioner, Lord Mersey, interrupted, wanting to know whether or not there were many people close at hand. 'I do not know, there was no one visible certainly,' Cosmo replied. This did not satisfy the Attorney General, who then asked whether Sir Cosmo thought there was nobody left on the ship. 'Oh, no,' he said, 'but I certainly thought all the women had got off. I had seen all the women in my part, and I knew in other parts of the ship they were lowering boats.'

The questioning then moved on to the subject of what happened after the lifeboat had been lowered into the water. How far had the boat travelled before the ship went down? 'Well, I have always said 1000 yards when telling anybody, but it is true I have only one eye [he had lost an eye in a shooting accident], and I am, therefore, presumed not to be a judge of distance, but I think it still.' Did he hear any cries? 'Yes, I heard the explosion first, and I heard, I will not say the cries, but a wail – one confused sound.' Were these the cries of people who were dying? 'Yes,' he said. There was no doubt about it? 'Yes, I think so without a doubt.' Had it occurred to him, with all the room he had in the boat, that it might have been possible to save some of those in the water? 'It is difficult to say what occurred to me. Again, I was minding my wife, and we were rather in an abnormal condition, you know. There were many things to think about, but of course it quite well occurred to one that people in the water could be saved by a boat, yes.'

Considering that there was room in the boat, and had it been possible to get some of these people from the water into his vessel, then was it safe to assume that they could have been saved? 'Yes, it is possible,' Sir Cosmo answered. Had he heard a suggestion that the lifeboat go back to the place from where the cries came? 'No, I did not,' he said. He never heard anything like that at all? 'I heard no suggestion of going back.' Which way did the crew row – was it away from the ship, away from the cries? At this point, Cosmo became a little confused, stating that he did not know which direction the crew were rowing. Surely he wasn't implying, the Attorney General continued, that the lifeboat was moving towards the cries? 'Oh no, I do not suggest that for a moment,' he said, falling into the trap.

The questioning continued. Did Sir Cosmo hear any of the ladies in the boat say anything about the danger of being swamped if they went back? 'No, I did not,' he said. Was there any discussion at all about being swamped? 'No, I did not hear the subject raised; the subject was not raised, I think.' So, in effect, nobody in Sir Cosmo's boat took any notice of the cries that came from the dying? 'No,' he replied. There was no conversation about it? 'No, I think there was no conversation.' He had no thoughts of going back to help? 'I do not think it would have been possible, for one thing,' said Sir Cosmo. The Attorney General pushed him on this point; would he mind answering the question? Sir Cosmo became confused, asking, 'What was the question?' It was repeated: had he no thoughts of going back to help? 'No, I suppose not.'

One of the previous witnesses to have been called – crew member Albert Horswell, who had been in Sir Cosmo's lifeboat – testified to the effect that actually it would have been quite safe to go back to the place where people were dying in the water. Sir Cosmo answered by saying it surely would not have been possible as they would not have known which way to row. The cries continued for quite some time, did they not? asked the judge. 'Yes, I believe they did,' said Sir Cosmo. As the men were rowing did the cries sound fainter? 'Oh, you could not hear the sound at all when the men were rowing,' he replied. And, for the record, the Attorney General continued, what was his opinion of Hendrickson's testimony? Had Sir Cosmo heard Hendrickson's claim that it had been suggested the boat go back to help save some of the people? 'I can only say I did not hear any suggestion, that is all I can say,' he said. And did Sir Cosmo know that it had been alleged that one of the ladies, identified as his wife, had been afraid to go back in case of being swamped? 'I heard that,' he said. Did he hear his wife say that? 'No,' insisted Duff Gordon. Or any lady or other person? 'No,' he replied. Did he mean to say that what had been claimed was not, in fact, true? 'It comes to that, of course,' he replied. The Attorney General pointed out then that had they gone back towards the cries they would surely have saved a good many people. 'I do not know that,' said Sir Cosmo.

Finally came the tricky question of the money. Had Sir Cosmo made any promise to the men in the boat? 'Yes, I did,' replied Duff Gordon. He then explained his version of what happened. He was sitting next to a member of the crew, whose identity he still did not know, who said to him, 'I suppose you have lost everything.' Sir Cosmo said that was correct, at which point the man commented that while he would be able to buy more things, he and his fellow crew members would not be able to replace their kit and that their pay would have been stopped. 'You fellows need not worry about that,' Sir Cosmo claimed to have said, 'I will give you a fiver each to start a new kit.' And that, he said, was 'the whole of that five pound note story', hoping to bring the matter to a close.[22]

He was not to get off so lightly. Sir Cosmo was recalled the following day and immediately he took the stand the Attorney

General returned to the interlinked issues of the five-pound note and the failure of the lifeboat to return to pick up the people in the water. Trying to catch Sir Cosmo out once again, the Attorney General asked at what point Duff Gordon offered to give the crew a sum of money: 'Was it before or after the boat had gone back to try to pick up the people?' Duff Gordon could only make the reply, 'I did not know about the boat going back.' Finally, he had been forced to admit, in his own words, that the lifeboat had not returned to help the dying. The wealthy aristocrat may not have committed a crime, but he was certainly culpable, in the eyes of the Attorney General and the general public, of falling short of an unwritten moral code.

Sir Cosmo thought the Attorney General had been a tough interrogator, but this was nothing compared with the snake-like approach of W.D. Harbinson, counsel for the third-class passengers. Harbinson asked Duff Gordon if it would be correct to say that the conversation about the money occurred around twenty minutes or so after the *Titanic* sank. 'Something of that sort, twenty minutes or half-an-hour, I should fancy,' said Sir Cosmo. So he was talking about money and gifts at the same time as the screams of the dying could be heard across the ocean? 'Oh, no,' said Sir Cosmo. At this point, Lord Mersey interrupted Harbinson's questioning and asked him to prove his statement. It was, said the Commissioner, highly irregular to assume facts that were not proved. Harbinson explained his point clearly – the cries of the passengers lasted for a good while after the sinking of the *Titanic* and surely they would have been audible twenty minutes after the ship had sunk. Lord Mersey, clearly on the side of those who dwelled in the upper echelons of society, warned Harbinson that he should not 'try to make out a case for this class or that class or another class'. Duly rebuked, the counsel for the steerage passengers continued, asking whether he had heard any cries twenty minutes after the

Titanic sank? 'No, I cannot tell you at all about that.' He could not remember? 'I do not think anything like that.' Did he tell the men in his boat to row to drown out the cries? 'No,' said Sir Cosmo. Was this not a rather strange moment, twenty minutes after the ship had sunk, to make suggestions about giving away five-pound notes? 'No, I think not,' he said. 'I think it was a most natural time. Everything was quiet; the men had stopped rowing, the men were quite quiet lying on their oars doing nothing for some time, and then the ship having gone I think it was a natural enough remark for a man to make to me, "I suppose you have lost everything?"' Would it not have been more appropriate, more in harmony with the traditions of seamanship, to suggest to the sailors that they try and rescue those who were dying? 'I have said that I did not consider the possibility – or, rather I should put it, the possibility of being able to help anybody never occurred to me at all.'

With these words, Sir Cosmo Duff Gordon had in effect damned himself. Harbinson was quick to pounce. So all that mattered was that he was safe. He had no concern for those who might perish? 'No, that is not quite the way to put it,' said Sir Cosmo. Harbinson's harsh questioning brought another admonishment from the Commissioner. 'The witness's position is bad enough,' he said. 'Do you think it is fair to put a question of that kind to him? I do not.' Harbinson agreed he would not pursue it any more, but did go on to ask whether Duff Gordon had heard any lady making any protests about the boat going back to help the dying. 'No,' he said. There were, of course, only two ladies in the lifeboat, were there not, asked Harbinson? 'Yes,' said Sir Cosmo. Did he have any conversation with Lady Duff Gordon? 'I spoke to her several times,' he said. Did he talk to her about an attempt to rescue the people in the water? 'I have said that the question did not arise in the boat.'

The questioning was then passed over to Clement Edwards MP, who represented the interests of the Dock, Wharf, Riverside and General Workers Union of Great Britain, and whose attitude was even more aggressive than Harbinson's. Edwards began with an examination of Duff Gordon's behaviour on the ship itself. How could Sir Cosmo explain the testimony of George Symons, the Captain of the lifeboat, who said that he saw two ladies – Lady Duff Gordon and her secretary Franks – rush from the saloon of the *Titanic* and ask an officer if they could get into the boat, soon followed by himself and two other men who did the same? That was not true, said Sir Cosmo. Once he was in the lifeboat, and the *Titanic* had gone down, was it true to say that he was so absorbed in paying attention to his wife that he could not think to go back to help the dying? 'Well, you may put it in that way,' said Duff Gordon. Did he think that, if it was perfectly natural to offer the sailors in his lifeboat five pounds to replace their kit, it might also have been natural to think there was a possibility of saving at least some of those poor people in the water? 'As I say, the possibility of being able to help I do not think occurred to anybody,' he said. Why did he suggest that it was more natural to think of offering this five pounds to the men than to help those screaming people? 'I do not suggest anything of the sort,' said Duff Gordon. So it was natural not to think of rescuing the dying? 'It is a difficult question to answer if you put it like that,' said Sir Cosmo. 'At the time I saw no possibility – I thought there was no possibility of doing so.' Did he still think it was natural not to think about going back to save some of those people? 'I think it was still natural, but I concede that it would have been a very splendid thing if it could have been done.'[23]

Such language only reminded the court of Duff Gordon's privileged position. The subtext of his testimony was that as Sir Cosmo was an aristocrat he need not worry about the welfare

– or existence – of 'lesser' human beings. At this stage, his behaviour in the lifeboat was hardly the point; the damage to his reputation had been done by insinuation and suggestion. 'It was,' wrote Lady Duff Gordon in her memoirs, 'a terrible spectacle, this man of old family, battling, pale-faced, almost pleading for something still dearer than life, fighting for honour and repute.'[24]

When Lady Duff Gordon took the stand, the mood lightened somewhat. The ladies, bedecked in 'light costumes, flower-decked hats and white blouses',[25] had flocked to the court partly to see what the great Lucile was wearing. She did not disappoint. Entering the box at 11.45 a.m. on day eleven of the inquiry, Lady Duff Gordon sported a black crepe dress 'with a touch of white at her neck and bosom'[26] and a big black picture hat which was tilted to one side, showing a mass of red curls, while her pale face was partially concealed by a black chiffon veil.[27]

After taking off her white gloves and swearing the oath, Lucile began to be questioned by Sir Rufus Isaacs, the Attorney General. He was particularly interested in what she had related to her own solicitor, especially the words, 'It is such an enormous boat, none of us know what the suction may be if she is a goner.' Had she heard such words spoken while she was in the lifeboat? 'Yes, I heard them speaking of the enormous boat,' she said. 'It was the word "suction" I was not sure of. I see what you mean.' The Attorney General was quick to correct her – it was not what *he* had meant, but what she herself had said to her own solicitor. 'Well, I may have said so,' she replied. She had talked about the possibility of suction? 'That was, I am sure, long before the *Titanic* sank,' she said. Did she not appreciate the question? 'No, I did not,' she said. But this was said before the *Titanic* sank? 'Yes, it was before,' she said. The questioning continued:

The Attorney General: Now after the *Titanic* sank you still continued to be seasick, I understand.

Lady Duff Gordon: Yes, terribly.

The Attorney General: I only want to ask you one question about that. Tell me first of all do you recollect very well what happened when you were in the boat?

Lady Duff Gordon: No.

The Attorney General: Your mind is hazy about it.

Lady Duff Gordon: Very.

The Attorney General: There may have been some talk which you would not recollect, I suppose?

Lady Duff Gordon: Well, I do not know.

The Attorney General: You think you might?

Lady Duff Gordon: I think I would.

The Attorney General: I will put to you definitely what is said with reference to yourself. Did you hear after the *Titanic* had sunk the cries of the people who were drowning?

Lady Duff Gordon: No, after the *Titanic* sank I never heard a cry.

The Attorney General: You never heard anything?

Lady Duff Gordon: No, not after the *Titanic* sank.

The Attorney General: Did not you hear cries at all?

Lady Duff Gordon: Yes, before she sank, terrible cries.

The Attorney General: Before she sank?

Lady Duff Gordon: Yes.

The Attorney General: Did you see her sink?

Lady Duff Gordon: I did.

The Attorney General: You mean you heard nothing at all after that?

Lady Duff Gordon: My impression was that there was absolute silence.

The Attorney General: Were your men rowing?

Lady Duff Gordon: Yes.

The Attorney General: What, all the time?

Lady Duff Gordon: No, they began to row as soon as the boat went down.

The Attorney General: Did you hear a proposal made that you should go back to where the *Titanic* was sunk?

Lady Duff Gordon: No.

The Attorney General: Did you hear any shouting in your boat? It would be better if you would attend to me.

Lady Duff Gordon: I am listening.

The Attorney General: Did you hear anybody shout out in the boat that you ought to go back?

Lady Duff Gordon: No.

The Attorney General: With the object of saving people who were in the *Titanic*?

Lady Duff Gordon: No.

The Attorney General: You knew there were people in the *Titanic*, did you not?

Lady Duff Gordon: No, I did not think so, I do not think I was thinking anything about it.

The Attorney General: Did you say that it would be dangerous to go back, that you might get swamped?

Lady Duff Gordon: No.

Although Harbinson had no questions for her, Clement Edwards certainly did. Had Lady Duff Gordon seen the article purported to be written by herself in the London *Daily News* and published on 20 April? Had she written such an article? Yes, she had seen it, and no, it most certainly had not been written by her. 'A man wrote it from what he thought he heard me saying,' she explained, describing the feature that was in fact a reprint of the piece that had appeared in the *American Weekly*. Edwards handed her a copy of the article, prompting her to protest, 'What am I supposed to say?' The Commissioner interrupted the questioning and asked whether she had seen it before. 'Never, this is the first time,' she said, immediately contradicting herself. And what about her signature at the bottom of the piece, asked Edwards. Was that a forgery? 'Oh, absolutely,' she said. The MP then focused his attention on some of the more outrageous statements Lucile was accused of making. When she had been standing on the deck, waiting to board a lifeboat, had she turned to her husband and remarked, 'Well, we might as well take a boat, although the trip will only be a little pleasure excursion until the morning'? No, that was quite untrue, she replied. Had she really written, in regard to the *Titanic*'s last moments, 'An awful silence seemed to hang over everything, and then from the water all about where the *Titanic* had been arose a Bedlam of shrieks and cries'? No, she had never said such a thing. Was the last cry she had heard that of a man shouting loudly, 'My God, My God'? That was absolutely untrue, she said. She then went on to explain the circumstances of how she had related her experiences to her great friend Merritt over supper and how he had asked her whether he could publish the story in the following day's issue of the *American Weekly*. He had then related her story to a 'clever reporter' who reworded it for publication, the offending feature then being syndicated around the world.[28]

The problem for Lady Duff Gordon was that, almost certainly, too many versions of that night now existed in her mind. She had lived through the horror of it all, but with each retelling of the narrative the reality of the sinking mutated and transformed until she did not know what was true and what was not. Had she really said to Cosmo that a trip on the lifeboat would be like a pleasure cruise? Certainly this kind of facile quip was not outside the realms of her emotional vocabulary; remember, for example, her comment about Franks's pretty nightdress going down with the ship.

Lady Duff Gordon's strategy was one of psychological

obfuscation, of avoiding the central charge of her and her husband's questionable behaviour both on board the stricken *Titanic* and afterwards in the lifeboat. Yet, on close analysis, it seems clear that – even disregarding the possibility of the inaccuracies and exaggerations that crept into the article that appeared in the *American Weekly* and the London *Daily News* – her accounts are full of contradictions. For instance, in Lucile's memoirs, which were published as *Discretions and Indiscretions* in 1932, she says that she *did* hear cries after the *Titanic* went down. As the men rowed away from the 'vast bulk' of the ship, she said the passengers in lifeboat number one did not speak to one another as their 'ears were too full of those terrible cries of despair from the poor souls she had carried down with her', a statement that runs counter to the evidence she gave to the official inquiry.[29] It seems likely that, while in the lifeboat, she had said that they should not go back to rescue the dying in case they got swamped, but this was in no way related to Sir Cosmo's present of the five-pound notes. From examining their statements, and the many contradictions within them, it appears that the Duff Gordons were guilty of some charges – the rowing away from the scene of the accident being the most serious – but not guilty of others (such as the allegation of bribery). Theirs was not simply a case of consequential behaviour – one cannot say that the fleeing from the scene of mass death was connected to the payment of a bribe. Rather, their situation was more complex, more human. Lady Duff Gordon, already feeling struck down by seasickness, did not want, or could not bear, to contemplate the horrors that she knew lurked in the sea nearby. She did not have the strength to face death on such a scale and so she asked the men in the boat to row away, rather than towards, the victims struggling in the water. It was only later that she learned the full scale of the tragedy – the death of over 1,500 people. Could she have made a difference? Almost certainly, the lifeboat could have saved thirty or so people. Could the boat have been swamped? This is unlikely, as the freezing temperatures of the water – it was minus two degrees centigrade – rendered those who had been thrown into the sea physically incapable of much movement after only a few minutes.

It was not the role of the inquiry, however, to unpick the tightly knotted matrix of motivation that, consciously and unconsciously, shaped the behaviour of the Duff Gordons. Instead, its primary duty was simply to investigate the causes and consequences of the sinking. While the court officially vindicated the Duff Gordons, the questioning process exposed the flaws in their evidence and the experience left them wounded. Sir Cosmo 'never lived down the shame of the charges that were brought against him,' said Lucile, 'and from that time he became a changed man. He never spoke much about it, but I know that his heart was broken . . . To the end of his life he grieved at the slur which had been cast on his honour.'[30]

The effect on Lucile was more complicated; her strident personality refused to let the slurs on her character puncture her near-monstrous ego, even when she heard strangers whisper as she passed by, 'That is Lady Duff Gordon, the woman who rowed away from the drowning.' Towards the end of her life, when she was asked whether she had any regrets regarding her actions on the night of the tragedy she replied that she had none. 'The *Titanic* disaster made me and my fortune. Look at the tremendous amount of publicity it gave me . . . When I opened my dress establishments in New York and Chicago, people mobbed the places. I made thousands and thousands of dollars.'[31]

In order to understand Lady Duff Gordon and her behaviour on the night the *Titanic* sank, it is necessary to travel back in time. If anyone was destined to be a survivor it was Lucy

Christiana Sutherland, who was born in St John's Wood, London, on 13 June 1863. After the death, from typhoid, of her Canadian-born engineer father, Douglas, in 1865 at the age of only twenty-eight, the young girl grew up in a house of mourning. One of her earliest memories was seeing her mother, Elinor, crying as she tried to sort out some of her dead husband's papers. Lucy would later write of the incident, 'It made a deep impression on me and I can recall to this day the consternation which came over me.'[32]

As she was left virtually penniless, Elinor Sutherland had no choice but to return to her parents' home in Canada. With her she took Lucy and her younger daughter, also called Elinor, who had been born in Jersey in October 1864 and who would grow up to be the bestselling author Elinor Glyn. At Summer Hill, a ranch near Guelph, Ontario, the two girls were tutored in the arts of living by their domineering grandmother, Lucy Saunders, who told the children that ladies should never cry nor show emotion of any kind. 'The common people can find that a relaxation,' she said. Lucy was, by her own admission, something of a tomboy; she was resourceful and independent and she spent her girlhood stealing apples, riding horses, climbing trees and fishing for minnows with a bent pin. In her memoirs she also confesses to manifesting a 'streak of cruelty'; her greatest joy was, she says, to watch the ranch workers killing chickens. 'I took a ghoulish delight in watching their struggles in the brawny hands of the yard man as he twisted their unfortunate necks, and danced up and down excitedly at their despairing "squawks",' she wrote. 'The final thrill of seeing them run jerkingly and horribly a few paces with headless and bleeding necks had for me all the fascination which the spectacle of a dozen Christian martyrs, delivered over to wild beasts, must have had for a Roman audience.'[33]

Later in life, Lucy was ashamed to recall how much she

The *Titanic* – the biggest moving object in the world in 1912 – setting off on its maiden voyage from Southampton to New York. Already on board were many of the passengers whose lives would be transformed by the sinking.

Southampton City Council

R M S "TITANIC

April 14, 1912.

LUNCHEON.

Consommé Fermier | Cockie Leekie

Fillets of Brill

Egg à l'Argenteuil

Chicken à la Maryland

Corned Beef, Vegetables, Dumplings

FROM THE GRILL.

Grilled Mutton Chops

Mashed, Fried & Baked Jacket Potatoes

Custard Pudding

Apple Meringue | Pastry

BUFFET.

Salmon Mayonnaise | Potted Shrimps

Norwegian Anchovies | Soused Herrings

Plain & Smoked Sardines

Roast Beef

Round of Spiced Beef

Veal & Ham Pie

Virginia & Cumberland Ham

Bologna Sausage | Brawn

Galantine of Chicken

Corned Ox Tongue

Lettuce | Beetroot | Tomatoes

CHEESE.

Cheshire, Stilton, Gorgonzola, Edam,

Camembert, Roquefort, St. Ivel.

Cheddar

Iced draught Munich Lager Beer 3d. & 6d. a Tankard.

Menu for the last lunch on the luxury liner. The *Titanic* carried 36,000 oranges and 16,000 lemons; 75,000 pounds of fresh meat; 40,000 fresh eggs; 6,000 pounds of fresh butter; 20,000 bottles of beer and 8,000 cigars. Just before lunch an ice warning had been received by the ship.

Southampton City Council

A drawing of the sinking of the *Titanic* as described by seventeen-year-old survivor Jack Thayer. He later recalled: 'I saw the ship in a sort of a red glare, and it seemed to me that she broke in two just in front of the third funnel. At this time I was sucked down, and as I came up I was pushed out again and twisted around by a large wave, coming up in the midst of a great deal of small wreckage. As I pushed it from around my head my hand touched the cork fender of an overturned lifeboat. I looked up and saw some men on the top and asked them to give me a hand.'

Courtesy of Robert Maguire

Library of Congress

A lifeboat arrives alongside the rescue ship *Carpathia* in the early morning of 15 April 1912. Conditions were harsh – some passengers even perished because of the cold that night – and many survivors remained haunted by their experiences in the lifeboats for the rest of their lives.

A group of *Titanic* survivors on board the *Carpathia*, the so-called 'ship of widows'. As one first-class passenger observed, 'for four days the company lived together . . . in this strange assortment of undress costume, some in ball gowns, many in night dresses and only a few fully clothed.'

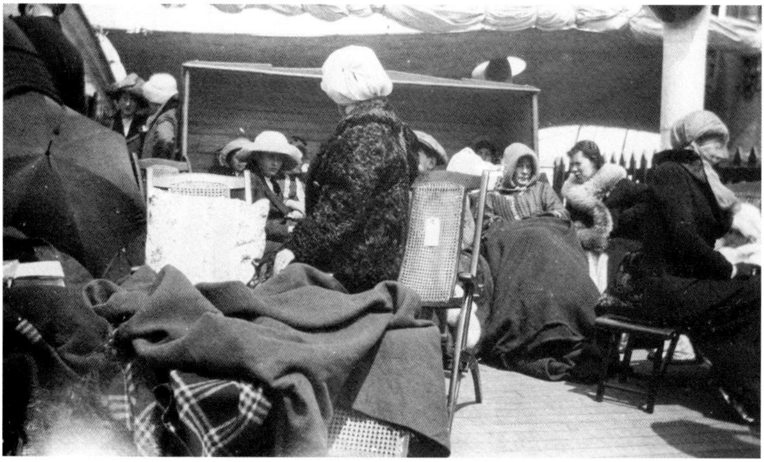

Library of Congress

Courtesy of Phillip Gowan

Renee Harris, who inherited her husband's business after he was killed in the sinking, transformed herself into America's first female theatre manager and producer. However, after decades of overspending – and devastating losses in the stockmarket crash of 1929 – she spent the rest of her long life in poverty.

John Jacob Astor, one of the richest men in the world, with his second wife, the eighteen-year-old Madeleine. She was five months pregnant when she escaped the *Titanic*; her husband went down with the ship.

© Getty Images

Library of Congress

Although Madeleine Astor inherited a $5 million trust fund from her husband after he was killed in the disaster, his will stipulated that she would have to forgo his fortune and Fifth Avenue mansion should she ever remarry.

Courtesy of Phillip Gowan

Madeleine Astor with her two sons from her second marriage. In 1916, Madeleine Astor had shocked New York society by marrying her childhood sweetheart William Karl Dick. Yet the marriage did not last.

Courtesy of Phillip Gowan

In early 1932, Madeleine decided she needed to escape from her failing marriage and try to improve the delicate state of her health. She told her doctor that the *Titanic* had 'ruined her nerves' – a trip to Europe would do her the world of good. On the *Vulcania* she met her third husband, the handsome Italian prize fighter Enzo Fiermonte, who would subsequently leach her of her money and use her as his punch bag.

Courtesy of Phillip Gowan

Robert Williams Daniel, who survived the *Titanic* in mysterious circumstances. He married fellow survivor Eloise Hughes Smith – who lost her husband in the sinking – and refused to talk about the events of that night for the rest of his life.

Courtesy of Phillip Gowan

Sir Cosmo Duff Gordon, whose reputation was ruined by allegations that he bribed the crew members of his lifeboat not to return to pick up passengers struggling to remain alive in the ice-cold sea.

Courtesy of Phillip Gowan

Lady Duff Gordon later recalled of the bribery allegations: 'I remember every word of that conversation, for it had a tremendous bearing on our future. I little thought then that because of those few words we should be disgraced and branded as cowards in every corner of the civilized world.' She went on to use the *Titanic* to further her own career as the high-society fashion designer Lucile, but her monstrous ego led to her downfall.

Titanic Historical Society (Helen Bishop)

Although first-class passengers Helen and Dickinson Bishop were rescued from the *Titanic*, their lives were touched by tragedy. After Helen suffered a serious head injury in a car accident, doctors fixed a silver plate over her skull, but friends said she started to behave erratically, and her marriage collapsed. She died in March 1916 after tripping over a rug.

Phillip Gowan (Dickinson Bishop)

After the death of Helen, Dickinson Bishop remarried. He died in February 1961, but relatives recalled that he never talked about the *Titanic*, nor the accident which killed his former wife.

J. Bruce Ismay, whose father created the White Star Line, built the *Titanic* as an act of hubris. His survival of the sinking brought about his destruction. Within days of the disaster, one newspaper ran a full-page cartoon of Ismay, showing him in a lifeboat, with the sinking ship in the distance and accompanied by the caption: 'THIS IS J. BRUTE ISMAY'.

© Getty Images

Ismay's marriage to his wife, Florence, was far from happy. She suffered from an early menopause at the age of thirty-seven and their relationship became a sexless one. Perhaps as a consequence of this, Ismay became obsessed with fellow *Titanic* survivor Marian Thayer, to whom he wrote a series of impassioned letters. 'I never want to see a ship again, and I loved them so . . .' he wrote to her. 'What an ending to my life. Perhaps I was too proud of the ships and this is my punishment.'

Library of Congress

After the sinking, Ismay retired from public view. Mention of the *Titanic* was strictly forbidden in his household. His granddaughter remembers: 'He returned [from the disaster] with a sense of self-loathing and was, in many ways, like a frozen corpse.'

Titanic Historical Society

Courtesy of Robert Maguire

Marian Thayer, who lost her husband in the disaster. His body was never found. Unable to deal with his death, she turned to a spiritualist in an effort to contact him.

Marian's son, first-class passenger Jack Thayer, whose survival was considered a miracle. Unlike J. Bruce Ismay, Thayer had shunned a place in the lifeboats and had waited on the sinking ship until the very end. He had taken his chance by jumping off the liner and plunging into the freezing sea. 'The shock of the water took the breath out of my lungs,' he said. 'Down and down I went, spinning in all directions . . . I finally came up with my lungs bursting, but not having taken any water.'

Courtesy of Robert Maguire

Jack Thayer in later life. After the death of his son aged twenty-two, killed in action in the Pacific in October 1943, and the loss of his mother, who died on the anniversary of the sinking of the *Titanic* in April 1944, Jack suffered from depression. In September 1945, he committed suicide by slitting his wrists and his throat. He was fifty years old.

Courtesy of Robert Maguire

Southampton City Council

Titanic stewardess Annie Robinson, who had survived a previous collision with an iceberg in the Atlantic. Two years after the *Titanic* disaster she was sailing into a foggy Boston harbour when memories of that fateful night came back to haunt her. She became so gripped by fear that she ran up on to the ship's deck and threw herself to her death.

Courtesy of Randy Bryan Bigham

Silent screen star Dorothy Gibson, who made the first film about the *Titanic* within four weeks of the disaster. She starred as herself, wearing the very dress she had worn that night.

One day, during the making of the silent film *Saved from the Titanic*, shooting had to be brought to a halt when Dorothy seemed to experience some sort of existential crisis. 'She had practically lost her reason,' wrote one observer, 'by virtue of the terrible strain she had been under to graphically portray her part.'

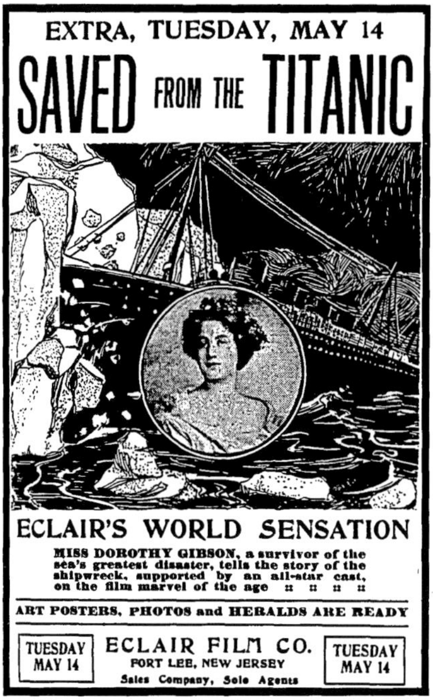

Courtesy of Frank Thompson

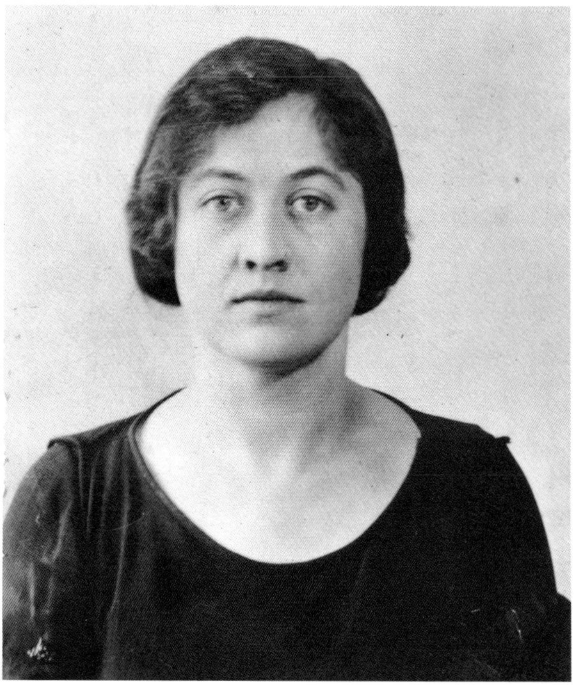

Courtesy of Phillip Gowan

Dorothy Gibson in later life. After an unsuccessful marriage, she left America for Europe, where she flirted with fascism, was imprisoned in a concentration camp, made a daring escape and died at the Paris Ritz in February 1946.

Marcelle Navratil with her two children, Michel and Edmond. The two boys had been snatched by their father, who had been travelling in second class on the *Titanic* under an assumed name. When he died in the sinking, the children were dubbed 'the orphans of the *Titanic*', but were finally reunited with their mother.

Library of Congress

Fashion journalist and buyer Edith Rosenbaum (later Russell) as a young woman. Soon after the sinking she cast herself in the role of spokeswoman for survivors with an authority that came naturally to her.

Courtesy of Phillip Gowan

MacQuitty International Photographic Collection

Edith's later life became increasingly dominated by the disaster. 'It was clear that the *Titanic* was the defining moment of Edith's life,' says family friend Jane MacQuitty. 'She was a battler, a fighter, tenacious, something of a dynamite character – and I'm not at all surprised that she made sure she survived. Yet afterwards, I got the sense that nothing ever lived up to that.'

Eva Hart was a seven-year-old girl when she sailed on the *Titanic* with her parents. She lost her father in the sinking. 'I have always been haunted by the thought that he must have tried, despite the intense cold, to swim for his life to reach a lifeboat,' she said.

Courtesy of Ronald C. Denney

Southampton City Council

When this photograph was taken in June 1992, there were only three survivors left alive in Britain: Eva Hart (left), Millvina Dean (standing) and Edith Haisman. Millvina Dean went on to enjoy the life of celebrity when she became the world's last *Titanic* survivor. 'Someone said of me that I am a tough old bird,' she said before her death on 31 May 2009 at the age of ninety-seven.

would look forward to the days she knew that the chickens would be killed, how eagerly she awaited the arrival of their executioner. After the slaughter she would be trembling with 'a sort of nervous ecstasy', fascinated by the thought that just an hour previously the birds, now no more than 'mangled corpses', had been pecking their way round the courtyard. She described her behaviour as a kind of 'infant sadism', and it is tempting to make a connection between her response to the culling of the birds and her actions on the night of the *Titanic*. There was something in her personality that flourished when it came in contact with the macabre or the ghoulish. Her violent trembling on seeing the slaughter of the chickens as a girl – described in her memoirs in near orgasmic terms – served as a kind of emotional blueprint for what would come later. The sight of death all around her made her feel more alive. On the night of the sinking she first lapsed into a seasickness, and then she became nearly ecstatic with the certainty that she would not, after all, perish in the disaster. This was manifested in her comment about Franks's nightdress – which in turn prompted Sir Cosmo's offer – and then her giddy behaviour at the Ritz on the night the *Carpathia* arrived in New York.

Lucy appears to have been conscious from an early age that she was quite different from other members of her own sex. The reason she gave for her divergence from the norm was an excess of originality. 'I have always had too much imagination,' she wrote in her memoirs, 'and splashed the blank canvas of my life with such brilliant colours that there had to be a good bas-relief of black to make them stand out.'[34] There was always a gap, she found, between the wild fantasies of her imagination and the realities of everyday life. She made it her mission to devote her existence to the creation of 'a dream world'; indeed, she was aware that she often took refuge in this alternative realm when the quotidian and the commonplace became too dull for her. She had a 'zest for living', and she was determined to make her extraordinary reveries come true.[35]

The young Lucy Sutherland channelled her creative energies into the making of clothes, first for her dolls and then later for herself. From early in her life, fashion was inextricably linked with emotion – she remembered the high spirits with which she received the arrival of the *tonneau bienvenu*, from her grandfather's family in France, which often contained beautiful garments. Later, after moving to Jersey with her mother and stepfather she became fascinated by the famous beauty Lily Langtry and her rather daring sense of style, as well as the extravagances of Versailles. She began to educate herself in the practice and history of fashion, taking inspiration from copies of eighteenth-century paintings to create her own dresses. One night at a dance, while wearing a black velvet dress, Lucy met a young captain, and the outfit was forever associated in her mind with the sensation of falling in love for the first time.

The liaison, however, did not last – it seems the captain rejected her – and after a series of arguments with her stepfather Lucy left the family home to stay with a friend in King's Walden, Hertfordshire. There, she met a wine merchant, James Wallace, who asked her to marry him. Still smarting from the breakdown of her relationship with the captain she had met in Jersey, she accepted him, and the wedding took place in September 1884. 'I cannot pretend that anything but pique would have made me listen to him [her new husband],' she said later, 'for we were hopelessly unsuited to one another in every way, and he was more than twenty years older than I was. Still, anything was better than eating out my heart for the man who had gone from me.'[36]

The marriage was an unhappy one and five years after the birth of her daughter, Esmé, in August 1885, Wallace left her for a girl who made her living from dancing in pantomime.

Lucy's subsequent divorce left her alienated from 'polite society' – she had always viewed the upper classes as stuffy and conventional – and, as a result, she started to mix with more bohemian types, such as the actress Ellen Terry. Now penniless, Lucy and her daughter went to live with her recently widowed mother in a small house in Davies Street, London, but she knew that she would have to do something to make a living. One day, while making a dress for Esmé, she had a flash of inspiration. 'Whatever I could or could not do, I could make clothes,' she said. 'I would be a dressmaker.'[37]

Her first commission was a tea-gown for the Hon. Mrs Arthur Brand – a last-minute job that she ran up in a matter of days and which led to more work. The business boomed and within a few years she turned her attention to the designing of underclothes and nightdresses. These garments, 'as delicate as cobwebs and as beautifully tinted as flowers', both scandalised and intrigued London society. Women flocked to see them, and although they were at first quite wary of purchasing such risqué items they soon became astonishingly popular. In the highly promiscuous atmosphere of late Victorian and Edwardian society – when it was the norm for a man to take a mistress – these 'flimsiest [of] undies', as one disapproving gentleman called them, became a tool by which a woman could sexualise herself, transforming her all too familiar body into something more erotic. 'Those cunning little lace motifs let in just over the heart,' said Lucy of her undergarments, 'those saucy velvet bows on the shoulder might surely be the weapons of the woman who was "not quite nice"?'[38]

Lucy tapped into the standards of a society that thrived on the contradictions between appearance and reality and by the turn of the century she had reinvented herself as 'Lucile'. Subsequently, she introduced the concept of the mannequin parade – a forerunner of today's catwalk show – and, at the same time as revolutionising fashion, she designed costumes for the theatre, invented the word 'chic' and established an incredibly successful business. 'In her heyday, Lucile's artistry was unique, her influence enormous,' said Cecil Beaton.[39] By 1909, the year in which Lucy's daughter married, her company was making £40,000 a year. The business, however, would not have been so lucrative had it not been for the investment of Sir Cosmo Duff Gordon, a tall, handsome Scot who had first met Lucy in the 1890s. The couple married on 24 May 1900, when Lucy was thirty-six, but only a year later she complained in a letter to her mother that her existence was 'deadly deadly dull'.[40] The problem was that Cosmo was something of a habitual talker and, as a result, this reduced Lucy to the role of the listener, something she clearly resented. She was an individualist at heart – she had to be the centre of attention, she had to be adored, she was the one who had to stand in the limelight. Her sister Elinor identified this trait in her, as she said in a letter to her mother, 'I think she is impossible with other people.'[41]

As Lucile's business grew, so did her ego – and her desire to accrue even greater riches. Her ambition, it seems, knew no bounds and she turned to America as a way of realising her dreams. In January 1908, from her suite at the Hotel Plaza, New York, she wrote to her husband, 'I'm sure we would make a fortune here, if we can find the money.'[42] With the help of her friend, the well-connected interior decorator Elsie de Wolfe, she hired a publicist whose job it was to bombard newspapers and magazines with her name. But the blanket coverage was perhaps too effective as Lucy soon came to be known in some circles as Lady Muff Boredom. Yet Lucile had no qualms about rejecting typically English values such as decorum and humility – what counted, she said, was 'self-advertisement of the most blatant sort'.[43] She would, she declared, be happy to blow her own trumpet with the loudest and the best, determined as she was to be heard above the crowd; she even went so far as to label some of her more expensive creations 'money dresses'.

Blinded by hubris, she was unable to see the warning signs of impending disaster, even when, in May 1911, her shop on West 36th Street was raided by officials and she was charged, in a New York court, of customs fraud. The American authorities accused her of avoidance of duty on the import of her dresses and she was fined $10,000. One might have expected the experiences on the *Titanic* to have served as something of a wake-up call for Lady Duff Gordon. Not so – if anything she became even more of a monster. Fresh from establishing Madame Lucile in America, in the summer of 1912 Lucy travelled to Paris to open a salon on the Rue de Penthièvre, which in turn became an enormous success. *Vogue* reported that, at the opening, her models sported a range of hair colours, including tango, blue, red and green. Personal success, and the indulgence of whim, shaped her actions and, soon after the declaration of the First World War, Lucy moved to America, a country which, at its most extreme, stood as a symbol of her bullish, selfish character. As Elinor, her sister, wrote, 'She loves America – it is exactly her affair. She means to live there . . . she is entirely satisfied with herself and every aspect of life.'[44] Lucy confessed her admiration for a country that mirrored her own ambitions, a nation that was happy to demolish its skyscrapers every five years or so to build bigger and better ones. She loathed the English upper classes, she said, and instead she would focus her business on the American middle classes, whom she assumed would lavish her with wealth. She opened a shop in Chicago, took a house on Long Island Sound, adored her extravagantly decorated apartment on Park Avenue, and surrounded herself with a gaggle of mostly homosexual men whose job it was to flatter her. 'The whole of America is now beginning to talk about me and I am coining money,' she wrote to her daughter.[45] In 1915, Sir Cosmo – unable to endure her emotional infatuation with one of her Russian 'boys', Bobbie (whose real name was Genia d'Agarioff) – returned to London to the comforts of a hotel. The couple never shared a home again.

The problem with Lucile was that not only had she created herself as a brand, but she had also become oblivious to the warnings of the people closest to her. She had always known best, she thought, so why change now? Perhaps surviving the *Titanic* had even encouraged the fattening of her ego. She was indestructible, she had cheated death, and she had gone on to prosper in America, while her weak-willed husband had given in to the mealy-mouthed class prejudices of England. She defined herself as a winner. Yet she knew that her own behaviour would not bear scrutiny, especially what had happened the night the *Titanic* had gone down. As she herself admitted, she would take refuge in a self-created dream world, and if anything was too painful she would 'step into it and shut the door behind me'. As it turned out, she spent the greater part of the rest of her life within the confines of this fantasy.[46]

Determined to surround herself with beautiful things, Lucile started to spend vastly beyond her means. She took houses for a few months and decided that they had to be completely refurbished – 'the silk flowers, the jewelled jade trees, the emerald lacquered walls, the antique furniture had to be perfect'.[47] She employed seven indoor servants, a sailor (for her motor boat), a chauffeur, and paid for the upkeep of her dear Bobbie and a number of his friends. This, of course, all came at a price – and there was no way she could survive on a mere two hundred dollars a week, the allowance she had received from the business when she had first arrived in America. Desperate to make more money, she started to work under the name 'Lady Duff Gordon' rather than 'Lucile' – the switch meant that she could wriggle out of her contract with the company and work on a freelance basis for other people, such as Sears Roebuck, who wanted her to design a number of mail-order dresses, and a Jewish rag trade manufacturer from New York, John Lang Shuloff, who had a plan to buy out her business completely. By this point, it was obvious that Lucile cared more about money than her husband – who had initially invested thousands in the fashion house – and she set about trying to force Cosmo to sell the company, causing a deeper rift between them. Yet she saw all the problems that threatened to undermine the business as originating from London, rather than closer to home. 'I'm so sick of the way Miles [the accountant] and Cosmo have managed Lucile since I left . . .' she wrote to her daughter in 1918. 'Nicely have they broken my trust while I am away here making the models, working and fighting for them . . . their vile croaking of economy is ruining the fine business I left in their hands and trusted to them.'[48]

Lucy was oblivious to the effects and consequences of the First World War, and aesthetically, totally at odds with the new mood of the times. After bleeding her bank account dry, she had no choice but to sell out to Shuloff, who suddenly began streamlining her business to get it ready for the mass production of garments. Her fantasy of fashions inspired by the eighteenth century practically disappeared overnight to be replaced by a more practical, austere look. 'I do not intend to write much of what happened to "Lucile's", there is too much bitterness left still . . .' she wrote in her memoirs.[49] Then, in early 1919, her close friend Bobbie died of influenza and pneumonia, a loss that nearly destroyed her. 'My heart is broken,' she told her mother.[50] Without her business or her dearest friend, she felt there was no other option but for her to return to Europe. She expected a grand welcome, but her arrival in London was rather muted – the commissionaire at the Hanover

Square business premises did not even recognise her. Cosmo, stung by her repeated rebuffs and betrayals, was determined to distance himself from her; and the glamour and *joie de vivre* of the pre-war fashion world had all but disappeared. She travelled to Paris but she found that equally dull and shabby. 'The old standard of extravagant dressing had gone for ever,' she said. 'It passed away with the day of the great courtesans, whose whims and follies had so delighted the Parisians of 1912.'[51]

Reality was all too painful and so, just as she had done during the tortuous experience of the *Titanic*, Lady Duff Gordon once more retreated into fantasy, believing herself to be the reincarnation of Marie Antoinette's dressmaker, Rose Bertin. One day, while walking through the palace of Versailles, Lucy stopped before a portrait of the queen, and commented to her new assistant, Howard Greer, how well she remembered the day she had finished that dress for the queen and how Her Majesty had been in such a delightful mood. As she fell increasingly out of fashion, so she became more deluded, more out of touch, until finally, as she continually haunted Versailles, she became a 'ghost among ghosts'.[52] She left Paris and returned to London, where, in 1923, she was declared bankrupt after running up debts of more than $100,000. During bankruptcy hearings, in response to an official who asked her a question about her shareholdings of the business, she replied, 'It's all Greek to me, I don't know what a share is.'[53]

Yet her naivety was not always entirely convincing. In the immediate years following her bankruptcy, she was contacted by the young designer Norman Hartnell, who wrote to her to ask about employment prospects. One day he visited her at her flat in Park Place, St James's, which he described as 'stuffy' and 'dimly-lit'. As he approached her, he noticed that she was wearing a turban fashioned from green and silver tissue on her head, and that strands of her bright red hair dangled down on either side of her face 'like a couple of fire escapes'. After examining his designs through a horn-rimmed lorgnette, she said that she would keep his drawings for the time being and get in touch when she had decided on his salary. A few weeks later, one of his designs appeared as an illustration in her 'Dorothy' column in *The Sketch*. 'My dear Dorothy,' she wrote, 'I've designed this lovely dress just for you.' He thought nothing more of it until, a little while later, another of his images was published, and then another. He wrote to her, first of all politely, and then, finally, when he received no answer, he had no choice but to involve a solicitor who sued her for the sum of £50 plus costs.[54] She had become so desperate that, feeling disconnected from the trends of modern fashion, she had resorted to plagiarism. She realised that her time had passed and the disengagement was almost too painful to bear. 'I could never walk through the big stores and see yards of materials, silks, chiffons and velvets without a feeling of homesickness for the studio,' she wrote in her memoirs. 'I was like an artist shut away from his colours, or a violinist deprived of his violin.'[55]

In 1931, Sir Cosmo died, and although she said she felt the loss keenly – the death, she said, 'left a blank in my life that will never be filled'[56] – the truth was that for the last twenty or so years of his life she had treated him with no more respect than an old, discarded garment that had seen better days. She survived on the income from his estate and the money she could eke out from her newspaper fashion columns and the publication of her autobiography. Finally, after she could no longer afford the upkeep of her little house on Villas-on-the Heath, Hampstead, she was moved to a nursing home in Putney. She was in pain, she told friends, from sciatica, but doctors diagnosed breast cancer. After a six-month illness she died on 20 April 1935 from pneumonia, aged seventy-one, and was buried alongside her husband in Brookwood Cemetery, Surrey.

'I do not think that, on the whole, it is good for a woman to have temperament,' she wrote in her memoirs. 'It is much better for her to be a vegetable, and certainly much safer, but I never had the choice. I have often secretly envied my normal and conventionally feminine friends, contented with their stolid husbands and commonplace children, for I have known that such contentment could never be mine . . . A woman's imagination is such a delicate and vivid thing that everyday life cannot keep pace with it, and realities, no matter how attractive they may have seemed from afar, will always disappoint her. At least that has been my own experience.'[57]

In a typically tangential way, this was the nearest thing to a confession that she ever wrote. Her genius, she maintained, was that she had the ability to create and see beauty in everyday life; her tragedy was that, in doing so, she erased the ugly, the hurtful, the unpleasant. Those close to her were able to see the stains on her character but she remained, for the most part, blind to them to the very end.

After her death, it was believed that the mauve kimono that Lady Duff Gordon had worn during her escape from the *Titanic*, the garment that bore the unpleasant traces of her seasickness, was passed down to her grandson, Lord Halsbury. In August 2001, author Phillip Gowan bought the kimono from fellow *Titanic* enthusiast Randy Bryan Bigham, who claimed that it had been presented to him as a gift. 'Randy wanted a swift sale and an offer I couldn't refuse was made,' says Phillip. 'The kimono would be mine for a set price if I could Fed Ex him the cash within twenty-four hours.'[58] Gowan claims he had seen two letters of provenance, including one from Lady Clare Lindsay, a daughter of Lord Halsbury, which stated that the family had good reason to believe that 'this was *the* kimono', and he was excited at the prospect of owning such an emblematic item, a garment which, in its very fabric, still carried the salt water and vomit stains of that night in 1912. 'It had a certain musty smell that was reminiscent of the aroma in some old homes containing furniture dating from the late 1800s,' says Gowan. 'There were a number of small yellow stains that ran up the front of the kimono, along the line of the buttons. And although it had not been kept in the best of conditions, I did not hesitate to buy it when given the opportunity, as it's very rare to be able to purchase anything that was actually on the *Titanic*.'[59]

When he first saw the kimono, at Bigham's home in Texas during the Christmas holidays of 2000, Phillip was astounded to see how it was kept – it lay scrunched up at the bottom of a cardboard box. As soon as he brought it back to his home in South Carolina, he purchased a special cabinet for the kimono, a metal box that would withstand both fires and hurricanes, and wrapped the garment in acid-free paper. He was proud of his new acquisition, describing it as the 'pre-eminent piece in his collection',[60] and was pleased to be able to lend it to Titanic: The World Class Exhibition, an exhibition that toured throughout the United Kingdom in 2003 and 2004. When that organisation ceased trading, the kimono was duly returned to Phillip Gowan, who reinstalled it inside its safe home within the specially adapted cabinet. The metal box may have been able to withstand natural disasters, but Phillip was not prepared for an attack from other quarters – firstly the relatives of Lady Duff Gordon herself, and then the man who had sold it to him, Randy Bigham. Two years later, in 2006, a fight broke out over the possession – and ultimately the authenticity – of the so-called *Titanic* kimono, a battle that would result in the breakdown of close friendships, the threatening of lawsuits and a good deal of bad feeling all round.

The nasty spat began when a display of some of Lady Duff Gordon's possessions was included in an exhibition at *Titanic*

Branson, a permanent museum attraction in Missouri shaped like the ship itself. Gowan had been contacted by Bigham with the proposal that he lend the kimono to the museum. When the surviving relatives of Lady Duff Gordon, the three children of the late Lord Halsbury, heard about the kimono they immediately demanded its return, claiming that their father had only loaned it to Randy Bigham and that he had no right to sell it. As Phillip Gowan tells it: 'There are a couple of considerations that came into play at this point. First, had Lord Halsbury *really* given the kimono to RBB [Randy Bryan Bigham] or was it only loaned to him as claimed by the great-grandchildren? RBB swore that Lord Halsbury had given the kimono to him but the old gent had been dead for about six or seven years.'[61]

Although Gowan's legal position was clear – he was, under American law, a 'possessor-in-fact', meaning that he owned the kimono no matter how he had acquired it – his moral position was more ambiguous. After a great deal of thought – and careful consultation with his lawyer – Gowan agreed that he would return the kimono to the Duff Gordon heirs on condition that he be reimbursed by Bigham. Over the course of the next eight months or so, the awkward triangle – Gowan, Bigham, and the Duff Gordon heirs – exchanged hundreds of emails. Finally, Bigham did send Gowan a sum of money as partial settlement, at which point, 'weary of the whole ordeal', Gowan agreed to return the kimono to the family if he could obtain a legal guarantee from Bigham that the remaining money would be paid to him.

'My attorney proposed drawing up a promissory note with detailed terms that would require RBB to make instalment payments over time until the entire amount was paid,' says Gowan. 'It was worded very carefully to prevent RBB from escaping the obligation via bankruptcy. While RBB did sign the promissory note, we believe he also obtained legal advice and added an addendum to the promissory note that basically allowed for him to avoid the commitment should he at any time file for bankruptcy. My attorney advised me strongly against signing the document after RBB had altered it. I then advised the Duff Gordon heirs (who had a copy of the proposal/ promissory note) that I was uncomfortable proceeding under those terms.'[62]

At this point, the Duff Gordon heirs made an offer – to pay Gowan the remaining lump sum if he would forward Bigham's payments to them as he received them – which he then accepted. However, just as Gowan thought the whole matter might be resolved, the family then began to question the authenticity of the kimono, claiming that they had come across evidence that suggested that the garment was not the one that Lady Duff Gordon had worn that night in 1912. However, they still said they would go ahead with the deal, but only if Gowan sent them the kimono immediately. According to Gowan, they demanded a deduction of the total sum of money they owed, maintaining that, as he had received a few payments for lending the kimono to the touring exhibition in Britain during 2003 and 2004, they should not have to pay this back. For Gowan, this was totally unacceptable, a piece of skewed logic 'similar to buying a house from someone, but offering to pay a purchase price less any rent that had been collected from it by the owner over the years'.[63]

Then the Duff Gordon heirs started to play tough. Lady Clare Lindsay first of all sent an email to Gowan demanding the return of the kimono and then, a few days later, at 4.30 in the morning, she dashed off another missive saying that she had been unable to sleep with worry. She and her sister, Lady Caroline Blois, stated that they would no longer honour their agreement to pay back the lump sum to Gowan, and then, another two days later, the family sent off another email, containing 'vague allusions' to posting what they now regarded as the true provenance of the kimono on various Titanica web forums. Indeed, Lady Caroline Blois did go ahead with her threat, quoting on the message board of Encyclopedia Titanica a recently discovered letter from Lady Duff Gordon to her sister, Elinor, regarding the kimono she had worn on the ship. The garment, Lucy is supposed to have written, was 'but a meagre one, which I'd taken unfinished from the shop and had not had time to sew properly'.[64]

Gowan was astonished to hear this, as this letter had never been mentioned in all the months of wrangling. Lady Caroline said to Gowan that the whole matter could be settled if he simply returned the kimono to them.

'That was the proverbial straw that broke the camel's back,' says Gowan. 'After all the months of trying to do what was morally right by the Duff Gordon heirs while trying to protect my own financial interest in the kimono, I made a decision that the matter should end unresolved. I advised both RBB and the Duff Gordon heirs that I would not be returning the kimono, that the sum already received from Randy would be returned to him, and that I did not wish to receive any further correspondence concerning it. I advised them that my attorney strongly suggested they pursue monetary relief from RBB. My attorney also advised that they pursue [the] value of the kimono [valued by an independent auctioneer at $50,000] – not the amount of the transaction between myself and RBB. They then replied that they were not interested in money, only in the kimono.

'In the next few weeks, I received numerous emails from them anyway and amazingly, RBB came up with the additional funds (or claimed to) and they demanded that the negotiations be re-opened. I declined that offer. I was then advised not to contact Lady Caroline (as if I would have done so) as the whole matter had impacted her health and she had "taken [to] her bed" over it.'[65]

After a lengthy discussion with the Duff Gordon heirs, Randy Bigham logged into the same forum and backed up Lady Caroline's claims, outlining that he now also believed that the kimono was not in fact the one Lady Duff Gordon had worn on the *Titanic*. Bigham tried to explain himself as best he could, saying that he had theorised, using family letters and published sources, that the kimono owned by Phillip Gowan was the 'so-called *Titanic* one'. Yet, after further consultation with the Duff Gordon heirs, he had no choice but to admit that he had been wrong. The sisters, he said, 'have forgiven me my error, and also for the lapse I made in ever selling the kimono entrusted to me by their late father, which I mistook for a gift rather than the extended loan he apparently intended it to be'. He had apologised to the family, he said, and they had made amends. 'Now, in deference to the family's wishes,' he said at the time, 'I will state nothing further on this issue, which we all now consider to be a closed one.'[66]

Today, Randy Bigham is embarrassed by his mistake, but at the time he 'sincerely believed Halsbury gave it [the kimono] to me', he says. 'He told me to keep it, that it was an old rag, not a Lucile design in any case. I was later informed by members of the family that I had misunderstood him – that he had meant me to have it on an extended loan. This was well after selling it to Phil G. The family forgave me this humiliating mistake, but they were determined to get it back just the same and I tried to help them to that end. Out of embarrassment I did initially try to shield the family from learning of the sale to Phil . . . I agreed to the plan to pay Phil back but he withdrew suddenly from the agreement, spouting his usual high-handed drivel, and returned my first instalment. We were all sure he had done so because he expected to make a fortune out of the old dress based on the provenance I had earlier determined and was now questioning. Making money had obviously been his motivation all along, as he had made quite a bit out of the touring show. The family only wanted the kimono returned so that it could join other family garments in the Museum at Bath. They were not trying to cash in on it as Phil was because by that time we were all sure the piece did not belong to Lucile but to her daughter, Esmé, Viscountess Tiverton (later Countess of Halsbury). I greatly regret my faith in Phil and that I ever sold the kimono at all to anyone. The family and I have moved on from this debacle and we maintain a friendship despite the past trouble.'[67]

Phillip Gowan finds it extraordinary that anybody would send over three hundred emails over the course of a nine-month period – emails that articulated the Duff Gordon heirs' desperation to regain possession of the kimono – if the garment was not authentic. 'The thing that convinces me that this was *the* kimono was the way in which the two sisters behaved,' says Gowan. 'In reality, the garment was nothing more than a stained old rag, but these women were acting as if their lives depended on it. Finally, I decided to sell the kimono and, as it was bought for a collector by an intermediary, I have no idea where it is today.'[68]

The Duff Gordon heirs and Randy Bigham, however, are adamant that the kimono is most definitely not the one worn by Lucile on the *Titanic*. 'The kimono in question is one worn by my grandmother, Esmé, and we've had all the tests done to prove it,' says Lady Caroline Blois. 'We tried to give it to the Museum of Costume in Bath, which holds a number of Lucile's designs, but they would not have it, as it was dated post-*Titanic* and the pattern was Fortuny, not Lucile. It was at this point that the kimono was lent to Randy. The next thing we knew, someone contacted us to tell us that the kimono was in a touring exhibition, and being advertised as having been worn by our great-grandmother. The only two letters of provenance that Mr Gowan could be referring to are one that was written by my sister in 1999 in which she says, 'Wouldn't it be exciting if it turned out to be [the kimono],' and another that says, 'I will bring the kimono to the House of Lords when you're meeting my father for lunch.' We tried on many, many occasions to get the kimono back from Mr Gowan, and he agreed to send it back. All I can say is that we now feel we have had to wash our hands of it, because of the people involved, and they know who they are. We feel we've been extremely let down. We've made our peace with Randy – he has made complete reparation – and as far as we are concerned this chapter is closed.'[69]

For his part, Gowan's conscience is clear; he maintains he tried his best to find a solution to the problem and even spent $700 in legal fees, while he says the Duff Gordon heirs 'contributed not one cent to the effort'. It is ironic, he adds, that Lady Duff Gordon became famous for her naughty lingerie; in his opinion the kimono saga is better referred to as the airing of 'dirty underwear'.[70]

What is interesting about this episode – apart from its sensational elements – is the way in which Lady Duff Gordon's kimono can be seen as a symbol of her experiences in the aftermath of the *Titanic*. The garment, complete with its stains, serves as a marker of the way her reputation was soiled in the weeks and months after the sinking of the ship. Yet it also stands for something more subtle. Just as the inquiry could not pin down the motivation or behaviour of the Duff Gordons in lifeboat number one – did they row away from the dying; did Sir Cosmo give a bribe? – so the kimono resists attempts to define itself. Is the garment authentic? Was Lady Duff Gordon really wearing it the night the *Titanic* sank? Are the stains it bears the marks of her seasickness and the splashes of salty water? Could it be the kimono once owned by Lady Duff Gordon's daughter, Esmé? If not, where did it come from? Why did the family believe it to be the *Titanic* kimono for such a long time?

Whatever the truth, the kimono carries the spirit of Lady Duff Gordon (if nothing else), a slippery quality that defies categorisation. She was notoriously elusive, constantly contradicting herself about her actions on the night of the *Titanic* and finally abandoning herself to what can only be interpreted as a permanent dream state. The kimono captures her ambiguity, her abstruseness. Any 'normal' person – her husband, for example – would have felt a certain amount of shame after the *Titanic*. Not Lucy. She existed on a different plane. As she explained in the closing pages of her memoirs, for her the realms of fantasy were always a better place to exist:

'I do regret the passing of so much of the romance which made the world a very pleasant place in the past. It is possible to look upon realities too much, so that you lose the power of make-believe, and I think that perhaps is a mistake which we are all making today.'[71]

Six

THE WORLD'S MOST WILLING WHIPPING BOY

Bruce Ismay twisted round in the lifeboat and turned his back on the *Titanic* as it sank deeper into the water. He could not bear to see the luxurious liner – which he described as 'the latest thing in the art of shipbuilding'[1] – disappear below the waves. Yet he had no choice but to listen to the awful screams of the dying, a sound that would stay with him for the rest of his life. During the course of the next five or so hours, the managing director of the White Star Line – a man who had been called 'King of the Atlantic' – stared into the darkness as he rowed, wishing he could disappear. By the time his lifeboat, collapsible C, drew up alongside the *Carpathia*, at around 6.15 a.m., he had already become so tortured that he could no longer communicate with the outside world; one witness described him as looking 'pitiable'.[2] Suffering from a form of traumatic shock so extreme that today it would almost be treated as a type of dissociative disorder, Ismay had to be confined to the doctor's cabin, where he was prescribed mind-numbing opiates. Ismay slipped further into a state of nervous collapse with each piece of bad news. First there was the incomprehensible statistic, the loss of over 1,500 lives, and then the slow torture of individual messages relating to the deaths of those close to him: his butler, John Richard Fry; his secretary, William Henry Harrison; the *Titanic*'s Captain, Edward Smith; the ship's chief designer and builder, Thomas Andrews, who was also the nephew of the chairman of Harland and Wolff, Lord Pirrie, and Dr O'Loughlin, who had worked with the White Star Line for thirty years and who had dined with Ismay the night of the collision.

On 15 April, Ismay managed to compose a short telegram, which was sent to the White Star Line. It read: 'Deeply regret advise you *Titanic* sank this morning after collision iceberg, resulting serious loss life. Full particulars later.' However, by the time seventeen-year-old Jack Thayer knocked on the door of his cabin, just as the ship was approaching New York, Ismay had entered what can only be described as a fugue state. 'He was seated, in his pajamas, on his bunk, staring straight ahead, shaking all over like a leaf,' observed Thayer. He did not register the presence of the boy in the cabin and neither did he respond when Thayer tried to reassure him that it was right that he had taken a place in one of the last lifeboats to leave the ship. Instead, the forty-nine-year-old man, who normally dominated a room with his six-foot-three frame, continued to stare straight ahead as if looking into an abyss. 'I am almost certain that on the *Titanic* his hair had been black with slight tinges of gray,' said Jack Thayer, 'but now his hair was virtually snow white. I have never seen a man so completely wrecked. Nothing I could do or say brought any response.'[3]

Ismay's self-imposed isolation – which appears to have been born out of an instinctive desire for self-preservation rather than any sense of shame or fear – did not earn him many friends aboard the rescue ship. A small group of recently widowed first-class women started to talk amongst themselves about how outrageous it was that they, who had been forced to sleep on blankets in public places on the *Carpathia*, had lost their husbands, while Ismay, cosseted away in the comfort of a cabin, had survived the disaster. Little did Ismay or anyone else for that matter realise at this stage how a few snide comments would mutate and grow into an international hate campaign against him. At issue was the fact that, while he had survived, at least 111 women and 54 children had died, along with at least 1,327 men. Ismay's trauma regarding this issue was witnessed at close quarters by Second Officer Lightoller.

'I may say that at that time Mr Ismay did not seem to me to be in a mental condition to finally decide anything,' he told the American inquiry. 'I tried my utmost to rouse Mr Ismay, for he was obsessed with the idea, and kept repeating, that he ought to have gone down with the ship because he found that women had gone down. I told him there was no such reason; I told him a very great deal; I tried to get that idea out of his head, but he was taken with it – and I know the doctor tried, too – but we had difficulty in arousing Mr Ismay, purely owing to that wholly and solely, that women had gone down in the boat and he had not.'[4]

Despite his delicate mental state, Ismay had no choice but to try and pull himself together. People started asking questions of him, they needed decisions to be made and, as the managing director of the White Star Line, one of the most high-profile survivors, he had to assume a certain level of responsibility. However, at times, he was uncertain not only what he should say, but also who he was – as a result of the trauma, his identity was fragmenting, his powers of reason were eluding him and his memory was beginning to fail. To the outside world, he appeared to display occasional moments of clarity – for example, as the *Carpathia* approached New York he signed a telegram using the personal, coded signature of 'Yamsi', to the White Star Line's New York office asking that the company's ship, the *Cedric*, be held in port until he arrived so that he, together with the crew, could use it to return to Britain. 'Please send outfit of clothes, including shoes, for me to *Cedric*,' he added. 'Have nothing of my own.'

Soon after the *Carpathia* docked at the Cunard pier, Phillip Franklin, vice-president of the International Mercantile Marine Company in New York, entered Ismay's cabin, and explained to him that outside there were two gentlemen who wanted to talk to him. There was going to be a Congressional inquiry into the disaster and these two men – Senator Charles Alden Smith of Michigan and Senator Francis Newlands of Nevada – would like to ask him a few questions. Ismay, who had in effect been playing a part demanded of him for many years, adopted as best he could the role that had been selected for him by his father. The mask he wore spoke of duty and diligence, repression and regularity. The words he spoke – jumbled, a little nonsensical to begin with – were those he knew were expected of him. The two senators entered the cabin and informed Ismay that the inquiry would open the next morning at the Waldorf Astoria Hotel and that he, together with some of the *Titanic*'s crew, should make themselves available for questioning. He nodded, and agreed that he would place himself at the disposal of the inquiry. After all, he said, he had nothing to hide. As Ismay walked down the gangway, he faced a barrage of reporters, to whom he handed a written statement:

'In the presence and under the shadow of a catastrophe so overwhelming my feelings are too deep for expression in words, I can only say that the White Star Line, its officers and employees will do everything humanly possible to alleviate the suffering and sorrow of the survivors and of the relatives of those who have perished. The *Titanic* was the last word in shipbuilding. Every regulation prescribed by the British Board of Trade had been strictly complied with, the master, officers and crew were the most experienced and skilful in the British service.

'I am informed that a committee at the United States Senate has been appointed to investigate the circumstances of the accident. I heartily welcome the most complete and exhaustive inquiry and any aid that I, or my associates, or our builders or navigators can render is at the service of the public and the Governments of both the United States and Great Britain.

'Under the circumstances I must respectfully defer making any further statement at this time.'[5]

Ismay spent the night at the Ritz Carlton, and the next day, just before 10.30 a.m., he arrived at the Waldorf Astoria Hotel to hear the opening declaration set out by Senator Smith. The Committee on Commerce had been authorised to investigate the causes of the wreck of the *Titanic*, 'with its attendant loss of life so shocking to the civilized world'.

Ismay was the first witness to be called to the stand. After asking Ismay to state his full name, age and place of residence, Senator Smith asked him to describe his occupation. 'Ship owner,' he said. Was he an officer of the White Star Line? He was, he said. In what capacity? 'Managing Director.' Was he officially designated to make the trial trip of the *Titanic*? 'No,' said Ismay. Was he a voluntary passenger? 'A voluntary passenger, yes,' he said. Ismay – who expressed his 'sincere grief at this deplorable catastrophe' – went on to outline the history of the ship, its trials, its arrival in Southampton, before describing the night of the collision, relating everything in a voice barely louder than a whisper. 'I presume the impact awakened me,' he said. 'I lay in bed for a moment or two afterwards, not realizing, probably, what had happened. Eventually I got up and walked along the passageway and met one of the stewards, and said, "What has happened?" He said, "I do not know, sir." I then went back into my room, put my coat on, and went up on the bridge, where I found Captain Smith. I asked him what had happened, and he said, "We have struck ice." I said, "Do you think the ship is seriously damaged?" He said, "I am afraid she is."'[6]

As far as he could recall he spent the best part of the rest of the night helping to launch the lifeboats and putting women and children into the rescue vessels. He stood on the starboard side of the ship until he left the *Titanic* in what he thought was 'the last boat to leave the ship'.[7]

The senator was keen to investigate the speed of the liner. On the run from Southampton to Cherbourg the *Titanic* was running at over 68 revolutions; the stretch between France and Ireland was covered at 70 revolutions; on the second day of the journey the ship's speed increased to about 72 revolutions, he said, while on the third it accelerated again to 75. 'I understand it has been stated that the ship was going at full speed,' said Ismay. 'The ship never had been at full speed. The full speed of the ship is 78 revolutions. She works up to 80. So far as I am aware, she never exceeded 75 revolutions. She had not all her boilers on . . . It was our intention, if we had fine weather on Monday afternoon or Tuesday, to drive the ship at full speed. That, owing to the unfortunate catastrophe, never eventuated.'

After examining other aspects of that tragic night, Senator Smith returned to the topic of speed once more, at which point Ismay's carefully constructed façade – his mask of normality – began to crack. Was he right to understand, asked Smith, that the ship was going more than 70 revolutions? 'Yes, sir,' said Ismay, 'she was going 75 revolutions on Tuesday.' On Tuesday? 'No, I am wrong – on Saturday. I am mixed up as to the days.'

Senator Smith asked a great many questions of Ismay, but the one that must have rankled was about the women and children on the ship – had they all been saved? 'I am afraid not, sir,' replied Ismay. What proportion was saved? 'I have no idea,' he said. 'I have not asked. Since the accident I have made very few inquiries of any sort.' Then the senator turned to his behaviour on board the *Carpathia*. Had he tried to interfere with the wireless communication on that ship? 'I was never out of my room from the time I got on board the *Carpathia* until the ship docked here last night,' he said. 'I never moved out of the room.' How had he been dressed? 'I had a suit of pajamas on, a pair of slippers, a suit of clothes, and an overcoat,' he said.[8]

Once Ismay had completed his evidence for that day – he would be recalled on day eleven – James A. Hughes, the Republican representative for West Virginia, whose daughter Mary Eloise Hughes Smith had lost her husband in the disaster, stood up and addressed the chairman. Before him he had a request from a West Virginian newspaper asking him to give his thoughts on the *Titanic* disaster, particularly in regard to a comment he was alleged to have made regarding the chairman of the White Star Line, 'that Ismay should be lynched'. He stated that he had sent a reply outlining the falsity of such reports. 'I may have said, if investigation showed neglect of any officer, no punishment was too severe for him,' said Hughes. 'Ismay was somewhat criticized by some for being among the men who were rescued.'[9]

Ismay's name was being used and abused by the popular press; statements were twisted, facts ignored, and opinions were proffered by journalists keen to bring down the mighty chairman. 'A queer jumbled business' was how eyewitness John Galsworthy described the inquiry. 'We heard the unfortunate Ismay gave his evidence very quietly and well. The system and public is to blame for the miserable calamity; and of course the same public is all agog to fix the blame on some unhappy shoulders.'[10]

Within a few days of stepping on to American soil, Ismay had been branded a coward. The starkest example of this was a full-page cartoon of Ismay, showing him in a lifeboat, with the sinking ship in the distance and accompanied by the caption, 'THIS IS J. BRUTE ISMAY'. The words underneath the cartoon stated, 'We respectfully suggest that the emblem of the

White Star be changed to that of a "Yellow Liver"', with the additional 'A Picture that will live in the public memory for ever, J. Bruce Ismay safe in a lifeboat while 1,500 people drown'.[11] Another newspaper claimed that Ismay cared for nobody but himself and that he had managed to come through the tragedy completely untouched and unmoved. 'He leaves his ship to sink with its powerless cargo of lives and does not care to lift his eyes,' it added. 'He crawls through unspeakable disgrace to his own safety, seizes upon the best accommodation in the *Carpathia* to hold communion with his own unapproachable conduct.'[12] Newspapers owned by William Randolph Hearst were particularly vicious about Ismay, partly due to the antipathy the media proprietor felt towards the chairman of the White Star Line. The two men had met a number of years previously at a New York party and had apparently taken an instant dislike to one another. Now, Hearst could get his revenge on a man he thought was standoffish and cold.

Ismay's case was not helped by the increasingly deafening call from relatives of high-profile victims, all keen to articulate their anger that he had survived while those close to them had perished. Typical were the words of Alfred Stead – the brother of writer and journalist William T. Stead who had died on the *Titanic* – who said, 'Speaking of Mr Ismay, by what right was he was saved? He was higher in the White Star service than the Captain of the *Titanic*. Why did he not stick to the ship and share the fate of the victims of the line's faults and misfortunes? If he had been picked out of the water, one could excuse him – but it is said here that he took a place in a boat – a place which certainly belonged to some woman or man for whose life White Star had assumed responsibility. True American indignation is easily understood and I hope all the facts in the affair will be ruthlessly brought to light.'[13] Attacks such as these did not, of course, help Ismay's already fragile state of mind and it was even rumoured back in Liverpool that he had committed suicide.

After the inquiry had moved from New York to Washington, Ismay took the stand once more. He began to display the same state of mind that he had demonstrated on the first day of his testimony. Had he occupied cabin B-56 on the *Titanic*? 'I am not sure whether I said 52 or 56,' he replied. 'But a gentleman who was on the stand yesterday said he had 52, and if he had, I could not have had it. I must have been in 56, I think.' Although Ismay actually occupied three rooms – B-52, B-54 and B-56 – the uncertainty with which he expressed something as simple as this undermined his response. How long had he been the managing director of the International Mercantile Marine Company? 'The general manager?' asked Ismay. Senator Smith repeated the question in a more straightforward manner – how long had he held his current office? 'I think since about 1910, sir,' he said. 'I succeeded Mr Griscom.' Ismay got the date wrong by six years – he took over the position in 1904 – an indication that by now his mind, his memory, his whole sense of self, was in the process of fragmenting and breaking down.

What is also notable is the contradictory evidence Ismay gave on how he came to save himself. How did he manage to secure a place in the last lifeboat to leave the starboard side of the ship? On day eleven of the American inquiry, he was asked by Senator Smith whether anyone had told him to enter the boat. 'No one, sir,' he said. Why did he then enter it? 'Because there was room in the boat,' he said. 'She was being lowered away. I felt the ship was going down, and I got into the boat.'[14] He repeated this statement during the British investigation into the disaster, even though it was a lie. According to evidence supplied by witness August Weikman, the ship's barber, in a number of press interviews and an affidavit sworn on 24 April 1912, Ismay had been ordered into the lifeboat by an officer.

Later, Bruce confessed to his sister-in-law, Constance, the truth of the matter: that Chief Officer Wilde, who did not survive the sinking, had indeed ordered him into the lifeboat.[15] If Ismay had related this at the inquiries, he might have been able to salvage enough remnants of his reputation to safeguard his position in society. As it was, it seems he made an unconscious decision to cast himself as an eager participant in the drama in which he played the role of the victim. In fact, the *Titanic* disaster and its brutal aftermath tapped into a deep-seated desire to be punished. Bruce Ismay was a masochist at heart and his thoroughly unpleasant treatment after the *Titanic* sank gave him the perfect opportunity to satisfy a clutch of previously unacknowledged impulses. He needed to be castigated, rejected, disciplined and maltreated and the *Titanic* provided him with the ideal circumstances through which he could mould himself into the world's most willing whipping boy.

Bruce Ismay's readiness to take on the role of scapegoat, his compulsion to punish himself in the years following the *Titanic* disaster, can be traced back to his early life. Born in Crosby, Merseyside, on 12 December 1862, Joseph Bruce Ismay was the eldest son of Margaret Bruce and Thomas Henry Ismay, a self-made man who transformed himself from an apprentice working in a Liverpool shipping firm to the millionaire owner of the White Star Line. T.H. Ismay was a typical product of the Victorian age: a man who defined himself by the concrete trappings of success – at the height of his career he owned a mansion on the Wirral with twenty-two indoor and ten outdoor servants. He was a sturdy, forceful presence who loathed sentiment, sickness and lack of success. He pushed the deaths of his children – Mary, known as Polly, who died at the age of eleven in 1871, and Henry Sealby, who died in 1866, aged only two years old – to the back of his mind, believing, as was customary, that to dwell on misery was self-indulgent. He wanted his eldest son to be everything he was and more: tough, self-reliant, bold, and exhibiting the kind of industrial strength that defined the age. 'From what I can gather,' says Bruce Ismay's granddaughter, Pauline Matarasso, 'he was not particularly kind to his son.'[16]

In 1880, after being educated at Elstree and Harrow schools, seventeen-year-old Bruce signed on for a term of five years as an apprentice at his father's firm, Ismay, Imrie and Company, in Liverpool. In his indenture of apprenticeship he promised to 'faithfully serve his said Masters [and] their Secrets keep, their lawful Commands gladly obey and do; hurt to his said Masters he shall not do, or suffer to be done by others, when it is in his power to prevent the same: . . . nor do any other Act, Matter, or Thing whatsoever, to the Prejudice of his said Masters but in all things shall demean and behave himself towards his Masters and all theirs as a faithful apprentice ought to do . . .'[17] On his first morning at work, Bruce hung his hat and coat in his father's office; when T.H. Ismay arrived he called for the clerk and told him to 'inform the new office boy that he is not to leave his coat and hat lying about my office'. By all accounts, it seems as though the relationship between the two men was seeped in mutual resentment, with the father regularly submitting his son to continued bouts of ritual humiliation, which the son then passed on to his subordinates.

As Bruce grew older, the circle of abuse widened to include his wife, Florence, the American-born daughter of George Schieffelin, a pretty, slim-waisted girl known in the society columns as 'The Belle of New York' whom Ismay married in Manhattan in December 1888. Florence, known within the family as Donna, was, according to her granddaughter, Pauline Matarasso, 'conventional, unimaginative but fun-loving', a woman who was 'made wretched by what passed for intimacy with her husband . . . Brought up to compliance and respectful of all conventions, she released the bully in her husband who took pleasure in snubbing her at dinner parties, leaving her floundering and the guests embarrassed.'[18]

Bruce's psychological difficulties were compounded by the loss of a six-month-old son, Thomas Henry, in October 1891 after a severe attack of enteritis, and the birth of a stillborn girl in 1900. Bruce Ismay loathed disability and sickness, associating it with failure and weakness, and the onset of polio in his second son, Thomas Bruce, born in 1894, affected him deeply. Thomas, who contracted the disease when he was only one year old, would be crippled for the rest of his life, and the boy grew up to be the butt of his father's jokes. Ismay 'shrank from anyone who was not physically perfect and after this [the onset of polio] his attitude to Tom was tinged with this involuntary repugnance which he tried not to show, but which the boy undoubtedly sensed'.[19]

After the birth of the couple's last child, George Bruce, born in June 1902, Florence began to suffer from an early menopause at the age of thirty-seven and, over the course of the next three years, she gradually absented herself from the marital bed until sexual relations between the couple ceased in 1905. 'Her relief was still plain,' says Pauline Matarasso, recalling a conversation she had had with her grandmother about her marriage, discussing the intimate details of her life while finishing a tapestry.[20] 'Their marriage was not a happy one – I don't see how it can have been. They never spent any time together and never went on holiday together.'[21]

Denied intimate contact with his wife, Bruce channelled his energies into his work. In 1902, the White Star Line had been absorbed into the International Mercantile Marine Company (IMM), the shipping conglomerate financed by John Pierpont Morgan. In 1904, five years after the death of his father, Ismay agreed to take on the position of president and managing director of the IMM. 'Although Bruce Ismay is often portrayed as something of a nincompoop, he was anything but that,' says Michael Manser, Ismay's great-nephew. 'When the shareholders sold the White Star Line to Pierpont Morgan they wanted Bruce to stay on as managing director. He must have been admired and respected for his abilities, otherwise this would have been the perfect time to get rid of him.'[22]

Colleagues regarded Ismay as a strict, but highly competent leader. He had, according to one who worked closely with him, a 'magnetic and dominating personality', yet he was 'quietly spoken and reserved and not the man to be on affable terms with. He was intolerant of inefficiency and inclined to be coldly cynical and critical to those who feared him.' On the day a new ship was launched, Ismay would take it upon himself to inspect the vessel, 'not hesitating to run his fingers over cornices in the alleyways to see if any dust had been left by a luckless steward'. This 'strikingly handsome man' with his 'strong figure and carriage, swarthy complexion and crisp black curly hair' took great care over his appearance – especially his carefully coiffeured moustache – while 'his clothes were always perfect and his shoes a dream – he kept a manservant'. For all the confidence he might have inspired in those who worked for him, it was difficult to get close to him. 'One got the impression that beyond maybe his wife and one or two members of his family he hadn't a real friend in the world, only business associates who admired, feared, or toadied up to him.'[23]

In the summer of 1907, Lord and Lady Pirrie invited Ismay and his wife to their house in Belgrave Square. After dinner, Lord Pirrie – who was a partner in Harland and Wolff, the Belfast shipbuilders favoured by the White Star Line – set out a daring proposal: to build a monster of a ship such as the world had never seen. Pirrie was worried about the White Star Line being outclassed by the Cunard liners the *Lusitania* and the *Mauretania*, and that night the two men outlined their plans for not just one, but a trio of colossal, luxurious ships – the *Olympic*, the *Titanic*, the *Gigantic* – that would dominate the Atlantic. Still haunted by the barbs and taunts of his father, who had died in 1899, Ismay believed that he still had something to prove. Bruce wanted to construct something monumental, something awe-inspiring, something truly majestic. The *Titanic* may seem to be the very definition of hubris – a concrete symbol of the machine age, an attempt by man to triumph over nature – but in fact it was born of insecurity.

Curiously, however, whatever drive Ismay had possessed seemed to disappear almost as soon as the *Titanic* had been built. In fact, it seems the ship began to suck the life out of Bruce Ismay many months before the collision, casting a curse on the man who had created her, like a mercantile reworking of Frankenstein and his monster. Suddenly the whole business started to tire him and, behind the scenes, Ismay began the slow process of extricating himself from his role as president of the IMM. In January 1912, he wrote to Harold Sanderson, his friend and deputy, saying that he was prepared to step down so as to make way for him to take over the role of 'the premier position in the business'. Ismay asked Sanderson, in a letter dated 10 January 1912, whether he would consider the proposition, 'namely that I will remain on as President of the IMM Co. until the 31 December 1912, during which period I would practically make London my headquarters, coming to Liverpool, say, once a week, in order to attend to my duties . . .'[24] Finally, after a great deal of correspondence between the interested parties – Ismay, Sanderson and Charles Steele, the secretary of J.P Morgan and Company of Wall Street, New York – it was decided that Ismay would retire from the job on 30 June 1913.

For his part, it seems Ismay had a strange sense that things would not go quite as planned. On 7 March, just over a month before the *Titanic* was due to sail on its maiden voyage, Ismay wrote to Albert Ballin, the director of the Hamburg-American Line, stating that he was worried about the fact there was no 'graving dock' – a dry dock where ships are maintained and repaired – in America that could accommodate big liners like the *Olympic* and the *Titanic*. This, he said, had given him 'much food for thought as to what would happen in the event of one of these vessels meeting with a serious accident while in American water'.[25]

Ismay also asked Charles Steele not to disclose the plans of his retirement, as 'the 30th June, 1913, is a "FAR CRY" and much may happen between now and then . . . No good purpose would be served by making any announcement, as it would only create a feeling of unrest, and the suggested changes may never come into force.'[26] The sentiment was duly repeated by Steele in his response of 2 March 1912, where, as he agreed wholeheartedly with Ismay's thoughts, he made a light-hearted joke about the existence of mental telepathy. Indeed, he added, 'There are lots of things that may happen before the 30th June, 1913.'[27]

Did Ismay think about those words as the *Titanic* began to sink? Did he perhaps reflect upon his past behaviour and the messy knot that was his psyche? Surely it was impossible that he had, albeit subconsciously, brought about the collision? He had created this monster of a ship, but had he also manufactured the conditions by which it would destroy itself? As he heard the screams of the dying in the freezing water did he think about how he had ruled against the construction of additional lifeboats? Did the memory of that ice warning that he had carried in his pocket for five or so hours begin to worry him? Was it a case of wish fulfilment on an epic scale?

Whatever thoughts passed through his mind at the time, as the *Titanic* sank so did a large part of his very being, slipping away under the cold ocean until he was no more than a living ghost. His death wish – his desire to punish himself for punishing others – was almost complete. He would spend the rest of his life in a kind of shadow land, a limbo, in which he searched endlessly for the spectre of his former self.

'The *Titanic* was most definitely a shadow over Bruce and the family,' says Pauline Matarasso. 'From that moment on, he was in a state of emotional trauma. It was said, and repeated, that nobody was to mention the subject of the *Titanic* in his presence. As far as his own marriage was concerned, I think the *Titanic* served to deepen the rift between him and his wife; it increased the sense of separation between them. It must have been hard for her to live with a man who was not only depressed, but deeply repressed, a man who cut down social life to an absolute minimum. Although he was not an unkind man, I think his unkindnesses within the family circle came from his own emotional problems. He returned [from the disaster] with a sense of self-loathing and was, in many ways, like a frozen corpse.'[28]

On 5 May 1912, Ismay – together with the surviving officers Lowe, Pitman, Lightoller and Boxall – returned to Britain on the *Adriatic*. In Queenstown, Ireland, he was met by his wife, Florence, his younger brother, Bower, and one of the company's managers, Henry Concannon, and the party continued to their final destination, Liverpool. There, Ismay waited until all the first-class passengers had disembarked, before he passed through the large number of newspapermen. He refused to answer any of their questions; instead, Concannon handed out a sheet of paper which read: 'Mr Ismay asks the gentlemen of the Press to extend their courtesy to him by not pressing for any statement from him. First, he is still suffering from the very great strain of the *Titanic* disaster and subsequent events.' He would not elaborate further, as he had yet to give his testimony before the British inquiry. However, he added that he would like to thank those who had sent him telegrams of support, 'which he appreciates in this, the greatest trial of his life'.[29]

In many respects it was a trial, but at issue was not so much Ismay's legal standing as his moral one. While he had not committed a crime in the eyes of the law, his survival meant that he had most certainly sinned against the 'natural' order of the Edwardian age. Ismay was, according to one commentator, 'thoroughly nervous as was natural for anyone as shy as he was, his features were set in a rather fixed smile, which were an attempt to hide his real feelings'.[30] The British inquiry also highlighted what many regarded as Ismay's lack of knowledge of basic seamanship. During questioning, the chairman of the White Star Line admitted, under oath, that he did not know the meaning of latitude and longitude, confessed that he was no navigator and even went so far as to say, 'I should say if a man can see far enough to clear ice, he is perfectly justified in going full speed.' Sir Robert Finlay pushed Ismay on this point. He did not expect the Captain to slow down when he had seen ice reports? 'No, certainly not,' replied Ismay. Understandably surprised by this, Thomas Scanlan, a representative of the Seafarers' Union, quizzed the chairman again on this issue. Did he or the crew take any extra precautions when they received news about the dangers of ice? 'No,' said Ismay. Really? 'No,' he repeated. Given the recent disaster, would it not be a reasonable precaution to put into action? 'That is a matter which is entirely in the hands of the Commander of the ship – he can put extra lookouts if he wishes to, at any time.' Another union representative asked him whether his company had considered the possibility of issuing instructions to its captains in regard to the navigation of ships when approaching ice? Or perhaps he had not had the time? 'I have not,' replied Ismay.

Clement Edwards MP, who represented the Dock, Wharf, Riverside and General Workers Union, questioned whether Ismay thought the *Titanic* was unsinkable. 'We thought she was,' he said. What was the reason for that belief? 'Because we thought she would float with two of the largest compartments full of water, and that the only way that those compartments were at all likely to be damaged was in case of collision,' he said. 'Another ship running into her and hitting her on the bulkhead.' Edwards then moved on to the subject of the *Baltic* telegram, which Ismay had read just before lunch on Sunday 14 April, about twelve hours before the ship hit the iceberg. Had he put the ice warning in his pocket in a fit of absent-mindedness? 'Yes, entirely,' he said. And he had carried it in his pocket for five hours until he had finally given it to the Captain in the early evening? 'Yes,' he admitted. Had he taken out the telegram at some point that afternoon and mentioned it to two ladies, Mrs Ryerson and Mrs Thayer? 'I mentioned it,' he said. Had he read it to them? 'Yes,' he said.

Edwards then moved on to discuss the number of lifeboats. If Ismay had not taken the view that the *Titanic* was unsinkable would he or would he not have insisted on provision being made for more lifeboats? 'I do not think so,' he said. So in his view the number of boats had nothing to do with the relative sinkability of the ship? 'The *Titanic* had more boats than were necessary by the Board of Trade regulations,' said Ismay. Would he please answer the question, Edwards insisted. 'What is the question?' Ismay replied. That, if he had taken the view that the ship was not unsinkable, would he not have had more lifeboats? 'No, I do not think so,' said Ismay. As managing director of the company was he one of the people responsible for determining the number of boats? 'Yes, in conjunction with the shipbuilders,' he said. When he got into the lifeboat did he know the ship was sinking? 'Yes,' he said. And that there were hundreds of people still on board? 'Yes.' People who would go down with the ship? 'Yes, I did,' he said. Had it occurred to him that, as managing director, a man who had decided on the number of boats, he owed his life to every other person on the ship? 'It has not,' he said.

If Ismay had, as he maintained, been successful in helping a number of women and children into the boats on the starboard side, why did he not do the same at other points on the ship? 'I presumed that there were people down below who were sending the people up,' Ismay replied. Yet he knew that there were hundreds of people who had not come up from the decks? He presumed that there were people below sending the passengers up? 'Yes,' Ismay said. Would it be right to say that everybody who wanted to was in the process of climbing up the ship? 'I knew that everybody could not be up,' Ismay admitted. What was the point of his answer then? 'Everybody that was on the deck got into that boat,' he said. At this point, the Commissioner interrupted Edwards to clarify his intent – in his view, was it Ismay's duty to remain on the *Titanic* until she went down? 'Frankly, that is so,' said Edwards. 'I do not flinch from it a little bit.'[31]

That night, at his grand house in Hill Street, Mayfair, Ismay broke down in front of his wife. 'He was completely exhausted mentally and physically,' said Wilton J. Oldham, who wrote a book about the White Star Line and became a close friend of the family, 'and, although he had managed to preserve some sort of self-control in court, now he was alone with Florence, the pent up emotion of the last months was released.'[32]

The following day, Ismay took the stand again. Of particular interest for the court was a recent interview that had appeared in the *Daily Mail* with Alexander Carlisle, the former managing director of Harland and Wolff. During the autumn of 1909 and the early part of 1910, when the *Titanic* and her sister ship the *Olympic* were being designed, Carlisle had presented the White Star Line with a plan to fit the liner with over forty lifeboats; Ismay, as managing director, had vetoed the plan, judging it to be too expensive. Turning to Ismay, Sir Robert Finlay asked him whether he had heard of such a design. 'No,' said Ismay. Was this quite new to him? 'It is,' he said.[33] However, in due course, Carlisle was called before the court. He not only confirmed the accuracy of the interview in the *Daily Mail*, but also stated that Ismay had personally seen and rejected the proposal. From Carlisle's point of view, he thought the *Titanic* should have carried a total of forty-eight lifeboats, three on each set of davits, vessels which would have had a capacity for nearly 2,900 people. Of course, if the plan had been approved most of *Titanic*'s passengers would have been saved.

At the end of the inquiry, Lord Mersey, the Commissioner, took it upon himself to say a few words about the conduct of Ismay. First of all, while he maintained that it was not within the jurisdiction of the court to examine the ship owner's moral behaviour, he felt he had to make a brief statement in case his silence was misinterpreted. Central to the issue was the question of whether Ismay, as managing director of the White Star Line, was under any moral duty to stay on the vessel until it sank. 'I do not agree,' said the Commissioner. 'Mr Ismay, after rending assistance to many passengers, found "C" collapsible, the last boat on the starboard side, actually being lowered. No other people were there at the time. There was room for him and he jumped in. Had he not jumped in he would merely have added one more life, namely his own, to the number of those lost.'[34]

Lord Mersey's report did little to lift Ismay's spirits. No

matter how many people wrote to him to tell him that his decision had been the right one – to go down with the ship would have been 'deliberate suicide'[35] – he couldn't shake off the depression that shadowed him. He started to take Sanatogen, a vitamin supplement, but after a few weeks he pushed it to one side. In some respects he embraced his suffering, seeing it as a small price to pay for the large loss of life for which he felt responsible. Those who had experienced hurt, loss, bereavement, depression and trauma identified with Bruce Ismay. Typical are the letters from a young girl, Elsie Stormont, who wrote to Ismay from Warrington, Merseyside. Although she had never met the chairman – and the social gulf between them was a wide one – she felt she could open her heart to him and reveal her inner pain as she instinctively knew that he would be able to understand.

'I am only a little stranger a country lassie a lonely one too because have very lately lost my mother & daddy,' she wrote. 'I have had a lot of sorrow grieving for them & I know tho' I am only a queer girl what pains in one's heart mean & awful loneliness & I have been so glad many a time for even the dumb love of my big dog who follows me everywhere.

'I know that no one can really understand your sorrow at present but will you accept from me pure beautiful sympathetic love. Even tho' I am no one but the helpless (to comfort you) lonely girl perhaps my loving sympathy may comfort you just as my big dog's dumb love comforts me often.

'It hurt me when I read you wished you had perished. God would never have let your life be spared had he not work for you to do. I have thought sometimes it would be easier to die & be with mother & daddy than live without their love but we haven't to wish for the easiest have we & your life is a useful one, not like mine where I am of no real use to anyone.

'I often wonder at God's plan but he plans all that is the best comfort. I know that is better comfort than all the sympathy in the world.

'Will you please take care of yourself & not look backwards. God spared you & I am very very grateful & tho' it may be harder at present to live than to have died God understands. There will be beautiful sunshine ahead for you.

'Forgive me intruding but if I could lessen your pains I would. Tho' I have never seen or heard you I am grateful God spared you & if my love can comfort you I ask God to let it.

Your little friend,

Elsie Stormont'[36]

Ismay responded to the girl's letter, outlining how he too, during recent moments of crisis, had received an unconditional, seemingly endless supply of love from his dog. His response made Elsie cry when she read out his words to her collie about how much he had felt sorry for her. Yet she was also heartened by his letter, as she realised that grief of this nature was no respecter of age or class. 'It hurts me to think of anyone suffering, but to suffer in one's soul is far worse than one's body,' she added.[37]

Ismay's soul was certainly in torment and he reached out for comfort in a rather indiscriminate manner. Florence, his wife, made a decision to forbid her husband or anyone within the family to mention the disaster or, in her words, 'that terrible inquiry',[38] believing that simply not talking about the *Titanic* would make the horror disappear. She took him to stay in Dalnaspidal, a remote shooting lodge rented by Bruce's brother, Bower, near Aviemore, Scotland, thinking that the peace and quiet would do him good. Yet the isolation only served to increase his anxiety and deepen his depression.

Relations between husband and wife were far from easy anyway and the couple had ceased having intimate contact in 1905. Deprived of sexual contact with his wife and forced to endure the agony of being unable to talk about the most traumatic event in his life, Bruce turned to someone who had experienced the nightmare of the *Titanic*, a woman who had lost her husband in the disaster – Marian Longstreth Morris Thayer. As a fellow victim, he assumed that they could embark on a mutually beneficial relationship of co-dependence and so he initiated a transatlantic survivors' support group, an exchange of letters that enabled Ismay to articulate aspects of his life and experience that were censored at home. Ten letters survive – documents written over the course of 1912 and 1913, which reveal both Ismay's utter wretchedness and his masochistic tendencies. In one letter he talks of how he is sitting by the open window, writing, while his wife has gone to church, his mind and body full of yearning for Marian: 'Oh, how I wish you were here and we could sit out in the garden and help each other. It would be lovely. I feel, now, that you are very close to me, I wonder if you are.'

He goes on to confess the sins of his personality – his awful undemonstrative nature, his inability to show his feelings to those of whom he is fond. As a result, he says, people assume he has a cold, distant, superior character. 'Of course one cannot hurt other people without hurting oneself,' he says. 'Very often a word would make things right, one's horrid pride slips in and this causes unhappiness. I wonder if you know all I mean. I can hear you saying what a horrible character and I agree. I absolutely hate myself. Tell me what I can do to cure myself.'

Of course, the reality was that he did not really want to cure himself; rather, part of him actually revelled in his new-found victimhood. Marian had told him not to be so repressed – 'don't lock yourself tight up' – and Ismay seized upon the phrase, using it as another opportunity through which he could torture himself. 'When did you notice that this was another of my failings,' he asked. 'Do you know I always put my worse side forward and very few people ever get under the surface. I cannot help it, can you help me to change my nature?'[39]

This constant pleading for Marian's spiritual or emotional assistance only served to push her further away and by June 1913 communication between them ceased. Ismay was left feeling rejected, irritated, frustrated and disappointed, complaining to her that a cable was no proper substitute for a letter. Yet Marian could take no more of his neediness. His pleading, pathetic tone was, at times, repellent. 'I never want to see a ship again, and I loved them so and took such an interest in the captains and officers,' he wrote to her. 'What an ending to my life. Perhaps I was too proud of the ships and this is my punishment.'[40] Unlike him, she did not want to spend the rest of her life as a victim. Although she brought their epistolary relationship to a close, she did keep a popular four-line verse that Bruce had sent her framed on her dressing table; the poem remained there for the rest of her life until she died on the thirtieth anniversary of the *Titanic* sinking in April 1942.

'With cheerful steps the path of duty run,
God never does, nor suffers to be done,
But what you would yourself, could you but see
The end of all things here, as well as He.'

It was an interesting choice of lines for Ismay. On the surface, the poem, which could be found reproduced in many religious books of the day, encourages those encountering difficulties to endure their fate and draw strength from an omniscient, omnipresent God. Yet, if one looks a little deeper into the subtext of the verse, one can also read the lines as an expression of Ismay's own peculiar psychology, an articulation of his masochistic appetites. He would have to be stoical about what had happened on and off the *Titanic*, but was it not also something he had unconsciously willed into being? God's actions were merely a reflection of his own dark psyche. He did not want to recover from the ordeal, neither did he want to forget it. Rather, he wallowed in its tragedy for the rest of his life, drowning in the turbulent waters of its aftermath for the next twenty-five years.

No matter how hard those close to him tried to alter his view, Ismay had decided that the *Titanic* had destroyed his existence. 'I am not belittling what you have been through, nor the effect it must have, but you are letting your mind dwell too much on morbid introspection,' wrote his friend William B. Boulton, in August 1912. 'You are arguing with yourself in a vicious circle which always lands you where you started . . . Now do not say again that your life is ruined – don't say it, or even admit it to yourself. You are still suffering from nervous shock which would have broken most men down and you are not competent to judge . . . The only cure is time and you can shorten or lengthen that according to how you live and how you think . . . Just now you are suffering from mental astigmatism and your perspective is all astray.'[41]

Ismay spent the rest of his life trying to make himself invisible. If he travelled by train he would make sure he journeyed at night and would reserve a whole compartment just for himself. His staff would prepare a cold supper for him so he wouldn't have to venture into the dining car and he would ensure that the blinds were drawn in his carriage. According to Frank Bustard, who worked closely with him at the White Star Line, he spent the last third of his life 'in seclusion . . . any reference to the *Titanic* disaster was absolutely taboo. What his own thoughts must have been, beggar the imagination.'[42] Even the continued love of his children did little to relieve his suffering. 'I very much hope that the worst is over now and that you will never again be misjudged and your words misinterpreted as they have been in the present inquiry,' wrote Thomas Bruce to his father, while Ismay was staying at Dalnaspidal, Scotland. 'I hope . . . that you will not be recognised as I know how you must hate to be before the public eye especially under the present trying circumstances.'[43]

It was while he was at Dalnaspidal that Ismay came across the details for The Lodge, Costelloe, a cottage in County Galway; the idea of being able to escape London and Liverpool for the wilds of Ireland appealed to him and he bought it unseen. Yet, as he contemplated his future, he began to worry about what he would do with the rest of his life; perhaps self-erasure wasn't such a good idea after all. The more time he had alone to contemplate what had happened, the more he loathed himself.

In the autumn of 1912, Ismay wrote to the directors of the Morgan Combine with a proposal: while he would stand down as president of the IMM he would still like to stay on as chairman of the White Star Line. After his plea was turned down, he wrote once again, stating that, 'I am bound to have a good deal of sentiment in connection with the White Star Line. I quite understand junior men will be promoted when I go and rightly so, but I cannot see how my remaining a director of the White Star Line will in any way hamper matters . . . I wish you would reconsider the matter, only so far as the White Star Line is concerned.'[44] His attempt to keep the position his father had bequeathed him can be seen as just another exercise in self-punishment and self-degradation. As he pleaded for his job he must have known what the answer would be; by now almost an addict of humiliation, he needed to be repeatedly rejected. After his begging letter was rejected by the board, Ismay went so far as to plead with Harold Sanderson, who had taken over as president of the IMM. Sanderson raised the issue with E.C. Grenfell, the chairman of the British committee of the

IMM, who in turn informed Ismay that the conglomerate would not change its mind.

At the end of December, Ismay finally sent off his letters of resignation, confiding to one friend, 'I do not expect to go to America again.'[45] Those who occupied Ismay's social circle – an environment that by now Bruce regarded as resembling one of Dante's circles of hell – did not, of course, understand the complexities of the situation.

'I would have liked you to remain head of the magnificent firm your dear father had built up,' wrote Lady Pirrie from her husband's yacht *Valiant*. 'You are so clever and *so* capable that it seems an awful thing you do . . . then my second feeling is – why at a certain age – when one has worked hard – should one not retire and enjoy the remaining years the fruits of one's work. You are just a bit too young to retire . . . I wish the last year of your connection had been a less sad and trying one – but one can only feel – "He knoweth what is best for us" – and that in time we may be able to see the great loss and sorrow was for some good purpose.'[46]

The passing of time did nothing to salve the psychological wounds inflicted by the *Titanic*. Nearly a year after the disaster, John Pierpont Morgan, head of the IMM, died at the age of seventy-five. A close friend wrote to Ismay saying it was 'that tragedy which broke his heart, even as it did yours'.[47] With each passing year, Ismay turned in upon himself. He spent the summers at the lodge in Costelloe – where he indulged his love of salmon and trout fishing. In London, he often attended afternoon concerts at St George's Hall, where he always bought two tickets – one for himself, another for his hat and coat. His routine was precise and unchangeable – a boiled egg for breakfast, a pot of tea and an apple; if he was in Liverpool, staying at the family home, Sandheys, he would take lunch at the Palatine Club; dinner, at home, would be fried Dover sole, a crust of bread, and another apple. If he was at the house in London he would ask the cooks to bake an old-fashioned cottage loaf from which the bottom had to be cut off – into the bread he would then sandwich dry bacon or cold meats. 'He would then eat that throughout the day,' remembers former kitchen maid Agnes Thwaite.[48]

Often Ismay would walk through the parks of London where he passed the time talking to tramps and down-and-outs, men he felt he could empathise with. In a way, these disenfranchised citizens were more blessed than he was – after all, they did not have to live with the burden of guilt that constantly shadowed his thoughts.

'He tormented himself with useless speculation as to how the disaster could possibly have been avoided,' said one family friend. 'If only he had not ordered the building of the ship in the first place or if only she had struck the iceberg in any other way; these and similar thoughts haunted him continually, but he was not able to have the relief of discussing the subject, which might have helped share the burden, as Florence would never have the subject mentioned.'[49]

At Christmas 1936, Bruce and Florence went to have lunch with their daughter, Evelyn, and her three children. One of the boys, who had a vague knowledge that his grandfather had been involved in the shipping industry, looked up from the table and asked, 'Grandpa, have you ever been shipwrecked?' The jovial atmosphere soured in an instant; the unmentionable had been mentioned. Ismay cleared his throat and replied, 'Yes, I was once in a ship which was believed to be unsinkable.' They were the first words he had spoken about the *Titanic* in nearly twenty-five years, but Florence was not going to have her husband upset, and she quickly changed the subject. 'My grandmother, Constance, who was Florence's sister, told me that Florence would not let Bruce talk about the *Titanic*,' says

Michael Manser. 'Constance felt it would have been better for him if he had been able to discuss it. As a result, the memory of it lingered on in the family. I remember in my grandmother's family it was forbidden for any of the staff to read the *Daily Mail*, as they had been particularly unpleasant about Bruce after the *Titanic*.'[50]

Agnes Thwaite, who worked in the kitchens at Bruce and Florence's house in Mayfair in the early 1930s, witnessed Ismay's ostracism by London society. Although master and servant never had much communication – as she says, 'I was downstairs and he was upstairs' – she observed at close quarters Ismay's lonely existence within the grand house on Hill Street. 'My overall impression of Bruce Ismay was that he was incredibly solitary,' says Agnes, now in her late nineties. 'London society rejected him and I remember he spent a lot of time just walking around, sitting in the park, going to the cinema by himself. The *Titanic* was never to be mentioned in the house, that was definitely off limits. Mr Ismay was a sad, lonely figure, but he was a very kind man – after I married the first footman, Angus, and had my first child, Bruce Ismay bought us a pram. His wife, who was American, was very nice, very small; she was a dainty little woman and only took a size two shoe. I also remember that, in the large front hall of the house, there were plans of all the ships. He would have had to see those drawings every day as he came in or went out of the house, something which must have been incredibly hard for him, as they must have reminded him of the *Titanic* and everything he had lost.'[51]

As Ismay aged, he developed diabetes and began to suffer from circulation problems in his legs. In the summer of 1936, while staying at Costelloe, the pain in his legs became so intense that he was forced to call upon the help of his former butler, John Smith. Smith felt at a loss about what to do, and thought it would be best if Ismay returned to London. The retired butler packed up his former employer's possessions from his beloved Lodge – a sanctuary that Ismay would never see again – and returned to Hill Street with him. There, in his bedroom, Ismay underwent an operation to amputate his right leg, the part running from below his knee down to his foot. 'Smith never left his side except to sleep and slowly Bruce regained his strength, but he withdrew more and more into himself,' remembers a family friend. 'He hated his disability and would no longer visit the theatres and concert halls which he loved. He was now in a wheel chair and had a set of crutches which he loathed.'[52]

The masochist in Bruce must have been satisfied. Finally, the punishment he was forced to endure was a physical one, a similar type of suffering to that borne by his own son, Tom, whom he had taunted and mocked all those years ago. The amputation also symbolised a kind of impotence, a sign of his own powerlessness, another excuse to hate himself even more. On the morning of 14 October 1937, Bruce began to ready himself to take a bath. In spite of his disability he tried to maintain a sense of independence and had overseen a system of pulleys that were designed to help him in and out of the tub. After turning on the taps, the butler, Warr, returned to the room to check on his master, only to find that he had collapsed in the armchair at the foot of the bed. Ismay was unconscious. The doctor who was called discovered that Ismay had suffered a stroke, which had left him blind and mute. Three days later, on Sunday 17 October, Ismay died, aged seventy-four.

The next day Florence received dozens of letters of condolence. One friend said that Ismay's death was 'a very merciful ending'[53] while another wrote how sad it had been 'to see him doomed to a life of suffering with no hope of enjoyment of his old activities. You will be thankful his days of suffering are over, and unknown worlds about him – the great adventure!'[54] Smith, his former butler, said that he would mourn his master's passing as much as any of his family, and another friend wrote to say that the flags of Liverpool, the town where the White Star Line had been born, were all flying at half-mast as a mark of respect. On Thursday, 21 October, at 2.30 in the afternoon, a funeral was held for Ismay at St Paul's, Knightsbridge, London. But even here, he could not escape the sea. The service, conducted by the Reverend Hamilton, included the reading of Psalm 121, verses from Revelation 21, 'Then I saw a new heaven and a new earth; for the first heaven and the first earth had passed away, and the sea was no more . . .', and the hymns 'Lead, Kindly Light', and 'Crossing the Bar', written by Tennyson:

Sunset and evening star,
And one clear call for me!
And may there be no moaning of the bar,
When I put out to sea.
But such a tide as moving seems asleep,
Too full for sound and foam,
When that which drew from out the boundless deep
Turns again home.

The obituary in *The Times*, headed 'An Able Shipowner', stated that Ismay 'was the subject of criticism, not well informed, both in England and in America, for his conduct in leaving the *Titanic* at all'. Although Lord Mersey exempted him from criticism, 'the affair cast a shadow over Mr Ismay'.[55] The *New York Times* noted how Ismay, after the disaster, had donated $50,000 to a pension fund for widows of the crew and how, in 1924, he had created the National Mercantile Marine Fund with an endowment of $125,000. The *Washington Post* took a more negative line – their headline read, 'Owner Who Fled Stricken

Titanic Dies a Recluse' – pointing out that while American icons such as John Jacob Astor, Benjamin Guggenheim and Major Archibald Butt chose to stay behind on the ship, Ismay saved his own skin. The newspaper also included an anonymous quote from one of the ship's officers who is supposed to have said, twenty-two years after the disaster, 'Ismay did the worst thing he ever did in his life when he got into that lifeboat.'[56] The *Journal of Commerce*, in its assessment of his life and career, stated that Ismay was, to most people, something of an enigma. 'He had the reputation of being austere, severe, aloof, and inflexible,' it said. 'Inflexible he certainly was, but it was a decision of character and not mere obstinacy.'[57]

Ismay left an estate, irrespective of property, valued at £693,305. To his son, Thomas Bruce, he bequeathed the casket in which the freedom of the city of Belfast had been presented to his own father, the illuminated address given to T.H. Ismay by the shareholders of the Oceanic Navigation Company, the silver salver left to Bruce by his grandfather, various lawn tennis prizes, and the gold cigarette case given to him by Florence. To his youngest son, George Bruce, he gave the watch and chain that had once belonged to his own grandfather, and the wristwatch given to him by his wife. He left a silver table centrepiece and one other piece of silver (of her choosing) to his youngest daughter, Evelyn, while to his eldest daughter, Margaret, he bequeathed a silver centrepiece passed down to him by his mother, and another one given to him by William Imrie, his father's partner. Yet it was the final object Ismay chose to leave to Margaret that perhaps carries the greatest emotional resonance: his ring, which bore the inscription, 'Be mindful'.

The words had been echoing in his head every day since the *Titanic* went down.

Seven

THE DARK SIDE OF SURVIVAL

At 10.30 on the night of 9 October 1914, forty-four-year-old Annie Robinson left the main saloon of the *Devonian* and ran out on deck. The liner had become shrouded in thick fog as the ship neared its final destination of Boston. The booming sound of the foghorn forced Annie to relive once again the awful experience on board the *Carpathia* as it approached New York, which in turn triggered the memory of her time on the *Titanic*. In an instant, the former ship's stewardess – who was travelling on the Leyland liner from Liverpool to Boston to see her daughter – was taken back to the moment two and a half years earlier when she had realised that the *Titanic* was sinking.

Soon after the *Titanic*'s collision, she had got out of bed, dressed quickly, and rushed along E deck, following the Captain and Thomas Andrews in the direction of the mail room. When she got to the top of the stairs, which led to the mail room, she looked down and saw two mail bags and a man's Gladstone bag floating in the water. Within half an hour of the collision the sea had reached within six steps of the top of the stairs and the water was rising higher with each minute. Annie's thoughts immediately turned to her charges – seven ladies in first class, a maid and a governess. She busied herself with the preparation of lifebelts and blankets, yet she gave little thought to herself. As she started to make her way up to A deck, she came across Andrews, who told her to 'put your lifebelt on and walk about and let the passengers see you'. Annie wasn't sure of this, replying, 'It looks rather mean,' at which point Andrews said, 'No, put it on. Well, if you value your life put your belt on.'[1]

Annie Robinson left the *Titanic* in lifeboat eleven, which was launched at 1.25 a.m. Fellow passengers included a number of young children, such as eleven-month-old Hudson Trevor Allison, who lost his parents and sister in the disaster; ten-month-old Philip Aks, whose mother was on another boat; four-year-old Marion Louise Becker and her one-year-old brother, Richard; and two-year-old Phyllis May Quick. Although the children were amused by the sight and sound of Edith Rosenbaum's toy pig – which played the melody of 'La Maxixe' – it was difficult for everyone to endure the cries of some of the women, who had, according to Edith, 'become half hysterical with apprehension'.[2] During the night, while the passengers in the lifeboat were searching for extra clothing for one of the stewards, they came across a man who had frozen to death at the bottom of the boat. The survivors tried to keep their spirits up – one seaman told the rest of the boat that this was his third shipwreck and that if he were to 'get out of this one' he would go 'back home to be a milkman' – yet for many it was hard to keep the dark tide of depression at bay. There was, said one young crew member, 'no use looking for good things when none are coming'.[3]

Remarkably, Annie Robinson had herself survived a previous collision with an iceberg. On 6 May 1909, the steamer *Lake Champlain*, travelling from Liverpool to Montreal with 1,000 passengers on board, hit an iceberg as it sailed through some dense fog off Cape Race. On that occasion no one died as the leak in the ship's bow was a minor one and the vessel managed to steam its way to St John's, Newfoundland, where it docked and underwent repairs. Annie survived that disaster, only to find herself on board a so-called 'unsinkable' ship that now lay at the bottom of the ocean. Had she been cursed in some way? Had she caused the disaster? Why did everything she touched seem to end in tragedy? That night in the lifeboat her spirits sank and, even after she had been rescued by the *Carpathia*, she felt she could not shake off the spectre of anxiety and dread that seemed a constant presence.

The tragedy affected many of the *Titanic* stewardesses in a particularly bad way, as one witness observed: 'I found myself walking unknowingly amid the survivors of the *Titanic*'s crew who had just landed from the *Carpathia* that very morning. Next, going through the first-class dining room I heard moans and sobbing and learned that some of the rescued stewardesses were in a semi-hysterical state. It was distinctly a funereal atmosphere . . . The next day the *Lapland* sailed, making the *Titanic*'s return voyage via Cherbourg . . . carrying back the survivors of the crew and many of the passengers originally booked for the *Titanic*. It was the saddest sailing I have ever witnessed.'[4]

On 29 April, Annie disembarked the *Lapland* at Plymouth. There, dressed in mourning with a black veil shrouding her rather severe features, she agreed to pose for a number of photographs with her fellow *Titanic* stewardesses. She spent the night in Plymouth, before travelling to Southampton the next day. Southampton was a city in despair, as it had been forced to endure the loss of a large number of its inhabitants, many of whom worked on ships such as the *Titanic* in order to support wives and children at home. Contemporary reports talked of 'the gloom which hangs over Southampton'[5] while the headmistress of Northam Girls' School wrote in the daily log, 'A great many girls are absent this afternoon owing to the sad news regarding the *Titanic* . . . So many of the crew belonged to Northam and it is pathetic to witness the children's grief.'[6]

Annie, a widow, did not have anyone to turn to and she felt the tragedy keenly. In May 1912, she was called before the

British Wreck Commissioner's Inquiry. Although she answered succinctly and correctly, never for a moment losing her composure, the experience forced her to relive the horrors of the night. She described how, soon after the collision, she had seen the ship's carpenter, Hutchinson, rush past her, looking 'absolutely bewildered, distracted', saying nothing; he perished with the ship. She remembered how the band was still playing as her lifeboat left the sinking liner. And she recalled the awful sight of that freezing cold water rising up the stairs by the mail room. The images and sounds would stay with her forever, no matter how hard she tried to erase them from her mind. She attempted to put the disaster behind her, but wherever she went it seemed people wanted to ask her about it. She attempted to keep busy working as a stewardess – she depended on a monthly wage of £3 10*s*. – and in July 1913, while aboard the *Galatea*, the Mersey Docks and Harbour Board's yacht, she talked about her experiences on the *Titanic* with King George V and Queen Mary who were in Liverpool to attend a lavish naval review.

From reading the jingoistic press reports of the occasion – detailing the pageant of the 109 ships, all sporting rainbow colours and carrying bands that blasted out the National Anthem – it would be easy to assume that the country had learned little from the loss of the *Titanic*. Indeed, it would seem national pride had made a full recovery – as is evident from the coverage in *The Times*, which said that the day was 'a manifestation of Britain's might'. The newspaper continued, 'It was obvious that their Majesties were deeply impressed with the spectacle . . . Arriving at the far end of the line, and passing the warships with bluejackets and marines at attention, the *Galatea* entered the Gladstone dock.' During this voyage the King and Queen had a 'long conversation' with Annie about what she had seen and heard on board the *Titanic*. 'Their Majesties were very interested in Mrs Robinson's narrative of her experiences, and asked her many questions on the subject of the great disaster.'[7] Annie Robinson responded to these enquiries with nothing but the greatest politeness, even though she was suffering agonies inside.

By the time she set foot on the *Devonian*, she was looking forward to some peaceful time with her daughter, who lived in the Jamaica Plain area of Boston and who had married a ticket seller at South Station. For the most part, the journey was a peaceful one. Then, on the night of 9 October 1914, as the steamship was 'groping through a heavy fog', the officers gave the orders for the foghorn to be sounded. Within an instant, Annie was taken back in time to the moment two and half years previously when she was on the *Carpathia* sailing into New York harbour. Every half a minute the foghorn had sounded, which was, in the words of the ship's Captain, 'particularly distressing for the survivors, and I was sorry for their state of mind'.[8] As Edith Rosenbaum remembered, the shock of seeing the blinding flash of the lightning, together with the awful noise of the thunder, combined with the 'monotonous wailing of the fog signals', added to an increased sense of anxiety. 'We were still very much on our nerves, and I suppose we felt that perhaps we had escaped one disaster only to run to a greater one,' she said.[9]

Annie could stand the sound of the fog signal no longer. She ran out of the dining saloon and up on to the deck, which was empty. If only that awful wail would stop. But wherever she went on the ship it followed her like a death knell. She tried to breathe deeply, but nothing could calm her down. She knew she had no choice but to end it all. She stepped over the rail, seeing nothing but a cloud of mist. For a moment, as she steadied herself on the very edge of the ship, she thought she could be in heaven. Then the wail of the foghorn rang once more in her head, sending its deep vibration through her body. Taking one last breath, she stepped out. At last, as she fell into the depths of the cold ocean, she felt free of the *Titanic*.

Annie Robinson was the first of ten *Titanic* survivors to commit suicide in the years after the disaster. Those who went on to take their own lives would include Dr Henry Frauenthal (who jumped from the seventh floor of a hospital building in 1927); third-class passenger Juha Niskanen (who shot himself, also in 1927, after failing to find gold); professional gambler George Brereton (who put a gun to his head in 1942); second-class passenger John Morgan Davies (who took an overdose in 1951 after going through a divorce); Phyllis May Quick (who had been only two years old at the time of the *Titanic*, who shot herself in 1954); and Frederick Fleet, the man who had first set eyes on the iceberg (who hanged himself in January 1965, two weeks after the death of his wife).

Many other passengers were plagued by mental illness for the rest of their lives. With symptoms such as anxiety, depression, nightmares, social withdrawal, emotional difficulties, physical disorders, and, in the most extreme cases, total mental collapse and the compulsion to commit suicide, we would now say that they all suffered from post-traumatic stress disorder. It would have been common for these passengers to display signs of what is now described as 'survivor syndrome', a condition that was not diagnosed until the 1960s and which is often marked by experiencing an overwhelming sense of guilt. Sufferers frequently torment themselves as they are unable to endure the fact that friends, families, work colleagues, even strangers, went to their deaths while they remain alive. Some *Titanic* passengers became obsessed with the idea of death, wishing it upon themselves, while others, such as Bruce Ismay, punished themselves for surviving, effectively transforming themselves into members of the 'living dead'.

One of the clearest manifestations of survivor guilt was the case of crew member William A. Lucas, who, according to reports, had behaved 'peculiarly' ever since the sinking.[10] He had joined the ship in Southampton as an able-bodied seaman at the very last minute – at ten minutes to twelve on the day of sailing. During the voyage he had worked on the watch, and on the night of the collision he had just left the mess room when the ship hit the iceberg. It was, he recalled, a hard shock; 'it very nearly sent me off my feet'. He did not see the iceberg, but he did notice the piles of 'darkish white' ice that had fallen on to the deck. After donning an extra jersey, he spent the next hour or so helping to launch the lifeboats. Just before two o'clock, Lucas ran over to the starboard side of the ship to find that all the lifeboats had gone. 'So I came back [to the port side] and the boat was riding off the deck,' he recalled, talking about the collapsible lifeboat that remained. 'The water was up under the bridge then. The ladies sung out there was no sailor in the boat and no plugs, so I was a sailor and I jumped into the boat.' In this boat – collapsible D, the last to leave the sinking ship – were the two Navratil boys; a couple of third-class passengers; and a number of first-class women, including Renee Harris, Jane Ann Hoyt, Gertrude Maybelle Thorne and Caroline Lane Lamson Brown. Lucas was so worried about the state of the flimsy vessel – it looked as though it was missing a plug, which meant that water seeped into it – that he made the decision to turn away two women who tried to board. 'Wait a minute,' he said to them, 'there's another boat going to be put down from the funnel for you.'[11] One of these women was Edith Evans, a thirty-six-year-old first-class passenger, who had already sacrificed her place in the lifeboat for her friend, Caroline Brown. 'Please take this lady, she has children,' said Edith, who subsequently died in the disaster. At a memorial service for Edith, held at Grace Church in New York, Caroline Brown told the congregation of her friend's noble spirit. 'It was a heroic sacrifice, and as long as life lasts I shall hold her memory dear as my preserver, who preferred to die so that I might live.'[12]

The story made headlines around the world, and it is highly likely that Lucas would have read or heard of Edith's sacrifice. The knowledge that perhaps he could have saved this young woman, and others like her, haunted the seaman for the rest of his life. He heard the cries of the dying when he slept and saw the bodies floating among the cupboards and chairs in the water in his dreams. He carried on working on ships, serving on the *War Mehtar*, the *Polynesia*, the *Dervent River*, the *Bellagio* and the *Constance*, but he could not get the disaster out of his mind. Finally, he could endure the psychological pain no longer. In November 1921, as he was travelling by train between Leeds and London, William Lucas put a gun to his head and blew his brains out. He was thirty-five years old.

Just as the iceberg smashed into the *Titanic*, puncturing a series of holes in the ship's side, so the tragedy violently collided with the consciousness of the survivors. But the extent of the damage on an individual's mental state depended on what they had witnessed or suffered that night, their general ability to cope in traumatic or stressful situations, their previous encounters with distressing or potentially dangerous situations, and their personality type. Some, such as thirty-six-year-old third-class passenger Anna De Messemaeker, were destroyed by the experience almost immediately. On the night of the sinking, she and her husband, Guillaume, whom she had married earlier that year, managed to work their way up the ship to the boat deck. As the liner plunged deeper into the sea, Anna became increasingly hysterical and refused to leave her husband's side. Finally, Guillaume – a Belgian who was taking his wife to Montana to start a new life – had to pick her up and force her into lifeboat number thirteen, which left the *Titanic* at 1.25 a.m.

Anna was convinced that she would never see her husband again, and as her lifeboat rowed away from the sinking ship her mind began to break down. By the time the couple were reunited on the *Carpathia* – Guillaume had been saved by responding to the call from the *Titanic*'s crew for men to help take charge of lifeboat number fifteen – Anna had become unhinged. After the rescue ship docked in New York, the couple travelled westward, but it was obvious to Guillaume that he had lost his wife forever. She was admitted to a mental hospital in Rochester, Minnesota, where she died in April 1918. Fellow third-class passenger Hanora or 'Norah' Healy, an unmarried servant from Athenry, Galway, also could not cope with the enormity of the tragedy. Soon after returning home to Ireland she started to exhibit signs of mental illness. In early 1919 she was certified and she spent the rest of her short life in the Ballinasloe asylum. She died there on 11 March 1919, aged thirty-six, after suffering a brain haemorrhage.

One Danish girl, a third-class passenger whose sweetheart died in the sinking, immediately 'lost her mind' and had to be sent from New York back to Denmark.[13] Meanwhile, Irish-born Bertha Mulvihill, again sailing in third class, showed such signs of mental disorder that her doctor in Rhode Island would not let her go to sleep in case when she woke up again she would not be in her right mind. One witness who observed the twenty-five-year-old woman, whose ribs had been broken when a man had landed on top of her as she was sitting in lifeboat number fifteen, noted that her eyes were full of 'privation and terror'.[14]

The deep psychological effects of the disaster affected passengers in all classes. After surviving the *Titanic*, first-class passenger Dr Washington Dodge, who had left the ship in lifeboat thirteen, tried to resume his busy life in San Francisco, where he worked as a local politician and banker. When he returned to the city, with his second wife, Ruth, and their four-and-a-half-year-old son, both of whom had also survived the sinking in a different lifeboat from Dodge's, rumours began to spread about the circumstances of his escape. Was he the man who had tried to escape the ship dressed as a woman? 'My father at the time was in San Francisco politics and some people tried to pin the legend on him,' recalled his son, also called Washington, many years later. 'This was absurd as he was about 6 feet 2 with a portly moustache and my mother a small woman. He actually stayed behind but as one of the boats was being lowered an officer asked him to volunteer to row because of his size. He naturally accepted.'[15]

On their return to California, newspapers ran a number of interviews with the Dodges. The *San Francisco Bulletin* featured Ruth Dodge in an article on 29 April 1912, which quoted her as saying: 'Was it cold? You can imagine how cold it was when I tell you that we passed fifty-six miles of icebergs after we got on the *Carpathia* . . . I think it is foolish to speak of the heroism displayed. There was none that I witnessed.'[16] Yet, according to Washington Dodge, his wife had not only never said such a thing, but she also had never even given a single interview on the subject. Dodge – who was described by contemporaries as 'eminently a self-made man'[17] – was also the kind of person who believed in discretion and it was not in his nature to be demonstrative. However, something would have to be done; the rumours, which spread quickly through west coast society circles, could not be allowed to continue and nor could the increasingly fictional 'reporting' of his and his wife's experiences. So, on 11 May 1912, he stood up in front of the members of the Commonwealth Club, and gave his account of the disaster.

He began by outlining the basic facts of the tragedy, before moving on to his own personal experience. He told his audience of how impressed he had been with the *Titanic*, how 'at all times one might walk the decks, with the same security as if walking down Market Street, so little motion was there to the vessel. It was hard to realise, when dining in the spacious dining saloon, that one was not in some large and sumptuous hotel.' He went on to describe how, that Sunday night, he and his wife were awakened by a slight shock. He was first informed that there was nothing to worry about, that there was a minor problem with the propeller but that all would be put right in a matter of minutes. Dodge, however, wanted to see for himself, and so, after throwing on some clothes, he ventured out on to the promenade deck, where he met some men who were talking about a collision with an iceberg. He also met a couple of stokers who told him that the ship had 'sprung a leak' and a steward who informed him that the order had been given for all passengers to put on their life preservers. Dodge returned to his cabin, told his wife to dress in some warm clothes and took down the three life jackets from the cupboard in their stateroom. 'We then quickly made our way to the boat deck . . .' he said. 'The officer in charge was calling for women and children to fill the boat, but seemed to have difficulty in finding those who were willing to enter. I myself hesitated to place my wife and child in this boat, being unable to decide whether it would be safer to keep them on the steamer, or to entrust them to this frail boat, which was the first to be launched, and which hung over eighty feet above the water.' Dodge placed his wife and son in the next starboard boat to leave the ship. 'As I saw this boat lowered, containing my wife and child, I was overwhelmed with doubts as to whether or not I was exposing them to *greater* danger, than if they had remained on board the ship.'

Dodge remained on the starboard side of the *Titanic*, helping women and children into the boats for the next half an hour or so until boat number thirteen was nearly full. The officers in charge repeatedly called for more women and children to come forward; when none did, Dodge, together with a small group of other men, tumbled into the boat. After about half an hour Dodge noticed that the ship had 'settled forwards into the water'; he could see this because of the line of light that came from the liner's portholes. Yet no one in the lifeboat ventured the possibility that the *Titanic* would ever sink. Indeed, a rather cheerful atmosphere prevailed in their vessel; some of the passengers joked, while others sang 'Pull for the Shore'. The mood, however, was soon to change. The lights on the *Titanic* finally went out, at which point Dodge saw the ship 'outlined as a great dark shadow on the water'. Yet everyone still assumed that all the passengers would have had a chance to get off the ship; no one was in danger.

'Suddenly, when I was looking at the dark outline of the steamer, I saw her stern rise high from the water, and then the vessel was seen to completely disappear from sight with startling rapidity,' he said. 'A series of loud explosions, three or four in number, were then heard, due, as we all believed, to bursting boilers.

'Any impression which I had had that there were no survivors aboard, was speedily removed from my mind by the faint, yet distinct, cries which were wafted across the waters. Some there were in our boat, who insisted that these cries came from occupants of the different lifeboats, which were nearer the scene of the wreck than we were, as they called to one another. To my ear, however, they had but one meaning – and the awful fact was borne upon me that many lives were perishing in those icy waters.'[18]

At this point, as he spoke to his audience at the Commonwealth Club, Washington Dodge lost control of himself. The memory took him back to the awful moment when he heard the terrible sound of death on a mass scale. Witnesses recall how he 'broke down' in tears and how he proceeded with his narrative with great difficulty.[19] 'With the disappearance of the steamer, a great sense of loneliness and depression seemed to take possession of those in our boat,' he continued. Despite his eventual rescue by the *Carpathia*, where he was happily reunited with his wife and son, Dodge never quite seemed to shake off this feeling. On board the *Carpathia* he used his training as a doctor – he was a graduate of the University of California – to resuscitate several men who had gone into heart failure as a result of hypothermia. He also listened to some of the experiences of passengers who had remained on the *Titanic* as she sank, stories which he said were 'almost too harrowing for repetition. These men, for hours after their arrival on the *Carpathia*, would burst forth in tears lamenting over the terrible scenes through which they passed.'[20]

That night, as Washington Dodge finished his narrative, he hoped that his account would put an end to the speculation about how he had survived. He could forget about the disaster and get on with his life. And to the outside world it appeared as though he had been successful in moving on and erasing the trauma of the *Titanic* from his mind. On returning home he resigned his position as the city's tax assessor, despite his enormous popularity with the electorate who praised his financial acumen and democratic spirit (he had famously taxed utility companies to fund improvements in housing). In July 1912, he accepted a role as vice-president with the Anglo & London Paris National Bank, and three years later he took on a role as public library trustee. He was regarded by his peers as 'frank and unassuming', and he spoke with a 'vein of humor running through his conversation, and with the ability to grasp without apparent effort, the most difficult or complex propositions'.[21]

In 1915, Dodge bought 7,000 acres of land northwest of Butte City, which he planned to lease to farmers to grow rice, while for himself he purchased a 200-acre plum-tree ranch near

Princeton, Colusa County, where he intended to retire after his latest job as president of the Federal Telegraph Company, a post he had held from 1917, came to an end. However, in late 1918 and early 1919, this man of honour – for Dodge it was a word that defined his very essence – experienced a crisis that threatened to destroy him. The trouble began when Dodge finalised a deal to sell a large number of shares in a company called Poulsen Wireless – a corporation that was controlled by Federal Telegraph – to the United States government, an undertaking worth $1.6 million. Central to this arrangement was a commission of $400,000 that Dodge's enemies said would be creamed off to a company owned by a member of the doctor's own family. Difficulties began when it became known that, just before shares in Federal Telegraph plummeted, Dodge had sold his interest at a high price. Fellow shareholders were furious that Dodge had made a profit while they had taken a fall. Sigmund Stern, the president of Levi Strauss, was especially angry with Dodge. Stern's wife, Rosalie, had had a brother, Edward Meyer, who had perished on the *Titanic*. The disaster would not disappear and the question of Washington Dodge's honour was raised once more. Just what kind of man was he? Not only had he managed to escape the *Titanic*, while many first-class men had died, but it seemed as if he had profited from insider information and siphoned money towards a member of his family at the expense of the other shareholders. For the Sterns, the double blow was too much and they started proceedings that would effectively ruin Dodge's reputation. On 14 January 1919, the shareholders of Federal Telegraph voted to have him sacked from the position of president of the company and joined forces with other interested parties to sue him. Dodge resigned, maintaining he had done nothing wrong. Yet, as his lawyer stated, this scandal 'preyed upon' the doctor's mind and 'reflected on his honor'.[22]

Dodge could not endure yet another attempt to sully his name. He became depressed and suicidal. It would have been better, he thought, if he had perished on the *Titanic*; at least then he would always have been remembered as an honourable man. His friend and physician Dr John Gallwey was so concerned about his welfare that in June 1919 he persuaded Dodge to seek psychiatric treatment at St Francis Hospital, San Francisco. There, he was attended by medics who put him on suicide watch. However, on the morning of 21 June he seemed a little brighter and responded to the suggestions made by Dr Gallwey that he take a trip to Santa Barbara with his wife. The break, said Gallwey, would do him the world of good. Dodge returned home to the Carlton Apartments, at 840 Powell Street, San Francisco, to collect a few things, while his wife went shopping for the trip. Just after four o'clock that afternoon, unable to bear living with himself for one moment longer, Washington Dodge made his way to the garage of the building, took out his .32-calibre revolver and shot himself in the right temple. The bullet fractured his skull and drove fragments of bone deep into his brain. As he fell on to the concrete floor his skull was fractured for a second time.

Dodge's death was far from instant. He managed to drag himself into the elevator and press the call button. On the floor above, the porter, George Hurd, heard the buzzer, but as Dodge had not closed the door of the elevator it did not move. 'Close the door,' shouted Hurd down the elevator shaft. Dodge managed to follow the order, and a moment later the elevator reached the lobby. Struggling to open the door, Dodge fell forward on to the floor. 'He said he wanted to go somewhere,' said the porter, but he couldn't make out what Dodge was saying.[23] The injured man was carried up to his apartment from where doctors were called and he was then driven back to St Francis Hospital. Surgeons thought it would be too dangerous to operate on him and, early the following week, it looked as though his condition was improving slightly.

'I have known Dr Dodge for forty years,' Dr Gallwey told the *San Francisco Chronicle*, 'and in all that time his integrity has never been doubted. A recent lawsuit in connection with the affairs of the Poulsen Company preyed upon his mind, however, and despite the assurance of Gavin McNab, his attorney, that the case would be dismissed without injury to his reputation, Dr Dodge became obsessed with the idea that he could not live in the face of the charge made against him.'[24]

The improvement in Dodge's condition was short-lived and a few days later he fell into unconsciousness. Doctors realised there was little they could do for him. On the morning of 30 June, with his relatives by his bedside – including his wife, his elderly mother, his two nieces, and Henry, his son by his first marriage – Dodge died. His funeral was held on 3 July 1919, after which he was cremated at Cypress Lawn Cemetery.

'Life puts a heavy strain and pressure on some of us,' said one of the men who attended the service, 'and unconsciously we find ourselves departing from the conventional standards set up by those whom nature, or the chance of birth, has favored. Not one of us is pure white nor solid black. We are a blend – a gray; rather a dark shade of gray at that . . . blindly groping toward the good.'[25]

Jack Thayer seemed to personify the word 'survivor'. In the very final moments of the sinking, the seventeen-year-old, who had been travelling with his parents, stood on the rail of the ship with Milton Long, the friend he had made on the voyage. The two young men turned to one another and said goodbye. Long asked if Thayer was ready to jump; the boy said he would join him in a minute or so. Milton 'did not jump clear, but slid down the side of the ship' and Jack never saw him again. Five seconds later, Jack jumped feet first from the ship into the depths of the freezing water.

'I was clear of the ship, went down, and as I came up I was pushed away from the ship by some force,' he explained when he told the remarkable story of his survival a few days later. 'I came up facing the ship and one of the funnels seemed to be lifted off and fell towards me about fifteen yards away with a mass of sparks and steam coming out of it. I saw the ship in a sort of a red glare, and it seemed to me that she broke in two just in front of the third funnel. At this time I was sucked down, and as I came up I was pushed out again and twisted around by a large wave, coming up in the midst of a great deal of small wreckage. As I pushed it from around my head my hand touched the cork fender of an overturned lifeboat. I looked up and saw some men on the top and asked them to give me a hand. One of them, who was a stoker, helped me up. In a short time the bottom [of the boat] was covered with about 25 or 30 men. When I got on this I was facing the ship. The stern then seemed to rise in the air and stopped at about an angle of 60 degrees. It seemed to hold there for a time and then with a hissing sound it shot right down out of sight with people jumping from the stern . . .

'We were then right in the midst of fairly large wreckage, with people swimming all around us. The sea was very calm and we kept the boat pretty steady, but every now and then a wave would wash over it.

'The assistant wireless operator [Harold Bride] was right next to me, holding on to me and kneeling in the water [in the bottom of the boat]. We all sang a hymn and said the Lord's prayer, and then waited for dawn to come.'[26]

Jack Thayer's survival was illuminated by the rosy glow of a seemingly permanent dawn, the iridescent aura of optimism. On his return to America, the boy was regarded as something of a hero, not only because he still had his life, but because of the extraordinary circumstances in which he had managed to survive. Typical was the headline that appeared in the Providence, *Rhode Island Journal* that read, 'Boy Sucked Down, Escapes'. Unlike Bruce Ismay, or some of the other men in first class, Thayer had shunned a place in the lifeboats and had waited on the sinking ship until the very end. He had taken his chance by jumping off the liner and plunging into the black, cold ocean. 'The shock of the water took the breath out of my lungs,' he said. 'Down and down I went, spinning in all directions.' There was something miraculous and mythical about his survival which appealed to the public. 'I finally came up with my lungs bursting, but not having taken any water,' he said.[27]

Thayer had lost his father, who went down with the *Titanic*, but he bore his grief with dignity and honour. As he climbed aboard the *Carpathia* he saw his mother. 'When she saw me, she thought, of course, that my Father must be with me,' he said. 'She was overjoyed to see me, but it was a terrible shock to hear that I had not seen Father since he had said goodbye to her.' A coffee mixed with brandy was pushed into his hands – his first taste of alcohol – and it warmed him almost like they had 'put hot coals in my stomach'. A kindly man gave him a set of pyjamas and lent him his bunk, his wet clothes were taken away, 'and with the help of the brandy' he slept until noon. 'I got up feeling fit and well,' he said, 'just as though nothing bad had happened.'[28]

On the *Carpathia* Thayer had the strength to try and rouse Bruce Ismay from his near-comatose state and managed to describe the horrific events of the night to Arthur Rostron, the Captain of the ship. Jack told him how 'the *Titanic* up-ended herself and remained poised like some colossal nightmare of a fish, her tail high in the air, her nose deep in the water, until she dived finally from human sight'.[29]

After docking in New York, Marian and Jack Thayer boarded the family's private train carriage, which took them back to their home in Haverford, Pennsylvania. Marian struggled to cope with the loss of her forty-nine-year-old husband; particularly difficult for her was the fact that his body was never recovered and she could not bear the thought of him lying at the bottom of the sea. Soon afterwards, she turned to a spiritualist in order to try and contact her deceased husband, something that at least brought her a little comfort. 'She was also something of a spiritualist herself,' says her granddaughter, Julie Vehr. 'I remember that she kept all these books full of handwriting, mirror writing, which she believed came from her late husband's spirit. She thought she was in touch with him and when I was a little girl I remember her as a spooky old lady.'[30]

Marian was also helped by the fact that John Thayer was regarded as a model of dignity and self-sacrifice. He was, in the words written in the programme of his memorial service held at the Church of the Redeemer, Bryn Mawr, Pennsylvania, 'a hero of the *Titanic* disaster, perfect in every relationship of life, he died as he lived, an example to all'. Uplifting and appropriately themed quotations were used to celebrate his life and mark his death: 'He rests where love, life and death all found him true, his memory as imperishable as his shroud, the sea'; 'I will bring my people again from the depths of the sea. And God shall wipe away all tears from their eyes'; and 'Greater love hath no man than this, that a man lay down his life for his friends'.

William D. Winsor, who had known John Thayer all his life, wrote that his friend was a 'worthy scion of the stock from which he came, a devoted son, a loyal brother, a loving husband'. He had, he added, a 'wonderful personality, and a power of adapting himself to those with whom he was thrown, and there was something almost magnetic in the contact of his presence'. Winsor also paid tribute to his friend's heroism in the face of adversity. 'There was not the excitement of the battlefield, the blare of trumpets, nor the hope of glory to aid him. Inch by inch the great vessel slowly settled into the water and he saw the approach of the dread inevitable, and the end of all. He was only sustained by his sense of duty to others. May we who survive him and mourn with tearful eyes his great loss, have, when the great end comes, as clear a record.'[31]

Jack felt proud of having such a brave and popular father – another friend said that John drew men towards him and 'bound them to him by hoops of steel'[32] – yet it wasn't that simple. With survival came a certain amount of guilt, but there was no outlet for him to express any dark emotions he may have had. Only a month or so after the disaster, Lucile Carter, a family friend who herself had escaped the *Titanic*, commented on his well-being, describing him in a letter as 'splendid'.[33]

Jack returned to his studies at Haverford School, where he graduated that spring, and then enrolled in the College of Arts and Science at Pennsylvania University. 'He had wanted to go to Princeton, but after the death of his father he decided to stay nearer home,' says his daughter Pauline Maguire.[34] There, he became active in the athletics club and was a member of the Phi Beta Junior Society, the Delta Psi Fraternity and the Sphinx Senior Society. From 1913, he began to spend an increasing amount of time with Lois Buchanan Cassatt, his exact contemporary in age, the granddaughter of Alexander Johnston Cassatt, the seventh president of the Pennsylvania Railroad, and the great-great-niece of James Buchanan, the former President of the United States. 'The two families were interconnected as they lived next door to one another,' says Pauline.[35] Lois was described as a 'rather shy, reserved woman', in contrast to Jack, who was 'the complete opposite, he was very outgoing'.[36] By 1917, the couple had announced their engagement and on

15 December of that year they married in Philadelphia. The following September, John, the first of their six children was born (one died in infancy from Spanish flu). Yet Jack was not there to see the birth of his first – and 'favourite' son[37] – as he was fighting in France, as a first lieutenant and then as captain in the 304th ammunition train of the Field Artillery, 79th 'Liberty' Division. On the Meuse–Argonne front, Jack would have witnessed death on a mass scale. During the ongoing battle – the southern part of the big triple offensive that broke the German lines on the Western Front – there were 117,000 American casualties alone, a figure that represented 40 per cent of the total US battlefield losses during the whole of the war. 'That must have been a horrible experience for him, but when he returned home I don't think he talked much about it,' says his daughter Julie. 'Like he never talked about the *Titanic*. In those days, a man did not talk about his feelings. In fact, nobody really talked about emotions at all. It just wasn't done.'[38]

In 1919, he took a job with the bank Lee, Higginson, becoming head of the company's Philadelphia office, where he stayed until 1932, when he moved across to be a partner at Yarnall and Company. He resigned from that firm in 1937 and accepted a job as treasurer of the University of Pennsylvania, before securing the position as the organisation's financial vice-president in February 1944. He led a busy, active, seemingly happy and fulfilled life. He was president of the Racquet Club, a member of the Rose Tree Fox Hunt and the Gulph Mills Golf Club, was a keen stamp collector and genealogist, and adored to figure skating. 'He loved to take his children ice skating,' says his daughter Julie. 'One year, when the Schuylkill River in Philadelphia was frozen over he took us down to skate. I remember being quite scared, in case the ice would give way and I would fall in and get trapped beneath it, but he said, "Don't worry, I've got my rope with me." It was a kind of pole with a rope wrapped around it that he said he could use to pull us out of the water if we fell in. Looking back, it is curious that he should want to go on frozen water after what he had been through with the *Titanic*. Of course, at the time I thought nothing of this, as he never, ever mentioned the disaster. That was one thing daddy never talked about. He was not afraid of water, and loved to swim, but he never sailed and would never go on an ocean liner.'[39] He may not have verbalised his recollections of the sinking and its aftermath, 'but he must have thought about that night a great deal,' says Pauline. 'I never knew anything about the *Titanic* as a child, as it was never mentioned in the family.'[40]

As his children began to approach the age he had been when he took that fateful voyage he began to think how best to deal with his memories of *Titanic* – images, conversations, emotions, fears he had kept to himself for nearly thirty years. 'I think he wanted us children to know what had happened that night and so he wrote an account of the sinking just for the family,' says Julie.[41] 'Perhaps it was easier for him to write these things down than talk about them,' says Pauline.[42] The resulting short text, which he entitled *The Sinking of the SS Titanic* and which he dedicated to the father he had lost, is an extraordinary piece of writing. Thayer also was able to situate the disaster within the context of modern history, observing that while other calamities such as the Johnstown Flood of 1889 (in which 2,200 people died) or the San Francisco Earthquake of 1906 (more than 3,000 perished) did stir the sleeping world they did not shock it 'enough to keep it from resuming its slumber'. The *Titanic* sinking, he said, 'not only made the world rub its eyes and awake, but woke it with a start, keeping it moving at a rapidly accelerating pace ever since, with less and less peace, satisfaction, and happiness'. In many ways, the disaster became symbolic of the modern age itself: an overture that served as a prelude to a century of disquiet and disorder. 'Today the individual has to be contented with rapidity of motion, nervous emotion, and economic insecurity,' he wrote. 'To my mind the world of today awoke April 15th, 1912.'[43] As he wrote those words, in 1940, little did he realise the full extent of the personal horrors he would still have to endure.

After writing his account of the sinking, he tried to contain and confine his recollections of the *Titanic*. Yet a messy spillage of fragmented memories began to emerge from the depths of the past. Could the act of remembrance – and its subsequent expression in words – have triggered this new wave of 'nervous emotion'? Had the articulation of past events, an act he had assumed would result in the calming of the sea of memory, actually done the opposite? Whatever the reason, Jack Thayer – respectable, honourable, extrovert, fun-loving, seemingly well-rounded as he was – began to experience an anxiousness that would not leave him, a realisation of his own mental vulnerability. The strength he had shown to the world over the past thirty or so years since the sinking began to slip away from him. Everything seemed to be connected to that night; whatever he did the *Titanic* was always there at the edge of his consciousness, taunting him with its presence. In October 1943, he learned the news that his twenty-two-year-old son, Second Lieutenant Edward Cassatt, a co-pilot of an army bomber, had been killed in action in the Pacific. The thought of his son's plane plunging into water forced the sinking of the *Titanic* to the front of his consciousness. 'Edward was lost over one of the islands in the Pacific,' says Pauline, 'and I think it must have brought back the memory of the water.'[44]

Then just six months later, his mother, who had been ill with a heart condition for a year, died, aged seventy-two. The double loss was hard enough to bear, but the date – 14 April 1944 – was the strange thing, as Marian had died on the thirty-second anniversary of the disaster. 'He started to suffer from depression,' says his daughter Julie. 'It was a result of everything that had happened to him over the years – the *Titanic*, losing his son and then his mother. Eventually, it seems he suffered a nervous breakdown. My mother sought medical help for him, but one day he slipped away from watchful eyes.'[45]

On the morning of 18 September 1945, fifty-year-old Jack Thayer left his office at the University of Pennsylvania and drove through the streets of Philadelphia. At the city's trolley loop, near 48th Street and Parkside Avenue, he slowed down and pulled over. He took out a cigar from his amber cigar case and lit it. He inhaled deeply, enjoying the smell and taste of the smoke, savouring it until it had burned down to within an inch of its holder. Then, from his briefcase, he grabbed a set of razor blades, placed one in each hand and took a deep breath. He raised his left hand and cut deeply into the wrist, ignoring the pain as he repeated the action with his right. Blood began to seep out of his veins, staining his grey business suit and shirt. Gripping a blade tightly between his fingers he brought it towards his face, hesitated a moment as he felt the sharp edge slice into the skin on his neck, before quickly making a slashing movement across his throat. As life seeped out of him and he began to drift into unconsciousness, he felt a sense of contentment, a realisation that the pain he had suffered would soon be over. His family reported him missing on the morning of 19 September, but his body, complete with a brown hat still on his head, lay there in the car, undetected, for two days until it was discovered by two Philadelphia Transportation Company employees on the morning of 21 September. The two men telephoned the police station, which sent out two officers who transported the body to the Presbyterian Hospital. In the morgue, the corpse was identified by Thayer's brother, Frederick, and his lifelong friend, the lawyer and politician, Lieutenant Governor John Cromwell Bell. Thayer had 'been suffering from a nervous breakdown during the last two weeks,' said Bell, 'due,

I believe, to worrying about the death of his son who was killed in service. A few days ago he seemed to develop amnesia.'[46]

After police examined his body, they discovered that Thayer had slashed his shirt with a razor blade, and that he had been carrying $1.88 in cash, an assortment of cards, and a routine letter to a bank. Missing, however, was a gold watch, which held a heavy gold chain carrying a locket that contained a photograph of a woman, presumably his wife, Lois, and a T-shaped fraternity pin. Apparently, the thief who had initially swiped the watch from the body had suffered from a guilty conscience and promptly, and stealthily, returned it, as the next day it turned up, wrapped in paper, on the running board of the family's station wagon in the garage of their home in Gray's Lane, Haverford. Understandably, the family was too upset to comment on this unpleasant development. The funeral was held in the afternoon of 28 September at the Church of the Redeemer, Bryn Mawr, after which Thayer's body was interred in the cemetery.

'Maybe my mother had had some warnings, but as children it was the last thing we expected,' says Julie. 'I was seventeen when he died, and it came as a complete shock. It was terribly, terribly sad.'[47] 'One of my sisters said she was embarrassed to go to school afterwards,' says Pauline, 'but I thought you shouldn't be embarrassed, because you would need so much courage to do it. At the time, he didn't do it because he was brave, however, he did it because he was desperate.'[48]

Eight

MISS MASQUERADER

Dorothy Gibson didn't like the look of the water that was seeping into her lifeboat. Boat number seven had just been launched into the flat, perfectly calm sea, but somehow, during the loading of its passengers, the drainage plug had been displaced from its bottom. The survivors acted quickly, filling the hole with what Dorothy described as 'volunteer contributions of lingerie from the women and garments from the men'.[1] Despite this, the leak was not completely sealed and, for the next few hours, the passengers had to sit with their feet submerged in the freezing water. The cold seemed to eat into their bones, but they knew it was nothing compared to the deadly bitterness of the ocean.

Dorothy, dressed in only a short coat and sweater over an evening gown, was beginning to shiver and so William Sloper, a friend she had made on the ship, passed his overcoat to her; she thanked him with a kiss. 'I never knew one could be so cold and live,' she said later. 'I ached from head to foot, and I was much more warmly clad than some of the women.'[2]

Ever since it had been launched, at 12.45 a.m., lifeboat seven had remained stationed only twenty yards away from the *Titanic* in case it could be used in a rescue operation. Dorothy and her mother, Pauline, watched as lifeboat after lifeboat left the vessel, but by just after two o'clock it was obvious that the vast majority of its passengers would not be able to escape from the liner. Realising that the ship's sinking was imminent, look-out George Hogg ordered that lifeboat seven be rowed away from the *Titanic*. The risk of being sucked down was high, he thought, and so the passengers and crew manning the oars rowed as hard as they could across the pitch-black sea. Dorothy could not take her eyes off the ship, its bow now underwater, its stern rising up into the sky.

'Suddenly there was a wild coming together of voices from the ship and we noticed an unusual commotion among the people about the railing,' she said. 'Then the awful thing happened, the thing that will remain in my memory until the day I die.'[3]

Dorothy listened as 1,500 people cried out to be saved, a noise she described as a horrific mixture of yells, shrieks, and moans. This was counterpointed by a deeper sound emanating from under the water, the noise of explosions that she likened to the terrific power of Niagara Falls. 'No one can describe the frightful sounds,' she said.[4]

Horrified by the scene, Hogg wanted to turn the lifeboat round and row to the spot of the sinking to pick up any survivors. He knew that, even though the majority of the stricken passengers wore lifebelts, they would not last long in the icy water. But, as soon as he voiced the suggestion, it was shouted down by the men and women in his lifeboat. Dorothy, when asked later about the reason why her lifeboat did not return to help the people in the water, could not explain it adequately.

'A minute, or probably two minutes, later she sank her nose into the ocean, swayed for a few minutes and disappeared, leaving nothing behind her on the face of the sea but a swirl of water, bobbing heads and lifeboats that were threatened by the suction of the waters. After the vessel had disappeared, the officer in command of our boat wanted to return, saying that there was room for several more passengers and pointing out the possibility of being able to rescue some of those who might be swimming. But immediately behind us was another lifeboat carrying forty people and as no one could be seen in the water some of the passengers in the other boat were transferred to ours.'[5]

Dorothy's account, published in a newspaper less than a week after the disaster, is full of contradictions. In the first sentence she states that immediately after the *Titanic* disappeared under the surface she could see the ocean full of 'bobbing heads'. Yet, in the same paragraph, she maintains that 'no one could be seen in the water'. Between the two observations lies a gap of time during which some of the struggling passengers could have been saved. The fact that there was another lifeboat near hers, filled with forty people, had nothing to do with the decision not to go back to rescue those dying in the water. In trying desperately to justify her actions, her words – and her jumbled reasoning – betray a sense of guilt.

Even at this early stage, Dorothy Gibson had already begun to shape her perception of the event so that she could psychologically survive the experience. She deliberately did not, could not, see the mass of bodies floating in the sea before her. With a couple of blinks of her light-blue, heavy-lidded eyes she had erased the corpses from her memory. Self-preservation was impossible, she had learned, without a certain element of self-deception.

Dorothy's knowledge of herself was confused. When she looked in the mirror she saw not only herself, but also a reflection of her screen image. Her life as a silent film star was dedicated to the supremacy of the visual. Before stepping on to the *Titanic* she had already transformed herself from an ordinary New Jersey girl into a model for the famous illustrator Harrison Fisher – whose lush images of idealised American beauty graced the covers of popular magazines – and then into a star of the silent screen. Her image had been reproduced so many times that her identity had become nothing but multiple layers of film laid over one another to form what looked like a whole.

A keen sense of opportunism drove Dorothy Gibson, and it was this overreaching ambition that would net her extraordinary material rewards, but would ultimately lead to her downfall. During the course of her early life she had two fellow strategists who would assist in her self-transformation – her mother, and fellow *Titanic* passenger, Pauline, and her older lover, the wealthy film pioneer Jules Brulatour. Pauline instilled in Dorothy an insatiable desire to succeed, fostering a relationship that can only be described as co-dependent. 'My mother has always managed me, and I have always let her do it,' she said.[6] Brulatour, who was nearly twenty years older than her and a married man when they met, took advantage of her hunger for fame. After the loss of the *Titanic* it was Brulatour who influenced, if not manipulated, her decision to write the scenario for a film and star in what could be called the world's first exploitation movie – *Saved from the Titanic*, which had its premiere only four weeks after the sinking.

Dorothy's perception of the tragedy, already skewed by her desire to rewrite what she saw on that clear, cold night in April, took on another level of unreality when she made the film. In effect, she became a character of her own imagining, a substitute self that was in many ways more heroic than the real one. However, this confusion between authentic and invented selves had its consequences. One day, during the making of the silent film, shooting had to be brought to a halt when Dorothy seemed to experience some sort of existential crisis. 'She had practically lost her reason,' wrote one contemporary observer, 'by virtue of the terrible strain she had been under to graphically portray her part.'[7]

* * *

Dorothy Gibson had, in many ways, been playing a part since she was a child. It was a role scripted for her by her mother, Pauline, a woman of German and Danish extraction whose father had emigrated to the United States from Denmark in the 1850s. Pauline, born in 1866, grew up in Hoboken, New Jersey, and in 1887 married a twenty-two-year-old builder from Scotland, John Brown. Yet soon after the birth of their only child, Dorothy, on 17 May 1889, Brown passed away. Pauline, always keen on self-advancement for herself and her daughter, set out to find a suitable second husband. She must have been quietly jubilant when she caught the attentions of a well-off merchant, Leonard Gibson. The couple were married in February 1894, three months before Dorothy's fifth birthday. Over the course of the next few years Pauline and Leonard tried to make a family but by 1900 two of their offspring had died in infancy. As a result of this loss, Dorothy became the sole focus of Pauline's attention. Mother and daughter constructed a seemingly impermeable unit, one that could happily survive without the attentions of the man Dorothy had learned to call her father. 'My father,' she said, 'is a great man of the spirit and is contented with the simple life. But I and my mother are bohemian and we find the pleasures of this lovely world irresistible!'[8]

In 1906, the family moved to Manhattan and Dorothy soon became entranced by the stage. For a time she worked in the chorus line of a number of productions under the name of Polly Stanley; apparently the pseudonym was used to protect the reputation of her stepfather. By the autumn of 1907 she had kicked the chorus line to the wall and had won a supporting role as a schoolgirl in the musical *The Dairymaids*. The same year she was taken on as a client of the Shubert Brothers, one of New York's biggest and most powerful agents and theatrical production companies. Their large-scale shows were known for their spectacle rather than their subtlety. They were mostly musical variety productions, often with a cast of 500, and were extravagances that aimed to stun and awe the 5,000-strong audience at the Hippodrome Theatre. 'All we did was stand around in pretty hats, lean on our parasols and purr through a few ditties,' said Dorothy later. 'It was easy to get into a Shubert show. The casts were so big, anybody could get in. I think my aunt was in one.'[9]

In autumn 1909, Dorothy was performing on stage at the Hippodrome when she was spotted by the successful illustrator Harrison Fisher, lauded by *Harper's Bazaar* as the 'greatest portrayer of American womanhood'. He went backstage and introduced himself to Gibson, told her that he admired her face and asked whether she would sit for him. 'I laughed until I realized he was in earnest,' she said. 'And then it dawned on me that here was *the* Harrison Fisher offering to engage me as a model! I went white and all the girls around me squealed.'[10] Soon, she was sitting for him, earning around $15 to $50 each time. With each new image – titles included 'Roses', 'My Queen', and 'Music Hath Charms' – Dorothy became more and more idealised. Fisher transformed and enhanced her beauty, softening the shape of her nose, extending the space between her round eyes and slightly lifting her jaw, until she became at once both more girlish and more sexualised. In one cover, for *Cosmopolitan*'s June 1911 issue, she is pictured drinking sarsaparilla from a tall glass, her long fingers caressing its base, the lips of her rosebud mouth closed around a straw. Dorothy's mix of ingénue innocence and barely concealed sexual energy was a winning combination for the illustrator. Yet Gibson claimed she was mystified by her appeal. 'I was fortunate to be discovered, in a manner of speaking, by Mr Fisher,' she said. 'But he had many models, and some of them were far prettier than I was. I do not know what he saw in me. Youthful charm I may have had but I never thought I was a great beauty.'[11]

Dorothy later claimed that she was nothing more than a 'child' at this time, frightened of life. This comment could, on a superficial level, explain the failure of her marriage to a young pharmacist, George Henry Battier, whom she had met in 1909. Although the couple married in February 1910, by the summer of the same year the union had disintegrated. Perhaps Battier had become confused by the mixed messages portrayed in Fisher's images of his sweetheart. Had he based his desire for Dorothy on her innocence or her sexuality? What did he want her to be – girl or woman? Was he shocked by her lack of experience in the bedroom or her rather too abundant knowledge?

From the reputation that Dorothy developed later – it was rumoured she was highly promiscuous – it's possible that her view of herself as an innocent child bewildered by the complexities of the world was just another of her many poses. In fact, some believe that the reason why her first marriage broke down was because Gibson had embarked on an affair with Harrison Fisher. There is no proof of this – neither party was ever questioned about the validity of the rumour – yet it would tally with her habit of seeking out and exploiting rich, powerful men to improve her lot in life. Sex was her bargaining tool, fame her goal.

By the time she came to be travelling on the *Titanic*, Dorothy had acquired not only a career as a silent film star – working for Éclair, which had its studio in Fort Lee, New Jersey – but had also fallen in love with Jules Brulatour, one of the most powerful men in the early movie industry. After arriving in New York from New Orleans in 1898, Brulatour had worked as a sales representative for the Manhattan Optical Company of New Jersey, selling photographic paper, lenses and cameras, before securing a position as sales chief for the Lumière North American Company. In the first decade of the new century, the manufacture and sale of motion picture stock, cameras and projection equipment was highly controlled by the Motion Picture Patents Company (headed by Thomas Edison and George Eastman). The MPP loathed the independents, viewing them as upstarts and preferring instead to sell their film and machinery to a small group of established film companies such as Biograph and Kalem. Brulatour – together with Carl Laemmle, who had given Dorothy one of her first jobs as a stock player at his studio, the Independent Motion Picture Company – challenged the monopoly, and in 1909 created the Motion Picture Distributing and Sales Company. The move heralded a death knell to the rigid control of film stock and gave Brulatour his status as a maverick within the movie industry.

It was clear that business – the making of money – is what drove Brulatour. He switched allegiances between Lumière and Eastman Kodak (his former sparring partner) with the same ease with which he slipped out of his sober business suit and changed into his dapper evening dress at cocktail hour. During his lifetime a certain mythology grew up around the amount of money he made from the sale of raw stock – it had been rumoured, according to *Variety*, that it ranged between half a cent to one penny per foot. Whatever the truth, it was clear that by the time he met Dorothy Gibson, Brulatour was a wealthy man.

The couple were introduced at a Motion Picture Distributing and Sales Company ball held at New York's Alhambra Hall in October 1911. He was forty-one, she twenty-two; both were married to other people and Brulatour had three children. 'It happened before I knew it,' she said later. 'Only in youth can we love so much and so unwisely.'[12] The attraction may have been instant but it was far from straightforward. Perhaps for Dorothy it was a case of falling in love with a fantasy figure of a father she never had. Brulatour was balding, with dark eyes and an aquiline nose, a strong Southern accent and a reputation for ruthlessness. For his part, it seems he was attracted to the simulacrum of Dorothy, rather than the reality. He told her that night that it seemed he already knew her, as he had, he said, 'admired your lovely photo in the papers'.[13]

The affair was a passionate one and conducted in secret. Brulatour was adamant that his wife of seventeen years, Clara, should not find out about the liaison. Yet Dorothy – together with her mother, who no doubt helped organise illicit meetings for the couple – was keen for Jules to divorce his wife and marry Dorothy. It's clear that Brulatour found in Dorothy the ideal mistress – she was beautiful, fun-loving, initially malleable – but she wanted to take on another, altogether more serious role: in her dreams she saw herself as playing the part of the perfect wife. At this point in their relationship, when sex and fame bound them together, they did not give voice to their mismatched desires. It was enough that they had each other; he was her 'Julie', she his 'Mutsie'. The couple spent their days working at the studio in New Jersey and nights together at the Great Northern and St Regis Hotels in Manhattan. In late 1911 and early 1912, Dorothy worked hard, churning out a string of light romantic comedies and heart-rending melodramas such as *The Musician's Daughter*, *Love Finds a Way*, *The Awakening*, *The Kodak Contest*, *Easter Bonnet*, and *Miss Masquerader*, a title which could stand as a neat character description of Gibson herself.

By the spring of 1912, Dorothy was feeling so overworked that she pleaded with her employers – in effect, Brulatour, who had now begun to produce films at Éclair – to let her have a holiday. The days were long, and she realised that, in effect, there was 'very little of the glamour connected with movie stars'. She may have been earning $175 a week – the equivalent of nearly $4,000 today – but she was exhausted; she even went so far as to consider quitting the studio. Perhaps this was

out of the general field, which, itself, was six to twelve feet above the water-line.'[21]

At around 6 a.m. the lifeboat carrying Dorothy Gibson, her mother, William Sloper and their fellow passengers drew up alongside the *Carpathia*. Although boat number seven had been the first to leave the *Titanic*, it was the third to reach the rescue ship. Dorothy looked up to see the rails lined with kindly, curious faces and, a few moments later, after she had climbed the rope ladder that had been lowered down from above, she found herself on deck. With William Sloper, Dorothy and her mother watched the arrival of the rest of the lifeboats. They saw one lifeboat – that containing Sir Cosmo and Lady Duff Gordon – draw up containing only twelve passengers. This must have made Dorothy feel momentarily less guilty – there were others in this world, after all, who were more self-centred than she and her mother.

Dorothy, still wearing her damp, windswept evening gown, was approached by *Carpathia* passengers James Russell Lowell and his wife, and asked whether she would like to share their cabin. She accepted their kindness and, after eating breakfast, retired to their quarters where she slept for the next twenty-six hours. The suffering of some of her fellow survivors – many of whom had lost husbands, sons, lovers – passed her by.

One of the first things Dorothy did on waking was to try and get a telegram to Jules Brulatour to let him know that she was safe. But the backlog of wireless messages was long and she was told she would have to wait. On 17 April, two days after the loss of the *Titanic*, she received a note from her lover. 'Will be worried to death till I hear from you, what awful agony – Julie.' The next day she borrowed some money to send a short missive to Brulatour at his home at 31 East 27th Street, New York. 'Safe, picked up by *Carpathia*, don't worry – Dorothy.' The actress was careful not to use her pet name in case his wife spotted the message.

Brulatour had always intended to send a film crew to the pier to record Dorothy's arrival in New York; he was one of the first to realise that the newsreel could be used as an effective and powerful publicity tool and that the star's return to America on board the world's most famous rescue ship would help boost box office numbers. But suddenly he found himself with an extraordinary story on his hands. Information about the loss of the *Titanic* was in short supply – initially some newspapers had claimed that all her passengers had survived. Captain Rostron had placed a blanket ban on information from the *Carpathia* being leaked out to the news media – the wireless service could be used, he said, only for the purpose of communication with the authorities and for the relay of messages between survivors and their families, as well as the task of providing a list of which of the *Titanic*'s passengers had perished.

If he played this right, Brulatour knew that he could pull off the scoop of the century. Together with the newspaper the *New York American*, whose publisher was William Randolph Hearst, Brulatour paid for a tug, the *Mary Scully*, to take a handful of newsreel cameramen and still photographers to the site of the disaster. News then came through that the *Carpathia* was on its way to New York with the survivors, and so the *Mary Scully*'s course was altered. But, by this time, the news had spread and many other publishers had had the same idea. As the *Carpathia* sailed into New York – on the dark, stormy night of Thursday 18 April – it was surrounded by a mass of tiny vessels, all chartered by news corporations desperate to break what would be one of the biggest stories of modern times. From their tugs, reporters shouted through megaphones offering terrific sums of money for information and exclusives, but Captain Rostron said that he would shoot any pressmen who dared venture aboard his ship.

Unknown to Rostron, however, one of his original passengers, Carlos F. Hurd, was a veteran journalist for the *St Louis*

Post-Dispatch, and over the course of the past four days he had spoken to many survivors, amassing enough information for a five-thousand-word story. Hurd's only problem was how to get the report off the ship. He managed to send a wireless message to a friend at the *New York Evening World*, which, in turn, charted a tug to sail to the *Carpathia*. Out of sight of the Captain, Hurd stuffed his manuscript into an oilskin bag, which he then threw down to the waiting boat. The final edition of the *New York Evening World*, published on 18 April, carried a digest of Hurd's report, which was published in full the next morning. The story – which carried the headline, 'Titanic Boilers Blew up Breaking Her in Two After Striking Berg' – began:

'Fifteen hundred lives – the figures will hardly vary in either direction by more than a few dozen – were lost in the sinking of the *Titanic*, which struck an iceberg at 11.45 p.m., Sunday, and was at the ocean's bottom two hours and thirty-five minutes after.'[22]

The public's appetite for more information and details – accounts of suffering, bravery, self-sacrifice and selfishness – seemed insatiable, and Jules Brulatour, who was as much an opportunist as his mistress, took advantage of it by employing the relatively new medium of newsreel to the greatest effect. His footage of the docking of the *Carpathia* – which was spliced together with scenes of Captain Smith walking on the bridge of the *Titanic*'s sister ship, the *Olympic*, and shots of icebergs from the area where the liner sank, together with images of the launching of the liner – premiered in east coast theatres on 22 April. Not only was Brulatour's *Animated Weekly* newsreel 'the first on the scene with specially chartered tugboats and an extra relay of cameramen', according to *Billboard* magazine, but it also showed that 'the motion picture may fairly equal the press in bringing out a timely subject and one of startling interest to the public at large'.[23]

Brulatour hyped the newsreel as 'the most famous film in the whole world', and so it proved, packing out theatres across America over the following weeks. The pioneering movie mogul organised a private screening for Guglielmo Marconi – the inventor of the wireless technology that had played a central part in the *Titanic* story – and gave a copy of the film to President William Howard Taft, whose close friend Major Archie Butt had died in the sinking.

Some showings of the newsreel were even accompanied by the vivid live presentation of third-class passenger Olaus Abelseth, a twenty-five-year-old Norwegian who was emigrating to South Dakota. Abelseth regaled the audience with thrilling tales of how he had survived by jumping off the ship at the very last moment. When he had hit the freezing water he had felt a rope snake itself around his legs and he was forced to let go of his brother-in-law's and cousin's hands, neither of whom could swim and neither of whom would survive. He fought himself free and surfaced, only to find a fellow passenger pressing down hard on his head, using him as a kind of buoy. 'I said to him, "Let go." Of course, he did not pay any attention to that, but I got away from him,' said Abelseth. 'Then there was another man, and he hung on to me for a while, but he let go. Then I swam; I could not say, but it must have been about 15 or 20 minutes. It could not have been over that. Then I saw something dark ahead of me. I did not know what it was, but I swam toward that, and it was one of those collapsible boats.'[24]

For the price of ten cents at the box office, spectators could immerse themselves in the representational complexities of the disaster. On the one hand it was a real event, a tragedy captured by press reports, documentary newsreel footage and the testimonies of surviving witnesses. And on the other, there was its uncanny resemblance to a piece of fiction: the story of the sinking of the ship took about the same time as the staging of a play and it possessed all the elements of a great drama (the hubris of the enterprise, followed by the resulting catharsis). It's no wonder then that Brulatour felt that the story had 'legs'. Spurred on by the success of his *Animated Weekly* feature, he decided to go ahead with a silent film based on the disaster, starring his lover, authentic *Titanic* survivor Dorothy Gibson.

'The nation and the world had been profoundly grieved by the sinking of the *Titanic*,' she said, 'and I had the opportunity to pay tribute to those who gave their lives on that awful night. That is all I tried to do.'[25]

But that was not quite the whole story.

As Dorothy Gibson stood on the deck of the *Carpathia* she could hardly make out the skyline of New York. In fact, the night seemed so black it was difficult to see anything. Only the occasional streak of lightning and the flash of the photographers' cameras lit up what seemed like a dark, silent mass gathered on the dock. Unknown to her, thousands of people had come out that rainy night to witness the arrival of the *Carpathia*. Dorothy 'ran crying down the ramp' into the arms of her stepfather, soon followed by her mother, who was also greeted by her sister and a number of Hoboken friends and neighbours. Leonard Gibson ushered his stepdaughter and wife through the crowd and into a taxi and whisked them off to a celebratory party at a New York restaurant. But there was only one thing on Dorothy's mind – her lover, Brulatour. She realised that it would have been inappropriate for him to meet her at the pier – this would have given rise to scandal – but she desperately needed to see him. And so, after a couple of hours regaling friends and family with tales of her dramatic escape, she excused herself. She was so tired with nerves she thought she might collapse, she said. In truth, she had never felt so alive. She took a taxi back to her Manhattan apartment, quickly changed into more presentable clothes and hurried through the rain into the comfort of the grey car Brulatour had given her. She drove through the stormy night to the hotel where she had arranged to meet her lover.

That night Brulatour presented her with an engagement ring – a cluster of diamonds worth $1,000 – and a plan: to make a dramatic one-reel film of her survival. Soon, he said, she would not only be his wife, but she would be more famous than ever before. The loss of the *Titanic* would make both things possible: had she not sailed on the ship – had he not experienced the agony of almost losing her – it's unlikely that she would have made the transition from mistress to wife, while the experience of surviving the disaster would supply her with the greatest role of her career.

Over the course of the next few days Dorothy sketched out a rough outline for a story. She would play Miss Dorothy, a young woman travelling in Europe who is due to return to America on the *Titanic* to marry her sweetheart, Ensign Jack, in service with the US navy. Jack – who has been promised a message from Dorothy – enlists the help of a friend, Jenkins, who works as a wireless operator, to send a missive to the ship. But that night, by the wireless station, they hear the *Titanic* send out its distress call. Jack is in agony as he listens to the news of the sinking – and the next day he has to call on Dorothy's parents to tell them of the disaster. They wait anxiously until they hear that she is safe.

The scene then shifts to post-disaster, with Dorothy sitting at a table together with her parents and Jack. She tells the story of the sinking (all relayed in dramatic subtitles, of course, as this was a silent film) but the strain is too much and she faints. It is clear to her mother that Dorothy has been through a terrible ordeal and she calls on Jack to resign his position in the navy. He has a night to decide his future – it is a question of love versus duty – but he settles on staying with the navy. 'A sailor's first duty is to his flag and country,' Jack tells Dorothy's father, who in turn is so moved by the young man's patriotism that he hands his daughter over to him. 'My daughter,' he says, 'there's your husband.'

If one can see through the fog of the romantic melodrama, it's possible to read Dorothy's treatment as a fictionalisation of her own predicament. Substitute Jack for Jules and the navy for Clara Brulatour and the plot reads like a straightforward wish fulfilment fantasy. In her fictionalised scenario, Dorothy's survival forces her lover to choose between outward honour and inner desire, but his ultimate choice brings about the reconciliation of the two, something that she knew was impossible in her society, motivated as it was by strict codes of public, if not private, decency. By penning this sketch for the film, Dorothy was able to fashion an alternative reality for herself. In doing so, she would be saved from the *Titanic* twice – once, in a concrete form, as a survivor of a disaster of historical record, and again, in her imagination, where she could unite the conflicting forces of her personal and public life to form an idealised whole.

Shooting began almost immediately at the Éclair's Fort Lee studio in New Jersey and on location on board a derelict freighter that lay in New York harbour. Wearing the same outfit she had worn the night she had escaped the sinking ship – a white silk evening dress, a sweater, overcoat, and black pumps – the verisimilitude of the experience was overwhelming. A reporter who attended the shoot described how 'the cameramen advanced upon her alone on the deck of this supposedly doomed ship', and how they 'witnessed a tragic bit of acting that stirred even their hearts, accustomed as they were to weekly scenes of the kind'.[26] Yet this wasn't so much acting, in its conventional form at least, as replaying. Dorothy drew on her memory and shaped it into a reconstruction, transforming herself – and her rather less than heroic actions – in the process. The true reason why she subsequently broke down on set – why she became 'overwhelmed' – was the momentary inability to reconcile her lived behaviour with the fantasy she was creating in front of the cameras. Perhaps she did feel some guilt, after all, a certain sense of shame that she had survived. She had not only listened to 1,500 or so fellow passengers go to their deaths, but, while in the lifeboat, she had colluded in the refusal to go back to help rescue the dying in the water. She was indeed *Saved from the Titanic*, but she was also damned.

The subtleties of the situation – the complex knot of actions, memories, desires, fantasies and meta-representations that competed for dominance in Dorothy's mind during and after the disaster – were lost on the popular press. When the film was released, on 16 May 1912, just a month after the sinking, it was simply celebrated for its technical realism and emotional power. 'The startling story of the sea's greatest . . . disaster is the sensation of the country,' stated the *Moving Picture News*. 'Miss Dorothy Gibson, a heroine of the shipwreck and one of the most talked-of survivors, tells in this motion picture masterpiece of the enthralling tragedy among the icebergs.'[27]

The actual film no longer survives, but a number of images from the one-reel feature are held by the US Library of Congress. In one, Miss Dorothy stands in front of a map of the Atlantic, pointing to the very spot where the ship hit the iceberg. In another she is sitting at her parents' dining table, telling the story of her survival. One of the very last pictures in the sequence shows Dorothy towards the end of the film leaning her head on her sweetheart's shoulder, her father looking on proudly. In all of the images Dorothy looks strangely blank and empty, her eyes drained of emotion. The experience had left her feeling hollow, disassociated from her reality. Confused by how she had manipulated the truth – and in turn, how she had been manipulated by her lover, Brulatour, and the Éclair film bosses – soon after the release of *Saved from the Titanic* Dorothy Gibson walked out of her dressing room at the Fort Lee studios and turned her back on the movie business. She was, she stated, 'dissatisfied'. She needed to feel connected to the world once more – she desired, she said, a husband (seemingly forgetting, for an instant, that she still had one, Battier, albeit not a rich, powerful or loving one), children, animals and a stress-free country life. Unfortunately, she believed Jules Brulatour would be able to provide all this for her – and more.

At some point during the summer or autumn of 1912 – just as Brulatour was forming, with Carl Laemmle, the Universal Film Manufacturing Company, later to become Universal Pictures – Clara Brulatour finally decided to bring the farce that was her marriage to an end. For all their secret meetings and clandestine behaviour Dorothy and Jules were a high-profile couple in an industry powered by gossip and innuendo, while Gibson's sudden exposure in one of the most sensational films of the era probably did not help. Clara could not bear the rumours or the pitying looks of her friends any longer and so she initiated divorce proceedings against her unfaithful, but rich, husband. Brulatour dreaded the bad publicity such an action would bring and, through the mediation of lawyers, he came up with a compromise – he would settle on her a large sum of money ($20,000), together with a $65,000 life insurance policy, which she would receive in the event of his death, if Clara agreed to his plan. Instead of a divorce, which would have to be heard in a court, he came up with the idea of a private separation contract. As he signed the document, Brulatour congratulated himself for containing the scandal.

Dorothy, meanwhile, had to content herself with her status as mistress. Jules promised that once all the legal complications had been sorted out they would marry, and, in order to keep her sweet, he gave her the use of his Long Island weekend home and treated her and her mother to regular holidays in Europe. As Dorothy was no longer working as an actress – despite requests to star in various features – she began to look for something to fill her free time and finally settled on training as an opera singer with tutors who had worked with the Metropolitan Opera House in New York. She had, she said, 'an uncommon voice' and, although she seems to have been a little deluded about its quality and range, she went on to take part in the chorus of productions such as Umberto Giordano's *Madame Sans-Gêne* at the Met.

After submitting an insurance claim, in January 1913, for the loss of possessions on board the *Titanic* – a sum that came to just under $4,000 for mother and daughter – Dorothy was determined to put the disaster behind her and create a future for herself that was not defined by her status as a survivor. The *Titanic* was, she tried to convince herself, a minor incident in her life. The fact that she had made a film about the sinking was of little consequence.

Yet, one day in the spring of 1913, she was forced to remember, albeit subconsciously, the horrors of that awful night. She was driving from New York to Brulatour's house in Long Island when she became momentarily distracted and lost control of her car. The vehicle mounted the sidewalk and hit a married couple – Julia Smith and her husband. Julia sustained major injuries in the accident, while her husband subsequently died.

What is notable about the incident is that Dorothy was driving the same car, the little grey Detroit that Brulatour had given her, which she had said was the thing she would miss most if she were to die on board the *Titanic*. 'I'll never ride in my little gray car again,' she had screamed, in the moments before jumping into the lifeboat. It's tempting to see the car as a kind of symbol – a representation of her repressed guilt – and the accident as a way in which she could punish herself for the fact that she had survived both in real life and in filmic form. Unconsciously, she was laying the foundations that would ultimately bring about her own self-destruction.

Brulatour managed to control the story for a while, but then, in May 1913, the news leaked out after it was revealed that Julia Smith was suing Dorothy for the death of her husband and the injuries that she had sustained in the accident. In court, Gibson was asked about her relationship with the owner of the car – Jules Brulatour. They were, she maintained, nothing more than 'good friends'. How long had she had the vehicle? Just over a year. Was she 'acquainted' with Mrs Brulatour? No, answered Dorothy. On 21 May, Justice Platzek ordered Dorothy to pay Julia Smith the sum of $4,500, a ruling which might have brought the lawsuit to a close had it not been for Brulatour's decision to plead his lover's case, in a statement which, in effect, contradicted Dorothy's earlier testimony. Gibson was, he stated, 'his fiancée' and although she was married and he was not divorced, he did intend to marry Dorothy once everything was settled. Clara was furious that her good name was linked with the scandal and started divorce proceedings once more, an on-off process that dragged on until 1917, by which point both Dorothy and Jules had succeeded in their attempts to legally separate themselves from their partners.[28]

Dorothy thought marriage would solve all her problems – not only would it legitimise her standing as the most important woman in Brulatour's life, but it would ease the unpleasant associations surrounding her survival of the *Titanic* as well as the scandal of the car accident and her exposure as a liar in court. Yet, almost as soon as the couple married – on 6 July 1917 in New York – their relationship started to deteriorate. It soon became obvious that whatever spark they had between them had been kept alive by the illicit nature of the relationship. Married life was nothing but an awful anticlimax and, as both were thrill-seekers at heart, they soon sought out new partners with whom they could indulge their desires – he with the young actress, Hope Hampton, whom he eventually married, while it was rumoured that Dorothy had dalliances with both the singer Johannes Sembach and the matinee idol Conrad Nagel. The only thing that tied them together was a string of complicated legal cases, centring on the authenticity of Brulatour's divorce – which was granted in Kentucky, where he was not a resident – and, as a result, the validity of their marriage.

By August 1919 Dorothy was in court appealing for alimony of $48,000. The request was refused and she was granted $10,000 a year. But the presiding judge, Justice Luce, was appalled by the pair's behaviour and went so far as to reprimand them for their 'unprincipled conduct'. He stated that 'the papers contain the story of the infidelity of both parties, an utter disregard of marital obligations, and resort by both parties to the court to be relieved of matrimonial vows as if they were nothing more than a mere contract'.[29] Finally, after an interminable number of hearings the couple were granted a divorce on 'common-law' grounds – a ruling that acknowledged the dubious legality of their marriage. After Brulatour married Hope Hampton, in 1923, Dorothy was so humiliated that she felt her only course of action was to leave America for Europe.

'I had a great deal of unhappiness and much less money,' she later said. 'Mr Brulatour had married again, and we still had many of the same friends . . . I was not very happy as my husband and his new wife were always around. Therefore I went to Paris to live with my mother . . . I already knew Paris very well . . . I talked it all over with my lawyer and friend, Max

Steuer, and he advised it most strongly. So my mother and I went to Paris.'[30]

Once in Europe, Pauline Gibson learned to hate America. She distanced herself from the country of her birth to such an extent that she chose not to return to the United States for the funeral of Leonard, her husband, in 1938, and admitted she did not know whether her sister was alive or dead. Pauline, whose mother had been German, resented the way the Germans had been treated in the USA during the First World War – a number of her friends in Hoboken, a city built by immigrants from the heartland of Europe, had been sent to Ellis Island for detention and parts of the neighbourhood had been subject to martial law.

Dorothy's reason for loving Europe was, at first, inspired not so much by a dissatisfaction with America as with a sense of having discovered a new freedom. In many ways, her life – post-*Titanic*, post-stardom, post-Brulatour, post-America – should have been one of pure hedonism. Settling in Paris, she had more than enough money from her alimony for everyday luxuries such as cocktails and champagne and entertained a wide range of bohemian friends including the writers Colette, H.G. Wells, and James Joyce, and actresses Fannie Ward and Pearl White. For her movie business set she would often throw what she called 'picture parties', during which she would show clips from a selection of old films, sometimes even her own. 'It is great fun for us and our friends to watch all those silly escapades and be reminded of the horrid fashions we wore,' she said.[31]

She saw Europe as a continent of unadulterated pleasures, a place where she could indulge her unconventional desires (she preferred the role of mistress to that of wife) without fear of moral reprimand or public scandal, while she associated

America with a certain puritanism that bored and annoyed her in equal measures.

'Oh my, what a time I am having!' she told a journalist in 1934. 'I never cared much for motion pictures, you see, and I am too glad to be free of that work. I tell you it was an immense burden. I have had my share of troubles, as you know, but since coming to France, I have recovered from that and feel happy at last. Who could not be deliriously happy in this country? I have such fun. But I fear it cannot go on like this always. I have had my dream life, and am sure that someday a dark cloud will come and wash it all away!'[32]

Dorothy's capacity for self-knowledge was, as we have seen, extremely limited, yet this prediction suggests an unusual degree of insight. She could sense that there was a 'dark cloud' on the horizon – little did she realise, though, that this shadow that she feared would destroy her dream life was nothing less than the Second World War. Displaying characteristically poor judgement, Dorothy and Pauline, believing that Hitler would win the war, aligned themselves with Fascist elements. Dorothy fell in love with Antonio Ramos, the press attaché for the Spanish Embassy in Paris. A photograph exists showing Ramos, a large, quite portly, moustachioed man, together with General Franco's brother, Nicholas, at the 1937 Nazi Party Congress in Nuremberg. Pauline, for her part, idolised Mussolini, and chose to base herself in Florence. Unfortunately, as Dorothy was driving from Paris to Florence, ostensibly to collect her mother and bring her back to France, Germany invaded Holland and Belgium. Unhindered travel suddenly proved more difficult, yet it would still have been possible for the two women to return to America. The reason they didn't? Certainly their experience on the *Titanic* was a factor.

'I must say I never wanted to make the Ocean trip to America at this time,' said Dorothy in an affidavit, 'as my mother and I were most timid on the ocean – we had been in a shipwreck – but I also never wanted to stay in Italy, but we just waited in Italy always hoping things would be better to travel.' Ideally, Dorothy wanted to go to either Portugal or Spain, but she said that her mother was not well enough to make the difficult journey. 'In the meantime our passports were always in order,' she continued in the same official statement. 'To my horror Mussolini and Hitler declared war on America – a thing I never thought possible. Two days later I wired Rome asking to be taken to America, I was advised I would be taken. My passport was good until December 20, 1941. I was told to do nothing about my passport. Finally when the boat did not seem to be ready to leave I applied for a Swiss protectorate passport. My passports and my money were returned to me saying it was not necessary as I was being repatriated . . . I wish to say I never wanted to remain in Italy and that I have brought myself nothing but unhappiness and have perhaps completely ruined my life trying to do the best – as I thought – for my mother.'[33]

Trying to make sense of Dorothy's life from this point onwards is a difficult task. What little cohesion there was holding her personality together seemed to disappear completely until all that was left was a series of seemingly disconnected contradictory acts and movements. At one moment she was the lover of Ramos, a high-ranking Spanish Fascist, the next a friend of Indro Montanelli, the well-known Italian left-wing journalist and historian. Perhaps she had become so used to acting a part – that of wife, model, mistress, movie star – that she no longer knew who she was. There were, quite simply, too many masks to choose from.

Dorothy Gibson's disintegrating sense of self cannot have been helped by the veiled portrayal of her in one of the most famous movies of all time – Orson Welles's *Citizen Kane*, released in 1941. Although William Randolph Hearst thought that he was the sole inspiration for the figure of Kane, some film scholars now believe that the media mogul was modelled on none other than Jules Brulatour – and that his talentless wife, Susan Alexander, the aspiring opera singer who takes to the bottle (played by Dorothy Comingore), was inspired in part by Dorothy Gibson. As Louella Parsons, the infamous gossip columnist, wrote in a letter, the film was 'not so much about Hearst as it was old Brulatour and his sad girls'.[34]

In the spring of 1944, Dorothy was in a vulnerable state – both psychologically and politically. That April, while still in Florence with her mother, she was informed by the Questura, the Italian police, that she would be taken to the German-controlled Fossoli internment centre. She tried to escape, travelling on foot towards the Swiss border, but on 16 April she was arrested in Cannobio and taken to a Nazi concentration camp. After being moved around various camps, she was imprisoned at San Vittore, which she described as a 'living death . . . you can speak to no one – and if you try and are caught the punishment is awful'. It's most likely Gibson would have died in this camp had it not been for the machinations of a double agent, Ugo Luca Osteria, known as 'Dr Ugo', who wanted to infiltrate Allied intelligence in Switzerland (something he subsequently failed to do). Gibson – together with Indro Montanelli and another man, who were also held at San Vittore – was smuggled out of the concentration camp under the pretence that she was a Nazi sympathiser and spy. Perhaps for Dorothy, this was one role too many – although the plan worked (she, together with her two companions, escaped the camp, and managed to cross into Switzerland), the experience left her understandably drained and exhausted. After being interrogated in Zurich, where she gave an affidavit to James C. Bell, Vice Consul of the American Consulate General, she was judged too stupid to have been a genuine spy. In Bell's words,

Dorothy 'hardly seems bright enough to be useful in such capacity'.[35]

Dorothy tried to resume a normal life after this episode, but the trauma of her survival – first the *Titanic*, then a concentration camp – took its toll. Already a sufferer of high blood pressure – in her statement to James Bell she claims she suffered from blood pressure of 260 – she was treated for the disorder at the American Hospital in Neuilly at the beginning of 1945, and spent the summer trying to recover in Vevey, Switzerland. After the war ended in 1945 she returned to Paris and enjoyed a few months at the Ritz, where, on 17 February 1946, she died in her suite, probably from a heart attack.

Intriguingly, no cause of death was cited on her death certificate; it's almost tempting to fill the empty space with the word 'Survivor'. If she had not travelled on the *Titanic* it's highly unlikely that she would ever have made the transition from Brulatour's mistress to wife, and neither would she have become so infamous that she had felt the need to flee America for Europe. The guilt that came with surviving the *Titanic*, and the subsequent exploitation of its memory, lay heavy upon her heart until finally it could stand it no longer.

Nine

TITANIC FEVER

The sinking of the world's most famous ship generated three waves of *Titanic* mania. The first, as we have seen, hit popular consciousness in the days and months immediately after the disaster, resulting in a range of contemporary cultural artefacts such as Brulatour's newsreel, Dorothy Gibson's film *Saved from the Titanic*, a clutch of books written by survivors (those by Archibald Gracie and Lawrence Beesley being among the best), poems like Edwin Drew's *The Chief Incidents of the Titanic Wreck* (published in May 1912) and Thomas Hardy's 'The Convergence of the Twain' (June 1912), and a flurry of songs (112 different pieces of music inspired by the loss of the *Titanic* were copyrighted in America in 1912 alone).

John Podesta, a fireman who had survived the *Titanic*, experienced the frenzy for himself when, a few days after docking in New York, he was walking through the streets of Manhattan with his fellow crew members and 'everyone seemed to want to mingle with us and ask questions about the disaster'. At the Seaman's Mission, Podesta was treated to tea and sandwiches, and later that day an elderly lady said she would pay him a dollar if he gave her his belt as a souvenir. When he asked why she might want such a thing, she replied, 'because it's off a survivor!'[1]

The onset of the First, and then the Second World Wars quietened the *Titanic* storm; the loss of hundreds of thousands of men on the battlefields of Europe, the whole-scale destruction of cities and communities around the world, and Hitler's single-minded plan to wipe out an entire race of people, together with other 'undesirables', placed the sinking of the ship, with its death toll of 1,500, towards the bottom end of the league of global tragedies. During the First World War and inter-war years, being concerned with the *Titanic* was regarded as unseemly, improper, unbecoming.

If anything, one was encouraged to laugh at it, as Noel Coward did in his 1931 play, *Cavalcade*, which charts the history of a British family, the Marryotts, from the beginning of the twentieth century to New Year's Eve 1929. Part Two, Scene Five opens with a honeymoon couple, Edith and Edward, standing on the deck of an ocean liner, discussing, in typically light Cowardian dialogue, the breadth and depth of the Atlantic. Wouldn't it be awful, posits Edith, if a magician told them that unless they counted every fish in the sea they would both die that evening? How much would they mind dying, asks Edith. 'I don't know – a good deal, I expect,' says Edward. 'I don't believe I should mind so very much now,' she replies. 'You see, we could never in our whole lives be happier than we are now, could we?' At the end of the scene, as Edith takes up her cloak, which has been draped over a lifebelt, the name of the *Titanic* is revealed. The lights fade and the orchestra strikes up the hymn 'Nearer My God to Thee'. In three and a half pages of glittering dialogue, Coward reduces everything about the *Titanic* – the death of its passengers and crew, the knot of metaphors and meanings surrounding its loss, the complex emotions that surfaced post-sinking – into a joke. The visual punch line revealed by the removal of Edith's cloak from the lifebelt may have had a generation of theatregoers in stitches, yet for many of the survivors the inclusion of it, firstly in the play and then in the 1933 film of *Cavalcade*, was an insult to the memory of those they had lost and the continuing difficulties they suffered as a result of the sinking of the ship.

May Futrelle – whose husband, the novelist Jacques Futrelle, had died in the disaster – voiced the thoughts of many survivors when she said that the scene was 'absurd'.[2] Indeed, she had become so frustrated with the way the *Titanic* had been represented that she felt, against her better nature, that it was time she should speak out. 'I have stacks and stacks of clippings, papers, magazines stories, and even records, all full of inaccuracies,' said May. 'Many are faked interviews with me. Many are the wild imaginings of frustrated reporters, etc, etc . . . Radio plays every year are the worst offenders and would be funny if they were not so horrible.'[3]

May Futrelle's letter was written in the mid-fifties, during what is generally considered to be the second wave of *Titanic* fever. In the midst of the Cold War – when there was a perceived threat that, at any moment, the world could end without warning or preparation in nuclear Armageddon– the *Titanic* represented a manageable, containable, understandable tragedy. A mist of nostalgia hung over the disaster – a nostalgia for a society that functioned with fixed roles, in which each man and woman knew his or her place; a nostalgia for a certain gentility, or at least an imagined gentility, by which people behaved according to a strict set of rules; and a nostalgia for a tragedy that gave its participants time to consider their fates. There was, as one commentator put it, something rather 'quaint' about the loss of the *Titanic*. 'A truly modern technological disaster would not give its victims time to die, would not necessarily allow for survivors, might not even have an aftermath,' says Steven Biel.[4]

Writers, producers, journalists and directors realised that they could project any number of stories against the backdrop of the *Titanic*, shaping each of them according to the needs of the particular medium, audience, and genre expectation. The first full-scale movie representation of the disaster in the fifties was a melodrama – a genre which was considered both popular, and more importantly, profitable – called simply *Titanic*, and starred one of the ruling queens of the 'woman's picture', Barbara Stanwyck. She plays Julia Sturges, a woman in the middle of an emotional crisis. Trapped in an unhappy marriage to a cold but rich husband, Richard (Clifton Webb), she boards the *Titanic* with the intention of stealing their two children away from him. She loathes the way her seventeen-year-old daughter, Annette, has been spoilt by the trappings of wealth and the narrow values of high society and wants to teach her some humanity by taking her back to her home town of Mackinac, Michigan. Just before the ship sails, Richard discovers her plan, buys a last-minute ticket and slips on board, where he confronts her. During one of their heated arguments she confesses that the youngest child, ten-year-old Norman, is not actually his, but the product of a brief liaison. Richard refuses to have anything to do with the boy – that is, until he discovers Norman has not taken a lifeboat with his mother and sister, but has decided to stay on board the stricken *Titanic* with his 'father'. At this point, Richard's steely resolve fails him and, realising that they face death – all the lifeboats have now left the ship – he clings to the boy, proclaiming the words, 'Whatever happens I love you very much. I've been proud of you every day of your life, Norman.'

As the plot – and the dialogue suggests – this film, directed by Jean Negulesco, was not so much about the loss of the liner as the loss, and the subsequent rekindling, of love. If the scenario – a broken marriage, a devious plan to steal the children away from their father, a revelation surrounding true parenthood – wasn't melodramatic enough, the charged emotional setting of the *Titanic* was used to heighten the levels of sentiment to satiation point. The trailer begins, interspersed with shots of icebergs falling into the sea, with the words: 'Four decades have passed since the *Titanic* screamed across the headlines of the world, yet no human drama has eclipsed its staggering impact and overwhelming power. Now, for the first time, the screen brings you the strange events, the monumental story of those four never to be forgotten days . . . Unforgettable drama in scene after scene, an immense canvas on which is thrown the gripping story of young love, of cowardice and heroism, of faithfulness and adultery, of sinner and saint.' The viewer is then assaulted by a series of graphic messages that leap out of the screen in huge capital letters: 'Titanic in Emotion! Titanic in Spectacle! Titanic in Climax! Titanic in Cast! . . . The Motion Picture as Overpowering as its Name!'[5]

When news was first released that Charles Brackett, the writer and producer behind *The Lost Weekend*, *Sunset Boulevard* and *Niagara*, was interested in making a film about the *Titanic*, his office at Twentieth Century Fox studios was inundated with offers from survivors and other experts willing to act as consultants. May Futrelle – who had experienced first hand how journalists twisted and exaggerated certain aspects of the story – was among those who offered her services to the producers. 'I should like to tell you for your picture the full and complete story of the *Titanic* in all its dramatic incident as I know it, lived it,' she said, 'and, if you wish, help to guide your scenarists through the maze of published mistakes and the confused stories upon which they no doubt are basing their stories.'[6]

William Sloper, the Connecticut stockbroker who had escaped the ship with Dorothy Gibson, put himself forward as a technical advisor, mainly, one suspects, to try and clear his name. For more than forty years rumours had circulated that one of the first-class men had managed to sneak into a lifeboat by disguising himself as a woman. Although a number of men had been accused of this, Sloper wanted to clear his name once and for all. In a letter to Brackett's secretary, Sloper refers to a recent Hollywood news snippet, which included the phrase, 'a man donned a dress to gain a place in a lifeboat', a reference he took to be about himself. This was an untrue statement, he said; 'I know because I am the man about whom this story was maliciously written and published on the front page of Hearst's *New York Journal-American* on the morning of April 18 [1912]. The article was written by an offended reporter for Hearst's International News whom my father and elder brother refused to allow to come into our rooms at the Waldorf Astoria at 11 o'clock at night and interview me while I was eating the first meal I had had since noon. In fact, my brother, who was also a 6-footer like myself, pushed the reporter back out through the door of my room, along with 25 other newspaper reporters who tried to crowd into the room, by pressing his forearm under the reporter's chin and throwing his weight angrily behind his forearm against the man's Adam's apple.'

This assault, together with the appearance of Sloper's personal account in a rival newspaper, piqued the reporter to write his story under the large-type headline, 'William T. Sloper, son of prominent Connecticut banker, rescued from the *Titanic* disguised in a woman's nightgown'. At the time Sloper thought about suing Hearst International News Service, but his father advised against it, as he would have had to prove in court that he had suffered some financial loss and would have had to subpoena his fellow passengers in lifeboat number seven. He was convinced that he could easily depend on the support of his three bridge companions of the night of 14 April – Dorothy and Pauline Gibson, and the lawyer Frederick Seward – but his father insisted he should not take up the case. 'As no New England newspaper (that I ever knew of) used this libellous International News dispatch, I would never have known about it if a few friends, acquaintances and "cranks" living in other parts of the country had not cut the paragraph out of their own local papers and sent it to me.'[7]

It seems that there was no shortage of 'cranks' – all keen to have their stories told in the film. One woman, Blanche Boyce, a waitress from New York, wrote to Charles Brackett's office of her dramatic escape from the *Titanic*, relating how on the night of the collision she returned to her cabin and was told by one of her fellow passengers, an Irish woman as nervous as a 'fluttery hen', that something awful was about to happen. 'She says, "Don't undress, Winnie dear, I know there is something going to happen to this boat so don't undress, I am telling you,"' she said. 'Well, I get cross and I tell her, [you] are spoiling my trip and tomorrow I will ask the stewardess to put me in another stateroom – and I go up on deck and on the top stairs the boat stops. The water is very calm.' She watches as the officers release a lifeboat into the ocean, but she is ordered down below. She knocks on the cabin door, but her cabin mate, still angry from their earlier confrontation, tells her to go away. 'I go through the corridors and it seems so silly,' she continues. 'There is a sailor swabbing the floor and big tears running down his cheeks. I say to him, "Don't scrub any more, no one will walk these floors again," but he cries harder . . .' Finally, she manages to secure a place in one of the lifeboats. 'My shoes are lost and one stocking gone, but I am thankful to be where I am, when a man's voice called down to us in the boat, "Who will take the baby?" and I holler, "I will," and down comes the baby in a coarse brown bag, asleep. Oh, how long is the night, but the dear baby sleeps on, but I have cramp in my shoulder, but carry on in fear of my moving I would wake the baby . . .' The mate in charge of the lifeboat tells his passengers to all start yelling in order to attract the attention of a ship, whose light they could see on the horizon. But Blanche is feeling terribly sick at the sight of so many people in the water around her. 'The poor things in the water swam up to our boat trying to clutch the side,' she said. 'The poor hands were knocked back into the water. This sounds cruel but it had to be – too many people would swamp the boat, but those poor stumps will haunt me for ever . . .' She tells how she is rescued by the *Carpathia*, how she is given tea with rum in it to warm her and the conversation she had with a lady, a fellow passenger, who asks her whether she had managed to save anything from the *Titanic*. 'I said just these duds I have on – as she said I have something I have saved and will share it with you. I said [to myself], this is where you will get something to wear, but the lady goes to a drawer and coming to me she unfolds some tissue paper rolled up and divides some face power among us. What a vain person – powder of all things to rave over.'[8]

Blanche's stirring account makes for powerful reading, until one checks the passenger lists and discovers no such person ever boarded the *Titanic*. Miss Boyce was, it seems, nothing more than a fantasist, yet a fantasist who could give voice to the common desires and expectations surrounding the *Titanic* that existed in society during the early fifties. Blanche's scenario fulfils many of the received opinions and prejudices, a mixture of sentiment, silliness and sinister class hatred. Her account was neither used nor published – Charles Brackett decided he didn't want any contact with any survivors, whether they be real or imaginary – yet the 1953 film tapped into the common consciousness, and, to some extent, helped satisfy a seemingly insatiable appetite for more *Titanic* stories.

It would be easy to assume that the plotline of the abducted children in Brackett's *Titanic* film was nothing more than the product of a Hollywood screenwriter's overheated imagination. Yet the story had, in fact, its roots in real life. Immediately after the *Carpathia* docked in New York it came to light that on board the liner were two young French boys – Lolo (Michel) and Momon (Edmond) – who had been kidnapped by their father (travelling on the *Titanic* under the assumed name of Louis Hoffman). Fellow second-class passenger Madeleine Mellenger, who was thirteen at the time, remembered the two dark-haired boys, one aged nearly four, the other two. 'They sat at our table . . . and we wondered where their mamma was,' she said. 'It turned out that he [the father] was taking them away from "mamma" to America and the name was not Hoffman but Navratil.'[9] In an interview later in his life Michel recalled the majesty of the *Titanic*. 'A magnificent ship! . . .' he said. 'I remember looking down the length of the hull – the ship looked splendid. My brother and I played on the forward deck and were thrilled to be there. One morning, my father, my brother and I were eating eggs in the second-class dining room. The sea was stunning. My feeling was one of total and utter well-being.' On the night of the sinking, he remembered his father entering their cabin and gently awakening the two boys. 'He dressed me very warmly and took me in his arms,' he said. 'A stranger did the same for my brother. When I think of it now, I am very moved. They knew they were going to die.'[10]

Despite this, the man calling himself Louis Hoffman – real name Michel Navratil – did everything in his power to help fellow passengers safely into the boats. 'The last kindness . . . [he] did was to put my new shoes on and tie them for me,' recalled Madeleine Mellenger.[11] Madeleine escaped to safety with her mother in lifeboat fourteen, leaving the sinking ship at 1.30 a.m., but Michel Navratil had to wait until 2.05 a.m. to place his sons in collapsible D, the last boat to be lowered. Witnesses recall seeing the man they knew as Hoffman crouching on his knees, ensuring that each of his boys was wrapped up warm. 'The younger boy was so thoroughly bundled that he could scarcely move, and lay prone and inert upon the deck,' wrote one commentator. 'The older boy, equally well covered, stood patiently beside him.'[12]

As he handed his elder son over to Second Officer Lightoller, who was responsible for loading the boat, Michel whispered something into the child's ear. With that, Michel stepped back, raised his hand in a salute and disappeared into the crowd on the port side of the ship, and the two boys were lowered into the lifeboat. Later in life, his son Michel recalled the feel of the lifeboat hitting the water. 'I remember the sound of the splash, and the sensation of shock, as the little boat shivered in its attempt to right itself after its irregular descent,' he said.[13] Fellow passenger in collapsible D, Renee Harris, believed the two young brothers, with their pretty faces and mops of curly hair, were girls. She remembered the children crying and whimpering throughout the night. She tried to comfort them, wrapping them in a blanket her husband had given her, while Hugh Woolner fed them the crackers he had stuffed into his pockets before leaving the ship.

On reaching the *Carpathia*, Michel vaguely recalled the 'indignity of being hauled up the side in an ash-bucket',[14] but nothing of the fact that he and his brother became momentarily separated, something which resulted in 'howls of distress'.[15] The children found it hard to make themselves understood, as they spoke no English. Fortunately, one passenger who took an interest in the boys, Margaret Bechstein Hays, spoke fluent French and noticed that the elder child seemed to speak with a southern accent. She also observed the brothers' physical appearance, their 'heavy black hair, their dark eyes, and their sallow complexion'. When Margaret Hays mentioned the place 'Nice', Michel replied, in French, 'That is where Maman lives!'[16]

After the rescue ship docked in New York, Margaret Hays took the two brothers to stay with her at her apartment at 304

West 83rd Street. She watched as the two brothers played together in the bath. 'Where's Papa?' asked Momon. 'He's gone,' replied Lolo. In an attempt to try and trace any of their surviving relatives, Margaret gave an interview to the *New York Times*, a report that appeared on 20 April. From that moment the two boys became instantly famous. Their dramatic experience on board the *Titanic*, together with the mystery surrounding their identities and their adorable looks, combined to make the perfect story. Journalists dubbed the boys the 'Orphans of the Deep' or the 'Waifs of the *Titanic*' and within days their pictures featured in every newspaper in America. Speculation was rife, but it was generally assumed that the two boys had been thrown into a lifeboat during the last moments of the sinking, an endeavour described in the press as 'the last despairing act of their mother who sought to save her babes when she knew she must go to death herself'.[17]

Margaret Hays was besieged by enquiries and offers of adoption. One man, François Lefebvre, appealed to the public to help finance his journey from Mystic, Iowa, to New York in the hope that the two boys would be the children he had left behind in France a year before. Lefebvre – who knew his wife and four children had been sailing as third-class passengers on the *Titanic* – stopped in Chicago, where via an intermediary he sent off pictures of his family to New York. The images were duly compared, and after it was discovered that their identities did not match, Lefebvre, who had lost his whole family in the sinking, returned home a sad and disappointed man. (Later, the publicity surrounding the case would expose Lefebvre as a philanderer, fraudster and illegal immigrant and in August 1912 the authorities deported him back to France.)

Back in Nice, Marcelle Navratil, desperate to know about the fate of her children, appealed to the British and French consulates. She showed the envoys a photograph of Michel, and when it was learned that Thomas Cook and Sons in Monte Carlo had sold a second-class ticket to a Louis Hoffman – a name Navratil had borrowed from one of their neighbours in Nice – she began to understand what her estranged husband had done. She gave a complete description of her two boys to a French representative of the *New York Times*, who then passed on the details to Margaret Hays. There seemed to be no doubt about it – the so-called 'Orphans of the Deep' were orphans no longer. The White Star Line promptly offered their mother a complimentary passage to New York on the *Oceanic*, leaving Cherbourg on 8 May. In America, their temporary guardian agreed for the boys to be placed in the care of Mrs George Tyler, the sister of Eleanor Widener (a first-class passenger who had survived the *Titanic*) who not only spoke fluent French, but also employed Marcelle's first cousin, Rose Bruno, as a governess. There, at their new home in Elkins Park, Pennsylvania, just north of Philadelphia, the brothers played with the Tylers' son, five-year-old Sidney, who later remembered the air of mystery that accompanied the two boys when they entered his house. Although he could communicate with them – he could speak French too – it was frustrating that they were too young to give the family more than the barest details of their identities. 'Perhaps they were also in a state of shock which blurred their recollection of who they were . . .' he said. 'As nearly as I can recall, from remarks made by my parents at the time, the father and mother of Momon and Lolo had a violent quarrel, and separated, sometime in early April 1912 . . . I remember very clearly that toward the end of their visit with us, the boys were happy and thoroughly adjusted to their temporary home away from home.'[18]

Their stay in the Tylers' home proved short-lived for the two '*Titanic* waifs' as only a matter of weeks later their mother arrived in New York. Marcelle, who was twenty-one years old, was described as a 'rather slender, lithe and graceful' woman, 'with a wealth of lustrous black hair, big brown eyes and a complexion of peach-bloom. She wore deep mourning . . . and dark shadows under her eyes told of the many days and nights of yearning she had spent for her children since she learned of their fate and came to recover them in a strange land.'[19] On 16 May, she was met at the White Star Line pier by her cousin Rose Bruno, Margaret Hays and her father, Miss Utley (a nurse supplied by the Children's Aid Society), and Superintendent Walsh of the same organisation. 'There was a fond embrace between the two kinswomen and then Miss Hays was introduced to Mme Navratil,' wrote a journalist who witnessed the encounter. 'Weeping, the young mother embraced her.' A taxi took the group to the Children's Aid Society, which had been besieged by photographers and reporters. 'The windows of the building opposite were lined with interested groups of shop-workers who had got wind of what was happening across the way and who were craning their necks and gesticulating wildly toward a window on the fifth floor where the children were believed to be.'[20] The young mother was accompanied through the crowds, up to the fifth floor, and into the nurses' parlour, where her children were playing. As she stepped into the room, the rest of the group fell back, and she was allowed to greet her boys alone. There, she found Michel sitting in a corner of the room, in the window seat, turning the pages of an illustrated alphabet book. Edmond was scrambling over the floor, playing with the pieces of a puzzle. When she entered, the boys looked anxious, but then, as they recognised their mother, a 'growing wonder spread over the face of the bigger boy, while the smaller one . . . stared in amazement at the figure in the doorway. He let out one long-drawn and lusty wail and ran blubbering into the outstretched arms of his mother. The mother was trembling with sobs and her eyes were dim with tears as she ran forward and seized both youngsters.'[21]

The experience was suddenly too much for Marcelle – she was reported to be suffering from exhaustion and was placed under the care of the Children's Aid Society's physician. The situation was not helped by the high level of media interest in the case, particularly the attentions of a representative of a 'moving picture concern' who sought permission to 'subject the mother and children to the cinematograph'. Mme Navratil was apparently horrified at the idea – in the words of the Children's Aid Society's Superintendent Walsh, 'she did not desire her children to be made the subject of any sensation'.[22] The next day, however, she said that she had recovered her spirits somewhat and, with her two boys, she toured New York, taking in Fifth Avenue, Central Park and Riverside Drive. On the way home, their car stopped at the apartment of Margaret Hays, where Lolo became upset. 'You will never forget this beautiful young lady, will you?' said Marcelle to her son, as he stroked Margaret's face. 'No, indeed,' he replied in French. 'She is my good friend.'[23] The next day, in front of a large crowd of spectators, Marcelle and her two sons arrived at the White Star pier for the return voyage on the *Oceanic* to France. Still dressed in mourning clothes, and heavily veiled, she 'looked pale and walked slowly, with weariness'. On board the ship the brothers enjoyed their new-found celebrity, posing for a number of photographs taken by the crew. On their return to Europe, however, they faded from the public eye – their mother, believing that they had had enough experience of fame, tried to establish a foundation of normality at the base of their childhood. With each year, their story faded from public consciousness, and no doubt it would have largely disappeared from history had it not been for the curiosity of Sidney Tyler, the boy who had played with the two 'orphans' in the spring of 1912.

For years, Sidney Tyler had been haunted by the memory of the brothers and, in the autumn of 1978, as he entered his seventies, he finally decided to try and discover the fate of the two Navratil boys. He knew their first names, remembered their faces, assumed they probably still lived in France, but little else. His first step was to write to Ed Kamuda, the founder of the Titanic Historical Society, based in Indian Orchard, Massachusetts. 'I have reached the stage in my life at which it is fun to try and solve these puzzles and mysteries to which I have been exposed,' he wrote, 'and if I can find the names and/or addresses of these boys, I propose to go to France and re-establish the friendship. Because I myself remember so clearly what they looked like at the time, and what fun we had together, I have no doubt that they, in their turn, would remember me, though I doubt that they would have any recollection of my name.'[24]

In turn, Kamuda sent Tyler their surnames, a brief outline of their story, and a couple of faded photographs – 'How very French those boys do look!' commented Sidney.[25] Armed with this information, Tyler sent off a number of letters to the authorities in France. He was hopeful that it wouldn't take too long to locate the two brothers, as Navratil was apparently quite an unusual name in the country. Yet by February 1979 he had failed to find them. 'The French consuls here decline to set any wheels in motion,' he said, 'on the notion that they are authorized to search for missing persons only if they are relatives of American families who have lost touch with errant kin.'[26] Ed Kamuda, his curiosity piqued by the story, did everything in his power to help and sent Tyler a list of names of people in France who might know the whereabouts of the brothers. It was one of these contacts – Professor José Sourillan, regarded by both Kamuda and Tyler as 'a wild stab in the dark'[27] – who helped locate Michel Navratil. Tyler duly wrote to Michel, then working as a Professor of Philosophy at the University of Montpellier, and after a lengthy correspondence – described by Tyler as 'warm and cordial'[28] – in the summer of 1979 Tyler flew to France to meet the man he had last seen nearly seventy years before.

As Tyler walked up the flight of stairs to Michel's apartment at 9 Rue Pasteur, 'there seemed to be wings beneath [his] feet'.[29] Navratil, a man of 'modest stature' greeted him and immediately made him feel at home. The next day, after a drive to Aigues Mortes, an ancient walled city, where Michel delighted in showing his old friend the battlements, he began to talk of certain memories he had long suppressed. 'It is strange,' he said, 'how your discovery of me and the correspondence which flowed between us has led me to recall things which I thought I had forgotten. Not that they came back to me easily, mind you. Many had to be dug from the corners of my brain by efforts of will which were almost physical, and which required frequent application. I am not sure that during all these years I really wanted my memories to emerge, because many of them were painful.'[30] He confessed that he remembered nothing of the circumstances in which his father took him and his brother away from their mother 'that fateful Easter weekend'. He did, however, recall being on a boat – most likely the vessel that ferried him across the English Channel to Southampton – which was being tossed about on the ocean, and which made him feel seasick. 'I know that my physical misery was made worse by the anguish of separation from my mother,' he said, 'to whom I naturally turned for comfort when in distress.'[31]

He remembered the sight of the *Titanic* for the first time, its 'long black hull with its dazzling white superstructure'. The memory was so strong, he said, not because of the enormous size of the ship, but for what it represented – a permanent separation from his mother. Navratil went on to tell Tyler of the night of the sinking and the strange dream his mother had had on the night of 15 April 1912. Apparently, her husband had entered her room, presented her with a letter inside a white envelope that sported an ominous black border, and then silently withdrew.

Michel told Tyler how he had devoted his life to philosophy, how he had married a fellow student, Charlotte Lebaudy, in 1933, and how they had had three children together, a son and two daughters. He related how his wife had died in 1970, and how his mother, Marcelle, had passed away in 1974. His younger brother, Edmond, had married, had two daughters and lived in Lourdes, where he worked as an interior designer, architect and builder, but he had died in 1953, aged only forty-three. Michel said reliving the past was difficult for him, but he found it cathartic. One day, during a meal at a Greek restaurant, his son, Henri, turned to Tyler and said to him, 'There is something about your visit which has transformed my father. We have heard him say things to you about our family past which he rarely mentions within the privacy of our home and which he has never disclosed to an outsider. I think you have done wonders for him by enabling him to unburden himself of things long buried within him. We find him a happier person as a result of your visit.'[32]

Michel's daughter Elisabeth recalls that her father made little or no mention of the *Titanic* throughout her childhood. It was only when she was a teenager that she heard him begin to discuss the disaster with her mother, Charlotte. 'He consistently refused approaches from journalists or historians to discuss the event,' says Elisabeth. 'Yet I knew instinctively that one day a catalyst would arrive which would force him to talk about his experiences. And that catalyst was Sidney Tyler.'[33]

With Michel's help, Tyler was able to piece together the missing pieces of the Navratils' tragic story. In 1902, his father, who had been born in Szered, forty miles east of what is now Bratislava, travelled to Nice where he started to work as a tailor. Four years later, Michel senior met sixteen-year-old Marcelle

Carretto, who had been born in Buenos Aires of Italian parents. Soon after their marriage, in 1907, the couple started to experience marital problems. 'Perhaps the contrast between the Slovak culture and the Mediterranean, and between the Latin character and the Slav, turned out to be less magnetic than initially hoped,' said Tyler. 'Perhaps the young bride did not yet possess the maturity to cope with the triple demands of motherhood, home and work . . . Marcelle was artistic, imaginative and inclined to be impulsive, whereas Michel was decisive, determined and at times peremptory. Matters were not helped by Michel's conviction that Angele [Marcelle's mother] . . . was turning his wife against him, and by his awareness that both women were virtually inseparable, in a kind of symbiotic interdependence which persisted as though the marriage had never been.'[34] Michel's daughter, Elisabeth, maintains that Marcelle had begun to have a number of affairs behind her husband's back. 'She also squandered a considerable amount of money, which drove him to head for a new life in the United States,' she says.[35]

In early 1912, Michel moved out of the family home and the couple filed for separation on grounds of incompatibility. The court awarded custody of the children to Angele's brother, Bruno, who also lived in Nice, but often he would hand them back to his niece, an action which incurred reprimands from the authorities. The couple attempted a reconciliation in early April, but it lasted a mere three days. That Easter weekend, Marcelle sent the boys to their father's for the holiday, but when she went to collect them she discovered they had disappeared with Michel.

As the two men – Tyler and Navratil – reconstructed the past, they found themselves forging a close bond once more. Tyler likened the experience to a rainbow of space and time. 'Of space in the sense it arches over the ocean and connects two people on different continents,' he said, 'and of time in the sense that two-thirds of a century are compressed and telescoped and made as though the separating years had never been, bringing our youth and later lives together.'[36]

Sidney Tyler was so moved by the meeting that he felt the need to write about how their paths had crossed, first as boys, then again as adults. Michel agreed to the publication of a short book about the '*Titanic* orphans', and in the summer of 1980, Tyler returned to France with a draft manuscript. Michel then both added to and deleted from this, believing that 'certain passages . . . [were] too personal and private for publication'.[37] In March 1981, Michel wrote a letter to the author outlining his feelings about how the experience had resonated with him.

'I would say to you also that one of the principles to which I have always adhered, especially from the time that my research in Philosophy made me a professional in that area, has been the resolve not to forget the most important events of my past, and at the same time to preserve in my memory whatever the future might bring me on my journey through life. In my eyes, one of the most essential disciplines which Philosophy teaches is a backward view through the tunnels of time and a simultaneous receptivity to the unanticipated pathways of the future, in which one's daily encounters are enriched by unforgettable friendships.'[38]

The reclamation of his past continued when Michel decided to take a couple of *Titanic*-themed trips, firstly, in April 1987, to the site of the wreck and then, nine years later, to Halifax, Nova Scotia, to pay his respects at his father's grave. As Navratil, a Roman Catholic, had been travelling under the assumed name of Hoffman, after his body had been recovered from the sea he had been buried in the Baron de Hirsch Cemetery, reserved for those of the Jewish faith. During the 1996 trip, the past came alive once more as Michel remembered the last words his father had whispered into his ear. 'My child,' he had said, 'when your mother comes for you, as she surely will, tell her that I loved her dearly and still do. Tell her that I expected her to follow us, so that we might all live happily together in the peace and freedom of the New World.'[39] This was not so much a statement of intent – it's highly unlikely that Navratil wanted anything more to do with his estranged wife – as a kind of emotional salve for the young boy. As he recalled the words, Michel was able to view the painful events of the past through a prism of forgiveness and understanding. The whole experience, although difficult to live through, felt like a kind of rebirth. He was, he said, reminded of the words of Horace, '*Multa renascentur quae jam cecidere*,' which he translated as, 'Many things which have been destroyed will come alive again later.'[40] Although he passed away on 30 January 2001, at the age of ninety-two, the last male survivor of the *Titanic* disaster, Michel always said, 'I died at four. Since then I have been a fare-dodger of life. A gleaner of time.'[41]

Ten

FAME IS THE SPUR

After the melodrama of *Titanic* – the movie that won an Academy Award in 1953 for Charles Brackett's screenplay – the public wanted to know more about the doomed liner, specifically facts about why it sank, who was on board and the behaviour of the passengers, before, during and after the disaster. The demand was satisfied by an unlikely source – Walter Lord, a bespectacled advertising copywriter who worked for J. Walter Thompson in New York. As a boy, Lord, the son of a Baltimore lawyer, had sailed on the *Titanic*'s sister ship, the *Olympic*, and he had always been fascinated by the story of the collision between the luxury liner and the iceberg. With an almost military precision – Lord had worked as both a code clerk in Washington and an intelligence analyst in London during the Second World War – he amassed a mountain of material about the ship, and, most importantly, managed to locate, and interview, over sixty survivors. The resulting book, *A Night to Remember*, is a masterpiece of restraint and concision, a work of narrative non-fiction that captures the full drama of the sinking in little more than one hundred and fifty pages. On its publication in the winter of 1955, the book was an immediate success – entering the *New York Times* bestseller list at number 12 in the week of 11 December – and since then it has never been out of print. 'In the creation of the *Titanic* myth there were two defining moments,' writes one commentator, '1912, of course, and 1955.'[1]

The publication of *A Night to Remember* – together with its serialisation in the magazine *Ladies Home Journal* in October 1955 – had an immediate effect on the remaining survivors, almost as if the *Titanic* had been raised from the murky depths of their collective consciousness. Memories were stirred to such an extent that many of them felt they were reliving the disaster all over again. 'My mother and myself were survivors of that tragedy and tho' we are not mentioned by name in it [the book] we were passengers in the boat manned by Lightoller,' wrote Madeleine Mellenger to Henry Holt, the publisher of Lord's book. 'We were in two lifeboats – the first one was the one sent back to pick up and the second one 14 was the one which picked up the people from a collapsible including Lightoller. He was almost frozen being only in a light navy suit [with a] seaman's sweater under it. My mother rubbed and tried to warm him up and she put a large cape with a monk's hood [on him] . . . and after a while he was able to get up and give orders . . . [I] can remember it all as tho' it were only yesterday that it happened.' In fact, reading the account transported her back to that night to such an extent that she said she was 'going around in a trance today thinking of it all afresh'.[2]

Three weeks later, Madeleine Mellenger wrote to Lord himself, telling him of her emotions when the *Carpathia* pulled into New York, feelings not so much of relief, but of terror. 'The noise, commotion and searchlights terrified me,' she said. 'I stood on the deck directly under the rigging on which Captain Arthur Rostron climbed to yell orders thru' a megaphone . . . I live it all over again and shall walk around in a daze for a few days.'[3] Memories of the experience came back in flashes – the generosity of an American couple, honeymooners on board the *Carpathia*, who gave her mother, who was shoeless, a pair of beautiful French bedroom slippers, which were knitted and topped with big pink satin bows; and the horror of being forced to spend what seemed like an eternity in a cabin with a woman, Jane Laver Herman, who had lost her husband in the sinking. 'I had no clothes but the little short skirt so I could not get out of the bunk which was still warm when they put me in.' Lord's book had stirred her memory to the point where every small detail seemed to come alive. 'The bunk was draped with flowery chintz and curtains the same,' she said. 'After the beautiful cabin we had on the *Titanic*, second-class with two bunks . . . it was humble . . . I can recall as tho' yesterday laying in the upper bunks singing some of the lovely hymns of that night [aboard the *Titanic*] . . . PS. It would be wonderful if some time we survivors could all get together, somewhere?'[4]

Even though it was impractical for many of the survivors actually to gather in one location – something that became easier, and more popular, the fewer there were of them – those who had experienced the disaster were keen to share their stories. Walter Lord became a receptacle into which they could spill their innermost thoughts, memories, and fears. He, in turn, collected survivors' tales, and memorabilia such as buttons, menus, tickets, and silver spoons, with a near-obsessive passion, hoarding information about the *Titanic*'s passengers long after he had sent his book off to the publishers. He entered into lifelong correspondence with a number of survivors, and the resulting documents contain much information and many insights, which he kept back from publication, even in his 1987 sequel to *A Night to Remember* which he entitled *The Night Lives On*.

Lord's method was one of 'literary pointillism',[5] a term borrowed from art history which describes the work of certain Neo-Impressionists who used a series of small dots of various pure colours which then come together to form a picture. Lord took the experience of each of the survivors and scattered his text with fragments of their memories to create the impression that the reader was there on the ship with them, that night. Of course, for those who had lived through it, reading the book was an even more powerful experience. As Marguerite Schwarzenbach, formerly Frolicher, a young woman of twenty-two when she had sailed on the *Titanic*, wrote to Lord, 'you make us survivors relive that dreadful night, you brought back to us the horror, but also the feeling of gratitude and sense of obligation toward the grace that spared us.'[6]

Following the swell of *Titanic* mania there was a rush to transfer Lord's book to the screen, firstly in an American TV drama made by Kraft Television Theatre, which had an audience of 28 million when it aired in March 1956, and then in a big-budget British movie, released in 1958. The rights to the book were bought by William MacQuitty, an Irish-born producer who, like Walter Lord, had been fascinated by the *Titanic* since he was a boy. As a child, growing up in Belfast, he remembered teams of twenty draught horses pulling the liner's enormous anchors through the cobbled streets of the city, from the foundry to the Harland and Wolff shipyard. Over the course of the *Titanic*'s construction – from 1909 to 1911 – he watched the 'huge mountain of a ship' rise from its dock, and remembered being impressed by the grandeur and spectacle of the liner's launch on 31 May 1911. From 7.30 that morning crowds started to gather at the yard and by noon there were an estimated 100,000 people ranged around the slipway. 'The smell of the sea mingled with the smells of the shipyard, where a vast throng of workers and spectators waited in awed silence,' he said.[7]

MacQuitty watched as the dignitaries began to gather – Bruce Ismay was there, together with his wife; there was designer Thomas Andrews; Lord Pirrie; and star guest

J. Pierpont Morgan, chairman of the International Mercantile Marine. Just after midday a rocket was launched – a signal that there was just five minutes to go – before a second rocket was fired, the sign for the launch to go ahead. The noise was deafening, recalled MacQuitty, a cacophony of pistons, bellows, engines, saws, hammers and the excited shouts from the crowd. For what seemed like a couple of minutes – in fact, a matter of seconds – the *Titanic* remained motionless. William held his breath, like many others, as they waited for movement. After the faintest of shudders, the ship began to move, slowly at first, before picking up speed, finally whooshing down its slipway, generously lubricated by twenty-one tons of tallow and soap, and into the River Lagan with an enormous splash. 'A great wave rose as her stern hit the sea,' he said. 'The noise was thunderous. All the ships in Belfast harbour sounded their sirens, the vast crowd cheered, the hull was buoyed up by the water.'[8]

The following year, on 2 April, MacQuitty witnessed the ship steam out of Belfast harbour to begin its maiden voyage. 'Before her lay the freedom of the oceans and I longed to be aboard,' he said. When, two weeks later, he heard the news of its sinking he could hardly comprehend it – how could something so huge, so graceful, so powerful, now lie at the bottom of the Atlantic? How could over 1,500 men, women and children have lost their lives? 'The inheritance of Victorian certainty was shattered and something had changed for ever,' he said.[9]

MacQuitty continued to be fascinated by the *Titanic*. Then, one day in June 1956, his wife, Betty, returned from hospital with both their new daughter, Miranda, and a glowing review of Walter Lord's book. As soon as he read *A Night to Remember*, MacQuitty, already an established producer, knew that he had found the subject for his next film. The challenge was to try and convince his studio, the Rank Organisation, of the viability of the project. 'Why do you want to make this film?' barked John

Davis, the managing director of Rank, based at Pinewood Studios. 'It's been made before. And why do you want to buy the book and give the writer two and a half per cent of the profits? The story's in the public domain . . . It's just another shipwreck, on which you want to spend half a million [pounds].' The memories of the ship being launched came flooding back – the majesty of it as it sailed down the Lagan and into the open sea – and as MacQuitty explained the significance of the project his voice became enthused with passion. 'It's not another shipwreck,' he replied. 'It's the end of an era.' Davis asked him to explain himself – in simple, honest terms; he didn't want any of his 'Irish blarney'. MacQuitty saw the ship as a symbol for a lost age – in many ways, an age of arrogance. One could see this, he said, in the demographics of the passengers and how much they had paid for their tickets to sail across the Atlantic. 'Stateroom passengers, to establish their wealth, paid £875 for the five-day crossing from Southampton to New York,' he said. 'Steerage passengers paid £12.' The rigidity of the class system was also reflected in the monument to the disaster. 'In Belfast, the names on the *Titanic* Memorial are in order of importance, while those on the nearby 1914–1918 war memorial are in alphabetical order.' MacQuitty added that he didn't want *A Night to Remember* to be a mere vehicle for famous actors or a backdrop on which to project a melodrama, but a true account of the sinking in which the ship would be the real star. After a moment's reflection, the notoriously difficult Davis nodded his approval. 'Make it,' he said.[10]

MacQuitty chose Roy Baker as director, Eric Ambler as scriptwriter and Walter Lord as a consultant on the project; his job was to ensure that the film was as accurate as possible. The overall effect he wanted to achieve was one of near-documentary realism. Alex Vetchinsky – the Pinewood art director known as 'Vetch' – employed his obsessive eye for detail to recreate the *Titanic* itself. Working from original blueprints of the ship, Vetch built the centre third of the liner, including two funnels and four lifeboats, an undertaking that required 4,000 tons of steel. This was constructed above a concrete platform, which had to be strong enough to support the 'ship' and the surging mass of hundreds of passengers who were shown clinging to the rails to the very last.

As MacQuitty was adamant that the production was to be ruled by the watchword of realism he went to great lengths to ensure that a suitable ship was found as a stand-in for the *Titanic*. After some negotiations he discovered that the boats of the Shaw Savill Line provided a near-match in terms of colour and details surrounding the davits. His team was promised the use of a ship for one weekend, while it was in dock in London, but two days before the shoot an official rang MacQuitty to tell him permission had been withdrawn. 'Later I heard that the chairman was a friend of the Ismay family,' he said.[11] And although MacQuitty was a friend of Harland and Wolff's chairman, Sir Frederick Rebbeck – he had been best man at his son's wedding – permission was refused to shoot at the shipyard in Belfast.

Not to be defeated, the producer then rang Lloyd's, who advised him to contact Thomas Ward, the Clyde shipbuilders who were breaking up the *Asturias*, a ship that had the same davits as the *Titanic*. MacQuitty took a flight to Helensburgh the same day, examined the ship and discovered it to be a perfect match. 'The port side was already being broken up, but the starboard side, next to the sea, was still intact,' he recalled. 'By fixing a mirror on the camera, and ensuring that all lettering was then written backwards, we could also transform it into the port side without difficulty.'[12] An agreement was made with the manager of the firm – he could use the ship for £100 for ten days. The next day a telegram arrived from the London shipping companies advising Thomas Ward not to have anything to do with the film producer, but it was too late as the contract had been signed and the shoot could go ahead.

Scenes of the *Titanic*'s lifeboats drifting in the cold Atlantic were filmed during the winter of 1957 in the Ruislip lido; although the water was only four feet deep it was freezing. Kenneth More – who played Second Officer Lightoller in the film – remembered the shoot as being one of absolute verisimilitude; the cold was so biting and deep he didn't need to act, but simply react. Jumping into the water was like stepping into a deep freeze. 'The shock forced the breath out of my body,' he said. 'My heart seemed to stop beating. I felt crushed, unable to think. I had *rigor mortis* without the *mortis* . . . We struck out for the boats, struggling and kicking anyone who got in our way. We weren't acting. We were desperate to be rescued. There were eight lifeboats, which would carry about sixty-four each. This meant that more than five hundred men and women in overcoats and fur coats were thrashing about in the lido for quite a long time before they could all haul themselves aboard the boats.'[13]

MacQuitty's team drew up a list of *Titanic* survivors, some of whom agreed to help with the filming. Fourth Officer Joseph Boxall – a well-regarded navigator who had been assigned by Captain Smith the job of updating the ship's charts during the *Titanic*'s maiden voyage – was appointed as a technical advisor. One day during filming MacQuitty called upon him to try and verify the story of a man named John Owen, who had written to him about his experience on the *Titanic*. Owen, wrote MacQuitty, 'claims to have been a stowaway on board the *Titanic*. He was apparently concealed by John Grogan, a carpenter, in either the carpenters' shop or stores. When the crash occurred he came up on deck and worked with the ship's crew. He says he met you [Boxall] and that he was picked up with a Mr Thayer, and when he got on board the *Carpathia* a man named Skidmore brought him dry clothing.' MacQuitty had also recently spoken to Captain Smith's daughter, Mrs Russell Cooke, who told him that she recalled that there had been some talk of there being at least one stowaway on board the ship. As John Owen seemed to be quite a reasonable person could Boxall remember meeting him or someone of his description?[14] Boxall, then living in Christchurch, Hampshire, wrote back to MacQuitty the following day, telling him that this was the first time he had heard such an astonishing piece of news. In addition, 'a thorough search was systematically made on board all White Star Line ships prior to sailing, in all Departments and reported to the Captain.'[15]

News of the making of *A Night to Remember* drew out yet more fantasists and fame-seekers, keen to claim a part of the *Titanic* story for themselves. There was an Alfonse Ross, a fifty-nine-year-old horticulturalist from Jackson, Mississippi, who maintained that, as a boy, he had survived the disaster by clinging to an iceberg for three hours. A woman from Detroit said that she thought she was Lorraine Allison, the daughter of first-class couple Hudson and Bess Allison, whom the authorities always believed had died, aged three, with her parents in the sinking. And then there was the curious case of a Miss Vera Edwards, from London, who had enlisted the help of a solicitor, L.M. Wilkins, to try and solve the mystery surrounding her birth.

The saga began, said Edwards, when the Ministry of Health wrote to her to tell her that she had not been born in 1908 as she had always believed, but either in 1910 or 1911. She had been brought up in institutions until the age of eighteen, had never known her parents, or her real name. Then in the early 1930s, a letter had been pushed through her letterbox, giving no indication of its sender, containing a number of newspaper cuttings about the *Titanic* disaster. On the top of the folder, printed in red ink, was written 'Master, Dulwich College' and the words 'Handed from A deck to Lifeboat 13'. In order to try and solve the mystery, Wilkins wrote to Walter Lord, now considered an expert on anything *Titanic*-related.

'She [Miss Edwards] never suspected any connection . . . with the *Titanic* before this "information" . . .' wrote Wilkins. 'I discovered that "Master, Dulwich College" was Mr Lawrence Beesley. I visited him and he confirmed he was on Lifeboat 13, and that he had handed a child (unknown) to a woman sitting next to him. He recalled this woman had sat opposite him at the Purser's Table (both being second-class passengers) and that they knew the same friends in Clonmel, Ireland. She joined the *Titanic* at Queenstown. He could not remember her name, nor the name of the mutual friend.'

Further research led the solicitor to a Julia Murphy, then living in Kenmare, County Kerry, who told him that she had had a friend, Elizabeth Dowdell, who had sailed as a third-class passenger on the *Titanic*. Elizabeth travelled from America to Britain with another female friend – whose name no one seemed to know – who then entrusted the safety of her child to her on the return trip to the United States. 'She was on the *Titanic* and she told me how this lady followed her to the boat and gave her a child to bring back to America to her own people,' said Julia Murphy.[16]

From this, and other sources, the mysterious Miss Edwards seems most likely to have been none other than Virginia Ethel Emanuel, the daughter of an opera singer, Estelle Emanuel. Estelle had been performing in London for six months when she had sent the little girl back to her grandparents, the Weills, on the *Titanic*. When the Weills, who lived at 605 West 113th Street, New York, were reunited with their grandchild, it was reported at the time that they exclaimed, 'Our dear little girl! And you, Miss Dowdell, how can we ever repay you for your noble deed in saving the treasure we prize above everything in the world – our little Virginia.'[17] Yet from what happened next it seems that the four-year-old child cannot have been that much of a prize – as within only a few years she was dispatched back to London, where she was first taken into a series of institutions, before being placed in the home of a Mrs Hylton of 93 Plumstead Common Road. She spent the rest of her life trying to make sense of both the ghostly memories of the past and the confusion surrounding her true origins.

Whether Virginia Emanuel – who had lived under the assumed surnames of Scott, Wise and Edwards – ever discovered her real name or who her parents were is hard to say; no records or testimonies exist to shed light on this mystery. What we do know is that, as Vera Edwards, she went on to marry a Mr Hanson, and that she died around 1972.

When Walter Lord received the initial request from Wilkins for help or information, in February 1957, he decided not to pursue the story, no doubt filing the case under 'miscellaneous'; in effect, letters from the deluded, the fame-obsessed, or those dubious personages who wanted to profit from the sudden newsworthiness of the *Titanic*. Yet, in the case of Vera Edwards – born Virginia Emanuel – it seems like her need was a genuine one. In the midst of publicity surrounding *A Night to Remember*, both the book and the film, she wasn't seeking fame, press attention, or money – all she wanted was to reclaim her lost self. An impoverished woman, who had to depend on the services of a 'poor man's lawyer', her quiet, dignified request for help was not heard among the more articulate cries of some of her fellow survivors.

One of the most forthright and determined of *Titanic* voices belonged to Edith Russell, the first-class passenger who said her life was saved by her musical toy pig. Although not so self-deluded or naive as Dorothy Gibson – Edith was a fiercely intelligent woman – the fashion buyer, journalist and stylist shared a common infatuation with fame. Like the silent screen star, Edith used the *Titanic* as a way to manipulate herself into the public arena with such an obsession that, towards the end of her life, it came to define her.

She was born Edith Rosenbaum, in Cincinnati, Ohio, on 12 June 1879, the daughter of a Jewish furrier. A bright, artistic child, she was attracted to the glamorous world of fashion from an early age and at eighteen she left Cincinnati for New York and then Paris. By the time she was twenty-nine she had secured a job as a saleswoman for Maison Cheruit, in the Place Vendôme. With an ease that seemed to define her early life, she moved into fashion writing, firstly for *La Dernière Heure à Paris*, which was published by Wanamaker Department Store's Paris bureau, and then, in 1910, for *Women's Wear Daily*, for whom she worked as a foreign correspondent. By 1912, Edith – who was far from conventionally beautiful, having a large, prominent nose and a rather horsy face – had established herself as a fashion buyer and consultant. She had even created her own label, which was named 'Elrose', for Lord and Taylor in New York. She was, it has been claimed, one of the world's first professional stylists, dispensing fashion tips and advice to a number of clients, including the opera star Geraldine Farrar, funny girl Ina Claire and the *Folies Bergère* showgirl Mistinguett. Travelling with Edith on the *Titanic* were several trunks packed with expensive clothes; so many, it was rumoured, that she had been forced to take an adjoining cabin.

Right from the time of the disaster she cast herself in the role of spokeswoman for the survivors with an authority that came naturally to her. Within days of the sinking, she posed for pictures on board the *Carpathia*, together with her lucky pig. On the night the rescue ship arrived in New York she gave a number of interviews; she also wrote a long article for *Cassell's Magazine* in 1913, a feature which was, she said, 'the best of its kind'[18], 'the most authentic written on the *Titanic*'.[19] In 1937, on the twenty-fifth anniversary of the disaster, she made a broadcast on Post Parisienne. 'On that occasion, every dress house in Paris closed their ateliers down so the workers could hear me, as I was a prominent figure in the fashion world, and they all knew me,' she said.[20]

In 1952, when Edith first heard that a Hollywood film was going to be made about the *Titanic*, she wrote to the producer, Charles Brackett, outlining her experiences and offering her services. He simply had to meet her, she said, because she was the single best source of information about the sinking of the ship. 'The fact that I was the last passenger in the last lifeboat would qualify me to have seen quite a lot,' she said, a claim that does not stand up to much scrutiny. Edith in fact left in lifeboat number eleven, which was launched at 1.25 a.m. – another nine lifeboats would leave the *Titanic* before it sank at 2.20 a.m., not counting the two collapsibles that floated off the liner as it was going under. This discrepancy, however, did not seem to bother her one jot. She had the experience, and the ability, to tell a damn good story – she was a journalist, after all – and she wanted to be properly remunerated for it.

After receiving no answer from Brackett, Edith wrote again:

'All I would like to do is to graphically outline the incident to you verbally, giving you all the highlights as I remember them, and I think you would find a great many situations and facts that never were referred to either in the newspapers or in the various records,' she said. 'I have always made a point of telling the story to someone during anniversary week. Why don't you let me come to you, tell you the story, and you decide what you think it is worth and send me a check accordingly . . . I could even give you almost the exact design of the furniture in the drawing room. Why don't you let me come over and tell you the story during the week of the 13th to 18th – that is the day we landed. I always seem to have a little more inspiration during this particular week than I have through the rest of the year.'[21]

But still the letter elicited no response, as Brackett had decided not to talk to any individual survivors. The film makers were more interested in constructing their own story, one that would meet all the criteria of melodrama without getting bogged down by the real-life experiences of people like Edith. Although the production team never responded to her offer, they did, however, invite her – and a number of other survivors – to a preview of *Titanic* in New York in April 1953. It was an emotional experience for many of them, not least third-class passengers Leah Aks, who had been eighteen at the time of the disaster, and her son, Philip, who had been only ten months old. Edith recalled how, in the panic, the baby Philip had been torn out of his mother's arms and thrown into her lifeboat. Leah tried to push her way into this vessel, but was directed into the next lifeboat to leave the ship. Edith had done her best to comfort the baby during that long, cold night in the middle of the Atlantic – repeatedly playing the tune of 'La Maxixe' by twisting the tail of her toy pig – before they were rescued. On board the *Carpathia*, Leah was overjoyed to see her baby son alive, but the relief turned to horror when she realised another woman was claiming the child as her own. Both women were summoned by the Captain of the ship to explain themselves – thankfully the matter was settled easily after Leah successfully identified the baby by a birthmark on his chest.

The reunion brought all these memories back. 'The baby, amongst other babies, for whom I played my little pig music box to the tune of "Maxixe" was there,' said Edith of the screening. 'He [Philip] is forty-one years old, is a rich steel magnate from Norfolk, Virginia, and the stewardess, who held him on her lap, was also there and his mother. It was a great and wonderful and unforgettable thrill for me to meet them again.'[22]

Edith enjoyed the event, she said, and had the opportunity of showing off the little musical pig, together with the dress she had worn on the night of the disaster. Edith congratulated Brackett on the film, yet, as a survivor, she said she had noticed some obvious errors. 'There was a rather glaring inadequacy letting people take seats in the lifeboat as most of them had to get up on the rail and jump into the boat which swung clear of the side of the boat,' she said. 'The narrow skirts of that day made it a dreadful experience as the boat deck was at least fourteen stories from the sea (in building terms). The boat also went down with the most awful rapidity. It fairly shot into the water whereas yours gracefully slid into the water.' Despite these points, she thought the film was 'splendid' – she conceded he had done a 'good job' – and, above all, it brought the night alive once more. 'It gave me a heartache and I could still see the sailors changing the watches, crunching over the ice and going down to stoke those engines from where they never returned,' she said.[23]

At the preview, Edith thought Renee Harris had behaved in what she regarded as a rather strange manner. Not only did Renee choose to sit apart from the rest of the survivors, but she also turned down the opportunity to have her photograph taken and said she would rather not join the group after the film for an informal drink. 'Why? That's something I'd like to know,' said Edith, who for all her intelligence and sharp wit, seemed on this occasion to lack any sense of empathy or emotional insight. Unlike Edith or Leah Aks, Renee Harris had lost a husband during the disaster, a loss she still found difficult to live with. In addition, she did not share Edith's zest for publicity or love of fame. A few months before the screening, Renee had been invited on to a radio show by broadcasters Mary Margaret McBride and Bill Slater, both of whom had tried to get her to speak about her experience on board the *Titanic*. 'But I couldn't – without emotion,' she said, 'and I despise emotions.'[24] It was, for her, not a night to remember, but a night to forget.

This concept of private, dignified grief was alien to Edith Russell, whose only loss had been her stash of evening gowns. She felt possessive of the *Titanic* story – she believed it was hers alone to tell – and she wanted to try and exploit it for all it was worth. When the historian Walter Lord came along and published what for many is the definitive book of the disaster, Edith was furious. On 28 April 1956, from her suite at the Washington Hotel on Curzon Street, London, Edith wrote Lord a letter that barely concealed her anger. 'I read your story with mixed emotions, interest, and at the same time with great regret that my story which was originally written for Sir Newman Flower of Cassell's Magazine has been materially worsened by your very successful book,' she said. She was particularly annoyed by his description of her in *A Night to Remember*, believing he had portrayed her as something of a 'dim-wit', which could not be further from the truth. 'As I am a well-known woman professionally, I feel like an ass reading in various languages that I carried a curious object, a musical toy pig,' she said. She was cross that he hadn't bothered to contact her while researching his book. 'How much better it would be in writing to not glean one's information entirely from the newspapers published at the time,' she wrote.[25]

Undaunted, Lord wrote a polite letter back, outlining how he had tried, but failed, to find Edith during his research. He tried to reassure her that her story had its own merits and that she should not be disheartened by the success of *A Night to*

Remember; it might even stimulate wider interest in the subject to the point that there was a demand for further accounts, such as her own. The charming letter did the trick, and the two started to correspond. Edith realised that Walter, with his connections in the publishing world, could help her get her memoir into print, while Lord, now even more fascinated by the *Titanic* than ever, could add Russell to his growing collection of survivors. Within a matter of months, the correspondence became friendly, flirtatious even (on Edith's part, at least), and soon the pair became close friends. Walter adored Edith's slightly wicked sense of humour, while she felt she could mine him for advice and contacts. The reason he could not find her during his research, she said, was that he had been looking in the wrong place – New York – when in fact at this point in her life she split her time between hotels in Paris and London.

'The Edith Russells in New York, either one or both, are Negro charwomen,' she wrote to him. 'I have had extremely funny experiences with friends of mine who have telephoned these ladies thinking that they were me. As a matter of fact one was invited to the Plaza for luncheon and actually came, that is in itself a story which maybe some day I will tell you.'[26]

Edith had tried many outlets for her *Titanic* story, but so far without success, mainly due to the overwhelming popularity of Lord's book. She was, however, particularly keen to talk on television in America and she wanted to know whether Lord's employers, the advertising agency J. Walter Thompson – which helped produce the Kraft TV drama based on his book – could help secure her an appearance. 'I was a great success here in England in the showing of The Little Pig [she had recently appeared on television with her mascot] which can be supplemented by the actual dress that I was saved in,' she said.[27]

The best Lord could do was to suggest that Edith contact Bill MacQuitty, who was producing a film version of his book.

Without a moment's hesitation she rang MacQuitty's office and asked to speak to the producer. 'Are you Mr MacQuitty, the producer of the new *Titanic* film?' she asked. Indeed he was. 'Mr MacQuitty, I can be of great help to you in making this film. I am in the dress business. I have the dress and the coat that I wore when the *Titanic* sank. I am an expert. I know what the passengers wore. I would like to be attached to the costume department. I would also like to help with publicity. I write for many magazines and newspapers. I spend a lot of time in Paris, where I am well-known, and I can be sure of getting you valuable publicity there. I am in London, staying at the Washington Hotel for two weeks. Can I come and see you at the studio?'[28]

MacQuitty, slightly taken aback by the force of her proposal, assented and asked her to make an appointment with his secretary, Genia. A few days later, at half past ten in the morning, Edith arrived at Pinewood Studios. 'She was a tiny woman, dressed all in black, which accentuated the four strands of large pearls around her neck,' he recalled. 'She glanced down at her front from time to time, as if to reassure herself that the pearls were still there. Her hair was brown, turning grey. It was plentiful, and beautifully set. She wore no hat nor did I ever see her wearing one.'[29]

When Edith spoke, he was surprised by the deepness of her voice, almost like a man's. They walked past the studio workshops before turning a corner where the central third of the ship had been constructed, rising out of its concrete bed. Edith looked up at the two funnels that stretched high into the winter sky and stopped in her tracks. 'I can't believe it,' she said. She was, for once, speechless. They then walked on to the boat deck, where she grabbed hold of the lifeline of one of the lifeboats. 'Her face was aged, but strong and determined,' MacQuitty remembered. 'Straight eyebrows, set widely apart, enhanced the deep-set eyes. Edith was completely overcome, her thoughts still far away.' Quietly, a photographer took some photos, yet Edith did not notice his presence. Slowly, she came back from the past to the present, and she moved along the reconstructed deck until she found the very spot where she had stood that night, the point from which she had stepped off the ship and into lifeboat number eleven – the boat which had then borne her into the darkness.

By the time she returned to MacQuitty's office, where they had tea, Edith had resumed her normal mode of communication – a mix of charm and flattery (she congratulated the producer on the authenticity of the ship) combined with a quite extraordinary ability to state what she wanted in the most forceful way imaginable. The intention was to make herself appear absolutely indispensable. 'The action, what the passengers do and the clothes they wear – that's where you're going to need help and that's where I come in,' she said. 'I want to be attached to this film. I want to check that everything is right.' Interestingly, she stated she did not want money; if she received it she said then she would give it to charity. What was more important, for her, was involvement.[30]

MacQuitty told her in no uncertain terms that what she was proposing was impossible – he could only employ people who were members of one of the trade unions associated with film-making – and although she was 'bitterly disappointed' she explained to the producer that she could be quite persistent. Obsessive-compulsive would be a more modern, medical description. If one examines the correspondence between Russell and Lord it becomes obvious that Edith had a deep psychological need to revisit a part of her life that many people would have gladly tried to put behind them. For her, this was a night to remember and remember and remember again.

The historian and the survivor met in March 1957 at a lunch given by MacQuitty at a Hungarian restaurant in

London. The gentleman writer and the grand lady of fashion hit it off immediately, drawn together by a shared passion for the *Titanic* and a sense of nostalgia, a longing for an era that had died somewhere between the sinking of the majestic liner and the beginning of the First World War. Driven by an equally obsessive interest in the subject, Lord fuelled Edith's compulsion, and over the course of the next few years he sent her a regular supply of information, articles and titbits of gossip regarding the ship and its passengers. In May 1957, Lord posted Edith, then living at the Hotel Lutetia in Paris, a newspaper article about first-class passenger Charlotte Cardeza and her magnificent wardrobe of clothes that had gone down with the ship, including ninety pairs of gloves. 'Mrs Cardeza has nothing on me,' Edith wrote back.[31]

During this time, Edith made regular visits to Pinewood to check on the film's progress. Although she was not officially employed by Rank, MacQuitty was wise enough to realise there was little point in making an enemy of her. In December 1957, during a tour of the set, Edith was aghast to find that the actress playing herself – Teresa Thorne – was not only wearing a tailored suit with an open neckline and a picture hat, but she was holding a musical pig that looked nothing like the real thing. In a letter to Walter Lord, in which she complains about the glaring inaccuracies, it's interesting to note that she describes Thorne as not playing her, but understudying her, as if she herself were the star, and the professional actress a mere cipher. One gets the sense that Edith wanted nobody other than herself to play the role.

Edith was furious at the discrepancies – she 'blew her top', she admitted – but MacQuitty tried to calm her down by explaining that the hat was a mere filmic device, a sort of symbol, 'so that everyone would see that it was Edith Russell'. Yet she could not be placated. 'It was the coldest night on earth and no one in my lifeboat wore a hat, including myself, but for dramatic effect, I am hatted and coated,' she said. At the bottom of the letter, in red pen, she added, 'I think it too foolish. Captain Smith is perfect – also the set – and the gala dinner, the dining room, perfect. They make me push my jewellery aside and take pig from stateroom – all different from fact and it's a factual film??'[32]

She even took it upon herself to write to the director, Roy Baker, telling him of the problems with how 'she' had been dressed in the film. Although she condescended to say that it was within his rights to use a little artistic licence, the way she had been portrayed was nonsensical. 'You will also note that I left the ship almost entirely disguised as my family did not recognise me, but disguised most expensively in a full-length broadtail coat which today would cost thousands and thousands of pounds,' she said. 'The attractive little open-necked suit of the lifeboat I am afraid I will never be reconciled to as anyone who left in that lifeboat on that cold night without some sort of coat would have perished before morning. Glamour or no glamour, I feel like the escaped village nitwit . . .'[33]

Yet Edith herself was not averse to bending the truth a little when it suited her own ends. When she first met MacQuitty, she shaved ten years off her age – claiming to have been born in 1888, not 1878 – and as a result, he cast a much younger actress in her role, a woman in her twenties rather than her thirties. 'She loved to keep people wondering the truth,' he said later.[34] The two became good friends, and she spent the Christmas of 1957 with MacQuitty and his family at their London home in Mill Hill, an invitation that soon became a regular fixture in her diary. Betty MacQuitty, the producer's widow, remembers Edith as being a small woman who was full of life. 'She was very short, something like five feet in heels, and yet she was a sensation,' she says. 'She was incredibly spirited, feisty and great fun. She would come to our house each Christmas and regale our two daughters with the most marvellous stories. She would tell them how she was a spy – a fashion spy – and would always carry a pair of small curved scissors in her handbag. At a showing of the clothes she would ask the models to turn around, at which point she would reach out to feel the material and cut a tiny piece of the dress using the scissors hidden in the palm of her hand, which she would then send off to America to be copied. She quite liked to shock, and she would tell this story about how she escaped unwanted attentions from a sheikh by saying she had a touch of VD. She loved to have an audience.'[35]

Betty's daughter Miranda recalls being mesmerised by an enormous emerald ring, which Edith would wear on her finger, a piece of jewellery that seemed to symbolise her independence. 'She never married, or had children, and she wanted us girls to be able to fight our corner, that was what she expected of us,' she says. 'But she was definitely interested in the male of the species. She was incredibly determined, she knew what she wanted, and I think she had what you might call a survivor mentality. She was a fighter, an independent woman in an age when that was not the norm. The thing that struck you about Edith was that she was this tiny, tottering old lady, but yet she was made of steel.'[36]

Betty's elder daughter, Jane, agrees. She describes her as being sparrow-like in appearance, but hawk-like in temperament. 'As a child, I remember thinking that she looked rather like a witch,' she says. 'She had a large, hooked nose, very wrinkled, grey skin and sprouted a few hairs on her chin. Her eyebrows were unruly, and around her cheekbones she would dab rouge which she never bothered to blend in to the rest of her face. I remember her smelling rather sweet, like violets, and dressing mostly in black. She would wear quite short skirts and would totter about in these slingback, platform shoes which seemed like they were from the 1940s. She was quite eccentric, and would bring us boxes of chocolate that had a few chocolates missing. Yet we were all terribly fond of her, as she was so charismatic and commanding.

'She adored men, loved being the centre of attention, and I remember one summer party when she was surrounded by a group of young men – there was one to fetch her drink, and so on. She was definitely the centre of her own world and I remember that often she would nod off at our table. When my father joked about this, she replied, in her harsh, quite tough accent, "I always nod off when other people are talking."'[37]

MacQuitty's widow recalls how Edith fought hard to try and get her memoirs published. She badgered MacQuitty to help her, yet when he sent along a writer to try and help get her memories in some sort of shape – the book would effectively be a ghostwritten one – each encounter would end in recriminations. Approaching the project on all fronts, she also attempted to enlist the services of Walter Lord, and repeatedly sent him drafts of her unpublished account of the sinking of the *Titanic*, which she entitled 'A Pig and a Prayer Saved Me from the Titanic'. 'The copy I am sending you is not exactly what I would desire,' she wrote to Lord in February 1958, 'but the young lady who has been doing the work has not been very well, hence several people have been at it and the result is disastrous.' She asked Lord for his honest opinion, since his story had eclipsed hers 'and taken all the wind out of my sails to date, be a dear and help me all you can'.[38] Lord wrote a polite letter back, pointing out that although he found her account quite charming – 'the story of an alert, lively young girl, just starting out in life, thrown suddenly into one of the most dramatic events of our time'[39] –unfortunately at that time the market for *Titanic* books was somewhat depressed. Yet she refused to be disheartened and, over the course of the next few years, she used a mixture of charm, sweet-talk and steely determination to try and get her book published. Eventually, she approached an American syndication agency with the plan of selling and distributing her story, but was horrified to learn that they had not received her manuscript. 'It has made me perfectly ill,' she wrote to Lord. 'I had a birthday the other night and was out with the MacQuittys. I am quite ill over this horrible shock.'[40]

Edith was also struck down by an attack of fibromyalgia, or what was then called fibrositis, which manifested itself by pain, tenderness of the muscles, joints and tendons, stiffness and a debilitating fatigue. 'I have not had one day free of pain,' she said, and she was 'adding on weight'.[41] As the years passed, she began to confine herself to her rooms at the Embassy Hotel, where she started to fill the available space with newspaper and magazine articles, many of which were about the *Titanic*. When the MacQuittys visited they were alarmed to see the sitting room piled floor to ceiling with papers; it was so cluttered that there was hardly any room left for the bird-sized woman. 'Her existence was reduced to what was virtually one room, albeit quite a large one,' says Jane MacQuitty. 'And this space was completely overwhelmed by boxes, old newspapers and clutter.' The more the chance to write about the *Titanic* escaped her, the more she became increasingly fixated on the disaster. 'It was clear that the *Titanic* was the defining moment of Edith's life,' says Jane. 'Edith was a survivor full stop, so my father used to say, and I agree with him. She was a battler, a fighter, tenacious, something of a dynamite character – and I'm not at all surprised that she made sure she survived. Yet afterwards, I got the sense that nothing ever lived up to that.'[42]

Edith also began to drop hints that, while travelling on the *Titanic*, she had been the mistress of J. Bruce Ismay. She made this known to both Walter Lord and Bill MacQuitty, and some *Titanic* experts, notably Charles Pellegrino, have seized on this as a way of interpreting her kindly view of the White Star Line chairman. In the days following the disaster, she told a reporter from the *New York Times* that she owed her life to Ismay. 'I believe that Mr Ismay must have entered his lifeboat at the very last moment, judging by the fact that I myself was among the last to leave the *Titanic*. I last saw him calling out, "Any more women? If so, all off now." I think that Mr Ismay should not be censured, as he took his chances after all the women in that part of the ship had been saved.'[43]

It's true that, on board the *Titanic*, she occupied a first-class stateroom, A-11, which did adjoin Ismay's, and it's likely that she had played the role of mistress at least once in her life, yet the idea that the pair were more than just acquaintances owes more to Edith's fantasy than reality. By the last years of her life, the most vocal of *Titanic* survivors had become so obsessed with the disaster that she was prepared to do and say anything to attract attention. 'As far as I know nothing happened between Edith and Bruce Ismay,' says Betty MacQuitty. 'People like Charles Pellegrino are desperate to try and make a story out of it, but I think that's all it was, a story.'[44] Her daughter Miranda agrees. 'She did have a few strange stories, many of which were complete inventions,' she says.[45]

The most compelling evidence to quash the rumour of the alleged affair is the file of letters which Bruce Ismay wrote to fellow *Titanic* survivor Marian Longstreth Morris Thayer in the weeks and months following the disaster. The correspondence, which is still in the hands of the Thayer family, shows that Ismay had formed a strong bond with Marian, a connection that he wanted to deepen and expand. 'I have read the letters to Mrs Thayer,' says Ismay's granddaughter Pauline Matarasso, 'and I am quite certain that at the time Bruce Ismay was very vulnerable, emotionally mixed up and inhibited (he admits as much), deeply unhappy, [he] found his wife unresponsive, and was for all those reasons very inclined to fancy himself in love [with Mrs Thayer].'[46] Much of the language in the letters is coded, yet it is clear that, at this low point in his life, Ismay felt he could turn to Marian Thayer for emotional support. If Ismay had been having an affair with Edith Russell, then surely she would have been the one to receive these kind of letters, not Thayer's widow. The only correspondence between Ismay and Edith that exists in the vast National Maritime Museum archive is one that he wrote in October 1912 in which he addresses her in a polite, but formal tone, thanking her for her support at the time of the disaster. The clue to their relationship lies in his form of address, 'Dear Miss Rosenbaum' – hardly the words one would use to one's mistress.[47]

As Edith aged, she became even more eccentric. She started to encourage pigeons into her hotel room, where she fed them. The rubbish on the floor accumulated to such an extent that it looked as though it might spill out into the corridor. The *Titanic* remained a constant obsession in Edith's life, her survival her main achievement. On 14 April 1970, she relished the chance to talk to Sheridan Morley on BBC radio, embellishing her account with hyperbole and high drama. Referring to the stretch of road in France between Rouen and Paris – where she had had a serious car accident that claimed the life of her close friend, Ludwig Loewe, who was at the wheel – she described it as the 'hill of death'. After the *Titanic* had sunk and she lost all her trunks – which were packed with clothes belonging to clients – she claimed it took her three and a half years of 'acute starvation' to pay back her debts. Looking back, she recalled 'every detail of the horror' of that night, which she described as 'inky black . . . starlit, not a ripple in the sea'. But her most extraordinary statement is one right at the end of the monologue – for the piece cannot be described as an interview – when she talks about how she had experienced every type of misfortune. (She often said how she had survived every kind of disaster except for a plane crash, bubonic plague and a husband.) Imprisoned by her ego, which at this point can only be described as monstrous, she says, '*I* sank the *Titanic.*'[48]

Bill MacQuitty had always said that Edith Russell was 'fearsome in her battle for existence',[49] but now, towards the very end of her life, as her physical strength weakened, she began to invest herself with the force and power of the iceberg that sank the *Titanic*. It was one of many delusions that helped her to continue, a strategy for coping in the shadow of something more terrifying than either the iceberg or the sight of the majestic ship splitting in two and sinking to the bottom of the ocean: death.

Edith's mind had always been as sharp as one of the splinters of ice that she had seen fall on to the deck of the *Titanic* in April 1912. But now, in the 1970s, her faculties started to fail. The staff of the hotel where she lived became increasingly worried about the state of her health and anxious that she was effectively turning her room – with its pigeons, its piles of newspapers, its rotting mess – into something that was uninhabitable, both for her and future guests. One day in March 1975, Betty MacQuitty remembers receiving a postcard from Edith telling her that she was in hospital and asking her if she could please visit. A distant relative from America, who had heard through the hotel management of Edith's ill health, had flown to London and decided that she was no longer capable of looking after herself and had moved her to the hospital. The suggestion was that she was losing her mind. When Betty arrived at St Stephen's Hospital, in West London, she was horrified.

'She was in bed and not at all well,' says Betty. 'She complained to me about bad treatment and kept saying over and over again, "Get me out, get me out." She told me that her mother always used to give her chicken soup when she was ill, and that was what she wanted. So I made chicken soup. It was terribly sad. We desperately wanted to try to get her out of hospital – she absolutely hated it – and Bill and I even considered carrying her out of there ourselves, she was so light, you see. But that would have been kidnapping an old lady. So I contacted the American Embassy and told them about the situation. But it was Easter by this point, nothing could be done, and eventually the hospital phoned to say that Edith had died that morning.'[50]

When Edith died, on 4 April 1975, she was ninety-six years old. The consummate survivor – the woman who defined herself by the very fact that she had managed to escape from the *Titanic* – was no more. Yet she left behind a substantial inheritance and a slew of *Titanic* stories. To Walter Lord – the man whose book she felt had overshadowed her own attempt – she pledged her famous musical pig. When Lord died in May 2002, he in turn left it to the National Maritime Museum, which also holds Edith's unpublished manuscript, 'A Pig and a Prayer Saved Me from the Titanic'.

In the opening paragraph of this account, she said: 'As a *Titanic* survivor, this event has shaped my life and has made me an object of curious interest on many occasions. Whenever I cross the Atlantic on passenger liners I meet numbers of people, and when it becomes known that I am a *Titanic* survivor, they immediately ply me with every sort of question. One of the more frequent questions is: "No, were you really saved?" (I have never learned quite how to answer this one.) Or, "Did you hear 'Nearer my God to Thee?'" And yet another, "Was the water rough?" and "Were you cold?" "How many were saved?" "Were you frightened?" "You certainly were lucky."'[51] She was, indeed, lucky to escape, but surviving the *Titanic* also proved to be something of a curse; it defined and yet destroyed her. Her failure to publish the definitive version of the sinking came to overshadow her life until it finally reduced her to near-madness. Yet her spirited personality enriched the lives of many of those she came in contact with, providing them with a seemingly endless source of amusing anecdotes and life-enhancing stories. 'It was a privilege to have her at our table,' says Jane MacQuitty. 'She had survived one of the worst marine disasters of the modern age and she lived to tell the tale.'[52] And it was a tale she felt compelled to tell over and over again.

Eleven

THE LAST SURVIVORS

In the years after *A Night to Remember* the storm that had gathered around the *Titanic* seemed to abate, despite the best efforts of the Titanic Enthusiasts of America, the organisation formed in 1963 with the purpose of 'investigating and perpetuating the history and memory of the White Star liners, *Olympic*, *Titanic*, and *Britannic*'.[1] The group, which later renamed itself the Titanic Historical Society, produced a quarterly newsletter, the *Titanic Commutator*, which over the years transformed into a glossy journal. Yet, at this time, the membership comprised a relatively small group of specialists, maritime history buffs and a clutch of survivors. By September 1973, when the group held its tenth anniversary meeting, the society had a membership of only two hundred and fifty people. The celebration, held in Greenwich, Connecticut, was attended by eighty-eight-year-old Mrs Edwina MacKenzie, who had sailed on the *Titanic* as twenty-seven-year-old second-class passenger Edwina Troutt. After more than sixty years she still remembered seeing the liner sink, 'one row of lighted portholes after another, gently like a lady,' she said.[2]

Interviews with survivors occasionally cropped up in the press, such as one given by Marjorie Newell Robb, who had travelled on the *Titanic* as a twenty-three-year-old first-class passenger. Talking to a journalist in 1981, the ninety-two-year-old said how she still felt a deep sense of melancholy when she thought about the disaster. She recalled how, on the night of 14 April 1912, she had finished dinner when her father turned to her and her elder sister, Madeleine, and said, 'Do you think you can last till morning?' Although he was referring to the girls' enormous appetites, the words take on a certain tragic resonance when read in retrospect. The girls' father, Arthur W. Newell, of Lexington, Massachusetts, was one of the many victims, and his loss was felt so keenly by his wife, who had not travelled to Europe with the family due to her delicate disposition, that she forbade her daughters ever to talk about that night and insisted on wearing black until her death at the age of one hundred and three.

In the interview, Marjorie recalled the shock she had felt on the morning of 15 April 1912 when, in lifeboat number six, she had seen the sea covered with icebergs. She realised then how irresponsible Captain Smith had been in charting a fast course through such dangerous seas. Yet, during those first hours after the disaster, she still assumed her father would have been saved from the ship. Then, as she climbed aboard the *Carpathia*, she felt the awful silence, an oppressive atmosphere that she likened to that of a funeral. 'We didn't realize how few had been saved . . .' she said. 'The *Carpathia* by that time was loaded with *Titanic* survivors. People were lying all over the deck, just trying to find someplace to rest. Father wasn't there. But I was so proud of him, that he'd abided by the rule of the sea: women and children first. Some men didn't. I know I sat beside a man on the *Carpathia* who had shoved aside women and children to save his own life.'

After docking in New York, the two Newell sisters were taken to a hotel in Manhattan where they met their mother. The reunion should have been a happy one – Arthur had taken his daughters on a European tour, also visiting the Pyramids and the Holy Land – but Marjorie can remember the awful expression on her mother's face when she realised that their father had not been saved. 'I can see her now in the hotel corridor, her arms outstretched, giving a howl of despair,' she said. Two weeks later, Arthur's body was washed up on the shores of Newfoundland.

Marjorie found the experience too painful to talk about, and for many years she politely refused all enquiries from reporters and authors. She tried to get on with her life – she married in 1918 and went on to help found the New Jersey Symphony Orchestra – but then, in 1960, after the death of both her mother and her husband, she took a trip to Europe. One stop on her itinerary was Lichfield, in Staffordshire, where she wanted to see the beautiful medieval cathedral and the statue of Edward J. Smith, the *Titanic*'s Captain, even though he was, in her opinion, 'a very unpopular man'. As she walked into the cathedral she heard the sound of the organ fill the vast space. 'I walked down the aisle and stood there, terribly, terribly moved,' she recalled. 'I didn't even seem to be on earth; I was somewhere else. It was as if I was ascending. I felt that here, at long last, was the end of the *Titanic* story. My father had given his life to save me, and now that I was free of everything else, it was up to me to make the decision as to what I wanted to do with the rest of my life. But the *Titanic*? For me, it was over with.'[3]

Many people assumed the same – that, after fifty years, the liner, and the myths surrounding it, would finally be allowed to rest in peace. Of course, each anniversary continued to be marked by a television documentary or an interview with one of the last remaining survivors, but the general perception was that the ship would gently slip away out of public consciousness. After all, who really wanted to read another *Raise the Titanic*, Clive Cussler's 1975 blockbuster novel about a mission to bring the famous liner to the surface and tow it into New York harbour. (The convoluted plot involves the quest for the strangely named mineral byzanium, which 'holds the key to the safety of the free world' and which just happens to be on board the *Titanic*.) After the 1980 film *Raise the Titanic*, starring Alec Guinness and Jason Robards, flopped at the box office and lost a substantial amount of money, Lew Grade, its producer, famously said that it would have been cheaper to lower the Atlantic.

But a surprise was in store for anybody who thought the *Titanic* story was over. In the early hours of 1 September 1985, oceanographer and underwater archaeologist Robert Ballard from the Woods Hole Oceanographic Institution – together with French explorer Jean-Louis Michel from the French organisation IFREMER – discovered the wreck of the *Titanic* lying at a depth of roughly two and half miles, and around 370 miles south-east of Mistaken Point, Newfoundland. 'The Titanic lies now in 13,000 feet of water on a gently sloping Alpine-looking countryside overlooking a small canyon below,' said Ballard, on returning to America a number of days later. 'Its bow faces north. The ship sits upright on its bottom with its mighty stacks pointed upward. There is no light at this great depth and little life can be found. It is a quiet and peaceful place – and a fitting place for the remains of this greatest of sea tragedies to rest. Forever may it remain that way. And may God bless these now-found souls.'[4]

With this discovery, the world went *Titanic*-crazy once more, a frenzy that was even more intense than the previous two bouts of fever. For the first time in almost three-quarters of a century people could see both still and moving images of the ship and its contents. There was something almost supernatural about the resulting pictures and films, almost as if a photographer had managed to capture images of a ghost for the first time.

Within a couple of years of the discovery, wealthy tourists

could pay thousands of dollars to descend to the site of the wreck and see the *Titanic* for themselves, an experience that many likened to stepping into another world. Journalist William F. Buckley Jr was one of the first observers outside the French and American exploratory teams to witness the ship at close quarters. 'We descend slowly to what looks like a yellow-white sandy beach, sprinkled with black rocklike objects,' he wrote in the *New York Times*. 'These, it transpires, are pieces of coal. There must be 100,000 of them in the area we survey, between the bow of the ship and the stern, a half-mile back. On my left is a man's outdoor shoe. Left shoe. Made, I would say, of suede of some sort. I cannot quite tell whether it is laced up. And then, just off to the right a few feet, a snow-white teacup. Just sitting there . . . on the sand. I liken the sheer neatness of the tableau to a display that might have been prepared for a painting by Salvador Dali.'[5]

Over the course of the next few years, around six thousand artefacts were recovered from the wreck, sent to a specialist laboratory in France and subsequently exhibited. The shows – the first of which was held at the National Maritime Museum in London in 1994 – proved to be enormous crowd-pleasers. Touring exhibitions such as Titanic Honour and Glory and Titanic: The Artefact Exhibition have been seen by millions of people all around the world. Items on display include a silver pocket watch, its hands stopped at 2.28 a.m., the time the *Titanic* sank into the ice-cold waters of the Atlantic; the Steiff teddy bear belonging to senior engineer William Moyes, who went down with the ship; the perfume vials belonging to Adolphe Saalfeld, a Manchester perfumier, who survived the disaster and who would have been astonished to learn that it was still possible to smell the delicate aromas of orange blossom and lavender nearly one hundred years later. Then there were beautiful cut-crystal decanters etched with the swallowtail flag of the

White Star Line; the white jacket of Athol Broome, a thirty-year-old steward who did not survive; a selection of children's marbles scooped up from the sea floor; brass buttons bearing the White Star insignia; a selection of silver serving plates and gratin dishes; a pair of spectacles and a gentleman's shaving kit. These objects of everyday life brought the great ship – and its passengers – back to life as never before. For the first time, the public could see – and in the case of Saalfeld's perfume vials, smell – what it was like to have sailed on the *Titanic*.

With each passing year – as more and more artefacts were recovered – the survivors of the tragedy grew fewer and fewer. By June 1992, at the time of the opening of the Titanic Voices exhibition in Southampton, there were only three remaining survivors left in Britain – Edith Haisman, ninety-five; Eva Hart, eighty-seven; and Millvina Dean, then eighty years old – and only a further nine left scattered in various countries around the world. *The Times* carried a report about the reconciliation of these 'three grand old ladies', quoting each in turn. 'I still remember it as vividly as if it were yesterday,' said Edith Haisman, who had been travelling as a second-class passenger with her parents. Edith recalled how she was asleep in her cabin when the ship hit the iceberg. 'Being young, I didn't realize we might be drowned. You could see the ice for miles across the sea . . . nobody worried about it, some of the people, from the third class, came up playing with ice on deck and people in the first class, well they couldn't believe it. They said, "no, she's unsinkable." They went back to bed.' Later that night her father escorted Edith and his wife to lifeboat number fourteen and walked away into the crowd. Edith never saw him again. 'I still miss my father,' she said. 'He was a good man.'[6]

In fact, Edith, Eva and Millvina each lost a father that night, the men freezing to death in the icy waters of the Atlantic – the temperature was minus two degrees centigrade.

The manner in which they died later found expression in their daughters' personalities, almost as if, years later, the men's rigid bodies rose from the deep and cast an icy shadow over them, paralysing certain aspects of their children's psychology. Certainly Eva Hart, who was seven years old when she sailed on the majestic liner, suppressed the memory of the disaster with a steely determination; if anyone mentioned the *Titanic* she would run out of the room. 'As I grew up, and during the whole of my adolescence, I tried to draw a complete curtain over my memory of the *Titanic* disaster,' she wrote in her autobiography. 'Because it was so painful and horrifying to me I had no wish to recall it unnecessarily.'[7] Eva was often plagued by thoughts of her father in the freezing water. Although he was a champion swimmer – he would have been able to survive for quite some time in warmer waters – the ice-cold water would have killed him in a matter of minutes. 'I have always been haunted by the thought that he must have tried, despite the intense cold, to swim for his life to reach a lifeboat,' she said.[8]

For many years, Eva chose to remain in the cold, passionless waters of life, deliberately avoiding situations or people that would threaten her steady existence. She never married and, from what she says in her autobiography, never enjoyed a close sexual relationship with anyone. She kept her private life a secret and it's only relatively recently that her friends and relatives learned of an engagement with a man who was a rubber planter in Penang – a fact that she deliberately erased from her life story. Her cousin, Stanley Seymour, remembers taking a day off school to wave her off at King George V dock in London. 'It was only much, much later that I learnt that she was going to stay with a man, a Mr Brown, to whom she had become engaged,' he says. 'But when she arrived in Penang she discovered that he had been waylaid by bandits. His remains were found the next day in his burnt-out Austin Seven. That was the second great tragedy of Eva's life.'[9]

In 1955, while on holiday in Llandudno, Wales, a nondescript, elderly woman approached Eva on the Great Orme and proceeded to tell her fortune. Although the clairvoyant made no mention of the *Titanic*, her analysis of her personality was, she said, uncannily accurate. Eva thrived on responsibility and duty, was able to form intensely loyal and sincere friendships, but she was not the type of person to fall in love easily. 'The thrills of life do not appeal to you as strongly as some people,' the psychic concluded, 'and your aims lean more towards security than sensationalism.'[10]

Eva Hart seemed destined to be a survivor from the very beginning. Her mother, Esther, had been married before, but the union had been an unhappy and violent one. Esther gave birth to nine children with her first husband, but lost each one within the first few months. 'This was due to a combination of physical assaults she suffered at the hands of her first husband during her pregnancies,' said Eva, 'and the rare blood group she possessed and which I have inherited.'[11] After the death of her husband, when she was in her early thirties, Esther vowed she would never marry again and returned to live with her parents. One day, when her father called upon the services of a local builder to construct a new house in Chadwell Heath, Esther met Benjamin Hart, whom she would marry in 1900. Their daughter, Eva, was born on 31 January 1905. 'I became the tenth child my mother had carried, but the only one to survive,' she said.[12]

Eva had fond memories of playing with her father in his carpentry workshop, recalling the smell of the freshly planed planks and the curious worm-like forms of the wood shavings that seemed to snake their way across the floor. She adored her father, with his wavy black hair – she loved running her hands through it as he sat at the table reading the newspaper. There was only one occasion on which he smacked her, she said. The day was 6 May 1910, the death of Edward VII. Father and daughter were on their way to feed the ducks in South Park, Seven Kings, when Benjamin met a friend who informed him of the news. He told his daughter he would have to return home to put on a black tie, at which point five-year-old Eva started to object; the ducks were more important to her than the death of the King. 'My father was so angry that without more ado he smacked me,' she said.[13]

Although Benjamin, a master builder, had enjoyed a certain level of prosperity – at one point he had even owned a car, a rarity among the middle classes in Edwardian Britain – by 1911 his business had begun to suffer. No matter how hard he tried to resolve the issue he was faced with the same problem – there was a surfeit of unlet houses and a shortfall of potential customers. As he looked into the future he 'could see only a continued period of uncertainty ahead'.[14] At the suggestion of a friend – who had settled in Canada – he made plans to emigrate with his family to begin a new life. He booked passage on the *Philadelphia* which was due to sail to New York, where he would visit his sister, before the family travelled on to Canada by train.

From the beginning, Eva's mother, Esther, had her misgivings. Known for her sensible, straightforward personality, she began to show signs of anxiety and felt haunted by an irrational fear she could not define. When she heard the news that the *Philadelphia* could not sail due to a miners' strike – a strike which affected many ocean-going vessels due to lack of coal during the spring of 1912 – she was momentarily relieved. But Benjamin was so determined to reshape his family's fortunes that he booked second-class passage on the *Titanic* instead. It was only when Esther heard the name of the ship that she was finally able to identify the source of her fear. 'This is the ship that they say is unsinkable,' she said to her husband. 'And that is flying in the face of the Almighty. That ship will never reach the other side.'[15] Esther tried to persuade Benjamin to alter their travel plans, but to no avail. And so, on the morning of 10 April 1912, as she boarded the *Titanic*, after travelling down from London on the White Star Line boat train, she told her husband and daughter that she would never let herself fall asleep at night on the boat, preferring to rest in the day. During those first few days at sea, Esther said that she felt as though an enormous black eagle was sitting on her shoulder and that she could not shake it off. Although father and daughter did not take her seriously, Eva realised later that 'it was only due to her determination and obduracy that I lived to tell the tale. Had she been asleep at the time of the disaster we would not have been on deck in time to get a lifeboat.'[16]

On the Sunday morning, 14 April 1912, after staying up all night, Esther decided not to go to bed, as was her normal practice, but to attend the church service at eleven o'clock, after which she agreed to stay up for lunch. During the meal, one of the ship's officers, knowing of Esther's unusual sleeping patterns, came over to talk to her. 'Does that mean that now we are getting across the Atlantic you have got over your fears?' he asked. 'Oh no,' she replied, 'I'm going to bed now.' 'Ah, well, we shall be quite safe if you look after us again tonight,' he said.

Before retiring, Esther took the trouble to write a letter to her mother back in Chadwell Heath, a letter that was never sent but which she carried off the ship. She described how they had enjoyed that morning's church service, and how Eva had sung 'O God, Our Help in Ages Past' so beautifully. They were both looking forward to the next day's concert in aid of the Sailors' Home and the chance of singing again. 'Well, the sailors say we have had a wonderful passage up to now,' she added.

'There has been no tempest, but God knows what it must be when there is one. This mighty expanse of water, no land in sight and the ship rolling from side to side is being wonderful. Tho they say this Ship does not roll on account of its size. Any how it rolls enough for me, I shall never forget it . . . I shall be looking forward to a line from somebody to cheer me up a bit. I am always shutting my eyes and I see everything as I left it . . . oh the long, long days and nights. It's the longest break I ever spent in my life.' She left a little space for her daughter to add something. 'Heaps of love and kisses to all from Eva,' she scribbled at the bottom of the letter, accompanied by lots of kisses.[17]

On the night of 14 April, after dinner, Benjamin had retired to his bunk in the family's cabin, while Esther remained fully dressed, alert to every moan and groan from deep within the ship. At around twenty or fifteen minutes before midnight, she felt a slight 'bump' which she likened to that of a train jerking. Although it was not strong enough to spill her glass of orange juice by her bedside she still felt so unnerved by it that she proceeded to wake Benjamin and Eva. Father and daughter were both cross at having been woken up from their slumbers, but Esther ignored their complaints. Benjamin pulled on a pair of trousers and a sheepskin coat over his pyjamas and, against his better judgement, went to find out the nature of what Esther had described to him. A few moments later, he returned to the cabin a changed man. His face had turned white, his composure shattered. He was 'not the man I knew as my father,' Eva remembered, 'and I was so frightened I started to scream. He didn't need to say anything to my mother, she knew what had happened.'[18]

The family made their way up to the boat deck, Benjamin directing them to the lifeboats. Eventually, mother and daughter found a place in lifeboat fourteen, the boat that carried a number of other mothers and daughters who would also lose husbands and fathers that night. Eva recalled that as the lifeboat filled up with people – around sixty passengers – the deck of the *Titanic* began to slope more and more. Finally, after helping a number of women and children into the lifeboat, Benjamin told his daughter to stay with her mother and to continue holding her hand like a good girl. 'I didn't know that I was never going to see him again,' said Eva.[19]

The men in the lifeboat rowed away from the ship over the calm, ice-cold sea. Eva and her mother watched as the liner began its final descent into the waters, the stern of the ship rising high into the sky. The sight – and sounds – would stay with Eva for the rest of her life. 'One minute the ship was there with its lights still ablaze and illuminating the sea all around, and the next minute it was gone and the only light was from the stars,' she said. 'At the same time there was a great noise from the screams and cries of hundreds of people plunged into the penetratingly cold, icy Atlantic with little hope of being saved.'[20] The cries were followed by an awful silence. 'The ship had gone, the lights had gone, the dreadful cries had gone and it sounded as if the whole world was holding its breath,' she said.[21]

Eva experienced even further trauma when, at some point that night, she became separated from her mother during the movement of survivors from one lifeboat to another. The seven-year-old girl who had experienced a double loss – first of her father and then of her mother – started screaming and crying. It was only when the two were reunited on the *Carpathia* that she began to stop. 'I have never forgotten what it was like to feel that I might have lost both my parents in that tragedy,' she said later.[22] For the rest of the journey back to New York, they did not let one another out of their sight, huddling up close together on one of the dining tables on the rescue ship with only a blanket to cover them.

On arrival in America, Esther and Eva were met by

Benjamin Hart's sister – who learned that her brother had died in the disaster – but, almost immediately, mother and daughter decided not to proceed on to Canada. They returned to Britain on the *Celtic*, departing on 25 April. Although Esther slept soundly during the return voyage – 'What I dreaded has happened, it's over and it can't happen again,' she said – Eva was terrified. She was, she remembered, 'absolutely hysterical with fright'. Even when they had arrived back in Britain, her nights were haunted by horrific nightmares and her thoughts were disturbed by awful memories of the tragedy in which she had lost her father. Her mother, too, was never quite the same again. The shadow of misery loomed large over Eva's childhood and went on to shape her personality. Mother and daughter moved into a house in Chadwell Heath, where they lived together until Esther's death in 1928, aged sixty-five. The family was so poor that Esther had to be buried in an unmarked grave; her remains lie in St Mary's Cemetery, Ilford.

In order to take her mind off the disaster, Eva immersed herself in music; she learned to play the piano and went on to develop her soprano voice. Soon after leaving school at the age of sixteen, she started to teach music to young children and even managed to secure the occasional booking as a professional singer. 'I would come home from school and listen to some of Eva's broadcasts on the BBC at lunchtime,' recalls her cousin, Stanley Seymour. 'I thought it was dreadful, but I had to sit there and listen and not breathe a word. I realise now that it was wonderful singing to be applauded.'[23]

Eva did everything in her power to quash the memory of the *Titanic*, viewing it with fear and loathing, until the time came in the late 1920s when she wanted to embark on a long voyage to see her mother's godson in Singapore and her uncle in Australia – in effect her closest family. As she prepared for the journey, she suffered agonising nightmares and she thought that she might die of fright the moment she stepped on the ship for the first time. Indeed, for the first two days and nights of the journey – the ship sailed through the Mediterranean, the Suez Canal and the Indian Ocean – she imprisoned herself in her cabin, immobilised by fear. 'Gradually, however, I realised that the ship was still afloat and I was still alive,' she said. 'To a certain extent I managed to overcome my fears and I think it did me a lot of good in starting to work the subconscious aspects of the *Titanic* out of my system.'[24]

During her two years out of Britain – from 1929 to 1931 – Eva realised that she suffered from a number of psychological problems. These difficulties remain vague – all Eva says in her autobiography is that, on her return to England, she hoped that 'there might be a chance of coming to terms with myself'.[25] From a close reading of her memoir, it is clear that, despite having conquered her fear of sea travel, there was still a handful of issues that she had failed to resolve. 'Even though I still did not like to talk or think about the *Titanic* and the tragedy, I had at least faced up to one part of the shadow that had been cast over my life,' she said.[26] She was from a class and a background that rejected therapy – even just talking about oneself was considered bad form – and so she continued to avoid these other shadows that were just too painful to confront. Witnessing the sinking of the *Titanic*, as it moved from a state of presence to one of absence, left a certain part of her emotional landscape frozen. 'One moment you are part of an active, thriving community,' she said, 'then all that changes and a little while later you are watching and hearing the death throes as it slowly slides below the waves, until it eventually disappears from sight leaving a great visual void and an emptiness inside you.'[27]

As Eva made her way through life – first working in the wholesale department of a car dealer's in Goodmayes, heading the 'Housewives' Service' in Dagenham, becoming a Justice of the Peace and finally a welfare officer – she devoted more and more time to helping others rather than herself. Her jobs never paid much, and for fifty-six years she lived in the same modest rented upstairs flat at 2a Japan Road, Chadwell Heath. The only extra money she ever had was a modest inheritance bequeathed to her by her music teacher, Kitty Blake, who, after her death in the late 1970s, left Eva her house in Upminster. 'But Eva was not interested in money for its own sake,' says Stanley Seymour. 'In many ways she was more concerned with the welfare of those around her than herself.'[28]

As a lifelong Conservative, Eva believed in the concepts of individual responsibility, fair play, duty and justice. During her time on the bench as a magistrate, she was known as the 'Restitution Queen', a reference to her belief that justice should include helping the victims of crime, and not concentrate solely on the punishment of the criminal. 'I always maintained that if an old lady was robbed of five pounds, which might be next week's rent or the price of that day's food,' she said, 'then giving that five pounds back to her was what she needed more than just knowing that the thug who stole it had gone to prison.'[29] This belief had, she realised, been shaped by her experience after the *Titanic*, when she and her mother had been left to fend for themselves. Those early years, in which her mother had had to scrimp and save, had certainly toughened Eva, and had left no room for sympathy for what she regarded as 'the dregs of society'.[30] As a magistrate she had had to listen to reams of psychiatric reports – documents that aimed to provide some cultural or societal 'explanation' for misdeeds – but, in the case of those who committed acts of vandalism, for instance, these notes were nothing more than a lot of 'pseudo-scientific clap-trap', she thought.[31] Her goddaughter Dinah Hall remembers Eva as 'a force to be reckoned with'. She was, she adds, 'Titanic in every way' – an impressive public speaker, a strong, independent woman, 'who had been strengthened by her experience on board the *Titanic*'.[32]

For Eva, outward achievement became more important than inner knowledge. As she suggests in her memoir, it was her public role – first as a Justice of the Peace, then as the recipient of an MBE, which she received in 1974 for her good works, and then later in life as a *Titanic* celebrity – that increasingly came to define her identity. 'She was incredibly guarded about her private life,' says Richard Clegg, a friend who knew Eva for the last fifteen years of her life. 'For instance, the issue of her romantic life was completely a no-go area, and, of course, I would never dream of asking her. In many ways, she was a closed book.'[33]

Richard Clegg first met Eva in 1980, after seeing an article about her and the *Titanic* in a magazine. He read that she lived in Chadwell Heath, looked her up in the phone directory, found her address and wrote her a letter. Eva promptly replied, inviting him for a cup of tea. From then on the two became such good friends that Clegg was the one she chose to accompany her on lecture tours about being a *Titanic* survivor. She appeared on the BBC chat show *Wogan* and even a television quiz programme called *Find the Link*, in which panellists such as Kenneth Horne and Moira Lister had to guess the hidden connection between two people – in this case Eva and an elderly man who had been one of the *Titanic*'s crew. 'Question followed question and the team started to look rather bewildered,' remembered Eva. 'I thought we were going to get away with it, but on the very last question, almost in desperation, or by telepathy, one of the team said, "The *Titanic*," and we had lost . . . I think he [the crew member] was as disappointed as I that we had failed to win. But it showed us both how vividly the memory of the *Titanic* still remained.'[34]

Clegg witnessed at close quarters how Eva was transformed

from 'ordinary' elderly lady to *Titanic* celebrity. 'As the survivors began to die out, so Eva became increasingly in demand,' he says. 'Not just in Britain, but in America and around the world. I would go to her room in the mornings to collect her for breakfast and often there would be a queue of people waiting outside her room, hoping to speak to her or get her autograph. She was always very gracious and willing to talk. She was very generous with her time, and often went into schools to give talks. I remember on one occasion, after one of her lectures, one little boy put his hand up and asked if she had ever met Henry VIII. That made her laugh. Of course, part of her did enjoy the attention, the taste of the celebrity life, being treated like royalty.'[35]

According to her goddaughter, Eva adored her new-found status as a *Titanic* celebrity – not only for the chance to step into the limelight. 'One must remember that it also made her some money,' says Dinah Hall.[36] Towards the end of her life, however, there developed a rivalry for the title of reigning *Titanic* queen between Eva and fellow survivor Millvina Dean. Friends say that Eva thought Millvina to be something of an 'impostor'. She had only been a nine-week-old baby at the time of the sinking so she had no actual memories of the disaster. Plus, she had 'hit the *Titanic* trail' relatively late in life. Eva also had a problem with her fellow survivor's name – on the *Titanic* she sailed as Elizabeth Gladys, not 'Millvina'. 'The only time I saw Eva get cross was when Millvina Dean's name was mentioned,' says Richard. 'Let's just say, the chemistry was not good between them.'[37]

Eva battled with osteoporosis and cancer, but refused to sink into self-pity even when she was in great pain. Finally, however, at the age of ninety-one, she died on 14 February 1996 at her home in Chadwell Heath. At her memorial service, on 14 March 1996, at the Church of St Chad, Chadwell Heath, she was remembered 'for the kind of person she was – for her love of life itself, her energy, her courage, her determination, her love of people, her integrity and her commitment to all those values which enhance human life and dignity'.[38] In April of the same year, a tree was planted in St Chad's Park, where Eva used to love to go and sit; beneath the tree, her friends and family spread her ashes. Two years after her death, Wetherspoon's opened a pub in a converted police station on the high street in Chadwell Heath bearing her name; it's debatable whether Eva would have approved.

One thing would have rankled for certain: she was not the last survivor. Eva went to her grave knowing that her greatest rival, Millvina Dean, had beaten her in the *Titanic* celebrity game by the mere virtue of staying alive a little longer.

Millvina Dean first became a *Titanic* celebrity at the age of three months when she, together with her mother, Georgette Eva, and her brother, Bertram Frank, known as Vere, travelled back after the disaster to England on board the *Adriatic*. Passengers were so curious to see, hold, and have their photographs taken with the baby girl that stewards had to impose some kind of queuing system. 'She was the pet of the liner during the voyage,' reported the *Daily Mirror* at the time, 'and so keen was the rivalry between women to nurse this lovable mite of humanity that one of the officers decreed that first- and second-class passengers might hold her in turn for no more than ten minutes.'[39]

After returning to Britain, Millvina grew up to lead what, at first sight, seems to be a quiet, uneventful life. Then, in 1985, Ballard discovered the wreck at the bottom of the sea. 'Nobody knew about me and the *Titanic*, to be honest, nobody took any interest, so I took no interest either,' she said. 'But then they found the wreck, and after they found the wreck, they found me.'[40] This was followed in 1997 by the release of James Cameron's blockbuster film, *Titanic*, starring Kate Winslet and

Leonardo di Caprio as two lovers from vastly different backgrounds who meet on board the doomed ship. Suddenly, in old age, Millvina was famous once more. 'The telephone rang all day long,' she told me. 'I think I spoke to every radio station in England. Everybody wanted interviews. Then I wished I had never been on the *Titanic*, it became too much at times.'[41]

Of course, Millvina had no memories of the disaster – she was only nine weeks old at the time – but this did not seem to bother either her legion of fans or the mass media. As the last living survivor of the *Titanic*, Millvina Dean became an emblem for every survivor. She stood as a symbol of courage, dignity, strength, and endurance in the face of adversity. The public, desperate for someone who could embody what it meant to triumph over this and other tragedies, projected on to her a range of emotions and fantasies. In their eyes, she became part Millvina Dean and part Rose DeWitt Bukater, the fictional heroine in James Cameron's 1997 film who, in old age, is played by the elderly Gloria Stuart. 'Are you ready to go back to *Titanic*?' asks modern-day treasure hunter Brock Lovett, played by Bill Paxton. 'Will you share it with us?' Rose stands in front of one of the monitors on board Lovett's ship, her hand reaching out to touch the grainy images of the wreck sent up from the bottom of the ocean. For a moment it all seems too much for her as she breaks down in tears, but she is determined to carry on. 'It's been eighty-four years and I can still smell the fresh paint,' she says. 'The china had never been used, the sheets had never been slept in. They called it the ship of dreams and it was, it really was . . .'[42]

In the same way, Millvina was often asked to repeat her story of that night, but her account was second-hand, most of it pieced together from what her mother had told her together with fragments from newspapers and magazines.

'All I really know is that my parents were on the ship,' she told me. 'We were emigrating to Wichita, Kansas, where my father wanted to open a tobacconist's shop – and one night we were in bed. My father heard a crash and he went up to see what it was about. He came back and said, "Get the children out of bed and on deck as quickly as possible." I think that saved our lives because we were in third class and so many people thought the ship to be unsinkable. I was put in a sack because I was too small to hold and rescued by the *Carpathia*, which took us back to New York. We stayed there for a few weeks, before travelling back to Britain. My mother never talked about it, and I didn't know anything about the *Titanic* until I was eight years old and she married again. But from then on the *Titanic* was, for the most part, never mentioned.'[43]

The *Titanic* came to represent a ship of dreams for Millvina too, a vessel which would take her on a surreal journey to the outer realms of celebrity culture. In 1997, she travelled on the QE2 to America as a guest of the Titanic Historical Society, first calling at New York and then flying on to Kansas, to see the home she would have grown up in had her father not died in the disaster. As she stood outside the porch of 3659 Harrison Street, Wichita, she had a glimpse of a parallel existence that could have been hers had it not been for the *Titanic*. She also appeared on the chat shows *Wogan* and *Larry King*, had a street and a bus route in Southampton named after her, travelled around the world giving lectures about the disaster, and, in 2008, generated headlines around the globe when it was revealed that she planned to sell off some of her *Titanic* memorabilia in order to pay for her nursing home fees. One day, in October 2008, as she was sitting in her bedroom in Woodlands, on the edge of the New Forest, a strange-looking man, together with a reporter and a photographer from the *Sun* newspaper, turned up at her bedside. The man, David Gest, whom she thought resembled an alien and who is best known for being the ex-husband of Liza Minnelli, presented her with a cheque for a few thousand pounds. The couple posed – or rather Gest did (Millvina appears to be wincing as the *I'm a Celebrity Get Me Out of Here* 'star' pushed his cosmetically enhanced face into hers). It was all rather odd, she recalled. 'To be honest I had never heard of him before,' she said. 'He just turned up here, with four or five others. I didn't know any of them, had never seen any of them before.'[44]

Nevertheless, Millvina carried it off with her usual grace and charm, qualities that she put to good use during her reign as the last *Titanic* queen. Diplomacy is an absolute essential, she said. She remembered one occasion, in 2003, when a British couple, Sanya and Adam Ward, wanted to name their baby after her and came to ask for her permission, which she duly granted. 'It's really flattering to have a baby named after me,' said Millvina.[45] Five years later, however, when the two Millvinas met for the first time, she was forced to draw upon her best diplomatic skills as it was clear that neither she nor the little girl liked one other. 'She didn't like me, and, to be honest, I didn't like her,' she told me. 'I thought she was utterly spoilt. The parents kept saying things like "Millvina is having ballet classes, aren't you, Millvina?" and the girl would say, "Yes." "Millvina is having piano lessons, aren't you, Millvina?" at which point she would answer, "Yes." Oh, I got so fed up with her, but of course I didn't say anything.'[46]

One should not assume, however, that Millvina was incapable of speaking up for herself. She was far from a shrinking violet. Halfway through my interview with her she turned to me and asked whether I was paying her for her time. When I said I was not, she told me that she usually got five hundred pounds for an interview. At a later point in the interview she broke off from what she was saying to point out, 'To think you are having all of this for nothing when all those people paid.' She did have to be careful, though, she added. She had one 'friend' who, she said, 'was trying to make money' out of her on the internet.[47] *Titanic* author and expert Brian Ticehurst confirmed the truth of this statement – some people had tried to get close to Millvina so that she would sign letters or postcards, documents which they then proceeded to sell on the internet. 'It's big business,' said Millvina, with a twinkle in her eye.

On the day I met Millvina, at her nursing home in Southampton, she was holding a teddy bear, which wore a T-shirt that said, 'Over the hill and picking up speed', an appropriate motto for Millvina herself. At ninety-six, for the most part bedridden, sporting a large grey wig, and wearing thick spectacles that seemed to magnify her eyes, she may have appeared the personification of old age. Outside the window of her room one could see the reds, russets, and oranges of the trees that symbolised the autumnal stage of her life. Yet in many ways she seemed to sparkle with life. Her mind was fresh and alert. Three miniature bottles of brandy and a bottle of apple blossom *eau de parfum* wrestled for space on her cluttered bedside table, beside the piles of letters from her fans and friends from around the world.

For many years, Millvina suffered from an inferiority complex; she used to stutter and, by her own admission, she experienced trouble with what she described as her 'nerves'. But the *Titanic* – or rather, her status as a *Titanic* survivor – had given her something of a second chance, an opportunity to live again. 'I was a very highly strung child,' she said.[48] She was plagued by worries and fears, a sense of anxiety that she picked up from her mother, who was determined to repress her memories of the disaster. Occasionally, strangers would point at young Millvina on the street and whisper, 'There goes Girlie Dean, she was on the *Titanic*!' One of her most poignant memories is when she and her mother opened a trunk that had remained closed for years.

Inside were the clothes that she and her brother had worn as small children, in the years following the disaster. As the women took the garments in their hands they crumbled away in their fingers, the fabric eaten away by moths.

As a child Millvina took refuge in the world of books, and would never leave the house without one. 'My grandfather and my mother were so worried about me because I didn't do anything but read,' she said. 'Eventually my mother took me to the doctor because she was so concerned, and he told her to give me a patch of garden to look after, which I think did the trick.'[49]

She left school at sixteen, but stayed at home in Southampton, with her mother and stepfather, Leonard Burden, a vet. Often, during holiday periods or if people were ill, the family would take in animals and look after them; she remembered on one occasion there were as many as forty cats and forty-five dogs. She would feed the cats a mix of milk and fish and it was her job to take every single bone out of the fish before serving it up. During the Second World War she was forced to leave home to work in the Ordnance Survey Office, in Hinchley Wood, Surrey, where she remained for four years. A photograph of her taken during the war shows her as a woman with a long face, intelligent, but sad eyes, dressed in a uniform complete with shirt and tie. There is more than a passing resemblance to Vita Sackville-West. 'I enjoyed the war tremendously,' said Millvina. 'Everybody was your friend.'[50]

It was while working in the Ordnance Survey Office that she met a woman, Yolande Christopher, who became one of her closest companions. Millvina refused to reveal the exact nature of their friendship, but obviously it was so deep and so committed that when Yolande left for India where she had grown up, Millvina suffered from a nervous breakdown. 'She wanted me to go with her, but I just couldn't do it,' Millvina told me. 'Her father was a colonel over there, and although she wanted me very much to go, I said, "India, with all those snakes?" After the war, I was at home for a year, I believe, with my nerves. Finally, the doctor said, "Look, you have had enough time to think about yourself, you need to get a job." Each day I would walk past this tobacconist's shop and one day I popped inside and asked if he needed anyone to help. "Well, you've got me," I said. But then the nerves got the better of me and I couldn't start. A whole week passed by, I went back and apologised and asked if he would give me another chance, which he did. And so I worked there. I think it helped me with my nerves; it cured me, I would say. I never married. I liked too many people, I suppose. And I don't know whether I would have made a good wife, anyhow.' She tried not to think of Yolande, whom she called Chris. It was just too painful. 'I am the type who believes what can't be cured must be endured.'[51]

After working in the purchasing department of a Southampton engineering company, Millvina cared for her mother, who died in September 1975, at the age of ninety-six. 'Whatever other *Titanic* stories she had, she took to her grave because to the best of my knowledge she never really gave interviews about it and didn't want to be reminded of it,' she said.[52] In contrast, since the mid to late eighties, Millvina devoted her life to the *Titanic*. The transition from obscurity to celebrity was a relatively smooth one for her, precisely because she had lived so many years with an overwhelming sense of self-denial. She had said 'no' to herself so many times – particularly to her friend Yolande, who wanted her to accompany her to India – that now, given the chance, she was going to say 'yes' to everything and to everyone. As a result, she transformed herself not only into a celebrity but also, as she freely admitted, into a piece of 'living history'.

'For many people I somehow represent the *Titanic*,' she

said. 'I expect that's why they want to write to me. Sometimes people get very emotional and burst into tears when I meet them. All I can say is, "there, there" and hope they'll be alright.'[53] Millvina's brother, Vere, often accompanied his sister to *Titanic* events, and would freely give his time to talk about the disaster. Like Millvina he didn't remember anything of the event itself, but, as he said, he 'lived it over and over again as my mother told me'.[54]

On 15 April 1992, the day of the eightieth anniversary of the sinking, Vere died in his sleep while in hospital in Southampton. Millvina too had her health problems – she broke her hip when she was in her early eighties, suffered from cataracts, and contracted a blood infection while having another hip operation in her nineties. In 2006, she entered Woodlands nursing home, dependent on oxygen and in a terribly weak state. 'When I came in here the matron said, "That's the end of her, she'll never recover." But I did. Someone said of me that I am a tough old bird.' Would she describe herself as a fighter? 'Oh yes, definitely.'[55] After a short illness, Millvina died on 31 May 2009; she was ninety-seven. The last survivor of the *Titanic* was no more.

AFTERWORD

A few weeks after the *Titanic* disaster, Thomas Hardy wrote 'The Convergence of the Twain', his famous poem about the conjunction between the sublime iceberg and the majestic liner. First published in *Fortnightly Review* in June 1912, it articulates the 'intimate wedding' between a natural phenomenon and a symbol of the machine age. The marriage of the 'shape of ice' and the 'smart ship' is described as a 'consummation', a grotesque union that 'jars two hemispheres'. One hundred years after the sinking we are still feeling the aftershocks of the wreck as the 'twin halves' of this 'august event' continue to fascinate and disturb us in equal measure.

With the death of Millvina Dean a piece of living history has been lost; now there is no longer anybody alive who has a direct connection with the ship. Yet the night, the journey, the ship and its passengers (both victims and survivors) continue to live on in the collective imagination. Indeed, the disaster has become so invested with mythical status – it's been said that the name *Titanic* is the third most widely recognised word in the world, after 'God' and 'Coca-Cola' – that it almost seems like a constant, an event that repeats itself on a never-ending loop.

As we have seen, a great number of lives were 'sea-changed in the disaster',[1] with the ripples felt many years later. For the majority of survivors, the spot where the *Titanic* went down would always be suffused with a special significance. Some of those who escaped, such as third-class passenger Frank Goldsmith – who had been nine at the time of the sinking and who lost his father that night – felt so connected to that particular stretch of sea that he requested his ashes be scattered there. In April 1982, on the seventieth anniversary of the disaster, relatives of Frank – who had died on 27 January 1982, aged seventy-nine – sailed out to the spot off the Newfoundland coast, took out the urn that contained his remains and scattered the ashes over the ocean. 'He would tell me part of the story,' remembers Frank's grandson, Tom Goldsmith, 'but I would never get it from beginning to end. He would tell portions of it like he was still a child.'[2]

As Ben Goldsmith, Frank's great-great-grandson testifies, the fact that one of his ancestors survived the *Titanic* holds a special significance. Had his great-great-grandfather not escaped the sinking ship, he would not have been born. 'When I tell people I had family that was on the *Titanic* they always say, "They survived?"' adds Ben. 'But I wouldn't be here if they didn't.'[3]

Today there must be thousands of people who exist thanks to the fact that one of their relatives survived the *Titanic*. Robert Maguire, an American who now lives in London, is one such person. His grandfather was Jack Thayer, the seventeen-year-old boy who jumped off the ship as it was sinking and who committed suicide at the age of fifty. In August 1984, in Wayne, Pennsylvania, Maguire married Katherine Cobb Bucknell, a Ph.D. candidate and the daughter of the late John Addison Cobb Bucknell and Louise W. Carter. Years later, the couple were travelling in America when, in April 1992, on the eightieth anniversary of the sinking, Kate was reading a newspaper when she came across a list of *Titanic* survivors. Included in the register was the name of one of her ancestors, first-class passenger Emma Eliza Ward, a widow who had been sixty when she had travelled on the *Titanic*. 'It wasn't until that point that we realised we both had direct relatives who had survived the *Titanic*,' says Kate, who is now an author. One of the couple's young sons, Jack, is fascinated by our conversation. To try and explain the significance of the information, Kate turns to her son and says, 'If Daddy's grandfather – the one who was seventeen – had died on the ship you wouldn't have Daddy.' If Kate's great-great-grandmother, Emma Eliza Ward, had perished in the sinking the boy would not have his mother either. The consequences of all this are almost too much for the child to understand, but he looks intrigued and amused. To perplex and baffle the boy even more, Robert adds, 'And that means you, Jack, wouldn't exist.'[4]

The survivors of the night continue to live on.

ACKNOWLEDGEMENTS

This book could not have been written without the resources of one man: the late Walter Lord, author of *A Night to Remember*. During the course of his research into the sinking he had become a *Titanic* obsessive and after the publication of his 1955 book he continued to correspond with the survivors. These documents – letters and diaries that detail the disaster and its aftermath over the course of the last century – are a fascinating insight into that night and what happened afterwards. I am grateful to the National Maritime Museum, Greenwich, London and its Caird Library for access to the material and permission to quote from these previously unpublished documents. All the staff there – especially Andrew Davis, Hannah Dunmow, Gareth Bellis, Mike Bevan and Melanie Oelgeschläger – helped guide me through the enormous collection and made my research all the more enjoyable.

I also consulted archival material held at the J. Welles Henderson Archives and Library at the Independence Seaport Museum, Philadelphia, and I must thank Matt Herbison, its director, and Craig Bruns, for their help. I drew on the resources and expertise of the *Titanic* Historical Society (thanks to Karen Kamuda, its vice-president), the *Titanic* International Society (Mary Ann Whitley, Cathy Bernstein), as well as the phenomenal Encyclopedia *Titanic* (www.encyclopedia-titanica.org). I must thank the Library of Congress (particularly Amber Paranick, Paul Hogroian, Valerie Moore and Kenny Johnson) for their help. I also drew on materials held by Southampton City Council – thanks go to Maria Newbury, curator of maritime and local collections, archivist Sue Hill and Vicky Green from the city's Central Library.

I hope this book serves as a tribute to the passengers on the *Titanic*, both to those who died and those who survived. I have drawn upon the testimonies of many survivors of the *Titanic*, and their relatives, friends and carers, together with contemporary witness accounts, and I would like to acknowledge: Olaus Abelseth, Mildred Addison, Madeleine Astor, Lawrence Beesley, Karl Behr, Ruth Becker Blanchard, May R. Birkhead, Helen Bishop, Lida Fleitmann Bloodgood, Larry Boyd, William B. Boulton, Harold Bride, Frank Bustard, Helen Churchill Candee, Gus Cohen, Charlotte Collyer, Edwina Corrigan, Charles Dienz, W.H. Dobbyn, Washington Dodge Snr, Washington Dodge Jnr, Marjorie Dutton (formerly Collyer), Millvina Dean, Lady Duff Gordon, Sir Cosmo Duff Gordon, Archibald Gracie, Renee Harris, Esther Hart, Eva Hart, Julie Hedgepeth, Charles Hendrickson, Enzo Fiermonte, Frederick Fleet, Laura Mabel Francatelli, Phillip Franklin, May Futrelle, Dorothy and Pauline Gibson, Frederic A. Hamilton, George Harder, Robert Hitchens, Annie Hopkins, Carlos F. Hurd, J. Bruce Ismay, Thomas Bruce Ismay, Violet Jessop, George Kemish, Anna Kincaid (formerly Sjoblom), Seymour Leslie, Charles Lightoller, William Lucas, Jim Lyons, William MacQuitty, Bertha Marshall, Madeleine Mellenger Mann, Sylvia Mercherle (formerly Mrs Albert Caldwell), Daisy Minahan, Bertha Mulvihill, Julia Murphy, Michel Navratil, August Ogden, Lady Pirrie, John Podesta, George Rheims, Arnold A. Robert, Annie Robinson, Helen Rodman, the Countess of Rothes, George Rowe, Sir Arthur Rostron, Edith

Russell (formerly Rosenbaum), Emily Ryerson, Harold Sanderson, Mrs Paul Schabert, Marguerite Schwarzenbach, Elizabeth W. Shutes, Mary Sloan, Andrew Jackson Sloper, William Thomson Sloper, H.M. Alderson Smith, Eloise Hughes Smith, Jane Stern, Elsie Stormont, John B. Thayer, Marian Thayer, Sidney Tyler, Robert Vaughan, William D. Winsor, Hugh Woolner, Marion Wright.

In the course of researching and writing this book I also drew on a number of newspapers and periodicals including: The *American Weekly*, *Atlantic Daily Bulletin*, *Boston Evening Transcript*, *Chicago Daily Tribune*, *Collier's Weekly*, *Daily Mail*, *Daily Mirror*, *Daily Sketch*, *Detroit News Times*, *Dowagiac Daily News*, *Dowagiac Times*, *Evening Bulletin* (Philadelphia), *Eugene Register-Guard*, *Evening World*, *Harrisburg Leader*, *Huntington Quarterly*, *Los Angeles Times*, *Meriden Morning Record*, *Milwaukee Journal*, *Newark Star*, *New York American*, *New York Evening World*, *New York Herald*, *New York Morning Telegraph*, *New York Times*, *Paris Herald*, *Pittsburgh Post-Gazette*, *Providence Journal*, *San Francisco Bulletin*, *San Francisco Chronicle*, *Sarasota Journal*, *Semi-Monthly Magazine*, *Semi-Weekly Iowegian*, the *Shipbuilder Magazine*, *Southern Daily Echo*, *Sturgis Times Democrat*, *Time*, *The Times*, various issues of the *Titanic Commutator*, *Town and Country*, *True Story Magazine*, *Women's Wear Daily*, *Yankee Magazine*.

I consulted a wide range of books during my research but I must single out the following for being particularly useful:

A Rainbow of Time and Space: Orphans of the Titanic, Sidney F. Tyler, Aztex Corporation, Tucson, Arizona, 1981

A Voyage Closed and Done, Pauline Matarasso, Michael Russell, Norwich, 2005

Discretions and Indiscretions, Lady Duff Gordon, Jarrolds, London, 1932

Down With the Old Canoe: A Cultural History of the Titanic Disaster, Steven Biel, W.W. Norton, New York, 1996

Finding Dorothy: An Appreciation of the Life and Career of Dorothy

Gibson Brulatour, Randy Bryan Bigham, *Titanic* Star Publications, Dallas, Texas, 2005

The Ismay Line, Wilton J. Oldham, The Journal of Commerce, Liverpool, 1961

The 'It' Girls, Meredith Etherington-Smith and Jeremy Pilcher, Hamish Hamilton, London, 1986

Shadow of the Titanic: A Survivor's Story, Eva Hart and Ronald C. Denney, Greenwich University, Dartford, 1994

The Sinking of the S.S. Titanic, John B. Thayer, 1940, reprinted in *Titanic: A Survivor's Story*, Colonel Archibald Gracie and *The Sinking of the S.S. Titanic*, Academy Chicago Publishers, 1998

Titanic, John Wilson Foster (ed.), Penguin, London, 1999

Titanic: The Last Survivor, the Life of Millvina Dean, Anthony Cunningham, Sheila Jemima, with Millvina Dean, Waterfront, Kingfisher Productions, Settle, 2008

Titanic Memories: the Making of A Night to Remember, William MacQuitty, National Maritime Museum, London, 2000

Titanic: A Survivor's Story, Colonel Archibald Gracie, first published in 1913, republished Academy Chicago Publishers, Chicago, 1998

Titanic: Women and Children First, Judith B. Geller, Patrick Stephens Ltd, Sparkford, 1998,

The Loss of the Titanic, Sir Arthur Rostron, Titanic Signals Archive, Westbury, Wiltshire, 1991

The Loss of the S.S. Titanic: Its Story and Its Lessons, Lawrence Beesley, Forgotten Books, 2008, originally published by William Heinemann, London, 1912

Unsinkable: the Full Story of the RMS Titanic, Daniel Allen Butler, Da Capo Press, Cambridge, MA, 2002, originally published by Stackpole Books, 1998

The American and British inquiries into the sinking are great resources for researchers and now can be found online at:

www.titanicinquiry.org/

For use of photographs and images in the book I am grateful to: Randy Bryan Bigham, Ronald C. Denney, Getty Images, Phillip Gowan, the Library of Congress, MacQuitty International Photographic Collection, Robert Maguire, Southampton City Council, Frank Thompson, and the *Titanic* Historical Society.

I would also like to acknowledge the help and assistance of the following. Some provided leads and contacts, others wrote letters or granted interviews (or both). Their help proved invaluable in the research and writing of the book: Lady Caroline Blois, Randy Bryan Bigham, Elisabeth Bouillon, Kate Bucknell, Malcolm Cheape, Richard Clegg, Stratford Caldecott, Vanessa Cotton, Charles Darwent, the late Millvina Dean, Ronald Denney, Alice Fowler, Phillip Gowan, Dinah Hall, Clifford Ismay, Gautier Landivier, Alice Leader, Betty MacQuitty, Jane MacQuitty, Miranda MacQuitty, Robert Maguire (both father and son), Pauline Maguire, Michael Manser, Pauline Matarasso, Catriona Munro, Stanley Seymour, George Sinclair, Julie Sutherland (at Woodlands Ridge), Brian Ticehurst, Frank Thompson, Agnes Thwaite, Julie Vehr, Mandy Woodard.

I would like to thank the great team at Simon & Schuster, especially Mike Jones and Peter Borland (who commissioned the book), Talya Baker, Nick Simonds, Rory Scarfe, Nigel Stoneman and everyone in publicity, Kerr Macrae, James Horobin, Sarah Birdsey, Gill Richardson, Rob Cox, Gill Clack, Malinda Zerefos, Emily Husain, David Atkinson (for the index) and Martin Soames (for expert legal advice).

At Aitken Alexander in London I would like to thank my agent Clare Alexander for her enthusiasm about the project and her continuing support and friendship throughout the research and writing of the book. Also, Leah Middleton, Sally Riley and Cassie Metcalf-Slovo.

Finally, I would like to thank my parents, all my friends in London and Spain, and Marcus Field, without whom I could not have written this book.

NOTES

Abbreviations used throughout:
NMM: Caird Library, National Maritime Museum, London
WL: Walter Lord
AW: Andrew Wilson
TC: *Titanic Commutator*

INTRODUCTION

1. 'How I Was Saved from the *Titanic*', Charlotte Collyer, *Semi-Monthly Magazine*, 26 May 1912
2. Letter from George Kemish to WL, 19 June 1955, LMQ/7/1/49, NMM
3. Letter from George Rheims to his wife, 19 April 1912, LMQ/7/2/16, NMM
4. 'I Took a Voyage on the RMS *Titanic*', Scott Eyman, *Yankee Magazine*, June 1981
5. Letter from Hugh Woolner, written on board the *Carpathia*, April 1912, LMQ/7/2/46, NMM
6. 'I Went Down with the *Titanic*', *Daily Mail*, 1912
7. 'Miss Dorothy Gibson Tells of her Rescue', *New York Telegraph*, 20 April 1912, reproduced in TC, Vol. 30, Number 175, 2006
8. Affidavit of Daisy Minahan, United States Senate Inquiry, Day 16
9. Testimony of George A. Harder, United States Senate Inquiry, Day 13
10. Ruth Becker Blanchard, TC, Vol. 10, No. 4, Winter 1986
11. Letter from Edwina Corrigan to William MacQuitty, 20 March 1958, LMQ/7/19, NMM
12. *Ghosts of the Titanic*, Charles Pellegrino, William Morrow, NY, 2000, p 97
13. 'The *Titanic* Disaster' as told by Gus Cohen, TC, Vol. 1, Issue 3, 1963

14. *Ghosts of the Titanic*, p 97
15. Letter from Julie Hedgepeth to WL, 5 April 1987, LMQ/7/1, NMM
16. Letter from Jane Stern to WL, 1 June 1955, LMQ/2/5, NMM
17. *A Voyage Closed and Done*, Pauline Matarasso, Michael Russell, Norwich, 2005, pp 18–19
18. Letter from Larry Boyd to WL, 3 March 1998, LMQ/7/2/42, NMM
19. Ibid.
20. Ibid.
21. Letter from May Futrelle to Helen Hernandez, quoted in letter from Helen Hernandez to WL, 14 June 1955, LMQ/2/4/122, NMM
22. Letter from Bertha Marshall to WL, 10 April 1963, LMQ/7/2/37, NMM
23. Letter from Marjorie Dutton to WL, 27 November 1955, LMQ/2/4/72, NMM
24. Letter from Marjorie Dutton to WL, 7 August 1956, LMQ/2/4/72, NMM
25. Letter from Marjorie Dutton, to WL, 31 August 1956, LMQ/2/4/72, NMM
26. 'A Night to Forget', Renee Harris, unpublished manuscript, 1977, LMQ/7/1, NMM
27. Ibid.
28. Letter from Countess of Rothes to WL, 7 August 1955, LMQ/7/2/20, NMM
29. Letter from Jim Lyons to WL, 14 March 1972, LMQ/7/2/24, NMM

CHAPTER ONE

1. *Titanic: A Survivor's Story*, Colonel Archibald Gracie, first published in 1913, republished Academy Chicago Publishers, Chicago, 1998, p 4
2. Ibid.
3. 'I Took a Voyage on the RMS *Titanic,*' Scott Eyman, *Yankee Magazine*, June 1981
4. Letter from Julie Hedgepeth to WL, 5 April 1987, regarding her great uncle Albert Caldwell, LMQ/7/1, NMM
5. Letter from Marion Wright to her father, 11 April 1912, HSR/Z/30/1-17, NMM
6. Letter from Madeleine Mellenger Mann to WL, 24 February 1969, LMQ/7/2/5, NMM

7. Ibid.
8. *Shipbuilder magazine*, special issue devoted to the *Titanic* and the *Olympic*, 1911
9. Ibid.
10. Ibid.
11. Ibid.
12. Letter from Sylvia Mercherle (then Mrs Albert Caldwell) to WL, 13 July 1955, LMQ/2/5/14, NMM
13. Interview with Captain Smith, unnamed New York newspaper, 1907, quoted in *Unsinkable: the Full Story of the RMS Titanic*, Daniel Allen Butler, Da Capo Press, Cambridge, MA, 2002, p 48, originally published by Stackpole Books, 1998
14. *The Sinking of the SS Titanic*, John B. Thayer, 1940, reprinted in *Titanic: A Survivor's Story, Colonel Archibald Gracie and The Sinking of the SS Titanic*, Academy Chicago Publishers, 1998, p 329
15. Ibid.
16. Thayer, p 334
17. Marconi message from *Baltic* to *Titanic*, related by the Attorney General during testimony of J. Bruce Ismay, British Wreck Commissioner's Inquiry, Day 16
18. Statement of Emily Ryerson, 18 April 1913, LMQ/7/2/22, NMM
19. 'A Pig and a Prayer Saved Me from the Titanic', Edith Russell, unpublished memoir, LMQ/5/2/1, NMM
20. Ibid.
21. Ibid.
22. Edith Rosenbaum to Horace J. Shaw, 11 April 1912, quoted in 'A Pig and a Prayer', LMQ/5/2/1, NMM
23. Ibid.
24. Gracie, p 11
25. 'Sealed Orders', Helen Churchill Candee, *Collier's Weekly*, 4 May 1912
26. *Discretions and Indiscretions*, Lady Duff Gordon, Jarrolds, London, 1932, p 150
27. Thayer, p 334
28. 'Motion Picture Actress Tells of *Titanic* Wreck', *New York Morning Telegraph*, 21 April 1912
29. *Discretions and Indiscretions*, Lady Duff Gordon, p 147
30. Thayer, p 335
31. Testimony of Frederick Fleet, British Wreck Commissioner's Inquiry, Day 15

32. *A Night to Remember*, Walter Lord, originally published 1955, republished in 2005 by Owl Books, Henry Holt, New York, p 2
33. Testimony of Frederick Fleet, British Wreck Commissioner's Inquiry, Day 15
34. Ibid.
35. Letter from Sylvia Mercherle (then Mrs Albert Caldwell) to WL, 13 July 1955, LMQ/W/5/14, NMM
36. 'When the *Titanic* Went Down', Elizabeth W. Shutes, in Gracie, p 252
37. 'Motion Picture Actress Tells of *Titanic* Wreck', *New York Morning Telegraph*, 21 April 1912
38. Thayer, pp 335–6
39. Thayer, p 336
40. 'A Night to Forget', Renee Harris, LMQ/7/1, NMM
41. Letter from Laura Mabel Francatelli to Marion Taylor, 28 April 1912, LMQ/7/1/28, NMM
42. 'A Pig and a Prayer', Edith Russell, LMQ/5/2/1, NMM
43. May R. Birkhead, *New York Herald*, 19 April 1912
44. Letter from George Rowe to WL, undated, LMQ/7/2/21, NMM
45. Testimony of Robert Hitchens, United States Senate Inquiry, Day 5
46. *A Night to Remember*, WL, p 21
47. Letter from Laura Mabel Francatelli to Marion Taylor, 28 April 1912, LMQ/7/1/28, NMM
48. 'Motion Picture Actress Tells of *Titanic* Wreck', *New York Morning Telegraph*, 21 April 1912
49. Letter from Mary Sloan to her sister, Maggie, 27 April 1912, LMQ/7/2/28, NMM
50. Thayer, p 337
51. 'A Pig and a Prayer', LMQ/5/2/1, NMM
52. Ibid.
53. 'Sealed Orders', Helen Churchill Candee, *Collier's Weekly*, 4 May 1912
54. *The Loss of the SS Titanic: Its Story and Its Lessons*, Lawrence Beesley, Forgotten Books, 2008, p 33, originally published by William Heinemann, London, 1912
55. 'Motion Picture Actress Tells of *Titanic* Wreck,' *New York Morning Telegraph*, 21 April 1912
56. Written account of *Titanic* disaster, from the scrapbook of Karl H. Behr, LMQ/7/1/5, NMM
57. 'The *Titanic* Disaster' as told by Gus Cohen, TC, Volume 1, Issue 3, 1963

58. 'A *Titanic* Survivor Story: Coosan Coleen, Bertha Mulvihill', Tad Fitch, TC, Issue 166, 2004
59. 'Two Survivors Call on Mayor to Ask Relief', *Evening World*, 22 April 1912
60. Letter from Laura Mabel Francatelli to Marion Taylor, 28 April 1912, LMQ/7/1/28, NMM
61. 'A Pig and a Prayer', LMQ/5/2/1, NMM
62. Sheridan Morley radio interview with Edith Russell, BBC, 14 April 1970, http://www.bbc.co.uk/archive/*titanic*/5051.shtml
63. 'A Pig and a Prayer', LMQ/5/2/1, NMM
64. Ibid.
65. 'How I Was Saved from the *Titanic*', Charlotte Collyer, *Semi-Monthly Magazine*, 26 May 1912
66. Thayer, p 341
67. John B. Thayer Jr's statement to the press regarding the sinking of the RMS *Titanic*, The Pennsylvania Railroad Information for the Press, 20 April 1912
68. Unidentified newspaper, but it is thought to be either the *New York American* or *Herald*, 22–25 April 1912
69. 'A Night to Forget', Renee Harris, LMQ/7/1, NMM
70. Ibid.
71. Thayer, p 343
72. *Titanic and Other Ships*, Charles Lightoller, 1935, quoted in *Titanic*, John Wilson Foster (ed.), Penguin, London, 1999, p 97
73. Ibid.
74. 'Thrilling Tale by *Titanic*'s Surviving Wireless Man', *New York Times*, 28 April 1912
75. Thayer, pp 343–4
76. Ibid.
77. Thayer, p 345
78. Letter from George Rowe to WL, undated, LMQ/7/2/21, NMM
79. Letter from George Rheims to his wife, 19 April 1912, LMQ/7/2/16, NMM
80. Thayer, p 348
81. 'How I Was Saved from the *Titanic*', Charlotte Collyer, *Semi-Monthly Magazine*, 26 May 1912
82. 'A Pig and a Prayer', LMQ/5/2/1, NMM

CHAPTER TWO

1. 'A Night to Forget', Renee Harris, LMQ/7/1, NMM
2. Renee Harris obituary, *New York Times*, 3 September 1969
3. 'A Night to Forget', LMQ/7/1, NMM
4. Karl H. Behr, written account of the disaster in his scrapbook, LMQ/7/1/5, NMM
5. Letter from George Rheims to his wife, 19 April 1912, LMQ/7/2/16, NMM
6. 'A Pig and a Prayer', Edith Russell, LMQ/5/2/1, NMM
7. Letter from Marjorie Dutton (born Collyer) to WL, 27 November 1955, LMQ/2/4/72, NMM
8. 'Thrilling Tale by *Titanic*'s Surviving Wireless Man', *New York Times*, 28 April 1912
9. 'I Remember', Robert H. Vaughan, 20 January 1962, LMQ/7/2/36, NMM
10. May R. Birkhead, *New York Herald*, 19 April 1912
11. *The Loss of the Titanic*, Sir Arthur Rostron, Titanic Signals Archive, Westbury, Wiltshire, 1991, p 25
12. *The Loss of the Titanic*, p 24
13. 'I Remember', Robert H. Vaughan, LMQ/7/2/36, NMM
14. *A Night to Remember*, p 136
15. Letter from Julie Hedgepeth to WL, regarding her great-uncle Albert Caldwell, 5 April 1987, LMQ/7/1, NMM
16. Letter from Augusta Ogden to WL, 19 July 1955, LMQ/7/2/7, NMM
17. *The Titanic Man*, Carlos F. Hurd, (ed.) Vera and John Gillespie, 1997, LMQ/1/13/1, NMM
18. 'I Remember', Robert H. Vaughan, LMQ/7/2/36, NMM
19. Letter from Mrs White regarding the experience of her cousin Ella Holmes White, 22 April 1912, LMQ/7/2/40, NMM
20. Letter from Marion Wright to her father, 16 April 1912, HSR/Z/30/1-17, NMM
21. Letter from Mrs Paul Schabert to Countess Martha Butler-Clonebough, 18 April 1912, LMQ/7/2/25, NMM
22. Karl H. Behr, written account of the disaster in his scrapbook, LMQ/7/1/5, NMM
23. Letter from Bertha Marshall, then Watt, to WL, 10 April 1963, LMQ/7/2/37, NMM
24. Letter from Madeleine Mellenger Mann to Henry Holt Publishers, 31 October 1955, LMQ/7/2/5, NMM

25. Letter from Madeleine Mellenger Mann to WL, 13 January 1962, LMQ/7/2/5, NMM
26. 'A Pig and a Prayer', Edith Russell, LMQ/5/2/1, NMM
27. Wireless messages from Marian Thayer, private wireless traffic from and to the *Carpathia*, LMQ/5/1/, NMM
28. 'A Night to Forget', LMQ/7/1, NMM
29. 'A Pig and a Prayer', LMQ/5/2/1, NMM
30. 'A Night to Forget', LMQ/7/1, NMM
31. Letter from Marian Thayer to President William Howard Taft, 21 April 1912, Library of Congress, Case File 303, Series 7, reel 459
32. 'Memorial Services for *Titanic*'s Dead', *New York Times*, 20 April 1912
33. 'How *Titanic* Fund is Being Disbursed', *New York Times*, 3 June 1912
34. Ibid.
35. 'Thanksgiving Gift for *Titanic* Widows', *New York Times*, 29 November 1912
36. Ibid.
37. 'Relief for Victims of the *Titanic*', *Meriden Morning Record*, 5 August 1912
38. 'Dead of the *Titanic* Honored in Church', *New York Times*, 14 April 1913
39. 'Widows to Mourn at Great Ocean Grave', *Milwaukee Journal*, 5 April 1913
40. Renee Harris obituary, *New York Times*, 3 September 1969
41. 'A Night to Forget', LMQ/7/1, NMM
42. *Prostitution and Victorian Society: Women, Class and the State*, Judith R. Walkowitz, Cambridge University Press, 1982, p 50
43. Preface to *Damaged Goods*, George Bernard Shaw, Brentano's, New York, 1912, p iii
44. *The Social Significance of the Modern Drama*, Emma Goldman, Gorham Press, Boston, 1914, p 147 ff
45. 'Did I Do the Right Thing?' Renee Harris, *American Weekly*, 23 January 1949
46. 'Did I Do the Right Thing?' *American Weekly*, 24 April 1949
47. Renee Harris obituary, *New York Times*, 3 September 1969
48. Ibid.
49. 'A Night to Forget', LMQ/7/1, NMM
50. Ibid.
51. *Discretions and Indiscretions*, Lady Duff Gordon, Jarrolds, London, 1932, p 154

52. Letter from Renee Harris to Lady Duff Gordon, 17 June 1932, courtesy of Randy Bigham
53. Renee Harris obituary, *New York Times*, 3 September 1969

CHAPTER THREE

1. 'Widow of Astor Hunts Happiness at 42', Guy Murchie Jr, *Chicago Daily Tribune*, 17 March 1935
2. 'Colonel Astor to Wed Madeleine Force', *New York Times*, 2 August 1911
3. 'Col. Astor Sails Away', *New York Times*, 3 August 1911
4. 'Col. Astor's Fiancée to live in Newport', *New York Times*, 4 August 1911
5. 'Col. Astor Marries Madeleine Force', *New York Times*, 10 September 1911
6. Ibid.
7. Unidentified newspaper, but Randy Bigham believes it to be either the *New York American* or *Herald*, 22 or 25 April 1912
8. *Titanic Survivor: The Memoirs of Violet Jessop, Stewardess*, introduced, edited and annotated by John Maxtone-Graham, Sutton Publishing, Stroud, 1998, p 133, originally published in 1997
9. Letter from W.H. Dobbyn to Robert Ferguson, 15 May 1912, LMQ/7/1/2, NMM
10. Elbert Hubbard, quoted in *The Sway of the Grand Saloon*, John Malcolm Brinnin, Delacorte Press, New York, pp 380–1, 1971
11. 'An Echo of a Past Tragedy', taken from the diary of Frederick A. Hamilton, JOD/221/1, NMM
12. Ibid.
13. Letter from Seymour Leslie to WL, 20 July 1956, LMQ/7/1/50, NMM
14. 'Astor Family Funeral Hymn Omitted at Rites for Millionaire *Titanic* Victim', *Milwaukee Journal*, 4 May 1912
15. 'Vincent Astor in Full Control', *New York Times*, 8 May 1912
16. 'New Vogue for White Mourning', *Women's Wear Daily*, 22 May 1912
17. 'Sea Heroes Were Guests of Mrs Madeleine Force Astor Last Week in New York City', *Palm Beach Post*, 6 June 1912
18. 'Mrs Astor Inconvenienced by the Curious in Taking her Daily Drive', *New York Times*, 7 August 1912
19. 'Teas Are Machine Guns of Social War', *Pittsburgh Post-Gazette*, 19 February 1916

20. 'New York Society', *Chicago Daily Tribune*, 25 June 1915
21. 'Teas Are Machine Guns of Social War', *Pittsburgh Post-Gazette*, 19 February 1916
22. 'Astor Baby's $20,000 a Year Not Enough', *New York Times*, 6 June 1915
23. '$27,593 to Maintain Astor Baby a Year', *New York Times*, 29 April 1916
24. 'New York Society', *Chicago Daily Tribune*, 25 June 1915
25. 'Four Years a Widow, She Gives up Income of Millions of Dollars for Love of Girlhood Friend', *New York Times*, 18 June 1916
26. 'Kept Husband', Enzo Fiermonte, *True Story Magazine*, February 1939
27. Ibid.
28. 'Kept Husband', Enzo Fiermonte, *True Story Magazine*, March 1939
29. 'Boxer Denies He'll Wed', *New York Times*, 18 June 1933
30. 'Kept Husband', Enzo Fiermonte, *True Story Magazine*, April 1939
31. *Time Magazine*, 13 November 1933
32. 'Widow of Astor Hunts Happiness at 42', Guy Murchie Jr, *Chicago Daily Tribune*, 17 March 1935
33. 'Enzo Fiermonte is through with Ring "Forever"', *Chicago Daily Tribune*, 23 July 1934
34. 'He Wants Marital Ties Cut Speedily', *Los Angeles Times*, 10 August 1934
35. 'Italy to Keep Fiermonte', unnamed newspaper, 12 February 1935
36. *Chicago Daily Tribune*, 31 January 1935
37. 'Agile Enzo Skips Nimbly between His Two Wives', *Pittsburgh Post-Gazette*, 10 February 1935
38. 'Mrs Fiermonte and Spouse Face Bigamy Charges', *Chicago Daily Tribune*, 12 February 1935
39. 'Italy to Keep Fiermonte', unnamed newspaper, 12 February 1935
40. 'Widow of Astor Hunts Happiness at 42', Guy Murchie Jr, *Chicago Daily Tribune*, 17 March 1935
41. 'As Wife No. 1 Comes In, Enzo and Wife No. 2 Slip Out', *Milwaukee Journal*, 9 March 1935
42. 'Mrs Fiermonte Braves Newport Social Front', *Chicago Tribune*, 18 August 1935
43. 'Widow of Astor Hunts Happiness at 42', Guy Murchie Jr, *Chicago Daily Tribune*, 17 March 1935
44. 'Sparring Mate is Divorced by Widow of Astor, Tired of Being Punched by Ex-Fighter', *Chicago Tribune*, 12 June 1938
45. Ibid.

46. 'Divorced, One-time Pugilist Enzo Fiermonte, 30, by Madeleine Force Astor Dick Fiermonte, 45', *Time Magazine*, 20 June 1938
47. 'Kept Husband', Enzo Fiermonte, *True Story Magazine*, February 1939
48. 'Kept Husband', Enzo Fiermonte, *True Story Magazine*, March 1939
49. 'John Jacob Astor VI Dies in Miami Beach', Howard Matson, TC, Vol. 16, No. 3, November 1992–January 1993
50. 'A Night of Ice and Death', James Villas, *Town and Country*, April 1992

CHAPTER FOUR

1. Letter from Marion Woolcott to her parents, 24 April 1912, HSR/Z/30/1-17, NMM
2. 'Yeovil's Girl's Ordeal', unnamed newspaper, Cottage Grove Museum
3. Letter from Marion Woolcott to her parents, 3 May 1912, HSR/Z/30/1-17, NMM
4. Ibid.
5. Ibid.
6. Ibid.
7. Ibid.
8. Letter from Marion Woolcott to her mother, copy erroneously dated Monday 1 May 1912, this is more likely to be Monday 13 May 1912, HSR/Z/30/1-17, NMM
9. Ibid.
10. 'A Tale from the *Titanic*', Elaine Beebe, *Eugene Register-Guard*, April 1962
11. Ibid.
12. Written account of *Titanic* disaster, from the scrapbook of Karl H. Behr, LMQ/ 7/1/5, NMM
13. Ibid.
14. Ibid.
15. Ibid.
16. '*Titanic* Survivors Honor Capt. Rostron', *New York Times*, 30 May 1912
17. Ibid.
18. '*Titanic* Survivors Marry', *New York Times*, 2 March 1913
19. Written account of *Titanic* disaster, from the scrapbook of Karl H. Behr, LMQ/ 7/1/5, NMM
20. Letter from Eloise Hughes Smith to her parents, quoted in *The Huntington Quarterly*, Autumn 1997, reprinted in *Titanic: Women and*

Children First, Judith B. Geller, Patrick Stephens Ltd, Sparkford, 1998, p 66
21. Statement of Mrs Lucian P. Smith, United States Senate Inquiry, Day 18
22. *Titanic: Women and Children First*, p 67
23. Statement of Mrs Lucian P. Smith, United States Senate Inquiry, Day 18
24. Ibid.
25. Ibid.
26. Letter from Helen Rodman to WL, 29 June 1992, LMQ/7/1/21, NMM
27. Letter from WL to Helen Rodman, 14 July 1992, LMQ/7/1/21, NMM
28. Letter from Mrs William L. Rodman to WL, 29 June 1992, LMQ/7/1/21, NMM
29. *Titanic: Women and Children First*, p 67
30. Statement of Mrs Lucian P. Smith, United States Senate Inquiry, Day 18
31. *New York Herald*, 27 October 1914
32. '*Titanic* Survivors Keep Their Wedding Quiet', *New York Herald*, 27 October 1914
33. 'Reading Man Announces Wedding', *Reading Eagle*, 26 October 1914
34. '*Titanic* Survivors Keep Their Wedding Quiet', *New York Herald*, 27 October 1914
35. 'Robert W. Daniel, Ex-Banker Here, 56', obituary, *New York Times*, 21 December 1940
36. *Titanic: Women and Children First*, p 66
37. *Titanic: Women and Children First*, p 69
38. *Titanic: Women and Children First*, pp 69, 70
39. 'After Escape from Viking Princess Smith Family: Just Happy to Get Home in Venice', *Sarasota Journal*, 12 April 1966
40. Statement of Mrs Helen Bishop, United States Senate Inquiry, Day 11
41. 'The *Titanic* disaster was but one of many troubles . . . The Tragic Marriage of Helen and Dick Bishop', Don Lynch, TC, Vol. 20, No. 3, November 1996–January 1997
42. *Detroit News Times*, 21 April 1912
43. 'The *Titanic* disaster was but one of many troubles . . . The Tragic Marriage of Helen and Dick Bishop', Don Lynch, TC, Vol. 20, No. 3, November 1996–January 1997

44. 'Sturgis Survivors Tell Experiences', *Sturgis Times Democrat*, 22 April 1912
45. Statement of Mrs Helen Bishop, United States Senate Inquiry, Day 11
46. *Dowagiac Daily News*, 7 November 1911
47. 'The *Titanic* disaster was but one of many troubles . . . The Tragic Marriage of Helen and Dick Bishop', Don Lynch, TC, Vol. 20, No. 3, November 1996–January 1997
48. 'Auto Accident May Result in Death', *Dowagiac Times*, 6 November 1913
49. *Dowagiac Daily News*, quoted in: 'The *Titanic* disaster was but one of many troubles . . .'
50. *Dowagiac Daily News*, 15 March 1916

CHAPTER FIVE

1. Edith Rosenbaum, *Women's Wear Daily*, 19 April 1912
2. *Discretions and Indiscretions* (hereafter DI), Lady Duff Gordon, Jarrolds, London, 1932, p 155
3. DI, p 158
4. DI, p 159
5. DI, p 160
6. Ibid.
7. DI, p 161
8. Edith Rosenbaum, *Women's Wear Daily*, 19 April 1912
9. 'Lady Duff Gordon: Saved from the *Titanic*', Randy Bryan Bigham, TC, Vol. 15, No. 1, Spring 1991, p 10
10. DI, p 165
11. DI, pp 165–6
12. Testimony of Bainbridge Colby, quoted in *The 'It' Girls* (hereafter IG), Meredith Etherington-Smith and Jeremy Pilcher, Hamish Hamilton, London, 1986, p 157
13. 'Two Survivors Call on Mayor to Ask Relief', *Evening World*, 22 April 1912
14. 'Stengel Denies Bribes Were Given to Sailors', *Newark Star*, 24 April 1912
15. DI, p 167
16. Letter from Lida Fleitmann Bloodgood to WL, 28 January 1959, LMQ/2/4/23, NMM
17. Letter from Charles Dienz to WL, summer 1955, LMQ/2/4/64, NMM

18. 'Surviving the *Titanic* Disaster: Economic, Natural and Social Determinants', Bruno S. Frey, David A. Savage, Benno Torgler, Center for Research in Economics, Management and the Arts, 2009
19. DI, p 172
20. Testimony of Charles Hendrickson, British Wreck Commissioner's Inquiry, Day 10
21. DI, pp 172–3
22. Testimony of Sir Cosmo Duff Gordon, British Wreck Commissioner's Inquiry, Day 10
23. Testimony of Sir Cosmo Duff Gordon, British Wreck Commissioner's Inquiry, Day 11
24. DI, p 175
25. *Daily Sketch*, 21 May 1912
26. Ibid.
27. *Women's Wear Daily*, 21 May 1912
28. Testimony of Lady Duff Gordon, British Wreck Commissioner's Inquiry, Day 11
29. DI, p 157
30. DI, pp 171–81
31. 'Lucile's Frills: Old Threads, New Focus', Randy Bigham and Helene Drousais, TC, Issue 170, 2005
32. DI, p 15
33. DI, p 18
34. DI, pp 11–12
35. DI, p 12
36. DI, p 28
37. DI, p 40
38. DI, p 45
39. *The Glass of Fashion*, Cecil Beaton, Weidenfeld & Nicolson, London, 1954, p 34
40. Letter from Lady Duff Gordon to her mother, quoted in IG, p 86
41. Letter from Elinor Glyn to her mother, quoted in IG, p 87
42. Letter from Lady Duff Gordon to Sir Cosmo Duff Gordon, January 1908, quoted in IG, p 112
43. IG, p 127
44. Letter from Elinor Glyn to her mother, quoted in IG, p 168
45. Letter from Lady Duff Gordon to her daughter, quoted in IG, p 179
46. DI, p 12
47. IG, p 196

48. Letter from Lady Duff Gordon to her daughter, 1918, quoted in IG, p 198
49. DI, p 254
50. Letter from Lady Duff Gordon to her mother, quoted in IG, p 199
51. DI, p 258
52. IG, p 210
53. Lady Duff Gordon, obituary, *New York Times*, 22 April 1935
54. *Silver and Gold*, Norman Hartnell, Evans Brothers, London, 1955, p 24
55. DI, p 276
56. DI, p 282
57. DI, pp 11–12
58. Letter from Phillip Gowan to AW, 9 September 2010
59. Interview with Phillip Gowan, 7 January 2011
60. Ibid.
61. Letter from Phillip Gowan to AW, 9 September 2010
62. Ibid.
63. Ibid.
64. Letter from Lucy Duff Gordon to her sister, quoted by Lady Caroline Blois, Encyclopedia Titanica, 16 August 2007
65. Letter from Phillip Gowan to AW, 9 September 2010
66. Randy Bryan Bigham, Encyclopedia Titanica, 16 August 2007
67. Letter from Randy Bigham to AW, 18 April 2011
68. Interview with Phillip Gowan, 7 January 2011
69. Interviews with Lady Caroline Blois, 20, 21 April 2011
70. Letter from Phillip Gowan to AW, 9 September 2010
71. DI, p 288

CHAPTER SIX

1. Testimony of J. Bruce Ismay, United States Senate Inquiry, Day 1
2. May R. Birkhead quoted in the *New York Herald*, 19 April 1912
3. *The Sinking of the SS Titanic*, Thayer, p 356
4. Testimony of Charles Lightoller, United States Senate Inquiry, Day 5
5. Press statement, J. Bruce Ismay, 18 April 1912
6. Testimony of J. Bruce Ismay, United States Senate Inquiry, Day 1
7. Ibid.
8. Ibid.
9. James Hughes, United States Senate Inquiry, Day 1

10. *The Life and Letters of John Galsworthy*, H.V. Marrot (ed.), William Heinemann, London, 1936, p 340
11. Quoted in *The Ismay Line*, Wilton J. Oldham, Journal of Commerce, Liverpool, 1961, p 199
12. Quoted in 'The *Titanic* and the Chairman', Part IV, Wilton J. Oldham, TC, Vol. 12, No. 1, 1988
13. 'Stead's Brother Indignant – Asks What Right Ismay Saved from Wreck', *Providence Journal*, 20 April 1912
14. Testimony of J. Bruce Ismay, United States Senate Inquiry, Day 11
15. *The Ismay Line*, pp 216-17
16. Interview with Pauline Matarasso, 19 June 2009
17. Indenture of apprenticeship signed by Joseph Bruce Ismay, 13 September 1880, TRNISM/2/1, NMM
18. *A Voyage Closed and Done*, Pauline Matarasso, p 17
19. 'The *Titanic* and the Chairman', Wilton J. Oldham, TC, Vol. 11, No. 1, Spring 1987
20. *A Voyage Closed and Done*, pp 24–5
21. Interview with Pauline Matarasso, 19 June 2009
22. Interview with Michael Manser, 19 June 2009
23. Unpublished autobiography of Frank Bustard, section reproduced in TC, June 1974
24. Letter from J. Bruce Ismay to Harold Sanderson, 10 January 1912, TRNISM/2/4, NMM
25. Letter from J. Bruce Ismay to Albert Ballin, 7 March 1912, LMQ/7/1/20, NMM
26. Letter from J. Bruce Ismay to Charles Steele, 19 February 1912, TRNISM/2/4, NMM
27. Letter from Charles Steele to J. Bruce Ismay, 2 March 1912, TRNISM/2/4, NMM
28. Interview with Pauline Matarasso, 19 June 2009
29. Statement to the press, 11 May 1912, quoted in *The Ismay Line*, pp 206–7
30. 'The *Titanic* and the Chairman', Part VII, Wilton J. Oldham, TC, Vol. 12, No. 2, 1988, p 61
31. Testimony of J. Bruce Ismay, British Wreck Commissioner's Inquiry, Day 16
32. 'The *Titanic* and the Chairman', Part IX, Wilton J. Oldham, TC, Vol. 12, No. 4, 1988, p 36
33. Testimony of J. Bruce Ismay, British Wreck Commissioner's Inquiry, Day 17

34. Account of the Saving and Rescue of those who Survived, Conduct of Sir Cosmo Duff Gordon and Mr Ismay, British Wreck Commissioner's Inquiry, Report, 1912
35. Letter from Phillip Franklin to J. Bruce Ismay, May 1912, quoted in 'The *Titanic* and the Chairman', Part VII, Wilton J. Oldham, TC, Vol. 12, No. 2, 1988, p 58
36. Letter from Elsie Stormont to J. Bruce Ismay, 28 April 1912, courtesy of Malcolm Cheape
37. Letter from Elsie Stormont to J. Bruce Ismay, 21 May 1912, courtesy of Malcolm Cheape
38. 'The *Titanic* and the Chairman', Part IX, Wilton J. Oldham, TC, Vol. 12, No. 4, 1988, p 40
39. Letter from J. Bruce Ismay to Marian Thayer, quoted in *A Voyage Closed and Done*, p 25
40. Letter from J. Bruce Ismay to Marian Thayer, quoted in *A Voyage Closed and Done*, p 26
41. Letter from William B. Boulton to J. Bruce Ismay, 7 August 1912, TRNISM/1/4, NMM
42. Unpublished autobiography of Frank Bustard, section reproduced in TC, June 1974
43. Letter from Thomas Bruce to J. Bruce Ismay, undated, TRNISM/1/4, NMM
44. Letter from J. Bruce Ismay to E.C. Grenfell, 23 October 1912, quoted in *The Ismay Line*, p 220
45. Letter from J. Bruce Ismay to Phillip Franklin, 14 December 1912, quoted in 'The *Titanic* and the Chairman', TC, Chapter 17
46. Letter from Lady Pirrie to J. Bruce Ismay, 6 January 1913, TRNISM/2/4, NMM
47. Letter from Blanche Gordon Lennox to J. Bruce Ismay, 29 April 1913, TRNISM/2/4, NMM
48. Interview with Michael Manser, 20 June 2009
49. 'The *Titanic* and the Chairman', TC, Vol. 13, No. 3, 1989, p 50
50. Interview with Michael Manser, 19 June 2009
51. Interview with Agnes Thwaite, 20 June 2009.
52. 'The *Titanic* and the Chairman', TC, Vol. 13, No. 3, 1989, p 57
53. Letter from H.M. Alderson Smith to Florence Ismay, 18 October 1937, TRNISM/10, NMM
54. Letter from Mildred Addison to Florence Ismay, 18 October 1937, TRNISM/10, NMM
55. Obituary of J. Bruce Ismay, *The Times*, 18 October 1937

56. Obituary of J. Bruce Ismay, *Washington Post*, 18 October 1937
57. *Journal of Commerce*, October 1937

CHAPTER SEVEN

1. Testimony of Annie Robinson, British Wreck Commissioner's Inquiry, Day 11
2. 'A Pig and a Prayer', Edith Russell, LMQ/5/2/1, NMM
3. Ibid.
4. Letter from Arnold A. Robert to WL, 7 February 1956, LMQ/2/5/59, NMM
5. *Daily Mirror*, April 1912, quoted in *Titanic Voices: Memories from the Fateful Voyage*, Donald Hyslop, Alastair Forsyth, Sheila Jemima, Budding Book, Southampton City Council, 1994 and 1999, p 169
6. Northam Girls' School log, Miss Annie Hopkins, 15 and 17 April 1912, Southampton City Archives, quoted in *Titanic Voices*, p 170
7. *The Times*, 12 July 1913
8. *The Loss of the Titanic*, Sir Arthur Rostron, p 25
9. 'A Pig and a Prayer', LMQ/5/2/1, NMM
10. '*Titanic* Survivor is Suicide', *Toledo News-Bee*, 17 November 1921
11. Testimony of William Lucas, British Wreck Commissioner's Inquiry, Day 3
12. *New York Herald*, 20 April 1912
13. Letter from Anna Kincaid (then Sjoblom) to WL, 18 July 1955, LMQ/7/2/27, NMM
14. Bertha Mulvihill by Tad Fitch, TC, Issue 166, 2004
15. Letter from Washington Dodge Jr to WL, 1 December 1952, LMQ/2/4/67, NMM
16. 'Dr Dodge's Wife Tells Story of *Titanic* Wreck', *San Francisco Bulletin*, 30 April 1912
17. *San Francisco: A Brief Biographical Sketch of Some of the Most Prominent Men Who Will Preside Over her Destiny for at least Two Years*, Evarts I. Blake, San Francisco Press Pacific Publ. Company 1902, p 56, quoted by Jan C. Nielsen, 'Iceberg at the Golden Gate', ET Research, 12 February 2002
18. 'The Loss of the *Titanic*', Washington Dodge, Commonwealth Club, 11 May 1912, LMQ/1/13/3, NMM
19. 'Dr Washington Dodge Gives History of *Titanic* Disaster at Commonwealth Club', *San Francisco Chronicle*, 12 May 1912

20. 'The Loss of the *Titanic*', Washington Dodge, LMQ/1/13/3, NMM
21. Evarts I. Blake, quoted by Nielsen
22. 'Dr Dodge Attempts Suicide', *San Francisco Chronicle*, 22 June 1919
23. Ibid.
24. 'Dr Dodge May Recover: Had Been Guarded', *San Francisco Chronicle*, 24 June 1919
25. *Fremont Older, My Own Story*, Call Publishing Company, San Francisco, 1919, quoted by Nielsen
26. John B. Thayer, statement to the press, 20 April 1912, Independence Seaport Museum Library, Philadelphia, Folder 4
27. *The Sinking of the SS Titanic*, Thayer, p 345
28. Thayer, p 355
29. *The Loss of the Titanic*, Sir Arthur Rostron, p 22
30. Interview with Julie Vehr, 6 December 2010
31. Eulogy for John Borland Thayer, William D. Winsor, 1912, Independence Seaport Museum Library, Philadelphia, Folder 23
32. John B. Thayer, *Boston Evening Transcript*, 22 April 1912
33. Letter from Lucile Carter to J. Bruce Ismay, 24 May 1912, courtesy of Malcolm Cheape
34. Interview with Pauline Maguire, 15 October 2009
35. Ibid.
36. Interview with Julie Vehr, 6 December 2010
37. Ibid.
38. Ibid.
39. Ibid.
40. Interview with Pauline Maguire, 15 October 2009
41. Interview with Julie Vehr, 6 December 2010
42. Interview with Pauline Maguire, 15 October 2009
43. Thayer, p 330
44. Interview with Pauline Maguire, 15 October 2009
45. Interview with Julie Vehr, 6 December 2010
46. 'John B. Thayer, 3d, Ends Life in Auto', *Evening Bulletin*, Philadelphia, 21 September 1945
47. Interview with Julie Vehr, 6 December 2010
48. Interview with Pauline Maguire, 15 October 2009

CHAPTER EIGHT

1. *Finding Dorothy: An Appreciation of the Life and Career of Dorothy Gibson Brulatour*, Randy Bryan Bigham, Titanic Star Publications, Dallas, Texas, 2005, p 54 (hereafter FD)
2. Ibid.
3. 'Motion Picture Actress Tells of *Titanic* Wreck', *New York Morning Telegraph*, 21 April 1912
4. Ibid.
5. Ibid.
6. FD, p 11
7. *Harrisburg Leader*, 21 April 1912
8. FD, p 10
9. FD, p 13
10. *New York American*, undated
11. FD, p 14
12. 'Yesterday's Stars Today: Dorothy Brulatour', Adela Rogers St Johns, unnamed newspaper, 16 May 1934
13. FD, p 34
14. FD, p 43
15. FD, p 49
16. FD, p 55
17. 'My Eyewitness Story of the *Titanic* Disaster', excerpted from *The Life and Times of Andrew Jackson Sloper 1849–1933*, reprinted in TC, Volume 26, No. 158, 2002
18. FD, p 56
19. 'My Eyewitness Story of the *Titanic* Disaster', Sloper
20. 'Motion Picture Actress Tells of *Titanic* Wreck', *New York Morning Telegraph*, 21 April 1912
21. *The Loss of the Titanic*, Sir Arthur Rostron, p 21
22. *Titanic* report, Carlos F. Hurd, *New York Evening World*, 18 April 1912
23. FD, p 62
24. Testimony of Olaus Abelseth, United States Senate Inquiry, Day 13
25. FD, p 58
26. *Harrisburg Leader*, 21 April 1912
27. FD, p 65
28. 'Auto Suit is Settled', *New York Times*, 22 May 1913
29. 'Refuses $48,000 Alimony', *New York Times*, 21 August 1919
30. FD, p 78

31. 'Miss Fannie Ward and Friends Give "Movie Parties"', *Paris Herald*, 12 December 1924
32. 'Yesterday's Stars Today: Dorothy Brulatour', Adela Rogers St Johns, 16 May 1934
33. Affidavit given to James C. Bell, Vice Consul of the American Consulate General in Zurich, quoted in 'The Saga of the Gibson Women', Phillip Gowan and Brian Meister, *Atlantic Daily Bulletin*, Vol. 3, 2002
34. FD, p 84
35. Affidavit, quoted in Gowan and Meister

CHAPTER NINE

1. 'I Survived the *Titanic* Disaster', John Podesta, TC, Issue 7, December 1964
2. Letter from May Futrelle to Helen Hernandez, quoted in letter from Helen Hernandez to WL, 28 June 1955, LMQ/2/4/122, NMM
3. Ibid.
4. *Down with the Old Canoe: A Cultural History of the Titanic Disaster*, Steven Biel, W.W. Norton, New York, 1996, p 158
5. Original theatrical trailer, *Titanic*, 1953, Twentieth Century Fox
6. Letter from May Futrelle to Helen Hernandez, 10 March 1952, forwarded to WL, 28 June 1955, LMQ/2/4/122, NMM
7. Letter from William Thomson Sloper to Helen Hernandez, 25 August 1952, forwarded to WL, 28 June 1955, LMQ/2/4/122, NMM
8. Letter from Blanche Boyce to Helen Hernandez, April 1952, quoted in letter to WL, 14 June 1955, LMQ/2/4/122, NMM
9. Letter from Madeleine Mellenger Mann to WL, 13 January 1962, LMQ/7/2/5, NMM
10. Encyclopedia Titanica, Michel Navratil: http://www.encyclopedia-titanica.org/titanic-biography/michel-marcel-navratil.html
11. Letter from Madeleine Mellenger Mann to WL, 13 January 1962, LMQ/7/2/5, NMM
12. *A Rainbow of Time and of Space: Orphans of the Titanic*, Sidney F. Tyler, Aztex Corporation, Tucson, Arizona, p 25 (hereafter *Rainbow*)
13. Rainbow, p 72
14. Ibid.
15. Rainbow, p 27
16. Rainbow, p 29

17. 'French Children May Be His, Frank Lefebvre Goes to New York from Mystic to Identify Two Unknown French Children', *Semi-Weekly Iowegian*, 23 April 1912
18. Letter from Sidney Tyler to Ed Kamuda, Titanic Historical Society, 27 September 1978, quoted in *A Rainbow of Time and of Space*, TC, Vol. 19, No. 4, February–April 1996
19. *New York Times*, 17 May 1912
20. Ibid.
21. Ibid.
22. *New York Times*, 18 May 1912
23. Ibid.
24. Letter from Sidney Tyler to Ed Kamuda, Titanic Historical Society, 27 September 1978, quoted in *A Rainbow of Time and of Space*, TC, Vol. 19, No. 4, February–April 1996
25. Letter from Sidney Tyler to Ed Kamuda, 7 October 1978, quoted in TC, Vol. 19, No. 4, February–April 1996
26. Letter from Sidney Tyler to Ed Kamuda, 20 February 1979, TC, Vol. 19, No. 4, February–April 1996
27. Letter from Sidney Tyler to Ed Kamuda, 5 April 1979, TC, 1996
28. Letter from Sidney Tyler to Ed Kamuda, 1 August 1979, TC, 1996
29. Rainbow, p 63
30. Rainbow, pp 65–6
31. Rainbow, p 66
32. Rainbow, p 73
33. Interview with Elisabeth Bouillon, 27 January 2011 (in French, carried out by Catriona Munro)
34. Rainbow, p 17
35. Interview with Elisabeth Bouillon, 27 January 2011
36. Rainbow, p 74
37. Letter from Sidney Tyler to Ed Kamuda, 12 February 1981, TC
38. Letter from Michel Navratil to Sidney Tyler, 6 March 1981, quoted in Rainbow, p 79
39. Rainbow, p 25
40. Letter from Michel Navratil to Sidney Tyler, quoted in Rainbow, p 61
41. 'Last Male Survivor of *Titanic* Dies', BBC News, 2 February 2001

CHAPTER TEN

1. *Down with the Old Canoe: A Cultural History of the Titanic Disaster*, Steven Biel, W.W. Norton, New York, 1996, p 158
2. Letter from Madeleine Mellenger to Henry Holt publishers, 31 October 1955, LMQ/7/2/5, NMM
3. Letter from Madeleine Mellenger to WL, 25 November 1955, LMQ/7/2/5, NMM
4. Ibid.
5. Obituary of Walter Lord, *New York Times*, 22 May 2002
6. Letter from Marguerite Schwarzenbach to WL, 27 December 1955, LMQ/2/5/71, NMM
7. *Titanic Memories: the Making of A Night to Remember*, William MacQuitty, National Maritime Museum, London, 2000, p 8
8. Ibid.
9. Ibid.
10. *Titanic Memories*, pp 9–10
11. *Titanic Memories*, p 13
12. *Titanic Memories*, p 14
13. *More or Less*, Kenneth More, quoted in *Titanic Memories*, p 14
14. Letter from William MacQuitty to Joseph Boxall, 9 July 1957, LMQ/7/1, NMM
15. Letter from Joseph Boxall to William MacQuitty, 10 July 1957, LMQ/7/1, NMM
16. Letter from Julia Murphy to L.M. Wilkins, 2 November 1952, sent to WL, LMQ/2/5/112, NMM
17. '*Titanic* Survivors Tell Dramatic Story of Sea's Greatest Disaster in History', *Hudson Dispatch*, 19 April 1912
18. Letter from Edith Russell to WL, 28 April 1956, LMQ/7/2/19, NMM
19. Letter from Edith Russell to Charles Brackett, 26 February 1952, LMQ/7/1/11, NMM
20. Ibid.
21. Letter from Edith Russell to Charles Brackett, 1 April 1952, LMQ/7/1/11, NMM
22. Ibid.
23. Ibid.
24. 'A Night to Forget', Renee Harris, LMQ/7/1, NMM
25. Letter from Edith Russell to WL, 28 April 1956, LMQ/7/2/19, NMM

26. Letter from Edith Russell to WL, 13 May 1956, LMQ/5/2/1, NMM
27. Ibid.
28. *Titanic Memories*, p 20
29. *Titanic Memories*, p 21
30. Ibid.
31. Letter from Edith Russell to WL, 11 May 1957, LMQ/5/2/1, NMM
32. Letter from Edith Russell to WL, 23 December 1957, LMQ/5/2/1, NMM
33. Letter from Edith Russell to Roy Baker, 18 February 1958, LMQ/5/2/1, NMM
34. Edith Russell discussion board, post from Michael Findlay, 16 March 2001, Encyclopedia Titanica: http://www.encyclopedia-titanica.org/discus/messages/5811/5501.html?984771331
35. Interview with Betty MacQuitty, 16 October 2009
36. Interview with Miranda MacQuitty, 16 October 2009
37. Interview with Jane MacQuitty, 8 February 2010
38. Letter from Edith Russell to WL, 3 February 1958, LMQ/5/2/1, NMM
39. Letter from WL to Edith Russell, 17 April 1958, LMQ/5/2/1, NMM
40. Letter from Edith Russell to WL, 15 June 1959, LMQ/5/2/1, NMM
41. Letter from Edith Russell to WL, 12 April 1959, LMQ/5/2/1, NMM
42. Interview with Jane MacQuitty, 8 February 2010
43. 'Girl Survivor Has Praise for Ismay', *New York Times*, 23 April 1912
44. Interview with Betty MacQuitty, 16 October 2009
45. Interview with Miranda MacQuitty, 16 October 2009
46. Letter from Pauline Matarasso to AW, 9 February 2010
47. Letter from J. Bruce Ismay to Edith Rosenbaum/Russell, 14 October 1912, LMQ/1/14/2, NMM
48. Sheridan Morley radio interview with Edith Russell, BBC, 14 April 1970, http://www.bbc.co.uk/archive/titanic/5051.shtml
49. *Titanic – Women and Children First*, Judith B. Geller, p 77
50. Interview with Betty MacQuitty, 16 October 2009
51. 'A Pig and a Prayer', Edith Russell, LMQ/5/2/1, NMM
52. Interview with Jane MacQuitty, 8 February 2010

CHAPTER ELEVEN

1. Edward C. Burks, *New York Times*, 9 October 1973
2. Ibid.

3. 'I Took a Voyage on the RMS *Titanic*', Scott Eyman, *Yankee Magazine*, June 1981
4. 'Explorer of the Sea: Robert Ballard', Erik Eckholm, *New York Times*, 10 September 1985
5. 'Down to the Great Ship', William F. Buckley Jr, *New York Times*, 18 October 1987
6. *The Times*, 16 June 1992
7. *Shadow of the Titanic: A Survivor's Story*, Eva Hart and Ronald C. Denney, Greenwich University, Dartford, 1994, p 63 (hereafter Hart)
8. Hart, p 42
9. The Eva Hart Story, Stan Seymour, privately recorded audio tape, courtesy of Stan Seymour
10. Hart, p 155
11. Hart, p 13
12. Hart, p 14
13. Hart, p 16
14. Ibid.
15. Hart, p 19
16. Hart, p 24
17. Letter from Esther Hart to her mother, 14 April 1912, quoted in Hart, pp 30–31
18. Hart, p 34
19. Hart, p 40
20. Hart, p 42
21. The Eva Hart Story, Stan Seymour, private audio recording
22. Hart, p 48
23. The Eva Hart Story, Stan Seymour, private audio recording
24. Hart, p 76
25. Hart, p 84
26. Hart, p 83
27. Hart, p 12
28. Interview with Stanley Seymour, 19 June 2010
29. Hart, p 138
30. Hart, p 144
31. Hart, p 130
32. Interview with Dinah Hall, 27 April 2010
33. Interview with Richard Clegg, 16 April 2010
34. Hart, pp 168, 169
35. Interview with Richard Clegg, 16 April 2010
36. Interview with Dinah Hall, 27 April 2010

37. Interview with Richard Clegg, 16 April 2010
38. Eva Hart memorial service, audio recording made by Ronald Denney, courtesy of Stanley Seymour
39. *Daily Mirror*, 12 May 1912
40. 'Millvina Dean, *Titanic*'s Last Survivor, Dies at 97', *New York Times*, 31 May 2009
41. Interview with Millvina Dean, 12 November 2008
42. *Titanic*, James Cameron, 1997
43. Interview with Millvina Dean, 12 November 2008
44. Ibid.
45. *Southern Daily Echo*, April 2003
46. Interview with Millvina Dean, 12 November 2008
47. Ibid.
48. Ibid.
49. Ibid.
50. Ibid.
51. Ibid.
52. *Titanic: The Last Survivor, the Life of Millvina Dean*, Anthony Cunningham, Sheila Jemima, with Millvina Dean, Waterfront, Kingfisher Productions, Settle, 2008, p 35
53. *Titanic: The Last Survivor*, p 39
54. *Titanic: The Last Survivor*, p 43
55. Interview with Millvina Dean, 12 November 2008

AFTERWORD

1. *Titanic*, John Wilson Foster (ed.), Penguin Books, London, 1999, p xiii
2. 'Great-grandson of *Titanic* Survivor Hopes to Marry on Replica', Larry Phillips, CentralOhio.com, 23 May 2010
3. Ibid.
4. Interview with Kate Bucknell and Robert Maguire, 13 November 2008

INDEX